FACKENHEIM'S JEWISH PHILOSOPHY

An Introduction

D0840698

Emil L. Fackenheim, one of the most significant Jewish thinkers of the twentieth century, is best known for his deep and rich engagement with the implications of the Nazi Holocaust on Jewish thought, Christian theology, and philosophy. However, his career as a philosopher and theologian began two decades prior to his first efforts to confront that horrific event. In this book, renowned Fackenheim expert Michael L. Morgan offers the first examination of the full scope of Fackenheim's sixty-year career, beyond simply his work on the Holocaust.

Fackenheim's Jewish Philosophy explores the most important themes of Fackenheim's philosophical and religious thought and how these remained central, if not always in immutable ways, over his entire career. Morgan also provides insight into Fackenheim's indebtedness to Kant, Hegel, and rabbinic midrash, as well as the changing character of his philosophical "voice." The work concludes with a chapter evaluating Fackenheim's legacy for present and future Jewish philosophy and philosophy more generally.

(The Kenneth Michael Tanenbaum Series in Jewish Studies)

MICHAEL L. MORGAN is Chancellor's Professor Emeritus of Philosophy and Jewish Studies at Indiana University, the Goldsmith Visiting Professor of Judaic Studies at Yale University, the Grafstein Visiting Chair in the Department of Philosophy at the University of Toronto, and Honorary Professor of the Australian Catholic University.

The Kenneth Michael Tanenbaum Series in Jewish Studies

The Kenneth Michael Tanenbaum Book Series features outstanding research on topics in all areas of Jewish Studies. This interdisciplinary series highlights especially research developed within the framework of the University of Toronto's Centre for Jewish Studies. The Centre is an interdisciplinary research and teaching unit with a large and diverse cohort of affiliated faculty and an impressive roster of annual conferences, symposia, and lectures. Reflecting the Centre's vibrancy, the series highlights the best new research by local and international scholars who contribute to the intellectual life of this interdisciplinary community. The series has been enabled by a generous donation from Kenneth Tanenbaum, whose family has long supported the Centre and helped make it a leader globally in Jewish Studies.

General Editor: Jeffrey Kopstein, Director, Centre for Jewish Studies, Professor of Political Science, University of Toronto

Fackenheim's Jewish Philosophy

An Introduction

MICHAEL L. MORGAN

UNIVERSITY OF TORONTO PRESS
Toronto Buffalo London

© University of Toronto Press 2013
Toronto Buffalo London
www.utppublishing.com
Printed in Canada

ISBN 978-1-4426-4441-0 (cloth)
ISBN 978-1-4426-1266-2 (paper)

Printed on acid-free, 100% post-consumer
recycled paper with vegetable-based inks.

Library and Archives Canada Cataloguing in Publication

Morgan, Michael L., 1944–, author

Fackenheim's Jewish philosophy: an introduction / Michael L. Morgan.
(Kenneth Michael Tanenbaum series in Jewish studies)
Includes bibliographical references and index.
ISBN 978-1-4426-4441-0 (bound). – ISBN 978-1-4426-1266-2 (pbk.)

1. Fackenheim, Emil L., 1916–2003 – Criticism and interpretation. 2. Jewish
philosophy. I. Title. II. Title: Jewish philosophy. III. Series: Kenneth
Michael Tanenbaum series in Jewish studies

B995.F334M67 2013   191   C2013-903468-4

University of Toronto Press acknowledges
the financial assistance to its publishing program
of the Canada Council for the Arts and the Ontario Arts Council.

Canada Council   Conseil des Arts
for the Arts   du Canada

ONTARIO ARTS COUNCIL
CONSEIL DES ARTS DE L'ONTARIO
50 YEARS OF ONTARIO GOVERNMENT SUPPORT OF THE ARTS
50 ANS DE SOUTIEN DU GOUVERNEMENT DE L'ONTARIO AUX ARTS

University of Toronto Press acknowledges the financial
support of the Government of Canada through
the Canada Book Fund for its publishing activities.

To the Future ——
Gabby, Sasha, Tyler, and Halle

Contents

Acknowledgments

This book is one that I never expected to write. I first met Emil in 1967, and in 1970 I became his student, his teaching assistant, his research assistant, and his friend. I taught his work at Indiana and in a host of other venues from the moment I was appointed at Indiana in 1975. In 2001 I thought that the chapters in *Beyond Auschwitz*, published that year, would be my last writing on him and his thought. But when he passed away in 2003, we had been friends – he had been my teacher and more, I his student and more – for thirty-five years. We had spent a great deal of time together; no one (other than Audrey, Debbie, and Sara) had meant more to me, intellectually and in many other ways. I took on the responsibility of seeing his memoirs through publication and provided a foreword to them; *An Epitaph for German Judaism* finally appeared in 2007, the same year my books *Discovering Levinas* and *On Shame* were published. I thought then that I had honoured him in the right way – I had paid a debt of friendship and also was increasingly doing my own work, which he would have enjoyed and approved of. But then came the invitation to deliver the Shier Lectures and to return "home" to Toronto, where Emil and I had first become teacher and student and fast friends. I returned to his writings and to his thinking – this time with that strange combination of intimacy and distance that is the mark of maturity and philosophical vision. I was returning home, as if for the first time, to a place where I already had seemingly spent a lifetime. This book is the outcome of that return.

The book began as the three lectures I gave as the Shoshana Shier Distinguished Visiting Professor at the University of Toronto in the fall of 2010. Chapters 1 to 3 are based on those lectures, and a lecture I gave at Beth Tzedec Congregation in Toronto is the core of chapter 4. I want to express my gratitude and appreciation to Joseph Shier and the other members of the Shier family for their generosity in sponsoring this wonderful lecture series and for their hospitality and kindnesses during the semester of my residency. When I suggested that I might give the lectures on Emil Fackenheim's work, the Shiers responded enthusiastically, and their support was confirmed by the large audiences that came to hear about one of the university's and the city's honoured intellectuals. I want to thank especially Hindy Najman, who was director of the Centre for Jewish Studies at the University of Toronto at the time, for arranging my visit to Toronto. I am indebted to Hindy as well for arranging with the University of Toronto Press for the book to be published by the university at which Fackenheim spent the bulk of his career. I also want to thank the audiences at the lectures and all those whose questions and comments provoked me to rethink what I had come to think about Fackenheim's work.

For more than thirty-five years, in various courses on modern Jewish thought and philosophy, I have taught the work of Emil Fackenheim. I have learned a great deal from my classes and from teaching Fackenheim's thought to students at Indiana University and, since my retirement, at the Leo Baeck College in London, as well as at Yale, Northwestern, Toronto, Stanford, and Princeton. I have also lectured on his work at the Hebrew Union College–Jewish Institute of Religion, both in Cincinnati and in New York; to numerous adult education audiences in the United States, Canada, Australia, and England; and to academic audiences in those countries and in Israel. For arranging various visiting appointments, I thank Marc Saperstein, Steve Weitzman, Ken Seeskin, and Leora Batnitzky.

Special thanks go to Donald Ainslie and Arthur Ripstein, past and current chairs of the Department of Philosophy at the University of Toronto, for arranging to have me fill the Senator Jerahmiel S. and Carole S. Grafstein Visiting Chair on two different occasions, and to Steven Fraade and his Yale colleagues for having me serve twice as the Horace W. Goldsmith Visiting Professor in Judaic Studies at Yale. The support of all of my friends and colleagues at those two institutions is warmly appreciated. Leora Batnitzky has been an especially strong supporter. At her invitation I was invited to teach at Princeton in the fall of 2011. She also arranged for me to convene a workshop at Princeton, under the auspices of the Tikvah Program in Jewish Thought, on the idea of messianism in Judaism. The three meetings of the workshop were tremendously exciting intellectually and provided a valuable opportunity for me to think about issues relevant to Fackenheim's reflections on messianism and the philosophy of history in Judaism. I thank the participants in those workshops – Elisheva Carlebach, Ken Seeskin, Annette Reed, Steve Wasserstrom, Shai Held, Steve Weitzman, and Ben Pollock.

Several friends have been constant conversation partners in recent years; their intellectual partnership has meant a great deal to me. Ever since he came to Indiana, Shaul Magid and I have regularly met to talk about matters of mutual interest, modern Jewish thought among them, and in so many areas I am the beneficiary of his learning and his intellectual excitement and creativity. Shaul introduced me to Shai Held, who has become a very close and valued partner in thinking about modern Jewish philosophers. No one I know has a more lively and penetrating sense of what is important and worthwhile in Jewish ideas and of what is central to Jewish life and its future. Ben Pollock and I have known each other for years, and I consider him one of my closest friends. When he organized the celebratory conference in Jerusalem honoring Emil on his eighty-fifth birthday in 2001, Ben was kind enough to consult with me and then, after the conference, to invite me to join with him in editing the proceedings. We had known each other before then, but since that conference, during the past decade, we have become fast friends and constant partners in conversation, often about Rosenweig and about Emil's work, and just as often about everything else that is on either of our minds. In 2004 Ben and I spent an intense week packing up all the books and papers left in Emil's apartment, preparing them to be sent to various libraries and to the archives in Ottawa. Ben had been one of Emil's research assistants in Israel, and another of those assistants, Sol Goldberg, was one of the participants in the conference. When Hindy arranged for me to come to Toronto as the Shier Lecturer, she introduced or reintroduced me to Sol, who was in Toronto as a post-doc and was working for the Centre for Jewish Studies. Since that time, Sol and I have become very close. Together we organized a Levinas reading group during my stay in Toronto, and we talk regularly and often about philosophy and Jewish philosophy.

My reading of Fackenheim has many debts. One significant one is to Peter Gordon, from whom I have learned so much and whose collaboration and friendship I value tremendously. We worked together to edit *The Cambridge Companion to Modern Jewish Philosophy* and for over a year were in constant touch about the contributions to that project and regarding its progress. There is nothing like the closeness that develops between joint editors who collect, read, discuss, edit, and judge the contributions to their project. The *Cambridge Companion* made Peter and myself constant companions, and while it was a time of enormous demands and boundless work, it was a joy and brought a friendship that is very important to me.

Over the years I have had valuable conversations on topics that have found a place in this book, and I owe a debt to all of those with whom I have had these conversations. They include Michael Stroh, Louis Greenspan, Steven Mulhall, Simon Glendinning, John Collins, Jon Levenson, Shai Held, Sol Goldberg, Ben Pollock, Paul Franks, Jim Conant, Dan Garber, Jeff Stout, Peter Gordon, Sam Fleischacker, Ken Seeskin, Martin Kavka, Shaul Magid, David Novak, Marc Goldman, Fred Beiser, Peter Knobel, Steve Aschheim, Zev Harvey, Bob Gibbs, Shelly Zimmerman, Alan Cooper, Alan Mittleman, Allan Arkush, Eugene Borowitz, Steve Weitzman, Mira Wasserman, David Ellenson, Michael Marmur, Dov Marmur, Bruce Hoffman, and Joshua Shaw.

I would like to thank Kevin Hart and to acknowledge Michael Signer (z"l), who invited me, some years ago, to talk about Fackenheim with their seminar on revelation at Notre Dame. Also, I thank Sandy Seltzer, Larry Raphael, Barbara and Larry Shuman, and the dozens, indeed hundreds of participants at the fifteen or so Kallot conducted by the Union of Reform Judaism at which I taught and talked about Fackenheim's writings and his thought. Their eagerness, excitement, and intellectual engagement confirmed my own belief about how worthwhile the study of Fackenheim's work can be.

Special thanks go to Ruth Podeswa and her family for allowing us to use a photograph of a painting by her husband, Yehuda Podesva, for our cover. Ralph and Kitty Wintrob, old and dear friends of the Fackenheim family, called to my attention the paintings of Emil that Podesva, a Toronto artist and Holocaust survivor, had done in the late 1970s. He had many one-man shows throughout Canada in Toronto, Montreal, Winnipeg, and Halifax, and his paintings are in many private collections. A year ago Yidel passed away. Ruth located this painting, along with another, dated 1978, and generously made it available for our use. Podesva was born in Poland in 1924 into a family of artists and trained there and in Germany. His impressionistic painting captures Emil at a typical daily, reflective moment, marking a passage in his reading. The oblique orientation of Emil's posture speaks to the direction of his thinking, angling in on the texts and ideas of the past, recovering fragments that – when reconfigured – may bring some measure of hope to our ordinary lives.

All that I do philosophically draws on what I have learned and continue to learn from three colleagues at Indiana from the early 1990s – David Finkelstein, Fred Beiser, and Paul Franks. The period when we were all colleagues was the most exciting of my philosophical career. David, Fred, and Paul are among my closest friends. Each has taught me more than I could ever estimate. My work is better and richer because of them.

I first became captivated by modern Jewish theology, thought, and philosophy when I was an undergraduate in the early 1960s. There has never been a time since those years when I have not been engaged with the figures, issues, and problems in this intellectual arena. But in recent years, my understanding has been deepened and enriched by conversations and collaboration with Paul Franks. Jewishly and philosophically, Paul brings remarkable background and talents to the table; our work together – on our Rosenzweig book and on our current joint project on modern Jewish philosophy – is more rewarding and more exciting than I can possibly convey. My friendship with Paul and his family – as with my friendships with Fred, David, Ben, Sol, and Shai – is a special treasure.

I owe a special debt to Emil's children – David Aryeh, Suzy Goodwin, and Yossi Fackenheim – and to their families. I have known them all for years. They have, on one occasion or another, shared thoughts with me about their father and mother. David and his wife Wendy have hosted Audrey and me in Jerusalem, as have Suzy and her husband Mark when we were living in London. I hope this book will provide their children, Rose's and Emil's grandchildren, with an additional route of access to the memory of their father.

I would also like to thank Len Husband and Wayne Herrington at the University of Toronto Press for their care in the production of this book and Yaniv Feller for his efforts in preparing the index.

As always, I want to express what is really beyond my powers to express – my love for our daughters, Deb and Sara, for Deb's husband Adam, and for our four grandchildren – Gabby, Sasha, Tyler, and Halle. To Aud and myself they bring joy beyond anything we could have imagined. They make us proud and fill our lives with laughter and the occasional tear.

Finally, Aud means everything; enough said.

FACKENHEIM'S JEWISH PHILOSOPHY

An Introduction

Introduction

What is Jewish philosophy? There is no answer to this question that does not consider the relationship between the attempt to articulate the meaning of Jewish existence and the historical situation in which that attempt has taken place – that is, that does not appreciate that Judaism is a very particular historical phenomenon of great complexity and richness. In view of this fact, it is a commonplace to some that the very expression "Jewish philosophy" incorporates a tension between what philosophy aspires to and what Judaism is, between the universal and the particular. However, if we understand philosophy as itself a historical inquiry shaped by the vocabulary it has inherited from the Western philosophical tradition, but an inquiry significantly framed by the historical conditions of the time, then the tension between philosophy and Jewish self-understanding may appear less paradoxical. It may be more apparent than real.

Over the years, I have come to characterize Jewish philosophy as a result of the encounter between a reflection upon Jewish existence and the tradition of Western philosophy. Both that reflection and that tradition are historical, even when they aspire to some kind of intellectual transcendence. Emil Fackenheim regularly claimed that Jewish theology was an intellectual project to understand Judaism conducted from the point of view of someone committed to Judaism and Jewish faith. For much (perhaps all) of his career, he took philosophy to be the thinking of an engaged and historically embedded participant or agent: the philosopher is a real person, living in a particular culture and society, at a particular moment historically, and influenced by much that constitutes the world in which he or she lives. Still, the philosopher may aim for detachment and for a kind of purity of perspective.[1] Should we then add that

Jewish philosophy is therefore conducted by an engaged philosopher who brackets Jewish belief or any religious belief and who aspires to as much detachment or neutrality as he or she can achieve? If we do, then we can ask whether there is, throughout Fackenheim's career and his works, a strand we can call "Jewish philosophy." I believe there is. In this book I try to clarify some of its most important characteristics.

Fackenheim often speaks as an advocate of Judaism, as a spokesperson for Jewish ideas and beliefs. He tries to clarify what they are and then to support them with arguments and analysis; he endorses them and advocates for them. But within this effort and also at times separate from it, Fackenheim manifests the virtues of serious and rigorous philosophical thinking about some important concepts and themes. Given the urgency and intensity with which he speaks, it is easy to forget that much of Fackenheim's work is philosophical. In this book, I explore some of the central philosophical themes of his work and say something about his persona as a philosopher and as a Jewish philosopher.

The lectures that form the core of this book were originally titled "Continuity and Discontinuity in Emil Fackenheim's Jewish Thought." My plan for those lectures had been to explore three philosophical issues that permeated Fackenheim's thinking. That is, I had planned to examine three philosophical strands in his work: the concept of revelation, freedom and selfhood, and the nature of philosophy. I also wanted to take note of the fact that around 1966, Fackenheim began to focus explicitly on the Nazi Holocaust and its importance for Jewish thinking, Christian theology, philosophy, and much else. Part of his new focus was his claim that the Holocaust had been an "epoch-making" event – that it had placed in question all our concepts and theories and put everyone under the obligation to reconsider them all in the process of seeking to continue on after these events. I therefore proposed to ask whether the encounter between the Holocaust and his three philosophical concepts or themes led him to maintain their meaning and content, to modify them, or to jettison them altogether. In short, I used the issue of "continuity and discontinuity" as a lens through which to examine three philosophical aspects of Fackenheim's thought and to consider in particular whether his thinking about them underwent transformation. What did he find compelling about these issues, and did his commitment to them remain largely stable?

In a sense, the present book retains that structure, although the special role of the Holocaust and exposure to it does not play quite the role I had anticipated. Moreover, I have added to those three themes several others: the role of messianism in Fackenheim's reflections about the State of Israel; the relationship between thought and history or the problem of historicism; Fackenheim's debt to Kant and Kantian philosophy; his relationship to Hegel; the role of midrash in his Jewish thought; his philosophical voice and its relationship to his understanding of philosophy and Jewish philosophy; and, finally, his legacy for Jewish philosophy today and in the future. The result is not a systematic presentation of his Jewish philosophy; indeed, I am not sure one could provide such a systematic account without distorting the way Fackenheim's thought developed and without ignoring the various contexts in which he presented it. Nor is the book an intellectual biography or even an intellectual study. It has a more precise focus. It is narrow in the sense that it focuses on a select number of themes and ideas that are of central importance in his work and that are of philosophical significance. It is also narrow in the sense that it tries to clarify and understand his arguments and analyses in the context of the works in which he presents them. I also pay attention to the chronology of his work, since one dimension of this present book is to consider whether his thinking underwent interesting and significant alterations on key issues.

One figure who does not play a large role in my account is Leo Strauss. Fackenheim was candid that Strauss was important for him, and several recent studies of Fackenheim's work consider his relationship to Strauss.[2] He himself encourages such a perspective on his work; he recalls the significance for his career of reading Strauss, while he was still in Germany, and then of meeting Strauss in New York and maintaining a correspondence with him.[3] I believe, however, that his reading of Strauss was highly selective and not comprehensive and that he never studied Strauss the way, say, he studied Kant and Hegel and other figures – Buber, Rosenzweig, and Kierkegaard. His debt to Strauss is of a different kind. Yet there is no denying that there is something enticing about regarding the two together, especially given the enormous interest in Strauss, from a number of perspectives, during the past few decades. I leave it to others, however, to carry out that critical comparison. In fact, even in the cases of Buber, Rosenzweig, Kierkegaard, and Heidegger, I only touch upon their significance for Fackenheim. I leave the full development of their influences to those more expert than myself.

Personally, I am as interested in how the issues, themes, and concepts that are central to Fackenheim's thought can be brought into conversation with other late-twentieth-century philosophers, although he knew little about most of them. As I have tried to do in my own work on

Levinas, Rosenzweig, and Buber, among others, I hope to point to the way in which twentieth-century Jewish thought and philosophy can be better understood and better appreciated when viewed as part of an embracing conversation about philosophical, political, religious, and ethical issues – that is, when no rigid boundary is placed between Anglo-American and continental philosophy and thought.[4] I would frame this project as an inquiry into meaningful human life, its character and possibility. There are late-twentieth-century philosophers on both sides of the so-called "divide" who figure into this conversation – among them Jürgen Habermas, Stanley Cavell, Charles Taylor, Alasdair MacIntyre, Cora Diamond, Hilary Putnam, Robert Brandom, John McDowell, Robert Pippin, Donald Davidson, Thomas Nagel, Richard Rorty, Jonathan Lear, and John Rawls. Elsewhere I have tried to place Emmanuel Levinas within that conversation.[5] In this book, I want to recommend the same thing for Emil Fackenheim, although to provide accounts of the kind one would like to see in support of this proposal will have to wait for another occasion.

Perhaps it will be helpful if I make clear at the outset which issues I take to be central to this inquiry into meaningful human existence – what is the point and purpose of human life? – insofar as Fackenheim contributes to that inquiry. First is the conception of the self as historically situated, which Fackenheim associates early on with his commitment to existentialism and later with what he calls a hermeneutical conception of the self. I will have more to say about this later, but I take it that this conception of the person or self as embedded in a natural and cultural world of enormous complexity – indeed, in such a way that this embeddedness or involvement is primordial and constitutive of selfhood – is a valuable discovery of twentieth-century thinking about human life and one that Fackenheim adheres to consistently. Second is the problem of historicity or relativism. One might take this to be a consequence of the conception of the self as historically situated – that is, that it leads to the relativity of all meaning and truth. One source for this problem was the inquiry into the natural and human sciences at the turn of the century, but it became a central problem throughout the twentieth century, one that arose in a host of venues – in sociology and the social sciences, in the philosophical inquiry into anthropology and ethnography, in the philosophical examination of the history of science, in religious thought and reflections on culture and religion, in literary theory, and in a host of other arenas. As I will show, this issue is so important to Fackenheim's thinking that one might argue it is central to everything he does.

Third is the question of transcendence. What I mean here is the question of whether one can and does acknowledge transcendence, what one means by it, how it is expressed, and what role or roles it plays. Much of twentieth-century reflection about this issue is concerned with religion, since transcendence is taken to point beyond nature and towards divinity. But figures as diverse as Lyotard, Derrida, and Levinas have other ways of thinking about transcendence, which is associated by many with difference and otherness, and Fackenheim finds a place in this conversation as well.[6] Fourth, there is the role of rupture, which for Fackenheim raises the question of how to understand the Holocaust and its place in Jewish experience and indeed in history as a whole.[7] Anglo-American philosophy has only recently begun to think about evil and suffering in terms that might allow it to appreciate the radical character of the Nazi atrocities and the world they shaped – *our* world. Yet continental thinkers of all kinds have made room for that project, and slowly it is becoming an issue for everyone.[8] One need not have in mind any mystification of the Holocaust to be serious about how that event has altered how we understand our world and our lives. Fackenheim contends uncompromisingly that we need to be serious about the event and to appreciate what was distinctive about it and why that should matter to us all. He may be highly selective about the historiography he reads and cites, but there is something profoundly right about his statement that the more we understand, the more we do not understand. This is not a truth about all historiography, but it is certainly true about those horrific years and those horrific events.

Finally, and to me most importantly, when we ask what makes human life worthwhile, we are regularly inclined to point to what is normative for our lives. That is, we want to know not only how we should act to satisfy our needs and our desires; we also want to understand how we ought to live and why. Often enough we can explain these matters by pointing to our nature as rational agents and rational persons, or we try to explain them by talking about what would provide us with a good life, or we turn to social practices and habits and communal interests. Fackenheim of course views the question as requiring some attention to that overarching and determinative relationship we have with the Absolute or the Infinite or what is called "God." In short, relationships provide the matrix, the framework, in which our actions and conduct take place and that give those actions a purpose and a meaning, yet finite or limited relationships can provide only an occasional and conditional purpose. To have an unconditional purpose or meaning is to have a relationship of an unconditional and inescapable kind in which or under which all else makes sense and matters. That is what the divine–human relationship provides for Fackenheim, as it did for Hegel, Kierkegaard, and perhaps Kant, and many others as well. On several occasions in the following pages, we will have an opportunity to consider this matter more fully, but for the moment it is sufficient to point to it as a venue – indeed, an absolutely critical one – in which Fackenheim's thought can and does play a vital role.

When I was a young philosopher and teacher, I often told my students that when it came to Jewish thought and philosophy in the twentieth century, Emil Fackenheim was among a small number of truly great figures. A statement like this is of course controversial: whenever we compile a list of "greats," we are exposing our prejudices and opening ourselves to criticism and debate. In this case, however, what I said then, refined in the crucible of the intervening decades of teaching and philosophical work, I would stand by today and indeed with more confidence. Figures like Hermann Cohen, Martin Buber, and Franz Rosenzweig were on my list then and are still on it. I would now include Joseph Soloveitchik and Emmanuel Levinas.[9] It is on this list that I include Emil Fackenheim. To be sure, Fackenheim's knowledge of Jewish texts is not that of Soloveitchik, and his philosophical work is not as extensive and systematic as that of Cohen or Levinas. But his work is deep and profound, and its philosophical richness is incontestable. He takes us into new territory and lets us see a new place. In this book I try to show why I think so and what might lead you to agree with me.

Let me try to clarify the structure and argument of this book in another way. Suppose we begin with Fackenheim's commitment to a view of human existence and the human condition that portrays persons as historically – culturally and socially – embedded agents. In his early years, Fackenheim would have associated this conception with existentialism; and in his later years, given the importance of its temporal and historical character, he would have associated it with a hermeneutical conception of human existence. Such a view is central to Fackenheim's philosophical thinking and to his philosophical understanding. As we will see, he formulates, develops, and ramifies but never abandons this conception of persons as historically embedded agents. That is the theme of chapter 2.

This conception of situated agency is central to his philosophy; it also is implicated in his conception of philosophy itself, its methods, and most importantly its goals or purpose. For Fackenheim, the philosopher must always remember that he or she is a historically situated agent and that this perspective is central to how philosophy proceeds. To what degree this limits philosophy is a matter of debate and analysis, and whether it makes traditional philosophical aspirations possible or not is, at one point in his career, vital to Fackenheim. For various reasons, the very character of philosophical inquiry and thought is a continuing puzzle for him, and his conception of it – and of the possibility of Jewish philosophy and its encounter with the Holocaust and radical evil – changes during his career. These are the themes of chapter 3.

Insofar as philosophy is a mode of thought, and perhaps – in Fackenheim's eyes – the pre-eminent mode of thought, it is determined and shaped by the historical situation out of which it arises – that is, by the historical situation of the philosopher as an embedded agent and thinker. In chapter 7, I take up this tension or, better, this dialectical relationship between thought and history – a major theme for Fackenheim throughout his career and certainly through the 1970s. This issue raises the question of whether relativism is possible and whether some kind of historicism is plausible or even necessary; it thus raises questions that philosophers associate with objectivity and foundationalism. The more Fackenheim enriches his existential way of thinking and immerses himself in Hegel, especially the *Phenomenology of Spirit*, the more he sees the historical demands placed upon philosophy. And then, when he decides to take up in all seriousness the importance and impact of the Nazi atrocities, the horrors of the death camps, he seems to find himself bound to accept the historicity of all thought, philosophical thought included. How this problematic develops for him and what it means after his engagement with Auschwitz are the themes of chapter 7.

Fackenheim's persona as a Jewish philosopher, then, includes these moments of philosophical thinking. But another constituent of his philosophical character, and an equally important one, involves his "conversations" with central figures in the history of philosophy. In the course of his career, Fackenheim engages with various philosophers, most notably Kant, Schelling, Hegel, Kierkegaard, Spinoza, and Heidegger.[10] The most important Jewish influences are Maimonides, Buber, and Rosenzweig. If we want to understand what contributes to Fackenheim's philosophical personality, however, arguably the primary two philosophical encounters are with Kant and Hegel, and in chapters 4 and 5 I explore those encounters. The importance of Hegel to Facken-heim is unparalleled, even if, in *To Mend the World*, a central confronta-tion is with Heidegger. In each chapter I explore how Auschwitz influ-enced what Kant and Hegel meant to Fackenheim, the most important considerations being Kant's argument for God's existence and Hegel's appreciation of history and his deeper appreciation of the divine–human relationship. In the end, from Fackenheim's perspective, there was no one like Hegel.

All of these chapters cannot avoid Fackenheim's Jewish preoccupa-tions, but their primary aim is to understand the depth and develop-ment of Fackenheim's philosophical sensibility. They explore the con-siderations that are most central to that aspect of his authorship. What makes Fackenheim a Jewish philosopher, however, is that these philo-sophical explorations are devoted to understanding what Jewish exis-tence is and ought to be. To accomplish this task, Fackenheim draws on traditional Jewish texts and reflects on central Jewish ideas. The texts with which Fackenheim is preoccupied, throughout his writings, are midrashic. To be sure, he does devote a late book, based on a set of lectures, to the Bible, but consistently, from the earliest writings through to the very latest, it is midrash to which Fackenheim turns as the great-est expression of classical Jewish theology. In chapter 8, I examine his use of midrash and his reflections on its nature throughout his career and ask, as I have in other chapters, how the encounter with the death camps had an impact on his reading and understanding of midrashic texts.

Among the central Jewish ideas that Fackenheim treated in his work, I focus on two. From the 1940s and at least through the 1980s, no idea was more central to Fackenheim's thinking about Judaism than the idea or concept of revelation, of the divine–human encounter. Probably his earliest Jewish writing, a student essay written while he was a rabbinic student in the late 1930s, was on revelation, and many of his essays of the postwar period were on that subject or dealt with it in one way or another. There is no better place to start to think about his work than to focus on revelation, as I do in chapter 1. But, as I note, for Fackenheim this is closely tied to redemption and to the question of what is incum-bent upon the individual Jew who stands between Creation and Re-demption. In Fackenheim's later thinking, in particular, the notions of ultimate redemption, history, and messianism are tied to his commit-ment to Zionism and the Jewish state. Especially after his aliyah in 1982, Fackenheim thought constantly and urgently about the situation of the

State of Israel and its political and theological roles; he was consumed with concern for its survival and well-being. Hence it would require a volume in itself to examine his Zionist commitments. In chapter 6, my project is more limited: I focus on his views about redemption, messianism, and history and say something about the role the State of Israel played for him in the context of such views.

In these chapters on Fackenheim's Jewish preoccupations, one can see at play the philosophical issues and concerns that were discussed earlier. Hence, we can see how he is a Jewish philosopher. There is no need here to set aside separate space to discuss the influence of figures like Buber and Rosenzweig. Once we have discussed his thinking about revelation, their influence is transparent and continuing. But it is helpful to appreciate how particularized the synthesis of Jewish commitment and philosophical inquiry is in Fackenheim's writings and in his thought. I do this in the book's two final chapters, 9 and 10, where I discuss on the one hand his literary style – his voice or persona as an author and its relation to his understanding of philosophy – and on the other his legacy. If the reader comes away convinced that Fackenheim is indeed a Jewish philosopher and not one thinker with two roles, that of a philosopher and that of a Jewish theologian, one way of deepening that conviction is to watch how his particular task is tied to the distinctiveness of his literary authorship and his philosophical voice. Another is to ask what is singular and important about his thinking and his work and what it might mean for the future of Jewish philosophy.

This narrative, then, gives some idea of the line of thinking, the argument, of the present book. As the reader can tell, however, the chapters are not organized to reflect that argument or to follow it. One might ask why not, and it is worth saying a word about that here. I have chosen to begin with the chapter on revelation. It is, as I have noted, the central concept for understanding his work in the early period, and it continues to play a central role for his work on Hegel, his response to Hegel, and his conception of post-Holocaust Jewish life. Moreover, it introduces the influence of Buber and Rosenzweig in the best way and allows one to appreciate why, later, Buber ceases to play a central role for him while Rosenzweig's influence becomes, in a sense, even more important.

I then turn to the philosophical side of Fackenheim in four chapters, on selfhood, philosophy, Kant, and Hegel. At that point the temptation is to examine Fackenheim's reading of midrash, but I resist it. It is better to take up first a Jewish theme and a philosophical one, each of which combines features that have already been discussed. The first is history, redemption, and Israel; the second is the dialectic between thought and history and the issue of historicism. With these in hand, I believe, the reader will appreciate more fully Fackenheim's use and understanding of midrash, which is then discussed. The final two chapters deal with his particularity as a Jewish philosopher, his authorship, and his legacy. To be sure, the reader can use my sketch of the book's argument and read the chapters in a different order, but I think that reading the chapters in the order presented will have advantages.

1

Can There Be Judaism without Revelation?

Revelation in the Early Years

In his earliest essay in Jewish theology, Fackenheim writes that the relation with God is central to what Judaism is and to why remaining Jewish is justified. That essay, a reaction to a liberal reading of the Akedah, appeared in *Commentary* in 1948 and was Fackenheim's first in a series of efforts to argue that Judaism required a commitment to the actuality of divine revelation in history and to the possibility of revelation in the present.[1] This was a hallmark of his philosophical and theological thinking in the postwar years, from 1948 through 1965: that revelation is necessary for Judaism.

The necessity of revelation is in part a response to the claims of Jewish naturalism that Judaism is a civilization or ethnicity, an identity grounded in nothing more than human nature and the particularities of tradition, folklore, and custom. What Judaism requires, in order to be justified in an unconditional and non-contingent way, is a link with transcendence; what it needs is an absolute ground, and this means a tie between Jews, the Jewish people, and God. That tie is constituted by an ongoing relationship, a covenant, and that covenant is grounded in events of divine–human encounter. Like a marriage or intimate friendship, this ongoing relationship is established by a real encounter and confirmed again and again by subsequent ones. Something like this reasoning, at any rate, is what Fackenheim proposes in this early period. His argument is framed to respond to a set of alternatives to understanding Judaism that fail, in his eyes, to secure the objectivity or absoluteness of Jewish existence.

These alternatives come from three quarters: from Jewish naturalism or secularism, from liberal Jewish theology, and from traditional

Judaism. Jewish naturalism fails to acknowledge revelation at all and so must accept the possibility that Judaism is just one way of life alongside others. Liberal Jewish theology may acknowledge revelation, but it reduces it to human reason or at least to human interpretation; and even traditional Judaism, which is grounded in revelation and divine transcendence, identifies revelation with its content, gives that content absolute authority, and thus fails to do justice to the human contribution in revelation. Fackenheim's concept of revelation is intended to avoid these and other errors and thereby to provide the core of a genuine understanding of modern Jewish existence.

One can discern in these early essays of 1948 to 1965 Fackenheim's deepest concerns. Although he never says so explicitly, the Nazi destruction of Jewish life in Eastern Europe and also in Germany and Western Europe may have been what motivated him to make such claims about the centrality of covenant, chosenness, and revelation.[2] For if Judaism is not somehow more than historical, more than contingent, then there may be some truth in the idea that Judaism has been superseded and that its survival has no current justification, and even in these early years Fackenheim could not endure or allow such a possibility. So on the one hand, for him, revelation came to be the strongest reason for continuing to be Jewish in a world that threatened the very existence of the Jewish people and that culturally offered secular alternatives for those who were willing or eager to opt out; and, on the other hand, revelation showed him that there is something fundamentally ahistorical about Judaism, something that makes it immune to historical destruction. Jewish existence is certainly a way of life and involves deep commitments and serious responsibilities that are worldly and social; but still, its ground is its link to the absolute, to the transcendent. So Fackenheim argued in the 1950s and 1960s.

His concept of revelation, furthermore, has the advantage that it confronts and copes with what he called the tragic element in the human situation. This tragic element is characterized by contradictions that reason can grasp but not solve – for example, the fact that there is a difference in kind between what the human condition is and what it ought to be, and the tension between human beings as natural beings whose every action can be understood and explained scientifically and human beings as agents some of whose choices are spontaneous and free. Living in the world, individuals must face up to these contradictions, Fackenheim claims, but only if God speaks to persons and they hear the divine address can these conflicts be resolved. Hence, Fackenheim poses the choice confronting the modern Jew: either accept a tragic existence or live a life with God, either be satisfied with what Rosenzweig called "paganism" or receive God's love and become whole.[3]

Here we have, then, an account of revelation's role in Judaism and in human existence. Revelation provides answers to the threat of meaninglessness and nihilism, what Fackenheim calls the "tragic element" in human existence; at the same time, revelation is essential to a Judaism that takes on a particular conception of the task to oppose nihilism and to live life meaningfully. Furthermore, God and hence the possibility of revelation applies to life in the world and (as we shall see) to history, and nothing in history can refute either God's existence or the possibility of revelation. As Fackenheim puts it, God is the Jew's existential a priori.[4] That is, the single person-like, historical God is an unassailable feature of Jewish existence and Jewish life. And since God is only present to the Jew in revelation or in the memory of past revelations, these too are irrefutable. And this in turn means that there is nothing that can count against the meaningfulness of Jewish life, of human existence, and of history.

We could say much more about all of this, but let me push on to the essential point, which is that revelation can solve these problems or perform these roles only if it is properly conceived. What, then, for Fackenheim, is revelation? How should we understand the divine–human relation?

Fackenheim's understanding of the tragic, contradictory character of human existence is indebted to Kierkegaard, Tillich, and others in the existential tradition.[5] The same goes for his concept of revelation; it too is indebted to Kierkegaard but also, and most importantly, to the two monuments of German-Jewish reflection on the divine–human encounter, Martin Buber and Franz Rosenzweig. In the postwar years in North America, for those Jewish intellectuals struggling to articulate what faith and religious life might mean in a secular world, Buber and Rosenzweig – as often as not a hyphenated unity – offered the most compelling models and the most salient vocabulary. Buber's dialogical account of human existence and his conception of God as the Eternal Thou and Rosenzweig's understanding of revelation as the divine love for a human beloved – these and various other ideas nourished the rise of what was called "the new Jewish theology" or "Jewish existential theology."[6] No one better than Fackenheim represented these developments; it was he who gave them their most philosophically sophisticated and articulate form.

The only way to encounter God is within revelation, and the human standpoint in revelation is the standpoint of the engaged participant, the situated agent. To begin, then, human existence is situated in the world together with other persons. The self is not detached and isolated but rather engaged and embedded. As Buber put it, there is no isolated I or self; rather the self is what it is only as it is related to objects and persons in contexts of use and experience and also, in especially determinative moments, in direct immediacy, in I–Thou meetings or encounters. In all of these relationships, direct and indirect, immediate and mediated, the self is an engaged agent and not a detached spectator or observer. Even when we seek to rise to a detached point of view, to become rationally reflective, we cannot wholly leave behind our embedded perspective. In science and philosophy, such detachment and the impersonal standpoint – to the degree that we can attain them – are necessary; in religious life, they are impossible. For, as Fackenheim argues, God can only be encountered in this engaged way. In relation to God, he says, objective detachment is impossible. God cannot be an object. This is Fackenheim's version of Buber's famous claim that God is the only Thou that can never become an It.[7] God is the only being with whom we are related that can only be encountered in an I–Thou and never in an I–It nexus, and hence God's existence cannot be subject to doubt or scepticism, even if His presence can elicit rebellion or rejection or offence.

What, however, occurs in this divine–human encounter that always involves a divine address to a human agent and a human response to a divine presence? To begin with, although revelation is a single event, the philosopher can distinguish in thought between the divine presence and the human response to it. Furthermore, as Fackenheim clarifies in "The Revealed Morality of Judaism and Modern Thought," we can distinguish in thought between the pristine moment of revelation and the commandment that follows from it.[8] Together these distinctions enable us to focus here on the way in which the divine presence engages the human in the pristine moment, prior to the full-fledged commandment and the human response. In so doing, we turn first to the divine contribution to the pristine moment.

The moment of divine presence is a spontaneous act of what Fackenheim often calls "singling out." Revelation, that is, is absolutely given. Man can prepare for it but cannot elicit it. It is divinely initiated, and the reason for it is wholly mysterious, if indeed it makes sense to speak of a divine reason at all. Hence, as an utterly particular act of

God's singling out a particular person, revelation is an act of love. Fackenheim shows that he is indebted to the account that Rosenzweig, in the section on revelation in Part Two of the *Star of Redemption*, gives of revelation as an act of love, love as a subtle dialectic of quest and bestowal, of affirmation and accepting, of acknowledgment and self-understanding.[9] It would be worthwhile to take the time to show how the details of Fackenheim's account of revelation, in papers such as "Self-Realization and the Search for God" and "Can There Be Judaism Without Revelation?," are appropriated precisely from Rosenzweig. For us, however, one example will have to suffice. Fackenheim says that in the moment of revelation, God commands man to love Him in return and this means to choose to submit to Him. Man makes the decision, but it is in reality no decision at all, since revelation is inescapable. If revelation requires decision yet is absolutely given, how is this decision possible? Only if, Fackenheim says, the freedom to choose is given in the love itself, yet at the same time, only if that decision is made with supreme humility. It is an act of submission yet self-affirmation; the decision is free yet modest, mitigated. But this is precisely what Rosenzweig tells us is characteristic of the self who is loved by God and who receives that love and becomes aware of himself as a beloved. His sense of himself, which had once been pride and characteristic of the tragic hero of antiquity, now at the moment of revelation becomes humility, characteristic of the recipient of divine love and command.[10] In this way, as Fackenheim points out, revelation is both command and love, and it acknowledges in man both his capacity for transcendence and his utter dependence. In the moment of revelation, God's love for the particular human being is manifest in the gift of freedom and in the commandment to love and obey Him; as Rosenzweig said, this one commandment is in fact the totality of all the subsequent ones. Or, as Fackenheim puts it, this is the meaning of the commandment to accept the "yoke of the Kingdom of Heaven," the burden of all the commandments prior to their being articulated. In his words, the love of God is the life of all the commandments. It is the individual's loving acceptance of God in return for God's loving acknowledgment of her. Divine love and divine command are inseparable; the individual is both obligated and enabled. And in being so determined, the human recipient, in accepting the Torah as a whole, the yoke of the Kingdom, accepts herself as one accepted by God in her humanity. She realizes that her life is meaningful and oriented and that such a condition is an absolute gift.

What role does revelation, conceived in this way, play in human existence? As we have pointed out, for Fackenheim revelation solves the problems posed by human existence, problems that are constitutive of the alternative, which is to live tragically. But Fackenheim does not leave it at that. On the one hand, revelation points towards redemption. There is something like this in Buber and most clearly in Rosenzweig, for whom redemptive human action is a response to the gift of divine love. But on the other hand, revelation and the orientation towards redemption are necessary both to make sense of the individual's existence and to make sense of history. How is this so?

In the essay "Can There Be Judaism Without Revelation?" (1952), Fackenheim claims that human existence is incomplete without revelation.[11] As created, man is an animal, a part of nature, and as yet-to-be-redeemed, he and nature are ultimately to be consummated. What revelation adds is the significance in this process of the here-and-now, of the unique individual in the course of history. Revelation, then, is a particular divine–human event in which the individual is called to reach out to others and to direct his life to the task of human community. Or, as Fackenheim puts it, it is the religious category of existence as such. It gives meaning to the life of each and every particular person. If revelation were impossible, then each particular existence would be a weight upon time and history. Rosenzweig had taken revelation to be orientation, an absolute point that determines for the individual how his life fits into the pattern of all of history. Fackenheim is here appropriating that idea: without revelation, without being singled out by God, the individual can only wait for the ultimate redemption; with it, he is called upon to work on its behalf. Without the hope for redemption, there is no reason to think that human work can consummate history; with such hope, the work of each individual is confirmed as a contribution to a task beyond any one person's accomplishment.

Over a decade later, in "Judaism and the Meaning of Life," Fackenheim elaborates the significance of this view of revelation for the meaning of life and history.[12] Revelation, which both obligates and enables the individual, creates a special relationship with those whom God singles out, both individuals one by one and the community as a whole. This is the covenant, a relationship that is historically ongoing, even when man fails to observe its commandments and when God fails to respond to human conduct. Moreover, the covenant is made both with the individual and with the community; it gives direction and orientation for both, and thereby it makes history meaningful and a unity.

History is meaningful both because God guarantees the ultimate redemption of nature and history and because it is dependent upon human action, and its meaningfulness cannot do without either the divine or the human contribution. Hence, revelation, as Fackenheim understands it, is the category of events that provides the time between creation and redemption, so to speak, with significance and that identifies individuals and communities as genuine historical agents. In philosophically precise terms, Fackenheim here is glossing the famous passage in *I and Thou* where Buber says that revelation is not a content but a force and that it is the ground of meaning for the individual's life in the world.[13]

This sketch of Fackenheim's early concept of revelation will do for the time being. In chapter 2, I will examine the elaboration of revelation in commandment and law and also the role of human freedom. In the pristine moment of divine presence, we have seen, there is not only divine love but also human reception and response; the individual is obligated to love God in return, to acknowledge his singled-out condition and accept its obligations, and is also enabled to respond; he is free to receive that love with a supreme humility. For the moment, that is all we need say about the human side of revelation. We can now ask what role the concept of revelation comes to play as Fackenheim turns to the Holocaust and whether that concept undergoes modification or revision.

Revelation at the Turning Point

Fackenheim's early view of revelation drew much of its detail and character from the thought of Buber and Rosenzweig – in particular, from Buber's *I and Thou* and Rosenzweig's *Star of Redemption* as well as the other writings translated and presented in Nahum Glatzer's *Franz Rosenzweig: His Life and Thought*, which Fackenheim reviewed shortly after its publication.[14] It was a philosopher's work to articulate and defend revelation as a *concept*; but when Fackenheim turned to its role in Judaism, he noted that its *actuality* required that God – the possibility of divine presence – be treated by the Jew as an irrefutable reality, so to speak. He had said as early as 1952 that God was the Jew's existential a priori.[15] God's existence could be confirmed through experience, but nothing that took place in history could refute that existence. In 1966, in the last of his five responses to the questions asked of Jewish intellectuals by *Commentary* magazine, he reaffirmed this point:[16] God is not a hypothesis that requires verification or that must in principle be falsifiable. Hence, the "death of God" theology, so prominent in Christian theological circles in the mid-1960s, was of no significance for Jews.

We need to be more precise about what Fackenheim is saying here. In a 1964 essay that is an early version of the themes that will take up chapter 2 of *God's Presence in History* – the title, which Fackenheim appropriates from Buber, is "On the Eclipse of God" – he does not refer to the irrefutability of God's existence but rather to the irrefutability of religious faith.[17] Such faith, he says, is empirically verifiable, yet at the same time, it cannot be falsified by anything that happens in the world and in history. Faith, as Fackenheim here uses it, refers to the continuing relationship between the human and the divine and specifically to the human attitudes, expectations, and concerns that are constituted in an original moment of revelation and then undergo later confirmation, modification, and occasionally disposal. That is, what Fackenheim seems to be saying here is that nothing that happens to the believer or to others, nothing that anyone does or feels, can destroy the ongoing relationship of lover and beloved, of commander and obedient respondent, that is the primary matrix for the believer's historical existence, his life. The way the believer lives in that relationship may change, but the relationship itself is inescapable. In the terms Fackenheim had earlier used, this is the covenant. Moreover, since it is grounded in revelation and can always be confirmed by subsequent moments of revelation, if it is inescapable, it is so because new revelations are always possible. No matter what happens, the relationship can be reconfirmed or redirected. In these terms, in "On the Eclipse of God," Fackenheim describes the current crisis of religious faith as a situation in which faith is misunderstood. It is taken by many to be a feeling or attitude that can be falsified or shown to be misguided or mistaken. That is, if faith is the feeling of absolute dependence, as Schleiermacher claimed, then nothing prevents someone from feeling and yet refusing to accept the inference that God must exist as its object. The sceptic might argue as follows: that there are natural, human reasons for how and why such a feeling arises that show it to involve an erroneous reference to some divine being or a mere projection of such a being's existence. In short, when faith is understood as a psychological condition, the existence of God can be understood as a human construction. When faith is reduced to psychology, scepticism is possible. But this, Fackenheim argues, is to misunderstand what faith and revelation really are and to make them vulnerable to easy refutation. The point of Fackenheim's essay, then, is to expose the error of such naturalistic or humanistic accounts and to promote the view we have seen, of revelation as a divine–human I–Thou encounter, of a pristine moment of divine presence and love and human openness and response. Moreover, it is faith and revelation, viewed in these terms, that he takes to be inescapable from the standpoint of believing openness.

But it is only when Fackenheim notices the *error* in this confidence that he is able to confront the demons of Auschwitz. Indeed, Fackenheim expresses this reluctance himself and tells us so. He had been glib and uncritical regarding his supreme confidence not only in faith but also in philosophical and scientific thought, and it was only when he realized that such confidence was misplaced that he was able to take the Holocaust with complete seriousness. That was his way of putting it, but what does it mean?

In the first chapter of *Quest for Past and Future*, a retrospective of his work over the previous two decades (i.e., the 1950s and 1960s), he refers to the midrashic literature of the rabbis as Judaism's greatest theology. It is, he says, a corpus of "stories, parables, and metaphors" that portrays as a whole the contradictory impulses of Jewish life. Since it is a whole (albeit not a system), it has a logic of its own, which he calls the "Midrashic framework."[18] Moreover, he then in 1967 notes that the Midrashic framework is "open." That is, "the Torah was given at Sinai, yet is given whenever a man receives it, and a man must often hear the old commandments in new ways."[19] The recovery of the articulated responses to old revelations in the present is always subject to reinterpretation, and those reinterpretations are sometimes revisionary, sometimes radical. Indeed, "such openness is necessary if history is to be serious." Furthermore, Fackenheim claims, until now the old framework has been revised but has "remained internally unbroken." But it is not "invulnerable," and today, after Auschwitz, "vulnerability is no mere theoretical possibility." This is the realization that philosophy should remain open to history – indeed, must remain so if it is to be genuinely historical; and also the realization that Judaism and revelation are vulnerable when confronted with the dark history of Auschwitz. It is these two insights that lead Fackenheim to conclude that the Midrashic framework is an open framework, always vulnerable to what he calls "radical surprise," to being stunned by what it sees into recoil – into suspicion or even scepticism – and in a radical, unconditional way. This claim, moreover, constitutes a direct reversal of his earlier one that religious faith can be verified historically but can never be falsified by history. It amounts to saying that nothing in Jewish faith, in the covenantal content of the

Jewish life lived in response to revelation and the tradition of revelation, is immune to modification and even rejection. There is no such thing as a Jewish existential a priori.

Do not think that I am here discovering something of which Fackenheim himself was not already aware. In his autobiographical introduction to the first edition of *To Mend the World*, written in 1981, he asks explicitly: If the Holocaust is to be taken seriously, if it can be a radical "countertestimony" to Judaism and Christianity and even philosophical reason, then how is this possible and what follows from it? In short, is Judaism let us say immune to *all* historical threats, or is it vulnerable to at least some? And if it is vulnerable, might such a threat – Auschwitz would be one – destroy Judaism, or might there be for Jewish faith "a commandment to resist its destructive implications, to say nothing of the will and the strength to obey it?"[20] His answer is that he could permit the radical seriousness of Auschwitz only because he had made "the greatest doctrinal change in [his] whole career" – his realization that "at least *Jewish faith* is, after all, not *absolutely* immune to *all* empirical events." That is, it was the realization that the Midrashic framework, while a fragmentary whole with dialectical features, is nonetheless always open, vulnerable at any historical moment to a dramatic and possibly even overwhelming reinterpretation. In the case of the Holocaust, this openness and vulnerability requires that the Jew today worry about whether continuing as a Jew is at all possible and hence ask what the Torah can mean in a post-Holocaust world, whether one must simply capitulate to the evils of Auschwitz or whether resistance to those evils is both necessary and possible. Clearly, then, Fackenheim recognizes the change in his conception of faith and revelation that we have noticed. Articulating this change and its implications is precisely the task that Fackenheim sets for himself in *To Mend the World*.[21]

We might reformulate these questions this way: After Auschwitz, for Fackenheim, must Jewish faith face commandments, and if so, what are they? We shall have more to say about these questions in the next chapter; for now, I want to ask a different one – whether this change in Fackenheim's thinking, a change regarding the status of Jewish theological self-understanding vis-à-vis history, also leads him to change his concept of revelation. Recall that for the early Fackenheim, revelation was understood, in Buberian terms, as one possible mode of human existence within the possibilities articulated by a dialogical anthropology, an account of human existence as engaged and embedded, as intrinsically relational. Within this framework, revelation is a direct divine–human encounter, constituted by a dialectic of love and response, commandment and self-understanding. Does the Holocaust threaten such a conception?

Clearly, to move quickly to the outcome, Fackenheim does not think so. In *To Mend the World*, in the introduction, he says: "By 'Jewish faith' I understand now, as I did then, a commitment to revelation; and by 'revelation' I understand now, as I did then, not propositions or laws backed by divine sanction, but rather, at least primordially, the *event* of divine *Presence*." Fackenheim then goes on to explain how the movement to a "return to revelation," which was associated in German-Jewish thought with Buber and Rosenzweig, a movement that was brought to Fackenheim's attention by reading Leo Strauss, had gripped him when he was young and continued to do so in his early theological writings. It led him to seek to understand how the incursion by the divine into the world could be understood, how a human appropriation of the impact of that event is possible, what hermeneutical roles applied to God and man, and then how to provide some content for the revelation.[22] Once he had turned his attention to the Holocaust, however, while his agenda had changed: he had no "second thoughts" about revelation. Indeed, the early view, he says in 1981, was one to which he remained committed.

Viewed from a certain angle, then, we can understand in part why Fackenheim refuses to treat the Holocaust within the framework of the traditional problem of theodicy. The God of the problem of evil, omnipotent and unqualifiedly benevolent, is not the God of revelation, at least not in the way that Fackenheim, following Buber and Rosenzweig, understands that notion. The God of theodicy is an object of reason and argument, a being with essential attributes. But for Fackenheim the only way to encounter God, as an engaged and embedded agent, is at moments of divine presence. This is Fackenheim's way of putting Buber's claim that God is the only being that can never be expressed but only addressed. In part, Fackenheim simply finds traditional responses to the problem of evil impossible to accept and live with, but it is also true that for him, such intellectualizing, as it were, is simply the wrong way to engage with the suffering and the atrocity and certainly the wrong way to encounter God.[23]

Revelation and the Changing Agenda

But before we move too quickly to the way Fackenheim exposes Jewish faith to the horrors of Nazism, we need to see if what we have said is satisfactory. Is it enough to say that the Holocaust, as an epoch-making event that exposed all thought and all life to radical revision, had no effect on Fackenheim's concept of revelation?

This question, which requires us to consider revelation as he examines it in his writings after 1967, will take up the remainder of this chapter. I will have to be selective. First, there is one place where he takes an even later look at his early views about revelation and what that notion came to mean to him in his later work. His comments from 1992 suggest that he did change his mind about certain features of his account of revelation. Second, we will look at *God's Presence in History* as most representative of how revelation occurs in his writings at the turning point of the late 1960s. Finally, we must say a word about the role of revelation in chapter 3 of *To Mend the World*, where he focuses on revelation after Spinoza and Rosenzweig.[24] I will try to take these three steps quickly, in order to highlight what is most important and with an eye to our question: whether the exposure to Auschwitz led Fackenheim, as a philosopher and theologian, to modify his conception of revelation in light of the horrific events.

In *Fackenheim: German Philosophy and Jewish Thought*, the volume of essays on his work edited by Louis Greenspan and Graeme Nicholson and published in Toronto in 1992, Fackenheim replies to his critics, one of whom, Reinier Munk, had written about Fackenheim's concept of revelation, which he called Fackenheim's highest commitment.[25] In the course of his response to Munk, Fackenheim says that "Munk attributes to me views about Revelation that I have long abandoned."[26] What are these views that Fackenheim took himself to have abandoned? First, the claim that revelation solves problems in the human condition that can otherwise not be solved requires modification. The very notion of "the human condition," he claims, has become suspect; it is a relic of the nineteenth and early twentieth centuries. Human existence is embedded and hence pluralistic. There is no *one* condition that needs to be confronted, no *single* set of problems requiring solutions, and no reason to think that human problems, given their variety and type, all require religious solutions. Whatever can be said on behalf of a continued belief in revelation and the need for it, one can no longer simply return to those old arguments.

Second, Fackenheim points out that in *God's Presence in History* he replaces the concept of revelation with the notion of a "root experience in Judaism." The significance of this change is multifaceted. To begin, the focus of the new expression is on the human experience of the divine–human encounter. What is foundational or most relevant in revelation is the human response to it and not the fact that it involves a divine presence. Judaism is certainly a way of life, and it may be or may understand itself to be established on the basis of divine–human encounters. Whether it actually *is* or *does* is a contingent and historical matter; in response to Auschwitz, there will be those who believe and those who do not. Some take the imperative to continue as a Jew to be a divine command; others do not. In *God's Presence in History*, if we can put it this way, the emphasis has shifted in Fackenheim's thinking from the divine aspect of revelation to its human appropriation and response.[27] This is not to say that Fackenheim does not call attention in these lectures to the divine presence and hold firm to it, but he does so only to focus his attention on the human – here, Jewish – response to it.

Furthermore, and Fackenheim makes note of this, the notion of a root experience in Judaism is specific and not general; what has replaced the concept of revelation in general is the notion of a foundational experience for Judaism and Jewish existence. The very fact that such root experiences in Judaism are taken to be moments of revelation is a function of the notion's historical specificity. Moreover, since such events in Judaism are the salvation at the Red Sea and the revelation at Sinai, the divine presence is a saving presence in the one case and a commanding presence in the other. The human responses to these moments of encounter with God – the song at the sea with a sense of jubilation and gratitude, and the articulation of the commandments and the law – these become standards for later re-enactments of these events in the course of Jewish life and for the conduct of Jewish life as part of a commitment to them.

Third, the notion of a "root experience in Judaism" is the core of a historical understanding of revelation and its re-enactment and recovery. Revelation is the central feature of a religious, hermeneutical process; it does not stand alone. Since it points to history, to the past, to the present, and to the future, this notion requires another new concept, one that introduces the possibility that later events will influence or alter the reappropriation of the root experiences. This further notion is that of "an epoch-making event." Here, Fackenheim points out, he breaks decisively with Rosenzweig and especially with his conception of Judaism. For Judaism, as Rosenzweig sees it, is charged with the task of praying for and anticipating eternity, the ultimate redemption; it is not responsible for working to bring that redemption by changing the social and political life of others in the world. As Fackenheim puts it, for Rosenzweig's Judaism, nothing of significance happens in history between Creation and Redemption.[28] After Auschwitz, however, Fackenheim understands Judaism as wholly immersed in history, and therefore the lessons of the root experiences of Judaism must be recoverable at any time but only in terms of the historical character of the moment. Hence, that recovery is always subject to the impact of "epoch-making events" that could lead to radical revision of those lessons. As Fackenheim puts it, "within Judaism, an event is epoch-making only if it *threatens the root experiences*, and the threat is removed only if a *response* is found; as for *God's Presence in History*, the Holocaust is perceived in it as a threat *without precedent*, moral unless and until a *truly adequate* response is found."[29] In the weeks leading up to and including the Six Day War, the threat was so great that Fackenheim admits, having lived all those years with revelation, he "no longer could, whatever the theological cost, shut [his] ears to the desperate words of the poet Jacob Glatstein: 'On Sinai we received the Torah, and in Lublin we gave it back.'" This, at least, is the risk that comes with taking Auschwitz seriously. Such is the impact of this epoch-making event on the recovery of the Sinaitic root experience.

Here, then, we come face to face with the fact of the openness of the Midrashic framework, as Fackenheim calls the ancient Jewish theology, in all its specificity and reality. If, for Rosenzweig, revelation is an act of divine love that commands and enables human love in return as well as a consciousness of selfhood and responsibility, the Holocaust shows that *recovering* at subsequent historical moments that seriousness and that responsibility is fraught with risk and uncertainty. It must involve rethinking what it means to love God, to love others, and to live in confidence that such love is not in vain. Can the Jew in a post-Holocaust world hear the old command, respond to it, and feel confident in that response, and what would be the content of such a response?

If the early Fackenheim took revelation in general to be an absolute solution to historical problems, the later Fackenheim is more restrained, more humble. After Auschwitz, revelation does not come with guarantees. It may provide a direction; it may provide the possibility of recovering confidence and of hope in the future; but whether such recovery actually occurs, only time will tell. That is, in the 1950s and 1960s, Fackenheim had taken for granted that the covenantal faith was always secure, even when challenged. At the critical turning point in the late 1960s, he came to appreciate that the resonance of the primordial encounters could be threatened to its core. To see how that faith can survive today is the project of *God's Presence in History*, but it is a project he carries out in the context of his earlier Buber–Rosenzweig conception of revelation and not as part of a rejection of it.

Fackenheim refers to *God's Presence in History* as his most widely read book. No doubt it is. It is beautifully and succinctly written, rich in reasoning and readings of the Bible, midrash, Buber, and much more. But Fackenheim is right: when it comes to revelation, the core concept remains, even while his agenda has changed or at least his emphasis has shifted. As I have already noted, that emphasis is on Jewish response. But even though the agenda has changed and his focus with it, Fackenheim does attend to the divine aspect of revelation, what he calls the divine presence. In fact, Fackenheim never gave a more nuanced and richer account of revelation as a divine–human encounter than he does in the first chapter of the book. Here he turns to the specific revelations that are Judaism's root experiences – both the redemptive and the commanding presence of God. In the case of God's saving presence, this involves the citation and examination of a remarkable passage from Buber's book *Moses* in which Buber describes the experience of a "miracle" as an "abiding astonishment" in which "the current system of cause and effect becomes, as it were, transparent and permits a glimpse of the sphere in which a sole power, not restricted by any other, is at work."[30] As Fackenheim explains, Buber here provides terms in which one can understand what it means to experience God's saving presence and how the re-enactment of that experience is possible.[31] Then, later in the same chapter, he quotes and analyses the famous midrash on the *Song of Songs*, which records how God softens or sweetens the first word of the Ten Commandments that threatens to destroy those who hear it.[32] He gives this subtle account of what it means to experience God's commanding presence, also in terms of the presence of a "sole Power" and the response of an "abiding astonishment":

> The divine commanding Presence can be divine, commanding, and present only if it is doubly present; and the human astonishment must be a double astonishment. As sole power, the divine commanding Presence destroys human freedom; as gracious power, it restores that freedom, and indeed exalts it, for human freedom is made part of a covenant with Divinity itself. And the human astonishment, which is terror at a Presence at once divine and commanding, turns into a second astonishment, which is joy, at a Grace which restores and exalts human freedom by its commanding Presence.

Here is a nuanced restatement of the earlier account of revelation that
Fackenheim had appropriated from Rosenzweig, with the outcome
that each new generation of Jews is called upon to re-enact the original
encounter at Sinai by re-enacting, as Fackenheim puts it, the double
astonishment of terror and joy, for without both features the Jew's recovery of the past experience is inadequately open to the divine or inadequately human.[33]

In the second chapter of *God's Presence in History*, Fackenheim elaborates what he calls the external challenge to the Midrashic framework.
That framework, recall, is the logic that explains the ongoing re-
enactments and recoveries of the root experiences of Judaism in story,
parable, and metaphor. It is Fackenheim's expression for the defining
features of Jewish tradition. The external challenge – the sceptical challenge – to this tradition comes from modern philosophy and other intellectual developments, from Marx, Freud, Nietzsche, and others.[34] But for
our purposes, the interesting question about what remains of revelation
comes in chapter 3, where Fackenheim turns to what he calls an *internal*
challenge posed by Auschwitz and the death camps. Here we have an
epoch-making event that threatens the root experiences and, this means,
that threatens the possibility of recovering and retaining a sense of gratitude and confidence in response to God's saving power and a sense of
obligation and direction in response to God's commanding grace.

Fackenheim concludes that the Holocaust cannot be explained or understood – religiously, scientifically, or philosophically. But a response
to that event is necessary, and as we shall see in the next chapter, the
content of that response takes shape as Jews now seek to understand
what resistance to that event requires. Famously, Fackenheim formulates the imperative to which that response is made as the 614th commandment. That is, Jewish response is interpreted as grounded in a
divine command that supplements the traditional 613 biblical commandments. For the moment, let me focus on its source, so to speak. In
what sense can one take its source or ground to be divine?

The details here are complex, but the gist of the point is this. In thinking through a Jewish secularist response to the demons of Auschwitz,
Fackenheim puts it this way: "Jewish opposition to Auschwitz cannot
be grasped in terms of humanly created ideals but only as an imposed
commandment. And the Jewish secularist, no less than the believer, is
absolutely singled out by a Voice as truly other than man-made ideals
– an imperative as truly given – as was the Voice of Sinai."[35] Fackenheim claims that Jewish response to the horrors of the Holocaust is not

a matter of whim or nostalgia; rather, it is a matter of an obligation or imperative, and that obligation or imperative is experienced as given or as received and not as grounded in an ideal that human reason constructs or constitutes. Let us assume for now that Fackenheim has made his case for this result.[36] He then distinguishes between the Jewish believer and the Jewish secularist. In this passage he tells us that the Jewish believer is "singled out" by a divine Voice that is as much a commanding presence as was the Voice that spoke at Sinai. That is, the believer takes himself or herself to be the recipient of a divine commandment. What, however, about the Jewish secularist, who presumably does not believe in a divine presence? As Fackenheim puts it elsewhere, using terms he appropriates from Rosenzweig, such a Jew hears the *mitzvah*, the commandment, even if he does not hear the voice of the *mitzaveh*, the commander.[37] He senses an obligation to respond to the horrors of Auschwitz by opposing its forces and forces like them, by opposing the demons of Auschwitz. In the text I quoted, Fackenheim does not say that the Jewish secularist hears the Voice; he says that he is *singled out* by that Voice. But that is to confuse the issue, for it is only from the point of view of the believer that the secularist is singled out by a divine commanding presence. *From his own point of view*, the Jewish secularist simply knows that he is obligated to oppose Nazi purposes; he may not have any idea about what grounds the force of that obligation and its unconditionality. Fackenheim often cites a passage from Nietzsche's *Ecce Homo* that Martin Buber regularly called to mind: there are times when "one takes and does not ask who gives."[38]

At this crucial point in *God's Presence in History*, then, Fackenheim employs the account of revelation that he had articulated in his earlier writings. It is here particularized to the situation of a Jew seeking to reenact the root experience of Sinai but now in a post-Holocaust situation. He even suggests that there are features of the experience of such a moment of re-enactment that a Jewish believer will be able to recover that are opaque to the "eye" of a Jewish secularist. Nonetheless, the concept of revelation at work in this pivotal book – albeit set in a historical and hermeneutical framework – is by and large the same as the one he had articulated earlier in his career.

Revelation in Fackenheim's Mature Thought

In Fackenheim's memoir *An Epitaph for German Judaism*, in Appendix B, the inaugural lecture that he gave in Kassel on 24 April 1997 for the

Franz Rosenzweig Lecture Series, he commented on the theme of revelation in his work:

> My main work has been – and still is – the problem and fate of revelation
> in modernity, except that in more recent years the Holocaust has replaced
> modernity. "Revelation" I understand as the incursion of the "Divine Oth-
> er" into the human world and hence include Christianity as a religion of
> revelation, a necessity if only because the most significant thinkers in mo-
> dernity were Christians. Under the influence of Leo Strauss, I first tried to
> go back to the Middle Ages … But after a few years I turned to modernity,
> and not only because it was impossible to avoid modern philosophy.
>
> Until 1967 my work fell into two parts, which remained separate be-
> cause of the objectivity required by scholarship. One … was scholarship,
> the other was my commitment to Judaism.
>
> The scholarship was devoted to philosophy from Kant through Fichte,
> Schelling, Hegel, and Kierkegaard: is it possible to embrace Kantian "au-
> tonomy" and hold fast to the "Other" of Biblical revelation? In my opin-
> ion "From Kant to Kierkegaard" is the deepest development of the theme
> "Revelation and Modernity," although – an insight that came later – it is
> not radical enough for "Revelation and the Holocaust."[39]

In his own eyes, then, revelation and its viability in the face of modernity and the Holocaust were the central problem of his entire career, for
he was still, up until one month prior to his death in September 2003,
revising these memoirs, and hence up until that time he had the opportunity to revise or exclude this comment on the importance of revelation to him and the fact that his conception of it was of a divine incursion into the human world, as he put it.

This understanding of revelation is Fackenheim's answer to a question that he asks more explicitly and answers more directly in 1987 in
his book *What Is Judaism?*: Can the Jew of today still receive the Jewish
book, the Bible, as Torah? Can she still read it as a response to the divine
presence and as an interpretation of what the divine incursion into history means? This question is the theme of that book's fourth chapter. It
is premised on the conviction that "revelation is primordially a divine
presence, an incursion into the world of man, necessitating a distinction
between the event of revelation itself and a text that it 'stimulates.'"
And Fackenheim reminds the reader that he had, as a student in Berlin,
in the *Hochschule*, learned this view from Rosenzweig and Buber and
still held it in 1987.[40] Hence, if this is what revelation is, the question for

the Jew today is whether the old text can still be read today as Torah, as a bridge to the divine presence that was its primordial sponsor. For our purposes, the key to Fackenheim's answer is that when the Bible is received as Torah, at any moment and hence even today, and when that reception takes the form of studying the Torah, following its commandments, and such, what is going on in fact is that the Jew is "accept[ing] anew his covenantal relation with the God of his fathers." Or, as Fackenheim points out, the Jew opens himself to this possibility on two conditions. One is that he can make sense of how revelation can be both divine and human, the gift of divine power and the reception of human freedom. As we have seen, this joint contribution is something that Fackenheim had explored as early as his first essays. The second condition is that the epoch-making events of the last century have not made such reception and such a renewal of the covenant impossible. For Fackenheim, of course, they have not. What the events of the Holocaust do require is that no reception be adequate that does not stay with history and maintain its integrity.

We have leaped ahead to a comment that Fackenheim made very late in life, and we have then returned to 1987 and the position he set out in *What Is Judaism?* In a sense, we have followed paths that took us from his early works to 1970 and now back from the end of his life. These two paths converge on his great work of 1982, *To Mend the World*. What does he say about revelation in that book?

We have one more step to take, then, as we turn to the role of revelation in *To Mend the World*.[41] What we say here will be elaborated in later chapters, but the central point about revelation in this book, his magnum opus, is clear and will confirm the account we have developed thus far.[42] If *God's Presence in History* is about the necessity for Jewish life to recover the Jewish past through the dark prism of Auschwitz, then *To Mend the World* is about how that obligation can be met. That is, it is about the human capacity to repair, if only in a fragmentary way, the shattered world. This will be an important issue for us in chapter 2, where we turn to human freedom, human capacity, and human response. But in the third chapter of *To Mend the World*, "The Shibboleth of Revelation," Fackenheim addresses the question of whether revelation is possible in the modern world – more precisely, the question of what revelation is and whether it can still, after Auschwitz, be reappropriated. My own way of putting the point of the chapter is that it asks what revelation is and whether it can be recovered after the challenges of naturalism and Idealism. The most important text for us to consider is the last section of his chapter 3, "The Shibboleth of Revelation in Jewish Modernity."

Fackenheim argues here that "every genuine religion is an actual relation between the human and the Divine" and that "in religion, the Divine is represented as Other" and remains represented and experienced as other to the end. This is importantly true of Judaism, which stands firm on the difference between God and man but also on their moving towards each other. Fackenheim portrays the firmness of this commitment by showing how Rosenzweig affirms Judaism in the face of a Hegelian challenge that sees it as superseded or overcome and thereby that affirms a divine–human identity. He takes Rosenzweig's achievement to be inadequate for our day precisely because the latter's Judaism is by and large ahistorical.[43] But one aspect of this commitment is secure – that Judaism is grounded in the possibility of *teshuvah*, of returning to an engaged relationship with God that is a "divine-human turning-toward-each-other, despite and indeed because of their persistent and unmitigated incommensurability."[44] That is, whatever else might be true and necessary for a post-Holocaust Judaism, it continues to adhere to a commitment to revelation and to the ongoing covenantal existence. It may be that an otherworldly fideism is no longer authentic, but however historical and worldly a genuine post-Holocaust Judaism must be, it cannot be so without clinging still to its sense of religious purpose, and this means to the possibility that Jewish action in the world is a response to the encounter with a divine commanding presence.

Conclusion

There is no more central idea in Fackenheim's thought than the concept of revelation. We have seen that in his early writings, he defends the integrity of covenant, faith, and revelation by arguing for the particular role of revelation and by defending it against critics and sceptics. In so doing, he articulates a concept of revelation based on the thinking of Buber and Rosenzweig, and there is good reason to believe that he held fast to that concept throughout his career. At the same time that he indicated his allegiance to it, however, Fackenheim himself recognized that with his engagement with the Holocaust, the concept underwent modification. At least, his attention to it came to focus on its historical specificity, on the very particular reality of revelation as it occurs within Judaism, and also on the human response to revelation as a historical, temporal, and hermeneutical account. In short, as he put it, the agenda for contemporary philosophy and contemporary Jewish thought had changed; it had become deeply historical and worldly. But for him to take that historical dimension seriously, he had to admit that revelation, faith, covenant, and the Midrashic framework, the logic of the textual articulation of the meaning grounded in revelation, all were open to historical modification and even refutation. In principle, this openness exposed the possibility that the very concept of revelation and the way God's presence is implicated in it could be rejected; in practice, however, Fackenheim saw no reason for such rejection. By and large, he remained a loyal advocate of the Buber–Rosenzweig conception of revelation as a divine incursion into the world. At one time that conception, as realized in the actuality of the Exodus and Sinai, had provided Jews with confidence, hope, and direction for their lives; since Auschwitz it had not had precisely these benefits. In his later writings, Fackenheim's attention is on how the Jew – as well as so many others – responds to the obligation or imperative that "speaks" to him or her from the ashes of Nazi Europe. God, as he indicates in *What Is Judaism?*, is not to be ignored, but for many – some believing and some more sceptical – finding one's way back to a relationship with Him may be a long and difficult process.[45]

2

Selfhood and Freedom:
From Situated Agency
to the Hermeneutical Self

Fackenheim praises the "return to revelation" in German philosophy and religious thought that took place during the decade of the First World War and in the Weimar years, and he takes himself to be part of the development of this movement in North America in the postwar period. The hallmarks of this return, as he sees them, are the formulation of a concept of revelation as an incursion of the divine into the world and into history, and the event of divine–human encounter. As we have seen, this concept of revelation, which Fackenheim develops in his own way, has both divine and human aspects: there is the event of revelation – God's loving presence to man; and there is the human response to that presence – in language and in action. What makes the moment of revelation more than a human construction of ideals or principles is that the force of the command is grounded in the presence of a real God; and what makes the response more than the movements of a puppet or the obedience of a slave is human self-determination, human freedom. Moreover, to take God seriously, it is necessary to realize that even that freedom is grounded in God's love and grace; in the very act of commanding that the beloved love Him in return, God grants man the freedom to choose to obey that command or to reject it. Without that freedom, loving obedience by human beings would be entirely slavish and could not for that reason be love at all. That is the gist of what Rosenzweig describes in the *Star of Redemption*.[1]

Fackenheim makes much the same argument in his early writings. Our questions in this chapter are what his view of selfhood, human freedom, and responsibility is and whether it survives exposure to the Holocaust.

Human Freedom and the Self in the Early Writings

For the early Fackenheim, the believer and indeed all persons are primarily participants in life and not spectators of it – that is, of the world and of other persons. Even individuals who detach themselves to a degree and take up an impersonal point of view are nonetheless embedded in a vast setting or situation in which they think and act. The first-person point of view is unavoidable.[2] Fackenheim develops this conception of situated or embedded agency in his early writings and adheres to it, with modifications, throughout his early career.[3]

To see how this is so and what it means for his understanding of human existence and human freedom, we need to look at two dimensions of his early work. One has to do with the ground and content of the human response to divine revelation. Insofar as Fackenheim emphasizes the role of faith in Judaism, the primary locus of his account of the human condition and human existence is the life of the Jew, and that means, for him, the life lived in response to revelation, faith, and the covenant. In chapter 1, we focused on the concept of revelation itself; here we turn to the role and character of the human response to it. The second dimension takes us to Fackenheim's more philosophical consideration of human existence as a process of what he calls "self-making" or self-constitution, a view that he develops most fully in his Aquinas Lecture delivered in 1960, "Metaphysics and Historicity."[4]

From his earliest essays to *God's Presence in History*, when Fackenheim discusses the human or the individual religious believer, he features human freedom. Primarily, it is the freedom to respond and in particular to respond to God's loving call. Since Fackenheim is disposed to recall from the midrash that man is both a natural being and a spiritual one – a distinction that calls to mind Kant as well as others in the philosophical tradition – he seems to be suggesting that what distinguishes the human is this capacity to appreciate and respond to divine love as well as to the command to love God in return. He sometimes calls this responsibility, which incorporates the capacity to respond to a very particular command and the obligation to respond to God. We might call this the capacity to understand one's life as meaningful and purposeful. It involves what Charles Taylor calls "strong evaluation."[5] At the same time, drawing on Rosenzweig's account, Fackenheim takes it that the capacity for response, for decision in behalf of God, is itself a divine gift.[6] Man's audacity and his humility both come from God:

"Revelation, which becomes revelation only through man's decision to accept it as such, is then at the same time absolutely given, because God's sovereignty includes man's decision." But revelation is also, once received, the capacity to choose for or against the one who gave it.[7] Love is a risk, as much for God as for man. Hence, revelation as divine love depends not only upon God's presence to man; it also depends upon man's response – to love God and then to love his neighbours. But that decision, while free, is also necessary; it is made with what Fackenheim calls "sublime humility." It is a kind of voluntary but enabled submission. All of this is in Fackenheim; it is also in Rosenzweig. The believer as agent, then, is situated and equipped with a sense of what is important and of directedness that he has freely appropriated.

As we have seen, revelation singles out the individual to play a role in the meaningful historical process, and this means to acknowledge moral responsibility for and towards others. It also singles out the Jew to become a participant in the Jewish people and to play a role in their destiny. Fackenheim explains this in 1954 in "An Outline of a Modern Jewish Theology."[8] If creation establishes time and history and redemption consummates and redeems them, revelation establishes the significance of each and every moment and this means the significance of each and every person, who is given the opportunity to accept that task for him or herself. Revelation is what gives a particular life its capacity to further the redemptive process: "a history in which revelation is possible is one in which every event, no matter how insignificant, may in its stark particularity acquire unique meaning." Moreover, revelation always occurs *within* history and hence to an individual who stands within a particular tradition. Thus, revelation calls upon the Jew to accept his covenantal responsibilities, to play a responsible role in the divine plan. Since God is both revealed and concealed, his plan is only partially known, through the past responses by Jews to His call and through a history of responses formulated in texts, stories, laws, and customs. But

in themselves, all customs, ceremonies and folklore (including those Jewish, and those contained in the book called Torah) are mere human self-expression, the self-expression of men alone among themselves. But through the leap of faith any one of them (and pre-eminently those of the Torah) have the potency of becoming human reflections of a real God-Israel encounter. And thus each of them has the potency of becoming Halachah, commanded and fulfilled ... Thus no particular set of ceremonies is, as such, divine law ... But, on the other hand, all customs which flow from the concreteness of Jewish life have the potency of becoming divine law, and are a challenge to fulfillment.[9]

Here Fackenheim draws on "The Builders," where Rosenzweig reads Buber's insights about becoming links in the chain of tradition regarding text and study as applying also to Jewish life and conduct.[10] As each Jew chooses to take up the resources of the Jewish past and to seek to appropriate them for himself, he has within himself the capacity to turn a law into a commandment, to recover for himself the utter particularity of being singled out by God, of being the recipient of revelation. He also has the capacity to become a link in the Jewish tradition. The children (*banayikh*) who receive the teachings of the past can (will) become builders (*bonayikh*) of the Jewish future.[11]

The self, as a recipient of revelation, is an active participant in a narrative project, which is, to articulate what is significant for one's life and for the life of the tradition in which one participates. If Fackenheim's account of revelation is compelling, then freedom is both possible and necessary to the relationship with God. It is also necessary for human existence itself insofar as human beings are more than natural beings. But freedom is one thing; autonomy or rational self-determination, in the Kantian sense, is another. If freedom is compatible with God and with a respect for the past and for traditional authority, is autonomy similarly compatible? Fackenheim confronted this set of problems in two essays, "The Dilemma of Liberal Judaism" and "The Revealed Morality of Judaism and Modern Thought."[12] In both cases, even when not explicit, the challenge he faced came from Kant's moral philosophy and the claim that the moral law that is an intrinsic feature of rational agency is essentially autonomous, authoritative, necessary, and universal precisely because it is freely appropriated and grounded in the self's control over itself.

In "The Dilemma of Liberal Judaism," for example, Fackenheim argues that true freedom, with regard to the past, is not always autonomy. The relation between the present self and the body of past learning or practices is not a relation between isolated entities. Rather it is an encounter, as Fackenheim puts it. He focuses on religion and morality, the domain of meanings and values, and he points out that "religious and moral truths, even if long discovered, must always be re-discovered; and they are re-discovered, not just by being re-thought but by being re-lived." That is, the lived situation of the embedded self is one of reciprocal encounter with the past, not of one-way relation to it. The self does not simply either submit the past to its own authority or submit itself to the past's authority. Rather the two are in a complex, dialectical relation, whereby the present is already shaped by the past in some ways and always constitutes the past to one degree or another. Yet the self of today can learn from the past, and become something that it was not before it learned, and accept what is new. Hence, what Fackenheim is really arguing here is that genuine freedom or autonomy is not absolute; it is not unqualified spontaneity or unconditional rational determination, but rather the already shaped and influenced character and capacities of an embedded self to take what it is and build itself from that point. In other words, Fackenheim realizes that there is no sharp and exclusive distinction between being free and being limited; all our choices are limited to one degree or another, and even the most freedom we have is linked to the limitations of who we are, what the past and our communities have bequeathed us, and what is possible and desirable for us. Fackenheim's is a kind of narrative conception of embedded self-constitution.[13]

The same holds for the Jew's relationship with God. It is not a matter either of being autonomous or of submitting to divine power and authority. Rather the Jew's situation, both within the immediacy of the moment of revelation and in the course of the life of faith lived in response to it, is marked by a fundamental relatedness to God. In "The Dilemma of Liberal Judaism," Fackenheim calls this "the crucial question." If God is God and man is man, then in their relationship, man is either wholly active or wholly passive, or so it seems. Fackenheim's first step is to argue that even traditional Judaism, when it is honest with itself, is a religion of *commandment* and not a religion of *law*. That is, it is based on a living relationship between a commanding God and those who receive the command and obey it in love and humility. "Traditional Judaism," Fackenheim concludes, "is not the mechanical observance of a system of laws. It is the living covenant between God and Israel."[14] Here Fackenheim recalls precisely Rosenzweig's claim that the goal of Jewish ritual life is to take a law (a *Gesetz*) and convert it into a commandment (a *Gebot*) – that is, to turn every act of Jewish life into a living relationship between the Jew and his God.[15] If this is so, then the self is not wholly passive, even in the moment of revelation, for the divine commanding presence must not destroy but rather respect human selfhood and also human freedom, at the very moment that God's love issues in commandment. All of this is possible because revelation is divine love and commandment, and neither arid and mechanical law nor an otherworldly union with the divine. Hence, just as the freedom of the Jew vis-à-vis the past is an embedded agency, so the freedom of the Jew vis-à-vis God is a beloved agency.[16] As Fackenheim puts it in "The Revealed Morality of Judaism and Modern Thought," in the pristine moment of revelation, human freedom of choice is neither autonomous nor heteronomous, but it is a choice. "The Kantian premise is that moral law is a *bar* between man and its divine Giver. The premise of Judaism is that it is a *bridge*."[17]

On the one hand, then, a central feature of Fackenheim's early notion of human freedom is that it is embedded and limited. It is not absolute in order to be genuine; indeed, there is no such thing as absolute freedom of choice. Even in the pristine moment of revelation, human freedom respects divine otherness, yet it makes the choice to appropriate the divine command or not. "Divine commanding Presence and appropriating human freedom ... point to one another." All freedom is situated freedom; all agency is situated agency. Selfhood is historically embedded.

On the other hand, if God is wholly other and man is human, Fackenheim asks, how can man choose to love other persons for the sake of God and to do so freely? That is, if God were simply a supremely powerful ruler, then man might be *forced* to care for others, but if so, his action would not be free. If that action is free, then how can morality be something that is performed freely but also done in response to God? Fackenheim's answer, as I have said, is to follow Rosenzweig very precisely and to argue that "it is possible if God Himself has made it possible." That is, if morality is grounded in commandment and divine commandment is given in love, then man, to use Fackenheim's terms, not only is singled out by God and commanded to love Him in return and to love others, but is given as well the very freedom without which that love cannot be love and without which the commandments cannot be performed in joy and not in fear. "In Judaism the primordial manifestation of divine love is not subsequent to but *in* the commandments; primordial human joy is not a future subsequent to the life of the commandments but in that life itself."[18]

Historicity and the Self

Fackenheim's early conception of situated, free, self-constitutive agency is not confined to his Jewish writings; nor is it essentially tied to revelation or even more specifically to Judaism and the notion of covenantal existence. The best place to see Fackenheim articulate this conception philosophically is in his important Aquinas Lecture "Metaphysics and Historicity."[19] The primary goal of this lecture is to show that philosophy is still possible and indeed necessary, even if one is committed to a conception of the self as a historically situated process of self-constitution or self-making. Basically, Fackenheim wants to allay any fears that a conception of human being as historical will lead to scepticism and relativism. In the course of his main argument for the viability of philosophy, Fackenheim formulates the conception of selfhood as situated agency, and it is this conception on which I want to focus.

Fackenheim calls the rejection of a concept of human nature and the adoption of a view of human situated self-constitution – of "man's very being as historical" – the "doctrine of historicity," and he claims that it is a metaphysical thesis and not an empirical generalization. My concern is with what he says about its meaning. What does it mean to say that a person's very being is historical? Fackenheim identifies those presuppositions without which the doctrine cannot be formulated. The first is that nature differs from action and hence that human beings act freely from their point of view as "planning, deciding, and performing agents."[20] The second is that there is no permanent human nature; man is a product of his actions in history. Combined in a certain way, we get the result that "in acting, man makes or constitutes himself."[21] He is embedded in the natural world, which affects him, and also in history and culture, which also bear on him, but overall, "human being is a self-making or self-constituting process." Moreover, Fackenheim argues, for this process to be historical, we need the notion of a situation, for with it one locates the natural, cultural, and factually given realities in relation to which the self constitutes itself. The self is in a dialectical relation with its situation; it is limited and affected by it, and in some cases it alters and shapes that situation. How one acts and what one becomes is influenced, therefore, by the self's past actions and by the past and present actions of others. The outcome is that "every historical situation, then, *qua* historical, is a conjunction of limitation and opportunity; as it were, of fate and freedom."[22]

But this is not the end of Fackenheim's examination of selfhood. He next turns to what he calls the "existential account" of the human situation and of human self-making. Here the critical point is that the self recognizes that the human situation is other than the self and other than the human in such a way that the self is no longer simply and exclusively a process of self-making or self-constitution. Much of who we are is shaped by our family, our culture, background, and so forth. Hence, who we are is not purely autonomous; the situational features are genuinely other. Rather, such selfhood is the accepting or choosing of something already constituted. It is both the accepting and the accepted self, a subtle dialectic of the two.[23] Indeed, to be more precise, the self involves a grasping of its identity, what is given to it and constitutes its character, followed by an interpretation of that content, and then a choosing with regard to whether to be that self. Moreover, Fackenheim claims that from this dialectic comes the distinction, in existential philosophy, between the self and the authentic self. "The self is self whether or not it chooses itself. But only through self-choice does it become authentic self." The self, then, is not pure self-making; it is a process of self-choosing.[24] And if that self-choosing is performed in an authentic way, the result is as much as one can achieve for oneself.

In Sartre's *Anti-Semite and Jew*, for example, even the anti-Semite chooses to be the self he or she is, and in Sartre's eyes, she is inauthentic because she chooses against her own freedom; she chooses to be configured by how others view her.[25] Similarly, the inauthentic Jew is one who chooses to be who she is, but what she chooses is to be the person others view her to be. Only the person who chooses to be a self that is constituted in some deep way by her own choices and decisions is authentic.[26]

In "Metaphysics and Historicity," Fackenheim takes one further step. When man recognizes that there is an Other that situates him and takes that Other to be God, he has stepped beyond one type of philosophy, at least. In a note, he points out that this step need not be a step beyond all philosophy, and it is certainly metaphysical. He refers to Schelling and Buber as predecessors. Like Fackenheim, both view philosophy as motivating its own pointing to a divine Other. On accounts like these, then, philosophy leads to metaphysics and perhaps even to the relation with God, in particular that relation which Rosenzweig called "Creation," as the experience of existence (including one's own existence), as contingent and dependent. It also leads to Fackenheim's own understanding of revelation and faith.

In 1960 Fackenheim refers to this conception of selfhood as embedded agency as "existentialist." Its central features are that selfhood is not a substance in the Cartesian tradition, but rather is an ongoing process of relational and dialogical activity, of the I and its situation; and that selfhood involves a conjunction of what is given and choice or spontaneity. Later, as we shall see, Fackenheim will call a ramified conception of this original picture "hermeneutical."[27]

Human Situated Agency at the Turning and Beyond

As we move to Fackenheim's self-exposure to the Holocaust, matters become more complicated. Let me turn first to the self as it responds to the imperative of resistance to Nazi purposes. At the moment that Fackenheim's attention turns to an encounter with Auschwitz, he seeks to understand two things. One is the event itself, its horrors and its atrocities; the other is response to it. In facing the Holocaust, Fackenheim continually asks why they did it, why the perpetrators and bystanders acted as they did; and in trying to understand how and why one should go on after that event, his focus is first on those who survived the horrors and then, as time goes on, increasingly on its victims, including its most singular victims, the *Muselmänner*. That is, insofar as Fackenheim's later thought focuses on selfhood and agency, he asks a variety of questions. Can we understand in all cases why agents act as they do? In particular, can we understand acts of radical evil? When agents act in behalf of a sense of obligation or duty, how do they identify the content of the obligation, and what provides the confidence that they can act on that duty or obligation, even once they have understood what it is?

Let me begin by turning to the act of responding to the imperative that comes from Auschwitz. To be sure, Fackenheim speaks often as if this imperative is the command of a divine Voice, and to the believer it may indeed be that. But as I pointed out in chapter 1, Fackenheim distinguishes the believer who hears the voice of the commander through the commandment from the secular Jew who hears only the commandment – or perhaps more accurately, only the imperative or the obligation. The question here, however, is not whether this obligation exists, or what its source is, but rather what its content is, and its realization. That is, what gives rise to its content, and how is it possible for the respondent to enact it? In 1967, in his presentation at the New York symposium "Jewish Values in the Post-Holocaust Future," Fackenheim identifies the imperative as the 614th commandment and gives it a formulation: "The authentic Jew of today is forbidden to hand Hitler yet another, posthumous victory."[28] He tells us no more than that from a confrontation with the Holocaust this commandment "emerges," and he hesitantly goes on to elaborate its four fragments. That is, he explains what this abstract obligation means. In "Jewish Faith and the Holocaust," published the following year, and then in *God's Presence in History*, he tells us no more.

We can fill in some of the details, however, that Fackenheim does not make explicit. We should recall that he takes the imperative to be a commandment, even if those who hear it do not yet hear the voice of the commander, and in the case of such commandments, the revelation itself is an event of divine presence, while the content and all that follows from it is human interpretation and response. There is an ineliminable hermeneutical character to living in terms of one's acknowledgment of the significance of an event such as the Holocaust. Fackenheim takes such a view from Rosenzweig and also from Buber; as Rosenzweig famously said, revelation is an event of divine presence, while all the rest is human interpretation.[29] The Torah is already a human response to a divine revelation. Even if Fackenheim comes to see human selfhood as a humanly situated self-choosing, we should not forget that that moment of self-choosing involves appropriating an identity that is shaped by the experiences of the past, by tradition, community, texts, motifs, and customs, and that identity has been constructed interpretively in a dialectical encounter with what is given to it – natural, historical, and cultural materials. In short, Fackenheim's articulation of the content of the imperative that emerges from Auschwitz is an interpretive component of his own act of self-choosing and self-appropriation. Fackenheim does not spell out the interpretive character of the content of the 614th commandment in his works of the late 1960s and early 1970s, but by the time he completes *To Mend the World* in 1981, he has come to make the status of this interpretive enterprise more explicit.[30]

The crucial text in *To Mend the World* for our purposes comes from Section 11, subsection B, of Chapter IV,[31] titled "Historicity, Hermeneutics, and Tikkun Olam after the Holocaust." Its content is a summary and elaboration of what Fackenheim calls "a hermeneutical teaching that begins with the acceptance of historical situatedness" and about which there is a consensus. This "new hermeneutic" is a view of human existence that is indebted to Heidegger and Gadamer especially but also, as he points out in a note, to Rudolf Bultmann, Paul Ricoeur, Buber, and Rosenzweig.[32] This hermeneutic is particularly concerned with the self's relation to the past – that is, with how the past is appropriated or recovered in the present. It is, I propose, the clearest statement Fackenheim gives of the interpretive approach that accounts for the content of the 614th commandment.

Fackenheim summarizes the hermeneutic in six points. First, both the agent of the recovery and the past to be recovered – whether it is a re-membered experience or a text or an event – are "situated *in* history." Hence, in a sense, the present agent is already shaped by the past or already has a view of it, prior to her recovery of it. The agent does not come to the past as a blank; she is always prejudiced to one degree or in one way or another. In Gadamer's terms, all experience and action comes with prejudgments. Second, this prejudice or this pre-understanding of the past is what gives the agent access to it; it is only because she has some view of it that she is able to return to it and reinterpret it. There is a fundamental, unbreakable continuity between the past and the future. Third, this "always-already-existing 'pre-understanding'" and the inter-pretive recovery that depends upon it occur in thought only insofar as they have already occurred in life. In other words, this hermeneutic is not in any restricted way about how to read texts or how to understand ideas; it is about existence itself, or, we might say, it is about one's identity.[33]

Fourth, the past or the past text "has a many-faceted meaning in its own right." We should not think that interpretive recovery works on wholly passive material. This is not so. The material has a truth in and of itself. To be sure, to bridge the gap between the present agent and the past event or text requires some activity, but Fackenheim points out that the activity cannot simply be unconstrained manipulation. It must be a "faithful, receptive 'listening.'" Fifth, this method, which might be called interpretive or historical, differs from a Platonic method, which makes the present agent wholly passive, and from the Hegelian method, which makes the past (and the other in general) wholly passive. The "histori-cist hermeneutic" is dialogical and always, Fackenheim points out, in-complete. Both poles are in constant dialectical interdependence.

Finally, the past texts may be human ones or they may have a more than human source. What speaks through them may be the voice of God. One must be at least open to this possibility. In the latter cases – Fackenheim mentions Buber here – the believer today hears echoes of the past interpretations of the divine Word.

Let us set aside the particular content of the imperative that emerges from Auschwitz, and here focus on how this hermeneutical account of human existence provides us with some details for understanding how believing and secular Jews interpret for themselves the obligations that bear on them in a post-Holocaust world. The new hermeneutic is about how an agent in the present recovers the past in order to go on in the present and future. Broadly speaking, then, we can ask: What does this new hermeneutic of the historically situated self tell us about how the Jew of today, secular or religious, can go on after the Holocaust? How can the concepts of commandment, covenantal responsibilities, and such be recovered?

To this question, Fackenheim responds with a number of suggestions. The Jew of today can have a notion of Jewish obligation, of commandment, but there will be Jews who accept the structure of authority that grounds such commandments and Jews who grasp the commandments or feel their force without grasping that structure of authority. They will take the obligations to be binding but have no notion of what requires them. Furthermore, recovering the Jewish past with its ideas, practices, and commitments should occur in the context of a modern world that has sought to eradicate Judaism and the Jewish people. Whether one calls this realism or a kind of responsibility to the memory of the victims of modern anti-Jewish attacks or something else, it may require reinterpreting the ideas, principles, and themes of Judaism in a new light. However, no responsible recovery of the Jewish past can simply reject that past. To do so would be to cut off the dialectical character of all engagements with the past and efforts to recover it, and would deny the very notion of a historically situated hermeneutic at work. Specifically, then, to be honest to the *present*, one cannot simply assimilate one's responsibilities as a Jew to the old commandments; and to be honest to the *past*, one cannot simply replace the old commandments with new ones. Rather, one must recover the old in a new way. For these reasons, when Fackenheim called the imperative for going on as a Jew and as a humane, caring person after Auschwitz "the 614th commandment," he was already trying to incorporate some of the suggestions that follow from the new hermeneutic that he came to outline more than a decade later.

But there is one problem with this account of Fackenheim's thinking, and he is the one who calls attention to it. The second feature of the new hermeneutic is that there is an "unbroken historical continuity between past and present." But, Fackenheim points out, the Holocaust is a rupture in this unbroken continuity.[34] What exactly does Fackenheim mean? I think he means, at the least, that no view of how we, as interpretive agents, articulate our contemporary identities in terms of a recovery of the past can assume that all of the past is always recoverable. That is, for any particular idea or practice or theme, we cannot presuppose that we can (and perhaps should) recover it for ourselves today. Its meaning may be wholly transformed, or its truth may be wholly in question. For every element of our identity that is shaped to some degree by the past or by what is given to us as a background condition for our identity, it may be the case that an intervening event, between that past and the present, makes it impossible for us to appropriate that element intentionally and knowingly, and indeed it may even be impossible to understand that element any longer as it once had been understood. This is not to say that at some level we simply will not be able to understand an element from the past at all; rather, it is to say that it may be that we can and should no longer appropriate it in the old way. To be sure, there may even be cases where we can no longer understand the term or idea, and then surely we cannot appropriate it. But even if we can understand it in some detached way, we may not be able honestly and responsibly to accept it.

What does Fackenheim have in mind? The notion of martyrdom might be one such idea, Kiddush ha-Shem; after Auschwitz, can Jewish death, even out of an allegiance to God, be acceptable? Can it mean what it once did?[35] Or consider the notion of God as Saviour and Redeemer. Can one acknowledge God's saving power in the past and the hope for His saving power in the future? Indeed, can one have confidence in that power, as one once had? Fackenheim's point, I think, is that after Auschwitz the Jew can no longer assume, without argument, that there are some Jewish commitments or ideas that are non-negotiable if one is to go on living as a Jew. After Auschwitz, there are no such ideas. All Jewish beliefs are vulnerable; nothing is non-negotiable.[36]

We return here to the "openness" that we spoke of in chapter 1. For in a sense, this vulnerability of the historically situated hermeneutical relatedness to the past is Fackenheim's way of reformulating his earlier claim that the Midrashic framework is open. *The possibility of radical discontinuity in the relationship between present and past* is another way for Fackenheim to express the claim that in Judaism the Midrashic framework, the logic of Jewish theological belief, is always open to historical modification and even rejection.[37] What *To Mend the World* adds to the earlier formulation, in addition to nuance about the new hermeneutic, is that to conceptualize philosophically the way in which that recovered link can be reforged after the rupture has occurred, philosophy requires an idea that is not found in its own vocabulary or discourse. It requires a notion of a radical rupture that can and should be nonetheless healed, even if only in a fragmentary way. This requires an absolute break and a response that opposes that absoluteness. For

Fackenheim, philosophy should turn to Judaism for such a concept – that is, to the concept of *tikkun olam*. We will return to this concept in chapter 3. For now, the critical point is that Fackenheim's account of the historically situated agent, the hermeneutical self, is indeed modified in an important way as a result of the exposure to Auschwitz and the Nazi atrocities.

If the hermeneutic provides the content of response to the imperative to resist Nazi purposes, the *why* is provided by the recognition of the imperative force of the commandment or obligation. But neither the content nor the explanation of the imperative is Fackenheim's main project in *To Mend the World*. Rather, the focus of his attention throughout the book – and especially in its central chapter, Chapter IV – is on *how* a response to the imperative is possible. How can those living today think that it is within their capacity to resist forces unleashed by or akin to the Nazi assault? When faced with this threat, what makes us think we can meet and overcome it? What gives us the courage and the self-confidence? How can one build a bridge over an unbridgeable chasm?

Fackenheim had come to be worried about glibness, about taking it for granted that we understood how terrible the camps were and that we were right to think that surely anyone could in principle have resisted, if only the will had been strong enough. I want to treat this as a question about the limits of agency or the limits of selfhood. Taking it for granted that anyone can respond by resisting would be a mockery of those who did succumb; it would be to belittle their suffering, to criticize their weakness, and to underestimate the courage of those who did resist. In other words, it would be to avoid taking their selfhood seriously by taking for granted a distortion of that selfhood. He felt that in *God's Presence in History* he had been guilty of such errors, because he had insufficiently immersed himself in the horrors of the camps, but ignorance is no excuse. Surely it does not excuse us with all that we do know of those events, those places. If any one of us could have become a *Muselmann*, what makes us think now that we could have resisted, responded, and transcended? I think that the important thing to remember here is that Fackenheim is making a very special kind of demand. He is requiring that we question any tendency on our part to assume that we would have had the capacity to cope with this extreme event. His point seems to be that to continue on after the event, without a justification for our capacity to do so, is to demean its extreme character. In everyday terms, we judge our strength of character, so to speak, by how traumatic an event or experience has been and how we go on after it and in view of it. In a sense, all of us, living now, have gone on with our lives subsequent to many horrific events that have occurred to us or in our world or in recent history. In many cases, perhaps most, we go on without giving a thought to what it takes to do so. But when the events are close to us, affect us personally, and are deeply challenging, then to go on requires more courage, more determination, and such. What, however, if the event is so serious, so challenging, so extreme that it makes it impossible to go on, and yet what if one does go on? Where does that strength of character come from? What enables one to go on? This is the kind of question that Fackenheim is asking. Moreover, since part of one's obligation is not to dishonour or demean those who did succumb in those years, one does not want to make it easy on oneself. One wants to ask what emboldens us today to do what they could not do then. Where do we get the resources, and in such a way that their failure to find them does not diminish them in our eyes? If selfhood requires some level of capacity, can those who did not have it still be selves?

Fackenheim's answer is that we can do it today, we can go on as Jews – or Christians or Germans or Canadians or Americans – because there were those then who did go on. Resistance during the Holocaust, being aware of the threat yet commanded to oppose it, is the ontological ground of the possibility of subsequent resistance. What was actual then is possible today.

Around 1968, Fackenheim had given a different answer to this question – that the very command that commands endurance gives the power to endure.[38] And he elaborated this formulation by saying that what it meant was either the Kantian claim that ought implies can or the neo-Orthodox one that in the command, God gives man the freedom to obey. But by 1981, he had come to realize that both these answers – the Kantian and the neo-Orthodox – were inadequate. How so? Both claims are about human freedom and responsibility. One expresses the Kantian commitment to the role of autonomy and freedom with regard to the moral law, which states that moral responsibility is impossible without autonomy and that autonomy is impossible without metaphysical freedom. The other, the neo-Orthodox, expresses the religious commitment to the compatibility of religious obligation, divine commandments, and God's omnipotence. In both cases, man can be responsible only insofar as he has within himself the capacity to act, to decide what he wants, and to act on that decision. But in *To Mend the World*, the issue is not about human freedom per se and hence not about selfhood and responsibility. Fackenheim is not concerned about whether those who live today can go on with their lives in the shadow of Auschwitz as free beings or whether they could do otherwise. It is about the freedom to act only to the degree that freedom could not take place without the ability to overcome fear and threat. In a sense, the question is about what it means to be human, to be a self, which means to act in terms of a dialectical relation to the past when that past may very well be cut off absolutely from us. If the rupture that cuts the past off from us is threatening and horrific, the issue is one of confidence and courage, where courage is a matter of being honest about who one is and living with oneself, about facing obstacles and overcoming them.

What makes us think that an absolute obstacle, a radical threat, can be faced and resisted? To be sure, we today do not face that threat directly; in general, our lives are not beset with atrocity, dehumanization, cruelty beyond imagination. But in order to go on with honesty, we must imagine that our situation is of this kind. We must, Fackenheim suggests, imagine that in resisting today, it is as if we were resisting then. Hence, we must imagine that in going on today as Jews in what appear to be benign or indifferent circumstances, we are going on as Jews in the most desperate and harrowing ones. To do otherwise would be to risk degrading the heroism and the victimization of those who did in fact live in those conditions. We would be demeaning the seriousness of the event itself.

Let me draw a preliminary conclusion about Fackenheim on the self after the Holocaust. To be a self in a post-Holocaust world is to be historically situated, to be shaped by the past, and to be in a dialectical relation with a past that is separated from us by a rupture that threatens any recovery of that past. Yet we are in the grip of a responsibility to others, to victims, to that past, and to much else, and we are enabled to go on by the fact of ontologically basic resistance that did occur during the Holocaust. We are burdened and we are enabled, and both are deeply true of our selfhood.

Situated Freedom: The Self as Self-Choosing and the Hermeneutical Self

It is tempting to conclude that Fackenheim's conception of the self and human freedom remained essentially the same throughout his career. That is, he always conceived of selfhood and human freedom as processes whereby a historically embedded individual engages in self-understanding, self-articulation, and then self-choosing. This conception is the one he adhered to in his early theological writings, in his lecture "Metaphysics and Historicity" and associated writings, and then in *God's Presence in History* and *To Mend the World*. From a formal point of view, one might conclude, this conception never changed. What did change, and this is a substantive matter, is that Fackenheim came to acknowledge that the past that every self recovers can be ruptured by a radical event that prevents much if not all of that past from continuing to have its customary influence and that may prevent the self's recovery of the past altogether. Furthermore, when that conception of the self is placed religiously – say, within Judaism – it may be that one must, in the wake of such an event, rethink the ground and the character of the freedom that is a central feature of selfhood. That is, as one reflects on Fackenheim's treatment of selfhood and human freedom, one may conclude that essentially his account remains the same, even if some of its accidental features change.

But this sort of conclusion may well be hasty. It assumes that Fackenheim's understanding of the human condition can be parsed into formal and substantive features – in particular, that one can separate analytically the structural account of the self as embedded agency from the concrete possibility – at a particular historical moment, a post-Holocaust moment – of recovering the past in the present. Let me suggest, however, that Fackenheim would resist such an analytical separation of the self and history. Rather, he would want us to ask, to consider, whether the fact of Auschwitz had introduced into the very idea we have of selfhood and freedom possibilities that at one time we would never have incorporated; and then he would want us to appreciate that indeed, as a result of those dark events, the very idea of the human is no longer what it was. Hannah Arendt, in the final pages of *The Origins of Totalitarianism*, said that the Nazi death camps experimented upon the very idea of human nature.[39] Would Fackenheim not have claimed that this experiment resulted in that conception being dramatically altered? Indeed, would he not have agreed with Elie Wiesel, who famously said that at Auschwitz not only did man die but also the very idea of man?

There is a great deal we could say about these matters, but I want to isolate the central issue by focusing on what Fackenheim says about the *Muselmänner* and the perpetrators. In a sense, both are products of the Holocaust Kingdom, yet both seem to defy Fackenheim's earlier conception of the free and situated self. There is no room in Fackenheim's early conception for a self or person in whom the capacity to engage with its world has been, so to speak, annihilated, neutralized, anesthetized. Nor is there room in Fackenheim's conception for a self or person whose decisions and actions simply cannot be explained or understood in terms of what is given to it – that is, as making sense within the story of its developing selfhood. But, I think, Fackenheim in his later writings proposes that the *Muselmänner*, on the one hand, and the evil perpetrators, on the other, represent just such possibilities; they are realities that expose the inadequacy of a concept of personhood, of human existence, that heretofore had seemed inviolable. Since Auschwitz, the range of human possibilities has expanded to include possibilities that deserve attention and possibly respect. And this means that the very notion of selfhood has taken on a more moral character than it once had.

Consider, for example, what Fackenheim says about the *Muselmänner*.[40] In "The Holocaust and Philosophy," first delivered as a paper at the Eastern Division Meetings of the American Philosophical Association in 1984 and published in the *Journal of Philosophy* in 1985, he says: "Maximally, Auschwitz *has made possible* what previously was *im*possible; for *it is a precedent* ... Philosophers must face a *novum* within a question as old as Socrates: what does it mean to be human?"[41] Philosophers, since Auschwitz, have had to face something new within the old question: What is human existence? Moreover, in *To Mend the World*, Fackenheim would identify the *Muselmänner* as the "sole, truly original contribution of the Third Reich to civilization" and the "true *novum* of the New Order."[42] Explicitly, then, Fackenheim takes the Holocaust to have altered the very meaning of human existence. In what way does that alteration require a change in his earlier conception of selfhood as free self-constitution and self-choosing embedded in a situation?

For Heidegger, Fackenheim notes, "to die one's own death is part of one's freedom" and "in Martin Heidegger's *Being and Time* his freedom is foundational."[43] That is, there is nothing more essential to one's distinctive individuality than living towards one's own death. In its own way, death is the ultimate object of one's freedom and the ultimate limitation on it. But human freedom cannot be what it is – and hence human existence cannot be what it is – without it, and this is as true for Fackenheim's conception of selfhood as situated free agency as it is for Heidegger's conception of human *Dasein* as being-in-the-world.[44] Hence, the *Muselmann* – whom Primo Levi described in *Survival in Auschwitz* in a paradigmatic way that Fackenheim cites again and again – is a wholly new phenomenon, a human being, worthy of respect and our deepest compassion, yet a non-man.[45] The *Muselmänner* are walking corpses, without individuality, "who march and labor in silence, the divine spark dead within them," whose death one hesitates to call death. Fackenheim calls the *Muselmann* a new aporia; it is an impasse that prevents our appropriating without modification the conception of human existence as free selfhood, a conception that had been so compelling prior to an exposure to the death camps. Fackenheim is cryptic. He points only to the role of being-towards-death in human freedom and by implication its role for understanding human existence as being-in-the-world. But the implication is that if we require that even the most extreme victims of Nazi dehumanization deserve our respect as human beings, then no conception of selfhood is acceptable that excludes them. Human existence must make room for those crippled by the loss of all that makes freedom possible and meaningful. The issue does not seem to be an ontological feature of selfhood; rather, it is an ethical one, of recognizing as human what deserves respect simply in virtue of being an other whose suffering, whose victimization, makes a claim upon us.

In a lecture on respect and martyrdom, where Fackenheim calls attention to midrashic passages regarding human dignity and the notion of human beings' having been created in the "image of God," he notes that the rabbinic conception of the human incorporates both an ethical component and an ontological one, and that the two are related. The commitment to "love one's neighbour as oneself" would be mere sentimentality if it were not grounded in the ontological commitment to the "divine image in man," and the fact of being created by God in His image would be "empty if not fraudulent without an ethics," that is, without a commitment to love and care for others.[46] It thus would seem that prior to Auschwitz, human dignity and respect required a commitment – in Judaism, to divine creation.

Since the Holocaust, however, the situation has changed. The Nazi empire, Fackenheim reminds us, "repudiated" knowledge of the divine image. "It sought to destroy the reality of the divine image so systematically as to make its rejection of the knowledge of it into a self-fulfilling prophecy."[47] In the Holocaust Kingdom, life was cheap, death banal, and murder glorified. That kingdom made the existence of the Jew a crime, and its hatred of human life culminated in the death camps, which, as Hannah Arendt had argued, were no accidental feature of the Nazi empire, but rather the very essence of Nazi fascism.[48] And hence, its most characteristic product is the *Muselmann*, "the living dead," in whom the divine spark is dead, that is, in whom the divine image is no longer acknowledged. The goal was to create beings without human dignity, unworthy of respect; yet, as Fackenheim argues, not all succumbed, and even the most extreme victims are deserving of concern and respect. No response to Nazi dehumanization, no conception of selfhood today, is acceptable "without exposing [themselves] *both* to the fact that the image of God was destroyed, *and* to the fact that the unsurpassable attempt to destroy it was successfully resisted, supremely so, by the survivor ... determined to *live and be human* in a world where murder was law and degradation holy."[49] Hence, as a moral response to the Holocaust, Fackenheim's own conception of situated free agency must be expanded. If his early view had associated human dignity with freedom and if for the Jew that freedom was grounded in God and the divine image, then his post-Holocaust view had to make room for human beings who had lost that dignity yet still warranted attention, concern, and even respect, and others who heroically sought to recover it and to defend it.

At the other extreme, Fackenheim then turns to the perpetrators. In brief, the question he asks is, can one be the agent of radical, unqualified evil and still be human? Does being a person require being a good person, and does goodness require not only formal characteristics – such as freedom or rational agency – but also the substantive propensity for moral goodness? Or is it true that even the devil was once an angel and that even the most demonic human being is still a person worthy of acceptance and respect, even if he or she comes in the form of opposition?[50]

Fackenheim himself puts the issue in terms of those who shaped the demonic kingdom and those who served it as underlings:

> If we accept and philosophically radicalize Eichmann's plea to have been a mere "cog in the wheel," we end up attributing to the few ... a power to mesmerize, manipulate, dominate, terrorize that is *beyond* all humanity and, to the many, a mesmerizability, manipulability, and craven cowardice that is *beneath* all humanity. Yet, whereas Auschwitz *was* a kingdom not of this world, its creators and operators were neither super- nor subhuman but rather – a terrifying thought! – human like ourselves.[51]

The conclusion Fackenheim draws from this realization is that the Nazi empire was a whole greater than its parts – not a mere whole or one with benign purposes but rather a whole that "was singlemindedly geared to the destruction of humanity (as well as the lives) of its victims; and in pursuing this goal, the victimizers destroyed their own humanity, even as they yielded to its being destroyed."[52]

Furthermore, the Nazi murderers did more than annihilate humanity – that is, free situated agency and the dignity that comes with it – in their victims and in themselves. They did so without our being able to understand or explain *why* they did it. Arendt said that such as Eichmann were "thoughtless." They were not without motives or reasons for what they did, but their motives, purposes, and reasons revolved around job security and mundane self-interest. They had nothing to do with the actual *intention* to perform the atrocities and horrific cruelties they carried out. Fackenheim admits that such an account of the "banal" character of the conduct of the henchmen, the underlings, may be accurate enough, but he adds that it does not refer to those who conceived, orchestrated, and engineered the Final Solution.[53] Moreover, it is in and of itself only "half" a thought, for it does not explain the manipulating and dominating acts of those in charge. Nor does it explain the willingness to be manipulated and dominated of those who carried out the tasks of destruction and murder. In the end, we are left without a sufficient and satisfying understanding. What does remain for us who come after is a *horrified surprise* that calls forth an uncompromising opposition to a previously inconceivable possibility – a whole of horror, as Fackenheim calls it – a system of agents and institutions that extended the domain of the human to persons without freedom and hope and to agents without goodness. Yet however inexplicable the agency of evil, it warrants still our judgment and our condemnation. Hence, the boundaries of selfhood, for Fackenheim, are extended. There are agents who morally deserve our concern and respect just as there are perpetrators who deserve our condemnation and opposition – even if neither are free situated agents in his earlier sense.[54]

The Self in the Shadows

In this chapter I have raised a question that Fackenheim addresses only indirectly and obliquely, yet it is a question that pervades his work. That question concerns the concepts of human nature and the human condition, the existentialist account of situated free agency that he employs in his early work, the role of human freedom and interpretation within the moment of revelation and thereafter, and much else. In brief, the question is this: What can we say about human existence, about selfhood and what it means to be human, after Auschwitz? In his early work, Fackenheim's reflections on the character of human existence, on what it means to be a person and a self, arise in the context of his account of revelation and the human response to it and also in the context of understanding how a hermeneutical and historical conception of selfhood does not deflate the traditional view of philosophy as an aspiration to absolute knowledge. Clearly, that early conception is altered by an exposure to the Holocaust and its horrors. But how?

One way of interpreting the changes in his conception of personhood as free situated agency is to say that Fackenheim came to see the account of personhood or human existence in a dramatic historical and moral context, rather than in earlier philosophical and theological contexts. An acceptable understanding of what it means to be a human being after Auschwitz must allow for extremes previously unheard of – of human beings without freedom and dignity yet worthy of respect and of agents so immersed in a system of atrocity and evil that the only acknowledgment of them that is appropriate is an uncompromising critique, resistance, or opposition. In contemporary philosophy, accounts of personhood typically focus on metaphysical considerations or on features such as rationality, freedom and autonomy, the capacity for reflection and rational agency, and even the narrative structure of self-constitution.[55] But if Fackenheim is right, not one of these features can, without failing to take the evil of Auschwitz and the dignity of its victims seriously, be considered inviolable. He does not offer a clear judgment about what this means. But if we are right, a central feature of this shift is to make selfhood primarily an ethical matter and one to be lived in all its complexity rather than to be made the subject of a narrowly conceived philosophical inquiry.

In the end, then, Fackenheim never abandons the account of selfhood as situated agency and self-constitution that he articulated in his early writings, under the influence of Western philosophy from Kant to Hegel to Kierkegaard and Heidegger and Sartre. But in his late writings, this existential or hermeneutical account is broadened to include persons with diminished rationality and self-determination and others with a horrific and repulsive character. Personhood becomes for him more than a formal matter; it must include the extremes, and hence must include those worthy of our greatest sympathy and concern as well as our most intense opposition and resistance. These later moral considerations arise in a post-Holocaust world and hence against the background of the contingencies of history. Not only selfhood itself but also our conceptions of it turn out to be both moral and historical in important ways.

Central as the concept of selfhood is to Fackenheim's entire corpus, it has not been obvious how to assess the way that his later thinking continues and also modifies his earlier conception of the self as situated, free, and self-constituting. Still, I have sought to do so and have concluded that Fackenheim's conception took on a decidedly moral dimension once he turned to the Holocaust and to those implicated in it. Thus we can ask: Is he right that particularities of history, of our history after the Holocaust and a century of war and atrocity, warn us against conceiving of selfhood and humanity outside of the very compelling historical events that characterize our worldly situation? What is the point of expanding selfhood to include the Nazi perpetrators, on the one hand, and the *Muselmänner*, on the other? The answer is that what Fackenheim came to see is that no conception of selfhood, human agency, and identity can be abstracted from the moral situations in which persons are engaged and implicated. To the degree that events and actions occur that extend our moral responses and judgments, to that same degree our conception of what it means to be human is modified and perhaps extended. As Fackenheim turned to the Nazi atrocities, to those who were its agents and to those who were its victims, he came to see that those who become the subjects of our judgments and evaluations, our sympathy and our opposition, may be persons who exhibit ordinary forms of agency but also extraordinary forms. Self-determination, self-constitution, and self-choosing may still be characteristic features of many whom we call human, but there are also those whose agency is more reactive and determined and others whose agency is effective and powerful but not rational in any way we normally comprehend. To the degree that we believe that human beings are the subjects of our moral "reactive attitudes," as P.F. Strawson calls them, from blame and praise to sympathy and opposition, we must allow the category of the human, of the self, to include the death-in-life that is associated with the *Muselmänner* and the inexplicable agents or perpetrators of the Nazi horrors and actions like them.[56]

For my proposal to be plausible as a reading of Fackenheim, however, it must be the case that he takes the situation of the *Muselmänner* to be worthy of our sympathy and respect and at the same time to be a form of death-in-life, without the capacity for wilful, intentional opposition and resistance. But Susan Shapiro, in an important criticism of Fackenheim's argument for the actuality of ontological resistance during the

Holocaust that makes possible current resistance to the dehumanization and assault that is for us the legacy of the Nazi atrocities, has argued that his account fails to take the *Muselmänner* seriously precisely *because* it is based on a kind of awareness and commitment that such persons lacked. As she puts it:

> However admirable, exemplary and reorienting is the testimony of resistance, its categorical and ontological privileging necessarily excludes and negates the claims of other testimonies to the event. Although Fackenheim in no way wants to slight or make secondary the mute testimony of the *Muselmänner*, his privileging of physical and spiritual resistance issues in such a denigration. This denigration is the other side of the legislative character of the testimony of resistance when privileged. The logic of privilege necessarily implies that something else is excluded or made secondary.[57]

If Shapiro is correct about Fackenheim's argument in *To Mend the World*, then there would seem to be some tension between what he claims about the *Muselmänner* in the writings I have discussed and the way in which his account of ontological resistance "denigrates" or "excludes" these victims. In response to Shapiro, Fackenheim argues that the dialectical movement of thought – one that exposes a moment of resistance to the Nazi assault that is cognizant of its goals and intentions and at the same time recoils in horror yet with opposition to it – does not leave behind the *Muselmänner*.[58] His point is that his reflections on the victims of Nazism reach an extreme when they focus on the living-dead; no victims suffered more dehumanization and indignity without being killed or exterminated than these victims. When his thought moves on, then, it turns to those who suffered and yet resisted. What is carried forward to that next stage is the actuality of suffering and assault, and what is added to it is the actuality of resistance. One might argue that to find such resistance, the thinker must turn to a form of victimhood that is not as extreme as that of the *Muselmänner*, and that is true. What was not possible for all victims was possible for some. This does not demean the dignity of the *Muselmänner*, I would argue, but it does begin the movement towards self-conscious, reflective suffering and resistance that becomes the "ontological condition" that makes subsequent resistance and opposition possible. As long as Fackenheim respects the *Muselmänner* as worthy of sympathy, concern, and respect, then his account has not "denigrated" or "excluded" them. To claim that it has is to beg the question against Fackenheim and in fact to beg the question against the way in which his later writings extend the notion of what it means to be a self, a person worthy of respect and of value.

Appreciating the error in Shapiro's criticism helps us see how Fackenheim has not, in his later writings, simply continued his earlier account of selfhood and identity. He has not abandoned that account; indeed, he has extended or expanded it and reconceived its foundations. What it means to be human, a self, is no longer a matter of metaphysics or philosophical anthropology; it is an ethical or moral matter that is tied to the moral urgencies of a world darkened by the shadow of the Holocaust and subsequent horrors and atrocities.

3

Philosophy after Auschwitz: The Primacy of the Ethical

I like to think that philosophy and the Western philosophical tradition begin historically with Plato. This is controversial. Most often, historians date the origins of Western philosophy to Anaximander, in Milesia, or perhaps even to Thales, if one takes him to have been a real person and not simply a mythic figure or a subject of folklore. And even if one does not take these early "Pre-Socratics" and those who followed them to be philosophers but rather *physikoi*, physical thinkers, one might still date philosophy from Pythagoras, who purportedly invented the term, or from Socrates, who was known by the late fifth century and thereafter as the paradigmatic philosopher.[1] Still, there are reasons to confer the title of founder on Plato, for it was he who wrote most extensively about what philosophy is and who argued that it was the pre-eminent mode of life and also a life of reason, learning, study, and understanding. He took the philosopher to be engaged in understanding timeless and unchangeable concepts and principles, the Forms, which provide structure for the natural and social worlds. When Fackenheim, in his early writings, refers to philosophy, one is tempted to think that he is referring to a mode of inquiry and way of life that is best described as Platonic.

Philosophy was a lifelong occupation and preoccupation for Fackenheim. He always thought of himself primarily as a philosopher, and throughout his career, he held views about philosophical thinking and its relationships to other disciplines – theology most pre-eminently but also the social sciences, historiography, and the natural sciences. Yet he rarely attended directly to its nature; nor did he, except for once, turn to the topic of this chapter, the question about what philosophy *is* after the Holocaust. Still, his claim that no thinking is immune to alteration or rejection when exposed to Auschwitz applies most of all to philosophy itself, and not just to its results but also, and even more importantly, to its mode of inquiry. Therefore, it is fully in the spirit of his thinking to ask what an honest encounter with the Holocaust means for his and our understanding of what philosophy today is and ought to be.

Do we, as many have claimed, live in the time of the end of philosophy, a time when philosophy is no longer and in which something else has replaced it? Such a claim takes philosophy to be a mode of thinking that is traditional in the West; it is conducted from a detached, impersonal point of view, seeks to understand the fundamental principles of all things, and then proceeds to understand the totality of things based on that account of foundations. With the end of philosophy has come the end of this tradition of Parmenides, Plato, Aristotle, Plotinus, Aquinas, Maimonides, Descartes, Spinoza, Hobbes, Leibniz, Kant, Hegel, and others. For some, what has replaced the old philosophy is a new type of philosophy; while for others, what has replaced philosophy is another mode of thinking altogether.[2] Famously, Rosenzweig advocates replacing the old thinking with the new; and Wittgenstein, at least on one reading, seeks to reconfigure philosophy as a mode of therapy whereby we return to an elucidation of the ordinary use of terms and concepts in order to liberate ourselves from the distortions of traditional philosophy. For someone like Levinas, philosophy as a totalizing mode of inquiry should be replaced by a phenomenological philosophy of the face-to-face encounter of the self and the other, in order to show that ethics and not epistemology or traditional metaphysics is first philosophy; this strategy is reminiscent of Kant's disposal of traditional metaphysics in favour of critical, transcendental philosophy. For Richard Rorty, philosophy has been replaced by literature, and for Heidegger by poetry and thinking.

Where does Fackenheim figure into this estimate of philosophy, its history and its destiny and purpose? How does his conception of the philosopher compare with those of Cavell and of Levinas, of Rorty and of Taylor? To deal with this question and to clarify such comparisons, we need to look first at Fackenheim's pre-Holocaust writings, both the theological essays and the philosophical work, and then to turn to his philosophy in such works as *Encounters between Judaism and Modern Philosophy* and *To Mend the World*. For unlike others, Fackenheim comes to the question of the future of philosophy not out of internal questions about method, but rather from an encounter with the Nazi atrocities and the reality of evil. We will find, I think, that through much of his career Fackenheim understands philosophy in traditional, Platonic terms: it is a rational inquiry that engages with perennial problems and aspires to knowledge of universal and unchanging truths. But he personally defends a view of philosophy along what he calls existentialist lines. This is as true for the way he treats philosophy in contrast to theology as it is for the way he conceives philosophy in his understanding of Hegel and Heidegger. But with books such as *Encounters between Judaism and Modern Philosophy* and *To Mend the World*, with the encounter with the horrors and evil of Auschwitz, his conception of philosophy or at least his conception of its role changes – although he is not very explicit about what changes philosophy undergoes and what philosophy comes to mean in a post-Holocaust world. Fackenheim never gave up on philosophical thinking, even when he realized its limitations and inadequacies, but his conception of its character and role did indeed change. It is time to see how.

Faith and Reason, Theology and Philosophy: Early Reflections

In a 1963 essay, "Human Freedom and Divine Power," Fackenheim begins by contending that the problem signalled by the essay's title is not the same problem as that of free will and determinism. Subsequently, he seeks to show what the problem of human freedom and divine power is and how the divine–human relationship should be understood. Who is the agent of this inquiry? And what is that agent's point of view? I want to focus our attention on this issue – that is, on the perspective from which Fackenheim examines the problem or, to put it differently, on who is its primary audience. As one reads the essay, it becomes increasingly clear that while the person for whom the tension between human freedom and divine power is a reality is the religious believer, the inquirer Fackenheim is addressing is the philosopher. Thus in the course of the inquiry he says a number of helpful things about what he takes philosophy to be.

"Philosophy," he says, "is an attempt at objective rational understanding."[3] In other words, philosophy attempts to solve problems by taking up a detached, impersonal point of view and by rationally examining evidence, concepts, and testimony in order to arrive at an understanding of reality – that is, of the way things are. He points out early that not all philosophy is well done. When the philosopher solves the problem but ends up denying the reality, we have bad philosophy. In the present case, that is, bad philosophy solves the apparent conflict between divine power and omnipotence, on the one hand, and human freedom and self-determination, on the other, by denying the existence or reality of one or the other.[4] What, then, is good philosophy? Presumably it still is an "objective" and rational inquiry. It involves analysis, examination of options, and argument, and it does so from an objective point of view. That point of view is detached from any particular subjective one – specifically, from the particular point of view of the religious believer. Nonetheless, good philosophy takes the testimony of such a believer seriously; it does not reject the claims of that testimony but seeks to understand its apparent contradictions. It respects the subjective point of view but nonetheless evaluates and analyses from a point of view independent of it. Fackenheim is saying, that is, that "it is possible for man to step outside [the experience and] to become an impartial bystander, and thus to discover the truth."[5] In his well-known book, Thomas Nagel, while admitting that the first-person point of view is unavoidable, nonetheless recognizes and lauds the aspiration to objectivity, to what he calls the "view from nowhere."[6] It is the natural aspiration of philosophy, science, and religion, and it is what Fackenheim seems to have in mind when he describes the philosophical point of view as detached from all particular points of view.

Yet it might seem that philosophy is doomed to failure when it comes to understanding religious faith and the human–divine relation. Fackenheim points out that there are religious believers – the prophets, say – who would "deny ... that a man can detach himself from participation, become an impartial, outside observer, and yet understand the human–divine relation," and that there are those who would deny that the philosopher can take up the posture of faith and belief. Hence, one might think we are at an impasse. Fackenheim here focuses on a particular case of a general problem: How can philosophy aspire to objective rational understanding and thus take up a detached point of view, the view of reason, yet also enter into the subjective, engaged, particular point of view? "How then can [philosophical reason] enter into the life of participation without losing its identity?"[7] The particular example of the essay concerns human freedom and divine power – that is, the divine–human relation and religious life. But the particular case simply highlights the general problem, which is how philosophy can understand human experience.[8]

At this point, Fackenheim offers a way of resolving the dilemma for the philosopher seeking to understand the fundamental religious relation between the divine and the human. What he says, however, applies beyond this special case and tells us something about how he conceives of philosophy itself. "The philosopher," he says,

> rather than compelled to remain an external observer, can sympathetically enter into this logic [i.e., in this case the logic of religious discourse] and take long steps toward understanding it. Too often the philosopher is pictured as a man in possession of some absolute and self-sufficient wisdom, proudly sitting in judgment upon life. At his best, he often appears in quite a different role. Recognizing that truth and wisdom already exist in *life*, he seeks to illuminate them in the light of *thought*.[9]

Here, then, we have a description of philosophical reflection that faces its object honestly and without distortion and then stands back in order to seek on articulation of what goes on in it in terms of its place within a broader whole. This is Fackenheim's general point, and it is one, I believe, that he learned from his early reading of Kierkegaard and later from his work on Hegel and especially the *Phenomenology of Spirit*.[10] He then remarks that this special role of philosophy as an external perspective that enters into an engaged point of view and then returns to reflect upon it is especially apt for religious belief.

But how exactly does the philosopher carry out this task? What commitments does he carry with him into the process of enacting the experience in question, and what commitments does he save for his impartial analysis and examination? Fackenheim's general description is that the philosopher "enter[s] into the logic of religious discourse" but retains "his philosophical duty to impartial objectivity" by entering "into religious discourse of the most varied and even conflicting types." Without prejudicing his decision about what types of experience and discourse to enact, the philosopher exhibits his commitment to impartiality; he is not biased against an appeal to certain types of emotions and experiences. That is, he "remains neutral as to its *truth* ... while trying to understand some of its *meaning*."[11] Broadly speaking, this description calls to mind the Husserlian requirement – one that Fackenheim himself never cites or refers to –that phenomenological description takes place when we bracket our natural, everyday commitment to the truth or falsity of an experience and focus instead on a precise description of what appears to consciousness, to the *meanings* present to the experiencing subject. And insofar as the range of experiences is varied and even conflicting, what Fackenheim appears to have done is to blend features of Hegel, Husserl, and even Heidegger into a philosophical method that is receptive enough to explore a wide range of human experience without the biases common to reductive traditional approaches. Later, he will describe the movement of philosophical thought as a hovering between various engaged perspectives, often articulated in testimony, on the one hand, and the detached perspective of reflective configuration and comprehension, on the other. This is akin to the method he takes Hegel to have employed in the *Phenomenology of Spirit* as philosophical thought tracks the dialectical steps from one form of natural consciousness to another by hovering between those steps and the point of view of absolute knowledge.[12]

Two years later, in the preface to "The Revealed Morality of Judaism and Modern Thought," Fackenheim uses this same account of philosophy as part of a brief discussion of the possibility of modern Jewish philosophy. His first point recapitulates his claim that philosophy inquires into the meaning of experience and discourse without making any commitments regarding their truth. The essay concerns revelation, but, he says, "it nowhere categorically affirms the reality of revelation … [for] to do so would transcend the scope of philosophy."[13] As he had come to see it, philosophy involves understanding human experience and reality as they are experienced by means of a phenomenological, dialectical, and reflective comprehension of what that experience and reality means; it is akin to conceptual clarification and is not a matter of dogmatic or reductive metaphysics or of pseudo-scientific inquiry.

His second point is that this method requires that "philosophical thinking … both presupposes, and stays with, objective detachment."[14] In life and lived experience, agents make commitments about what they experience and what reality is. Hence, to withhold such commitments involves a kind of detachment. We can imagine, then, how Fackenheim takes such a withholding of one's existential commitments to involve a form of objectivity, the taking up of an impersonal standpoint. It is at least part of what is involved in taking up the philosophical point of view.

Also in his preface, Fackenheim uses this picture to raise a problem about the very possibility of Jewish philosophy; in fact, however, one might think there is an analogous problem about *all* philosophy or at least that the problem for a Jewish philosophy is no more intractable than for any philosophy. He puts the problem this way: "How then can [Jewish philosophy] at once have the objectivity and universality which is required of it as philosophy, and yet be essentially committed to a content which has Jewish particularity? … Can there be a Jewish philosophy, then, which is at once genuinely philosophical and essentially Jewish?"[15] But all human experience is particular and essentially so. It may have universal features or features that one thinks are shared by all human beings, but their occurrence is particular and concrete.[16] Hence, any philosophical reflection on them will always face the problem of how to take them seriously in all their particularity even while generating universal, objective results from them. What applies to a philosophical inquiry into Jewish experience applies to a philosophical inquiry into all experience. But if that is so, then an account of philosophy that shows how Jewish philosophy is possible would not be different from one that shows how philosophical inquiry in general is possible.

How, then, does Fackenheim solve this apparent paradox? He points out first that the problem is a historical one, in the sense that it confronts the Jewish philosopher in the modern period in a different way than it did the Jewish philosopher in the medieval period. In fact, one could say there *was* no such problem in the Middle Ages, since both philosophers and religious believers agreed on the fundamental point: both took revelation to be a historical fact like any other. But in a modern world where such a view about revelation and authority is no longer acceptable to either believers or sceptics, the issue is whether one is a *committed* believer or a *detached* thinker, Fackenheim argues. That is, he says, there is "no basis for meeting." Or is there? Fackenheim then makes the same move as in the earlier essay: he claims that philosophy can enter into the experience of revelation if it "suspend[s] judgment as to the actuality of revelation," and he here calls this movement of thought a "sympathetic phenomenological re-enactment." He also calls this "understand[ing] some of the meaning of committed faith," and he argues that unless its possibility is accepted, one must conclude absurdly that a non-believer can never understand religious literature or that a taking upon oneself religious faith will always have to be an utterly blind act. Without the possibility of intercultural or interreligious understanding, cultures and religions would be radically insulated from one another and communications among them would be impossible.[17]

Although Fackenheim does not place this problematic and its solution in a larger context, his suggested solution does point beyond itself. If philosophical thinking is always detached and human experience is always committed and engaged, then all philosophical thinking will have this problem. Philosophy in general, if it is to explore human experience, must engage in a kind of sympathetic re-enactment of the experience it examines, and this result is helpful for understanding how

Fackenheim understood what philosophy is. Furthermore, if the detachment is from a particular point of view and yet if the philosopher is also an engaged participant but in her own experience, then the issue is at least analogous to the general problem, which is, how one person communicates with another. How is it possible for one person to understand another? How do we engage one another in conversation? What Fackenheim calls a "sympathetic phenomenological re-enactment" calls attention to an ability that all members of a community of discourse must have in order to communicate with one another. In short, philosophy shares something fundamental with everyday life, albeit in a special way.[18] Philosophy attends to meanings precisely as we all do when we communicate with one another. But in addition, it withholds existential commitment, although this too is not unlike everyday communication, which is facilitated by withholding one's commitments in order to understand one another, prior to re-engaging those commitments in order to assess what the other has said to us and whether we can or should accept and believe it.

As Fackenheim describes it, then, philosophy is a reflective articulation of the meaning of human experience that is taken up from a detached point of view. It requires withholding one's existential commitments; it explores the meaning of various experiences and their features; and it ultimately seeks an understanding of human experience. We need to ask now whether this conception of philosophy can also be found in Fackenheim's more strictly philosophical works of the 1960s, especially "Metaphysics and Historicity."

In the Aquinas Lecture "Metaphysics and Historicity," the word "metaphysics" refers to philosophy insofar as it inquires into and seeks to understand fundamental realities, and the word "historicity" refers to the doctrine that man's very being is historical. In short, the problem that Fackenheim confronts is whether one must abandon the notion of metaphysical truth by accepting the doctrine of the historical nature of human existence.[19] In the course of engaging with this problem, what does he take philosophy to mean?

First, Fackenheim argues that metaphysical inquiry is a historically situated activity in which the "metaphysician [seeks to rise] above history, to timeless truth," including truth about the human condition.[20] He denies that metaphysics fails at achieving "timeless truth" even though it only succeeds at understanding the human condition "from the standpoint and within the limits of an historical situation." He argues against all such forms of historicism or worse. Rather, he defends a version of the Hegelian claim that human being is the struggle between seeking and fleeing the poles of infinite and finite consciousness. Furthermore, he claims that a central insight of existential philosophy is that human beings *are* this struggle and yet can rise to "philosophical self-understanding" precisely insofar as they recognize themselves *as* this struggle. But in order to do this, this understanding must be a self-definition in which the self understands itself as seeking to transcend its limitations but as failing to do so. Moreover, although "these attempts [at radical self-transcendence] must be radically individual, made by each person for himself, the knowledge attained through them is radically universal. For this is not a person's mere knowledge of his or her personal situation. It is her knowledge that she is both in principle situated and yet able to recognize her situatedness. This knowledge is universal; and the person who has acquired it has risen to philosophical self-understanding."[21] This is not the end of Fackenheim's analysis of the content of this philosophical self-understanding. He elaborates on it by disclosing what he calls the existential understanding of the human situation and all it implies. But for us it is sufficient to have arrived at this point, where he defends a form of philosophical and precisely metaphysical knowledge, what he calls philosophical self-understanding. It is, as we have seen, a reflection on the human condition by a human being engaged in being human; it involves an aspiration to transcend the limitations of the human situation but also a recognition that those limitations cannot be completely transcended.

By and large, then, philosophical self-understanding is a form of philosophical thinking aimed at understanding what human being is, but its overall character – its detachment and its engagement – overlaps with the account of philosophy we found in his theological writings. That earlier account focused on religious experience and emphasized the philosopher's withholding of his existential commitments and his attention to meanings; this later account does not do so; but the overall structure of philosophical inquiry and its universal aims are the same. In the Aquinas Lecture, that is, the crucial point is that a doctrine of human nature must be rejected in favour of an account of human being as a form of self-making and self-choosing, because the former assumes that such a philosophical inquiry must be conducted from a detached point of view and hence must be objective, whereas the latter accurate inquiry must be carried out from an engaged perspective, albeit one that involves an element of reflection and a universal result.[22]

Philosophy in *God's Presence in History*

Our next task is to consider whether this conception of philosophy – as reflective, engaged, and situated and as aspiring to universal truth – survives exposure to the Holocaust in Fackenheim's thought. This conception is not Rosenzweig's old thinking; it is existential philosophy, arrived at through a reflective analysis of personal, embedded thinking and experience. In the postwar period Fackenheim had already left behind traditional philosophy and its methods; the question that remains is whether an encounter with Auschwitz marked the end of this existential type of philosophy. Our first step is to examine the role of philosophy in the most important work that marks the shift in Fackenheim's career, *God's Presence in History*.

The topic of that book's first chapter is "Jewish faith in God's presence in history" or, in somewhat different terms, the possibility and character of the experience of revelation in Judaism. Fackenheim's central task in that chapter is to defend an understanding of Jewish faith, of Jewish belief in the divine–human encounter, to provide a justification for testimony in its behalf. It is an account of what the experience of revelation means for the Judaism of that time. One dimension of this defence of Jewish faith is a philosophical reflection, and we want to consider what its character is as philosophy.

Not surprisingly, given the structure of *God's Presence in History*, Fackenheim's understanding of philosophy shows itself to be basically the same as the one he articulated in his earlier theological writings. The book has three chapters. In the first, he articulates some of the content of classical Jewish faith, and this involves a philosophical account of how we can understand that faith and a presentation of its central components. In the second chapter, he subjects that account to nineteenth-century philosophical and other intellectual challenges – what he calls challenges from the outside. Finally, in the last chapter, he exposes that faith to the Holocaust – which he calls an internal challenge – in order to clarify how Jewish faith can be exposed to that radical evil and yet go on into the future. Given this structure, we should expect that the philosophical dimension of the clarification of Jewish faith in Chapter One has not yet had to cope with Auschwitz and therefore should show no signs of an encounter with the Holocaust. In a sense, the philosophical dimension of Chapter One is an excellent example of the approach to philosophy we have already outlined.

Philosophical analysis and reflection appear in at least three places in Chapter One. First, Fackenheim provides a philosophical analysis of what he calls "root experiences" in Judaism. Even though this analysis focuses on the two root experiences in Judaism, the Exodus and Sinai, it is nonetheless a philosophical analysis that explores the essential features of those events that gave rise to Judaism. The results are abstract and general enough to apply to other faiths as well, but the specific role of the philosophical analysis is to anticipate the commitment of the faithful Jew. Second, since these root experiences are cases of a divine–human encounter in history, Fackenheim must give a philosophical account of what such a moment of revelation is, and he does so by providing a philosophical interpretation of a passage from Martin Buber's *Moses* that describes what Buber thinks takes place in the experience of a miracle.[23] Finally, philosophical reflection confronts the particular root experiences of Judaism and discloses several contradictions within them. Let me say a word about these three philosophical moments.

Fackenheim never refers to either the analysis of root experiences or the interpretation of Buber's description of the experience of a miracle as philosophical. But clearly they are. In both cases, Fackenheim considers particular subjects and identifies essential features of them; revelation is here a historical and epistemological category. In the case of root experience, which is the concept that takes the place of revelation in the present work, Fackenheim prefaces his analysis with these questions: "What, considered abstractly, are the characteristics of a root experience in Judaism? What are the conditions without which a past event cannot continue to make a present claim – the claim that God is present in history?"[24] He presupposes that root experiences are privileged originating events and that such events gave rise to Judaism and continue to make a claim upon Jews in subsequent generations. That is, he asks us to accept the claim that there *is* such a thing as Judaism and that it originated in events that gave rise to Judaism and that would continue to affect later Jews. He then asks: What conditions make it possible for events to serve these functions? This is a transcendental question. It begins with a reality, a state of affairs, and asks what conditions make such a state of affairs possible. Such a question, such a strategy, is appropriated from Kant, Hegel, and later philosophers. Moreover, by uncovering the dialectical relation between past and present, between the public and historical character of the event and its re-enactment, Fackenheim takes thought into the experience of the original event and into its re-enactment in subsequent generations. That is, he employs a mode of thinking that is engaged, expository, articulating, and interpretive all at once. Who can doubt that he owes in this regard a special debt to Hegel, whom he had been studying for more than a decade?[25] And, I suggest, he owes a debt to his reading of R.G. Collingwood, whose account of historical understanding also requires a process of sympathetic re-enactment.[26] The philosophical method that Fackenheim employs in understanding root experiences in Judaism, then, is the same method of reflective analysis that we have already uncovered in his earlier writings – one that hovers between detachment and the posture of engaged participation while at the same time withholding a commitment to the reality of its objects.

And he uses the same method of philosophical reflection for a second purpose – to clarify the notions of "sole Power" and "abiding astonishment" so as to penetrate Buber's description of biblical miracle. He then applies those notions to arrive at an understanding of the Red Sea (and its later re-enactment) and Sinai as root experiences in Judaism. In short, he puts philosophy to work. As a philosopher, he sympathetically re-enacts experiences and reflects upon what occurs in them, and he does so while withholding any commitment to the veracity of the experience or the reality of its objects.

These tasks, however, are all preparatory. Their result is to make available an understanding of what faith or revelation means in Judaism and how that understanding applies to two fundamental, determinative moments of faith and revelation in Judaism as well as to their recovery by subsequent generations of Jews. But after these stages of philosophical reflection, Fackenheim takes one more step before allowing himself to acknowledge, point out, and describe the way in which Jewish life expresses its commitments. After Kierkegaard, he calls the commitment of faith after such philosophical comprehension "immediacy after reflection," but there is, for him, one more step of philosophical thought prior to the reflection and its literary articulation.[27] "The root experience itself," he says, "is an immediacy" – that is, a direct encounter between the divine and the human – "and so is its reenactment by subsequent believers. It is the potential object, however, of *philosophical reflection*; and the moment such reflection occurs it reveals the root experience to be shot through with at least three all-pervasive, dialectical contradictions."[28] For Fackenheim, as we saw in chapter 1 above, the human condition is riddled with paradox and contradiction, and it is philosophy that reveals them but faith that enables human beings to confront and endure them. He holds to this Kierkegaardian theme at least through *God's Presence in History*. Here it manifests itself as what philosophical reflection discloses and what midrash, the venue for native Jewish theology, articulates, engages, leaves unresolved, holds firm to, and represents in literary form – in "story, parable, and metaphor." This is what Fackenheim calls the "Midrashic framework." It is the "world" of midrashic thinking that

> reflects upon the root experiences of Judaism … like philosophical reflection, becomes aware of the contradictions in the root experiences of Judaism … [but] unlike philosophical reflection, it a priori refuses to destroy these experiences, even as it stands outside and reflects upon them. For it remains inside even as it steps outside them, stubbornly committed to their truth … Midrashic thought, therefore, cannot resolve the contradictions in the root experiences of Judaism but only express them.[29]

At this point, we need not work out the details of these contradictions that philosophy exposes, faith experiences, and midrashic thought expresses. It is sufficient to note that the philosophical reflection Fackenheim describes here is precisely the method he adopted and developed in the course of replacing, in favour of modern philosophy, the old systematic philosophy we associate with Plato, Aristotle, Aquinas, Hobbes, Spinoza, and so many others in the tradition. It is this new picture of philosophy about which we must ask: Does it survive the exposure with Auschwitz and its radical evil? And to begin to answer this question, we shall turn first to Fackenheim's next great philosophical work, *Encounters between Judaism and Modern Philosophy* of 1973.

Judaism and Modern Philosophy: Lessons about Philosophy

Although three of the five chapters of *Encounters* were previously published in one form or another, the book has a coherence and unity that derives from its task and from the way the chapters deepen and enrich that task.[30] What Fackenheim proposes in *Encounters* is that we can learn something important about a philosophical position by asking how it deals, explicitly or implicitly, with Judaism. In the book's central chapters he stages three encounters in an order of increasing depth and seriousness. The first is an encounter in which a philosophical position – that being empiricism and its development in logical positivism and subsequent analytic philosophy – by and large ignores Judaism. The second is an encounter in which another philosophical position – Kant's moral philosophy and Kierkegaard's rejection of Kant – does find a place for Judaism, but one that is based on a faulty picture of Judaism

and its moral system. Finally, Fackenheim describes an encounter between Hegel and Judaism in which Hegel's early bias against Judaism
is mitigated by a richer and more nuanced picture, although in the end
the modern Jewish situation poses insurmountable problems for the
Hegelian system. Our interest in this project is in what it tells us about
how Fackenheim understands philosophical inquiry and reflection, especially insofar as the Holocaust poses special problems for it.

Let me move directly to the crucial point. At the end of Fackenheim's
lengthy analysis of Judaism and Hegelian philosophy, he turns to contemporary realities, to the Holocaust, and he asks: "Would Hegel today
be a Hegelian?"[31] This is Fackenheim's way of asking whether philosophy could survive unaltered an honest exposure to the horrors of the
Nazi death camps. For him the question is not a parochial or narrow
one, for he says that in Hegel's philosophy we have an engaged thinking that seeks a comprehensive understanding of all reality and yet is
fully exposed to history – "radically self-exposed to history," as he puts
it. The question about Hegel is meant to be a test of *all* philosophy;
Hegelian philosophy seeks complete understanding even while it does
not ignore history and situated human experience in order to do so. If it
cannot survive exposure to the Holocaust, what philosophy could?[32]

We need not pause here to survey details of the Hegelian system and
of Hegel's philosophical method; we shall say more about those in
chapter 5. But we must say enough about Hegel to clarify what Fackenheim thinks is at stake for philosophy when we expose it to the Holocaust. According to Fackenheim, Hegel claims to have attained a world-
historical standpoint that does justice to and then comprehends "the
totality of all points of view."[33] Hegel's philosophy, that is, follows and
articulates points of view within history but also transcends history to
place all those finite points of view within the totality of the whole. As
Fackenheim puts it, "Hegel's philosophy is *in* history and permits a
contingent history. It is *above* history and rules out an essential future."[34]
The question then becomes whether Hegel would still today be able to
occupy that world-historical perspective and, if he could not, what
would remain of a philosophy that is wholly immersed in history. Insofar as the world-historical standpoint acknowledges that history is not
exclusively human history but is in fact divine–human, Hegel believed
that in his own day culture had implicitly attained the unity of that divine–human relation. According to Fackenheim, then, what philosophy
does is acknowledge the contingent and then "remove" it and in so
doing articulate explicitly and in thought that divine–human unity. The

question is whether that task can survive the Holocaust or whether it is ruined or unconditionally impeded by it. Does the Holocaust make the unity of the divine–human relation impossible?

According to Hegel, Fackenheim says, the modern world allows for outmoded, anachronistic forms of spirit (i.e., of culture and society) and even leaves room for modes of abstract, technological thinking that lead to alienation and fragmentation. But, Fackenheim claims, the modern world as comprehended in thought cannot permit *radical anti-Spirit*.[35] Hegel would have seen Nazism for what it was, "an all-too-spiritual anti-Spirit that affirmed the modern identity of the divine nature and the human in an unprecedented, enthusiastic, self-sacrificing celebration of hatred, degradation, and murder." In short, the Hegelian mediation – the purported unity of the divine and the human in the modern world – would have been seen for what it is, a shambles, and with it the philosophical thought that claims to comprehend that unity. Hegel's philosophy is open to history, which means that it requires for its comprehension a history that is itself already somehow coherent and complete. The reality of the death camps renders this complete coherence impossible, and Hegel therefore has no way of insulating his system from their evil. "Claiming to mediate all things, divine as well as human, it requires a world in which, except for the sphere of philosophical thought, so total a mediation is already actual."[36] This is what Fackenheim takes to be the plight of philosophy after Auschwitz. To be sure, he may be wrong about Hegel; his interpretation could be contested. But for us, his proposal about Hegel and Auschwitz is sufficient evidence for what he believes philosophy would suffer as a result of taking the horrors of Nazism and the death camps seriously.

But where does this crisis leave the modern world, and where does it leave philosophy? Fackenheim goes on to say that in today's world, even with the Hegelian mediation having been broken or disrupted, there are "dialectical consequences" or traces, "unrecognized fragments ... appearing on every side."[37] What does he mean? He is referring to evidence in the world of how the religious or divine, on the one hand, and the secular or human, on the other, occur as related one to the other, even if there is no longer reason to be confident about their unity. As he puts it, "a return to the medieval divorce between heaven and earth is impossible, and the loss of Hegel's own claim for their modern union still leaves us with a world in which secular freedom and religious receptivity must be interrelated even as they are held apart."[38] But where does this leave philosophy and philosophical thought?

Fackenheim tells a subtle and dialectically complex story about what remains for philosophy, but we can be direct. On the one hand, in returning to history and life, philosophy looks for evidence of a form of life, indeed a form of religious life that combines the religious and the secular in a dialectically coordinated way. On the other, the evidence must not rest on the assumption that in history "reconciliation and redemption" have already taken place. Rather it must look forward to a messianic future yet to come. This means that Hegel would turn to Judaism, for, as Fackenheim proceeds to argue, in Judaism one finds this combination of human freedom and divine grace, dialectically interrelated, in the concept of the covenant, and "covenantal mutuality ... is shot through with a fragmentation in which 'redemption' is not attained and 'reconciliation' forever alternates with alienation and sin." Moreover, Jewish messianism has just the right features. It is itself dialectical and "doubly representational," as Fackenheim calls it, for "it is distorted alike by absolutization of human action, and by absolutization of divine action." And it is, he argues, an "*absolute* confidence ... which does not flee from history but rather stays with it ... [a messianism] whose world-historical point of view is not above history, but rather remains a humble testimony within it."[39]

Philosophy – and in particular Hegelian philosophy – has identified Jewish life as the venue in which the radical anti-Spirit of Nazism is recognized for what it is and is confronted with an uncompromising opposition. After Auschwitz, "Judaism is threatened with existential despair."[40] Fackenheim argues that this response, which has yet to find its philosophical or theological articulation, is "already actual ... in the life-commitment of a people." Moreover, it is not a "mediating" response that seeks to integrate the Holocaust into Jewish theology in some way and to accommodate it into a conventional, traditional pattern of thought; rather it is a "radical, normative opposition." Fackenheim describes this opposition in terms of the commingling of the religious and the secular:

> Only by virtue of a radical "secular" self-reliance that acts as though the God who once saved could save no more can even the most "religious" survivor hold fast either to the Sinaitic past or to the Messianic future. And only by virtue of a radical "religious" memory and hope can even the most "secularist" survivor rally either the courage or the motivation to decide to remain a Jew, when every natural impulse tempts him to seek forgetfulness and even bare safety elsewhere. After Auschwitz, the religious Jew still

submits to the commanding Voice of Sinai, which bids him witness to the one true God. He is now joined, however, by the secular Jew, who, by the sheer act of remaining a Jew, submits to a commanding Voice heard from Auschwitz that bids him testify *that some Gods are false.*[41]

Thus, the uncompromising opposition to the forces of Auschwitz combines secular self-reliance with religious purpose. This is how the fragments of the Hegelian unity are now manifest in a post-Holocaust world. Moreover, as Fackenheim goes on to argue, this

> commingling of religiosity and secularity has found historical embodiment in the rebirth of the Jewish state ... After the holocaust, the Israeli nation has become collectively what the survivor is individually. Except only for those who never became part of the modern world, all religious Israelis are willing, if required, to take up "secular" arms in defense of the state. And except for those who cannot extricate themselves from ideologies that do Jewish history no justice, all secular Israelis have the "religious" wish that the state be Jewish.[42]

I do not here want to consider this picture of what a paradigmatic Jewish response to the Holocaust and to the Nazi evil has been and ought to be.[43] To follow Fackenheim's argument and to accept his account, one must treat as given the Hegelian terms in which it is couched. Specifically, one must treat as fundamental to the dynamic of history and the synthesis of the modern world the relationship between the divine and the human, and then one must agree that if the Holocaust and Nazi evil have fractured the unity between the two, the historical mode of life worth taking seriously must now engage with both poles and their dialectical interaction. For the moment, let us accept Fackenheim's portrayal of an authentic post-Holocaust Jewish opposition to the horrors, the dehumanization, and the evil of the Nazi assault. What we now must ask is what this response, this opposition, means for philosophy.

Fackenheim asks: If Hegel were alive today, what would he say about this commingling of the religious and the secular? What would he say about the restoration of the Jewish state? What would he think about messianic action that is courageous and secular but at the same time religious and hopeful, albeit not absolutely confident so much as realistic? In every case, Fackenheim answers that Hegel would have responded positively. For Fackenheim, if we generalize, there is reason to think that a realistic and responsible post-Holocaust philosophy would abandon any attempt to assimilate all history into theory. Rather, it would return to history as it is being lived, follow the traces of a life-commitment to opposing today's assaults on human dignity, endorse them, and advocate in their behalf.

Philosophy as Ethical Action:
Philosophy after the Holocaust in *To Mend the World*

The picture of philosophy that emerges from Fackenheim's critical engagement between Judaism and Hegelian philosophy does not abandon altogether its role as thought – that is, its role as a reflective analysis and articulation of what takes place in life and in history. But it certainly gives up any attempt to reduce the historical to preconceived categories, principles, and patterns. Indeed, it focuses on how historical life should be framed ethically, in response to the claims made upon those who live it, in particular the claims of the Holocaust in behalf of human dignity and worth. As we turn finally to Fackenheim's magnum opus, *To Mend the World*, in which he engages in a philosophical prolegomenon to future Jewish thought and more, we will see that philosophy continues to have this ethical character; philosophy after Auschwitz cannot cease to be a mode of thought, but nonetheless it must also be a mode of resistance or opposition to the forces of evil. Moreover, philosophy is marked by what it recovers from the past as well as by what it cannot recover but must leave behind.

After the recovery of revelation and the commitment to historicity, what does philosophy tell us about the *possibility* of opposing the demons of Auschwitz and going on to "mend the world"? This is the task of the central chapter of *To Mend the World*, Chapter IV. The philosophical movement of thought in that chapter shows how a dialectical, phenomenological, and hermeneutical inquiry into the actions of the perpetrators and the lives of the victims of the Nazi atrocities discloses the ground of the possibility of resistance to Nazi purposes. In this sense it is a kind of transcendental enterprise. As philosophy, it involves a journey of thought that arrives at a grasp of the Holocaust world as a totality that is more than the sum of its parts. That world is also a whole that is evil and horrific through and through; nonetheless, it is a whole that at rare but illuminating moments was experienced as the horror it was, and that was resisted in view of this recognition of its character as an evil that had been ordered with the goal of dehumanizing and then eliminating its victims. In this remarkable tour de force, Fackenheim engages in a philosophical tracking of historical experience in order to expose an understanding of its horror, of the imperative of opposition that arises from it, and of the actuality of resistance that has since made possible obedience to that imperative. To me, in this philosophical project, there are resonances of Hegel and Rosenzweig and of many others, with the unique difference that the outcome is not an articulated comprehension of a unified whole but rather the confrontation with a fragmented totality that Fackenheim calls "a surprised acceptance and a horrified resistance." Indeed, it is more than this. It is a "horrified surprise and, since the thought that is in this surprise is forced to accept what is yet in all eternity unacceptable, thought is required to become 'ecstatic,' such as to point beyond resistance within its own native sphere, to a resistance that is beyond the sphere of thought altogether, and in the sphere of life."[44] What begins as philosophical thought, tracking awareness in life, becomes not only resisting thought but also resisting action.[45] In Heideggerian terms, ontic thought arrives at an ontological conclusion that becomes deontic opposition. From the conclusion that resistance during the Holocaust was a way of life, Fackenheim concludes that it became for those who lived thereafter an ontological category, one that pointed ahead to actual resistance. "[The] resisting thought [of some victims] pointed to and helped make possible a resisting life; our post-Holocaust thought, however authentic in other respects, would still lapse into inauthenticity if it remained in an academically self-enclosed circle – if it failed to point to, and help make possible, a post-Holocaust life."[46]

There is more that could be and should be said about the philosophical exploration that follows this moment in Fackenheim's thought, especially concerning the way in which philosophy must, as he sees it, turn to Judaism for conceptual clarity about how such resistance – how a post-Holocaust life – ought to take shape. But the central point for us is already clear – that for Fackenheim an authentic post-Holocaust philosophy must be historically situated, attentive to the historicity of human existence, and action-oriented. His next step in *To Mend the World* – that is, the turn to Judaism for the concept of *tikkun*, the mending of a cosmic, radical rupture, a mending that is nonetheless fragmentary – continues to bespeak that practical, ethical orientation. And later, when Fackenheim turns explicitly to describe "Philosophy after the Holocaust," his account is decidedly practical and ethical. Moreover, it is deeply historical. To clarify this last step in Fackenheim's reflections on the nature of philosophy, we must turn to his explicit discussion of that theme.

Three predecessors hover over Fackenheim's exploration of philosophy after Auschwitz: Leo Strauss, Martin Heidegger, and Franz Rosenzweig. Rosenzweig provides him with the distinction between the old thinking and the new, between a conception of philosophy as ahistorical and a conception of it as intrinsically historical, or, in other terms, between philosophy as conducted from a detached, impersonal standpoint that seeks and grasps eternal truths and philosophy as conducted from the point of the view of the particular historical agent that clings to the utter historicity of being itself. The question Fackenheim raises is not whether the Holocaust ruptures philosophy but rather *how* it does so, and this means how a presently enacted philosophical recovery of the past, one that resists the forces of evil, ought to proceed. If the Holocaust threatens any recovery of the extremes of the "old" and "new" thinking – represented for Fackenheim by Strauss and Heidegger – then does it threaten the recovery of philosophy altogether? Fackenheim has his own way of framing this challenge, but basically it can be put this way: Can philosophy go on at all, if it can be neither Platonic nor Aristotelian in character?

The ground of the possibility of going on after exposure to historical rupture is to be found in a case of philosophical resistance that occurred within the rupture. Fackenheim explicates the ethical response of Kurt Huber, a little-known professor of musicology and philosophy who was the mentor to and spokesperson for the Munich students known as the "White Rose."[47] In a document discovered after his death, a "Final Statement of the Accused," Huber gives an account to the court that tried him for his actions. He acted, he said, out of a responsibility for all Germany, as an attempt to restore legality in behalf of unwritten laws that were being distorted by written ones. Fackenheim takes his statement to conclude with words of the German post-Kantian philosopher Johann Gottlieb Fichte, that one should act as if everything German depended upon you and your act alone and as if the whole responsibility was yours.[48] Fackenheim has much to say about the significance of Huber's citing Fichte, about how Fichte's views differ from Kant's, about how Heidegger and Sartre might be viewed against the Kantian background, and more. But the crucial moment comes when Fackenheim asks what made Huber do what he did and, in particular, what *role* the philosophical Idea played in motivating him. Was philosophy alive in his action? Surely, Fackenheim argues, the philosophical Idea did not cause him to do what he did, but neither was it irrelevant. Fackenheim observes that Huber was irresolute – what person would not

be? – yet even so he acted. The philosophical Idea, the moral conceptions of Kant and Fichte, did give him strength. If in his day philosophy
was weak – "abandoned, betrayed, assailed and mocked on all sides"
– that weakness contributed to his resolve to act, alone (except for a
handful of comrades) and without regard for the consequences. "Thus,"
Fackenheim writes, "he gave strength to the Idea even as, in turn, he
was given strength by it."[49]

Fackenheim then observes that this dialectic between the philosophical Idea and the resisting action resembles the dialectic of *teshuvah* and
tikkun that he had invoked as conceptual clarifications of how resistance after the Holocaust ought to look. His conclusion is that "Huber's
action was a *Tikkun*," a mending. "In obeying the unwritten law [as
accessible as a Platonic idea and yet separated from him by a horrific
present] he restored that law … by writing it into his own heart. In acting in behalf of Kant's Idea of Humanity, he mended that Idea – it was
broken – for he recreated the matrix or *Boden* [soil or ground] of it in
actual humanity, even if only in his own person."[50] To paraphrase Fackenheim, philosophy was part of what moved Huber to act, and at the
same time his action provided the vehicle for the philosophical Idea to
express its normative force; it was a reason for Huber to act only insofar
as his appropriation of it enabled it to serve as a real, operative reason.
Huber's action and the philosophical Idea revived each other, if only
in a fragmented way. That is, philosophy and moral action, in Huber's
person, dialectically supported and shaped each other.

Furthermore, Fackenheim argues, Huber's recovery of the old philosophical Idea makes a present recovery today both necessary and possible. The very Idea of Humanity, of its dignity and worth, was destroyed and then, by such a one as Huber, recovered, at least to a degree.
Any recovery of philosophy today ought to serve that same purpose – to
continue in Huber's footsteps, to contribute to the reclaiming of the
ideas of human dignity and worth. Each act of philosophical thought
should take responsibility for all of humanity.

Finally, Fackenheim asks whether philosophical *tikkun* is an act of the
old or the new thinking. To the degree that the recovery of philosophical thought must face the radical rupture that is the Holocaust, that recovery is instrinsically historical. It certainly seems that no unqualified
affirmation of the old thinking, of a philosophical inquiry into eternal
truths from no particular point of view, is possible. But, he claims, however historical it is, philosophy ought to focus on the questions that are
as old as Socrates; What is the human? What are we? Are we noble

creatures or are we capable of the most horrific acts? What is it to live a human life? What matters to us? Where does our dignity lie? In a sense, then, authentic post-Holocaust philosophical thought must be a historically engaged response to an old question, but a response that is morally relevant through and through.[51]

Conclusion

There is no more complicated and recalcitrant issue in Fackenheim's thought than the meaning and role of philosophy. From very early in his career, he practised a mode of philosophical thinking that was attentive and responsive to history and to the place of the philosophical thinker in history. At the same time, he was aware that much of the Western philosophical tradition was an attempt to understand nature and human experience from the outside, from a privileged, impersonal position. Since the Holocaust, philosophy's character has remained fundamentally historical; what has changed is its goal. Philosophy can no longer seek comprehensive knowledge of the world and history, nor should it; what it can and must do is understand human existence in such a way that it contributes to meeting the moral challenges of living in a world of atrocity and horror. Philosophy today must be responsive and responsible to those who suffer and to those who make claims upon us for acknowledgment and concern. In so doing, philosophy and moral action become interdependent. Each is shaped by the other.

In a rare essay specifically about the Holocaust, Emmanuel Levinas proposes that the extremity of Auschwitz situates us in a new age. We live in a time, he says, of the "end of theodicy." His point is not in any narrow way about religious theodicies, that is, attempts to justify God in the face of innocent suffering and human atrocity. Rather, it is a broad point about all attempts to take as primary the task of understanding such suffering and evil. Throughout Western history, we have been tempted by the aspiration to theodicies, that is, to respond to suffering and atrocity by explaining them. Levinas's point is that the extraordinary suffering of the Nazi years and of all the genocidal events that have followed should convince us that the primary response to atrocity ought not to be the cognitive and intellectual one of explaining such events; it ought to be the human response of reaching out to help others, of respecting life and defending human dignity. The only other figure whom Levinas refers to in his essay is Fackenheim, whom he credits with a similar insight regarding the way in which the Holocaust marks a new era in history.[52] It is with special regard to philosophy that I would contend this insight applies. For Fackenheim, as for Levinas, no philosophical thought today is authentic if it does not contribute in some way to moral purposes – to opposing the forces of hatred and oppression, to supporting affirmations of human dignity and worth, to serving humanity. Philosophical thought provokes such action and in so doing is recovered if not redeemed by it. Such philosophical thought cannot avoid an engagement with life as it is lived, nor can it neglect some reflective articulation of what the engagement reveals. But it cannot stay with such tasks; it must go one step farther and look towards action in behalf of humanity as its ultimate goal and ours as well.

As we shall see, however, this moral project – which gives content to the Jewish idea of messianism – is a fragmentary and partial one for Fackenheim. It makes a claim on philosophers and also on others, but it comes with no confidence and perhaps with little hope. There is, in Fackenheim's early works, an admiration, indeed a reverence for philosophy and a fidelity to it. In his waning years, I believe, the fidelity remained but without the same confidence. Too much had happened to him and to the world, and too much had been recalled.[53]

4

Fackenheim and Kant

Although Fackenheim's doctoral dissertation dealt with medieval Arabic philosophy and themes that go back to Aristotle and Plotinus, his primary philosophical engagement throughout his career was with German philosophy.[1] To be sure, he was a student of a variety of central figures in the Western philosophical tradition, from Plato and Aristotle to Spinoza and Kierkegaard, but above all, Fackenheim developed his own Jewish and philosophical views in conversation with Kant, Schelling, Hegel, and Heidegger. A comprehensive understanding of that conversation would require a book, much more than we can consider here. But for our purposes, some discussion is nonetheless mandatory for any responsible appreciation of Fackenheim's career as a Jewish thinker and philosopher.

After completing his dissertation in 1945, at first during his years in Hamilton, Ontario, as a congregational rabbi, and then during his early years at the University of Toronto, from 1948 until the late 1950s, Fackenheim's primary project dealt with the relationship between religion and philosophy in modern philosophy. The title he used for the project was "Reason and Revelation from Kant to Kierkegaard." When he applied for and was awarded a Guggenheim Fellowship for 1957, this was the title of his project.[2] During the 1950s, it was the overarching plan that provided the context, the setting, for his various papers on Kant and Schelling. The year of the Guggenheim Fellowship saw that project come to a standstill, and the aporia that created the impasse was Hegel. For the next decade, although he would at times return to the encounter between revealed religion and Kant, it was Hegel who was most prominent in his thoughts. Later, once his thinking permits itself to be exposed to the Nazi horrors and the death camps, Heidegger comes to take a special place, for it is Heidegger who raises the question of how philosophy as historically situated can confront historical, radical evil and yet go on. Roughly, then, Fackenheim's main German philosophical interlocutors might seem to replace one another in a serial order: first Kant, then Hegel, and finally Heidegger. That is, insofar as Fackenheim was always committed to defending Judaism and its character as a revealed religion, he did so first against Enlightenment rationalism and naturalism, then against Hegelian historical philosophy, and finally against Heideggerian secular existentialism. This, at any rate, might seem to be the narrative of Fackenheim's career.

But we should not be tempted by such a simple, linear view. In fact, Fackenheim's philosophical thinking and its development are a much more complicated and nuanced matter. Other figures play important and continuing roles, from Kierkegaard, Buber, and Rosenzweig to Schelling, Barth, Strauss, and Spinoza. Moreover, Kant's influence is not simply replaced by Hegel's, nor are these two set aside as Heidegger becomes a more and more significant opponent. Arguably, once Hegel intrudes, he does so in diverse and continuing ways, and he becomes the dominant philosophical influence on Fackenheim's work.[3] But later, when he turns to the future of a post-Holocaust philosophy, it is Kant (and Fichte) whose concern for the primacy of the ethical is so important, who once again takes centre stage. Indeed, in order to get our bearings, a good first step would be to focus on one philosopher with whom Fackenheim always engaged and whose influence might have changed but never waned, and that figure is Immanuel Kant.

Introduction

I want to frame our examination of Kant's place in Fackenheim's thought by asking how the encounter with the horrors of Auschwitz affected his understanding of and appreciation for Kant. To carry out this task, first I will look at several papers of the 1950s and 1960s in which Fackenheim explored the themes of history, evil, and religion in Kant. On the face of it, these three papers examine Kant "on his own terms" – they are, that is, attempts to understand Kant on these themes. Fackenheim, however, has very specific reasons for examining Kant, and we want to see what those reasons are and how they influence his reading of Kant. Then I will turn to an important paper of the mid-1960s in which he conducts a debate between Judaism as a revealed religion and Kantian moral thought[4] – it is an essay, Fackenheim tells us, in which he engages in Jewish philosophy. We shall say a word about what he takes that to mean and then explore the outcome, as well as the picture he paints of the role of ethics in a religion based on revelation. The third step will be to consider the consequences of that encounter in a post-Holocaust context, and this is best shown by examining the second chapter of *Encounters between Judaism and Modern Philosophy*.[5] There Fackenheim incorporates his paper on Kantian morality and revealed religion but places it in a different context. Finally, I will turn to the role that Kant's moral philosophy plays in *To Mend the World*, especially in the section on philosophy after the Holocaust. Kant plays a role in Fackenheim's understanding of the evils of the death camps and of Nazism, as well as in his account of a genuine philosophical response to those horrors. Fackenheim considers Eichmann's famous use of Kant and also the Kantian and Fichtean spirit of Kurt Huber, the mentor of the White Rose, but the centrepiece for our purposes may be the way that Fackenheim responds to Hannah Arendt and her famous claim about the banality of evil. Does Fackenheim think that Nazism discloses a radical evil that Arendt simply does not grasp and that also eludes the Kantian account?

The Kant who is important to Fackenheim is the Kant of the moral writings, the *Foundations of a Metaphysic of Morals* and the *Critique of Practical Reason*, and the Kant of *Religion within the Limits of Reason Alone*. Fackenheim takes for granted the Kantian disposal of rational theology in the *Critique of Pure Reason*; what interests him is the way in which Kant reclaims a role for God and religion within the moral sphere and also how Kant's understanding of religion and ethics struggles to deal with the empirical, the contingent, and the historical. In rejecting the God of the philosophers, does Kant find his way back to the God of Abraham, Isaac, and Jacob? Certainly not. But one can still ask: Does Kant's conception of religion pose insurmountable problems for such a return, or can Kantian thought be refashioned so that Judaism and philosophy after the Holocaust can be thought together?

The place for us to begin is with three essays that Fackenheim wrote in the early 1950s, one on Kant's philosophy of religion, one on his view of evil, and a third on his conception of history.[6] I will focus on the first two: the one on God and the other on radical evil. For Kant, morality is about freedom and rationality. The first of these essays situates morality – freedom and rationality – in the concrete human situation; the second continues the examination of moral character and its lack; and the third places freedom and rationality in the fabric of society and human conduct, in nature and history. Overall, Fackenheim's fascination with Kant is a fascination with the ways in which universality engages particularity, or, to put it differently, he is fascinated with Kant's Platonism and by how Kant struggles with the Platonic dualisms of the abstract and the concrete, the universal and the particular, the noumenal and the phenomenal, and the transcendent and the natural – how he succeeds in addressing these dualisms and how he fails to do so.[7]

Kant on God and Religion

In the first of these three papers, Fackenheim offers a general account of Kant's moral philosophy and its treatment of religion – that is, an interpretation of Kant's argument in the second *Critique* that the moral agent must postulate the existence of God in order to guarantee that happiness will be commensurate with virtue. Fackenheim's question is basically this: For a philosopher for whom moral knowledge and character are pre-eminent, why should religion be of any importance, and if it is, how does Kant negotiate the "transition" from morality to religion? Kant's strategy here is to argue for the role of the Highest Good as the ultimate end of morality and then to argue that God is necessary in order for us to have confidence in the realization of the Highest Good; human conduct is insufficient in this regard, nor is nature itself suited to guarantee it. But, as Fackenheim realizes, Kant's attention to the Highest Good and happiness shows that Kant is sensitive to the reality of morality and to its historical, concrete context in human existence. Hence, the introduction of God and religion leads to a philosophy of history, to a conception of how moral experience and moral conduct are realized in history, and Fackenheim takes this to be a central feature of Kant's understanding of the role of religion in human life. Furthermore, it is in such a context, that of nature and history, that evil arises: evil characterizes a type of character that threatens in an important way the development of morality in history. Hence, as recent commentators have shown, for Kant, a cluster of ideas – God, religion, evil, and history – exhibit important interconnections and are in fact mutually illuminating. In recent discussion this cluster often has a naturalistic tone; here I am thinking of the accounts of Allen Wood and David Sussman as examples of accounts that have such a secular cast.[8] But there are other accounts – those of Gordon Michalson, Henry Allison, and Philip Rossi come to mind, as well as Fred Beiser's excellent historical analysis – that take seriously that for Kant this is overall a project of fashioning a religion of reason that is both genuinely rational and natural and also seriously religious.[9] Fackenheim never doubts that Kant has a deeply religious sensibility. Kant may have been suspicious of revealed religion, to be sure, but he was never, for Fackenheim, suspicious of religion itself.

If we start with Fackenheim's interpretation of the postulates of pure practical reason and the argument for God as a guarantor of the Highest Good, we see that he does not follow Kant's own argument in detail. He takes Kant to have given an account of finite moral existence and to have disclosed the contradictions at its heart. Religion, he argues, is the recognition of these contradictions and a commitment to beliefs that do not resolve them but rather reflect or express them. In short, for Fackenheim, Kant does not identify problems or contradictions in human experience that he then seeks to resolve; Fackenheim does not follow those who criticize the very formulation of such contradictions, nor does he follow those who take Kant's resolution to be confused or unsatisfactory. Instead, he takes Kant to have revealed accurately the contradictions that characterize finite human existence and to have responded seriously and genuinely to them. Let me show how this is so.

Fackenheim takes a clue from the fact that Kant distinguishes his own view about the ends of morality, the Highest Good, from two ancient schools, the Stoics on the one hand and the Epicureans on the other.[10] That is, while the Stoics took virtue to be the exclusive content of morality, the Epicureans claimed that happiness or pleasure was its exclusive content. Fackenheim takes this polarity, between virtue and happiness, to correspond to the Kantian distinction between the noumenal and the phenomenal and hence between idea and nature. Kant's project is to show that the poles of these dichotomies are excessive; true morality must avoid the failures of the extremes and find a way to accommodate both poles in a higher synthesis or resolution.[11] Although Fackenheim had been teaching Hegel since 1952 or so, he had not yet begun to write on Hegel; even so, his strategy for reading Kant in this essay is certainly Hegelian.[12] In this regard, Fackenheim finds Kant's claim that morality requires the Highest Good, which incorporates both virtue and happiness and involves a commitment to one and a desire for the other, to make every bit of sense. While he notes the criticism of people like Goethe and later Hermann Cohen that happiness is an impurity in the Kantian system, Fackenheim himself believes that Kant is absolutely right to acknowledge its important role in the moral project as a genuinely human one. Fackenheim claims that what presents itself as a "contradiction" is resolved by an act of "practical metaphysics," a commitment to the existence of God as the agency that guarantees the commensurability of virtue and happiness.[13] This is not the old metaphysics or an example of natural theology; it is something new – a commitment to a metaphysical claim from the point of view of a philosopher who is a finite moral agent, who is aware of that fact, and who takes his account therefore to disclose "ultimate moral reality."[14]

Furthermore, Kant's solution to the problem of the commensurability of virtue and happiness is to call upon a providential agency – outside of nature and outside of human autonomy – that guarantees that unity. Human beings are embodied, concrete actors, and God guarantees that this combination of body and soul is harmonious, not dissonant. As Hegel puts it, in a text Fackenheim is fond of citing, the self is the struggle between the finite and the infinite. In short, Fackenheim's approach to Kant's conception of religion is guided by two polarities and by the thought that Kant is one stage along the way to understanding human existence as the tension between them.[15]

If Hegel is one influence on Fackenheim's reading of Kant on religion, the other is Martin Buber. Although Fackenheim never mentions Buber in his essay on Kant's conception of religion, there is a passage in Buber's *I and Thou* that is, I think, present in his mind as the frame for his reading of Kant in this essay. That passage, which gives Buber's account of the kind of "essential and indissoluble" antinomy that characterizes the "religious" situation, as he calls it, cites the Kantian strategy for dealing with the antinomy of free will and causality in the *Critique of Pure Reason*. For Buber, there is no resolution or dissolution of the conflicted nature of the religious situation; it is to be lived in all its contradictoriness. As a comparison he draws upon Kant's strategy for dealing with the fact that human experience is marked by both spontaneity and causal determinism: "Kant can relativize the philosophical conflict of freedom and necessity by relegating the latter to the world of appearance and the former to that of being, so that the two positions no longer really oppose one another but rather get along with one another as well as do the two worlds in which each is valid." Buber contrasts this antinomy with the tension between the self-determination and unconditional submission that mark the encounter with God, on the one hand, and the way in which this tension must be endured and lived "both in one," on the other.[16]

Fackenheim's goal is to show that Kant, by his own lights, is engaged in a new kind of metaphysics. In one way, Fackenheim's essay is about how Kant makes the connection between morality and religion, especially the belief in God. But in another, it is about how this metaphysical result requires that Kant acknowledge the primacy of the finite agent's point of view yet also find a way for thought to rise to transcendence – that is, arrive at metaphysical results. Kant wants to show that the soul is immortal and that God exists and that the philosopher knows these truths, even if he cannot arrive at such results theoretically.[17] Fackenheim's strategy is to remind the reader that Kant had already argued for the existence of freedom and then to claim that Kant uses the same method in arguing for the immortality of the soul and the existence of God. This method requires that the philosopher recognize his perspective as finite moral agent but also that what he grasps from that point of view have the status of metaphysical truth. The passage from Buber helps him understand Kant's argument for freedom and its relationship to the totality of embodied human existence. He argues this way.

Fackenheim takes Kant's argument in the *Grundlegung* to conclude that "the belief in freedom is implicit in moral consciousness" – that is, that "moral consciousness alone can understand it, to the extent to which it can be understood at all."[18] In other words, freedom is not known by the philosopher from a detached, impersonal point of view; rather, it is known by the finite moral agent as a presupposition of the possibility of his own moral experience.[19] But it is one thing for the ordinary moral agent, in everyday life, to commit himself to this claim; it is another for the philosopher to make the same claim for everyone and as a metaphysical truth. Why can and why should the philosopher, reflecting on the situation of that finite moral agent and his experience, accept such a claim for himself? Fackenheim answers: "the philosopher *can* accept it as a reality because it does not contradict causality, and … he *must* accept it as a reality because he, too, is a moral agent."[20] Freedom is not incompatible with causality; the philosopher's rational scruples do not prevent him from believing such freedom. Moreover, the freedom in question is as necessary for the philosopher insofar as he is a moral agent as it is for any other moral agent; his own experience testifies to the need for it.

Fackenheim next turns to Kant's arguments for the immortality of the soul and for the existence of God. Broadly, "the structure of finite morality has certain inner contradictions," he says, precisely because it *is* finite. He means by this that human beings do not have complete control over their existence; they are finite because they are embodied, and being embodied they are natural beings subject to causality. There are limits to what human beings can do and how; physical nature constrains them.[21] The results are "inner contradictions." Philosophy explicates these contradictions and then clarifies how the beliefs in immortality and God "reflect" them. These beliefs, then, resolve the contradictions, Fackenheim says, but only by reflecting them. They remain, I take it, contradictions, but the philosopher sees them clearly and recognizes how believing in the soul's immortality and God's existence expresses them.

The key to Fackenheim's reading, then, is that moral agency as finite has these "inner contradictions." What are they, and why are they present in finite morality? As I have indicated, the contradictions arise because human beings are embodied, natural beings, and in this respect, they are finite or limited. There are features of their situation and their character that are beyond their complete control. Human beings have to cope with these features but cannot eradicate or eliminate them. Basically, there are two such features. One is the natural inclinations that move us to act; the other is the interests we have in happiness, our own and others – in security, well-being, and so forth.

The presence of natural inclinations in the moral agent as a natural being gives rise to the belief in immortality. As Fackenheim puts it, finite moral agents grasp the moral law as obligation, as what *ought* to be, because they are always struggling between their natural inclinations and what duty requires. "Finite moral existence is struggle and must always remain struggle."[22] To be sure, human beings can become increasingly virtuous, but they can never become holy or perfect or absolutely virtuous, nor can any stage along the way be sufficient in and of itself. The belief in the immortality of one's soul expresses this contradiction, for in Fackenheim's terms, it is the belief in "an infinite duration making possible through struggle an infinite approximation of holiness."[23] Furthermore, this need not be a conscious belief; rather, *"while he is in actual moral engagement this belief is necessarily implied in his engagement."*[24]

The second natural feature is the interest in happiness. The issue here concerns ends: "all *finite* willing must aim at ends."[25] Fackenheim takes Kant to be claiming that there are two kinds of ends, one where willing of the right kind can by itself achieve the end, and the other where it cannot and "which can be achieved only by the kind of overt acting which transforms the world."[26] Broadly speaking, we aim at virtue and happiness, that of others and also our own. Moreover, Fackenheim argues, they stand and fall together. He does not explore the claim in detail, but it is the familiar one that for Kant the Highest Good must include happiness as well as virtue and that "if the Highest Good is to be one whole, this must be happiness in proportion to virtue."[27] But since the world with its causal structure is beyond his control, the Highest Good is beyond his reach – or, as Fackenheim formulates it, since all willing is a willing to act, willing itself seems to be incoherent. It would be futile and pointless if he knew that the world was always recalcitrant, but while he has no reason to believe that it is, neither does he have any reason to think that it will conform to his will and his interests. "So far as the evidence is concerned, the question is open."[28] But as Kant argues, the finite moral agent does not leave it that way: he wills and acts, and thereby "whether he knows it or not, he believes in God" – that is, "his *actual* moral engagement implies the belief that that which moral law bids him realize in nature can be realized in it because there is a 'common author' of both."[29]

We have now followed Fackenheim in his reading of the ways in which the finitude of human moral existence, its embodied and natural character, leads to the beliefs in the soul's immortality and God's existence. Internally, in each case, there is a contradiction that the finite moral agent must live with; together there are contradictions as well. What Fackenheim has in mind is that the finite moral agent aims at two ends: one is perfect virtue or holiness; the other is happiness proportionate with virtue. The contradiction comes about because in each case there is a problem both with taking the end seriously and with *not* taking it seriously. In the case of holiness, the finite moral agent must aim for it but in a sense cannot, because for an embodied person holiness or unconditional virtue is unattainable; in the case of happiness, the other person's happiness is always a worthy end for him to aim at, yet his own happiness is never worthy of his willing. The upshot of Kant's account, for Fackenheim, is an understanding of religion: "the religion of finite moral existence does not supersede but reflects this contradiction."[30] That is, religion is not a resolution of a tension or struggle; it is acknowledging and living with that struggle. The struggle is the struggle between Kant's two definitions of religion, as the understanding of our moral duties as divine commands and as the hope for deserved happiness.

Why are these definitions in tension? For the former, we now see, means that God's role in morality is to guarantee the unity of happiness and virtue and hence that we should be confident that we can achieve the ends we aim at. But by itself this is inadequate as a definition of religion. As is the belief that we can hope for deserved happiness, since "genuine virtue can be acquired only if it is sought for its own sake."[31] Fackenheim takes this tension to recapitulate the excesses of a Stoic or an Epicurean account of the Highest Good. Neither virtue by itself nor happiness commensurate with virtue is satisfactory; genuine religion must include both.

This lesson is not one that Fackenheim sees in Kant directly but one he arrives at only by stepping back and reflecting on his work. It is not a lesson about Kant's moral faith, at least not in terms of its specific content. It is, rather, a matter of the *form* of Kant's conclusions about religion and its relation to the tensions characteristic of the human condition. Fackenheim puts it this way: "religion culminates at the point at which the finite moral agent recognizes his radical inability to understand the relation between that which must be achieved by himself and that which can be expected only from God."[32] In other words, Fackenheim takes the core of Kant's philosophy of religion to be its recapitulation of the theme of nature and grace or act and faith, in particular the dialectic between human conduct and divine assistance.[33] Or, more broadly, Kant takes religion to register the way in which our selfhood involves the struggle between the finite and the infinite.

But Fackenheim is not finished. He asks: What makes these results "practical metaphysics"? That is, this account of the structure of moral consciousness does not end with mere beliefs or "postulates." It ends with commitments about reality, with moral knowledge.[34] How is this so? Fackenheim puts it this way: "this analysis [of the structure of finite moral existence] ... turns into ['practical metaphysics'] only by virtue of the thesis that the *enaged* standpoint of finite moral existence is *metaphysically ultimate, for the philosopher no less than for the man in the street.*"[35] Like freedom, God and the immortal soul, "which appear as realities in the moment of moral engagement," are in fact realities and not simply useful fictions.[36] The comparison is not unproblematic, however. We should recall that freedom can be a reality because it is not incompatible with causality. But God and the immortal soul do not involve resolving a contradiction or paradox; rather, they reflect and leave untouched contradictions and in fact just those contradictions that characterize finite moral existence. Freedom, that is, is free from contradiction, whereas God and the immortal soul are not. The claim that we are free, therefore, can be taken in its literal sense; the claims that God exists and that the soul is immortal cannot be. They must be read "symbolically" – or "analogically," as Fackenheim puts it. Each contains a truth that is formulated as clearly as we, as incarnate beings, can grasp it, but each is represented anthropomorphically and indirectly. The soul in itself is not temporal, nor is God in itself wilful and rational. Hence, the "postulates" about God and the soul point to realities, even if in a limited way. Moreover, that limited way is the most we can expect for creatures like ourselves – finite, incarnate, natural, and limited. A commitment to their existence that arises out of our moral experience is, as Fackenheim puts it, ultimate. The philosopher realizes that as a philosopher and yet also a finite and limited being, he can attain no more ultimate standpoint, and if he seeks to flee his philosophical stance and take up one outside philosophy – say that of the mystic – he merely substitutes a real God with an image of his own making. With this defence of Kant's "practical metaphysics," Fackenheim brings his account of Kant's philosophy of religion to a close.

Fackenheim's claim about "practical metaphysics" is highly controversial. He seems to be claiming that the philosophical results of Kant's practical arguments are not merely subjective, nor is their status fixed by their relationship to evidence and justification. In the case of freedom, causality does not count against its existence. In the case of God and the immortal soul, the contradictions of finite human existence similarly do not count against their reality. But suppose we grant these conclusions. Beyond that, what does it mean to say that the "engaged standpoint of the finite moral agent is metaphysically ultimate"? At least part of what the claim means is that even for the philosopher, no more ultimate standpoint enables him to demonstrate God's existence; there are no theoretical arguments for God's existence that are compelling and without flaws. Yet if the practical standpoint – that is, the engaged standpoint of the finite moral agent – is available and indeed necessary, then what does it require? The issue is not whether such an engaged standpoint is sufficient to give rise to the belief that God and the immortal soul exist; it is whether the standpoint is sufficient to show their necessity. Basically, Kant's argument is that it does this insofar as without believing in their existence, such finite moral agency is futile. Has he shown, however, that finite moral agency would be futile without their existence? Only if believing in their existence cannot occur without their actually being realities. Or is this required? Is it not sufficient that such agency cannot occur without their existence, whether indeed the moral agent has the belief or is aware of having it or not? After all, it is not the ordinary person as moral agent who postulates God's existence and the soul's immortality; it is the philosopher as moral agent – that is, the reflective moral agent – who does so.

In short, religion, for Kant, is the recognition that we being finite moral agents, our individual moral conduct would be futile and pointless if it were not for God; as human beings, we are capable of acting on principle but not of accomplishing everything we thereby seek to accomplish. Religion occurs at the point where finite human capacity and divine assistance meet. Or so it might seem. But later Kant worries about the former, about what we are capable of choosing to do, about what moral evil involves and whether in fact we are capable of moral regeneration. It will turn out that here too, in order to avoid futility, Kant turns to God for assistance. If the concept of the Highest Good raises for Kant the issue of self-sufficiency and the need for divine grace, so does the concept of radical evil. It would be convenient if Fackenheim saw things this way; it would underscore Kant's role in developing a mediating position that takes seriously both human will and divine assistance. But in order to see if Fackenheim does view it this way, we must turn to his essay "Kant and Radical Evil."

Kant and Radical Evil

There has been a great deal of recent discussion of Kant's concept of radical evil, largely focused on his moral psychology and the meaning of the expression "radical evil."[37] What leads us to choose what is evil rather than what is good? Kant needs to explain, many commentators claim. And he also needs to explain how deep-seated in our nature is the disposition to evil and what it would take to overcome it. These are questions about our concrete moral situation, and recent commentators think that the need to clarify that situation is enough to warrant Kant's attention. Moreover, their interpretations of Kant's account are by and large naturalistic. But that account of moral evil comes in the first chapter of Kant's 1793 book on religion, *Religion within the Limits of Reason Alone*, which should and indeed does point to a need man has for divine assistance. Gordon Michalson, in his excellent book *Fallen Freedom: Kant on Radical Evil and Moral Regeneration*, takes this to be a primary feature of Kant's theory. Fackenheim surely takes seriously the religious context for Kant's account of radical evil, but one wonders if his treatment is along these lines or for other purposes.

Fackenheim begins by asking if Kant's doctrine of radical evil marks a shift for Kant, and he agrees that it does; but it is a shift conducted for legitimate philosophical reasons and not for theological or political ones.[38] Individuals are subject both to natural inclinations, desires and wants, and to the law of reason, the moral law. They are not ruled exclusively by the former, without any sense of what ought to be other than what causal necessity requires, or by the latter, such that what ought to be is the law of their being. Human beings, Fackenheim argues, are neither brute animals nor gods. Finite human beings have inclinations to satisfy their natural desires and also a respect for the moral law, the law of reason, and for what duty demands. In any given situation, then, what will he choose? Will it be to serve the purposes of morality or to satisfy his own interests, what Kant calls the interests of "self-love"? According to Fackenheim, moral obligation requires freedom. If pressed by his natural inclinations, the moral agent is free to act as duty demands. That is, moral responsibility requires the freedom to choose between natural desires and the moral law.

But what is this freedom? Fackenheim notes what he calls an ambiguity in Kant's understanding of moral evil. On the one hand, "man is free in the degree to which he is determined by the moral principle." According to this reading, moral freedom is autonomy; it is to be subject to the moral law. On the other hand, however, man "is free to choose good or evil."[39] This kind of freedom is not autonomy but something else, the capacity to determine the will – to choose – in one direction or another. Later commentators will call this Kant's distinction between *Wille* (autonomy) and *Willkür* (free choice). Fackenheim seems not to know this distinction, which has become a regular feature of the secondary literature. But he does understand the ambiguity or difference that it marks, and he sees at least part of what makes it important for Kant.

According to Fackenheim, Kant – in the *Grundlegung* and the *Critique of Practical Reason* – says that the will can only be free if it is self-determined and that means autonomous, determined by its own rational laws. But if so, then for Kant the will is free only if it is good, and this makes a responsible choice for evil or against the moral law impossible. To choose against the moral law and for one's natural desires or inclinations is not to choose freely but rather to be moved by an object outside oneself. Such an asymmetry, however, has a wholly unacceptable consequence: that one can be praised for making the right choice but not blamed for making the wrong one. Or, alternatively, that there is no such thing as an evil will. Fackenheim claims that this conundrum led Kant to explore the occurrence of moral evil and to give an account of how choosing against the moral law is possible.[40] Presumably, Fackenheim believes that prior to the *Religion* Kant did not make the distinction between choosing for the moral law and choosing against it and for one's natural inclinations or desires.[41] That is, Kant does not until the *Religion* acknowledge that the will is always faced with natural desires and the moral law and that in every situation it is the will's role to endorse a maxim that subordinates one to the other. I will return to this point later.

Fackenheim turns to Kant's essay and notes that Kant begins by noting historical and other empirical evidence that evil is a regular feature of daily life. From this Kant concludes that the possibility of moral evil, of acting against the good, is part of human nature. Furthermore, moral evil must be a free act; it cannot be grounded in some metaphysical principle or some innate condition connected, say, with the senses or with reason. Ultimately, moral evil, if man is to be held accountable, must be grounded in a free choice. It must be, as Fackenheim understands Kant, more than "the mere yielding to passion" and yet less than "the sheer diabolical defiance of the moral law simply because it is that law. Man may do evil, but he is no demon."[42]

As Fackenheim sees it, the key to moral evil is that the will is presented with two features: natural inclinations (desires and feelings) and the moral law. Whether a decision is good or evil is a matter of whether the natural relation between these is respected or perverted, whether natural inclinations are subordinated to the moral law or vice versa. When man freely chooses to subordinate moral principle to his natural desires, feelings, or interests, then his choice is evil. If such a view is correct, then man can choose freely between good and evil.[43]

But, as commentators regularly note, there is much more than this to Kant's account. For if this helps us understand how moral evil is possible, it does not tell us what makes such evil radical. Nor does it explain why Kant claims that moral evil is a feature of human nature. Fackenheim's response to these issues is to claim that for Kant, the appropriation of a maxim is the appropriation of "a rational, over-all principle governing a man's life as a whole."[44] Fackenheim does not engage in a careful analysis of Kant's terminology, of the terms "maxim," "disposition," and "propensity." But he is clearly on the right track.[45] What makes moral evil radical is that it involves the choice of an overall principle that guides one's whole life, an orienting principle regarding which consideration – one's natural inclinations or the moral law – will be primary and which will be subordinated. As Bernstein puts it, what makes a maxim good or evil is not what it contains, for all maxims contain both components: natural inclinations and the moral law. Rather, what makes a maxim good or evil is the order of subordination of the two components. Fackenheim draws a twofold conclusion: for Kant, man is not just occasionally good and occasionally evil; the choice is a radical one related to the overall tendency or disposition of one's life. Furthermore, all men as a species are in fact evil – that is, their self-chosen propensity or disposition is towards evil, towards the subordination of the moral law to natural inclinations or self-love.[46] Thus Fackenheim concludes that Kant is drawn to what might seem to be a paradoxical result: that evil is innate in human nature and is therefore radical, a matter of roots, and that nonetheless evil is up to each man himself – it is freely chosen. It must be innate, for otherwise evil would gain no foothold in a will wholly disposed to privilege the moral law; and it must be freely chosen, if man is to be ultimately responsible for the kind of person he is and hence for his choices and his actions. And there is no further, no higher ground or principle that determines the will. As Fackenheim puts it, "each decision of each man is metaphysically ultimate; and whichever choice is made, it is an ultimate irrationality."[47]

But if evil is innate in human nature, is man forever the victim of his original choice? Is there no hope for the good, no hope for what Michalson calls "moral regeneration" other than divine grace? Fackenheim, after arguing that radical evil is not original sin, recounts Kant's moral ideal, his conviction that all human beings are obligated to advance morally and to overcome the evil within them insofar as they are capable. Only if this is so is man genuinely free, not only to make an original commitment but then, also, to seek always to rectify it. Hence, "moral action [is] the core of the religious life."[48] But human life is not an either/or. It is not the case that human life is either wholly up to free choices to recover a human heart or wholly a matter of divine grace, of divine assistance. Rather, as Kant points out, we are obligated to better ourselves, to reshape our character, but at the same time we are imperfect beings who require assistance, divine aid. That aid, of course, will not come in this life, nor should one dwell on it, for that would lead to moral laziness. "Indeed, our sole concern with God's future aid should be to live in such a way as to be worthy of it. Thus it does not really make any difference to the life we ought to live now whether this future divine aid … is fact or fancy. In order to live the good life now, we do not require it."[49] To be sure, given the extreme perversion at the heart of human character, only a radical change can rid us of evil. Fackenheim refers to this radical change as "a total action of conversion, an act of redemption, the creation of a new man."[50]

But, as Fackenheim indicates, this situation is paradoxical. If man is by nature radically evil and if this means that he has a wholly perverted character, how can any choice he makes or act he performs overturn the priorities in his character? If moral evil is radical, how can he choose for the good? Is man either good or evil but not both? Fackenheim points out that Kant adamantly denies this dilemma.[51] People can become better; they can draw closer to moral goodness or virtue. Since we are talking about a change of character, of the overarching maxim that guides one's entire life, this change cannot be gradual. It is not, as Fackenheim says, reform; it is a revolution, a rebirth, the creation of a new person. But this conversion is ultimately inexplicable; nothing can be said about what brings it about. There is no higher determining ground than the free choice that would initiate it. It is not the moral law, nor is it his character. It is, to use Fackenheim's words, a *creatio ex nihilo* – a brute free act. Moreover, it is a remarkable one. But so, indeed, is the original act that man makes in behalf of evil. In short, both originally and at every subsequent moment, man alone among animals and gods is given this choice, between good and evil; it is the momentous fact that distinguishes the human from all else.

Michalson differs from Fackenheim. Michalson's treatment of Kant's doctrine of radical evil and his account of moral regeneration, in addition to his detailed analysis of the text of the *Religion* on these issues, ultimately show Kant to be focusing on a feature of human experience where human self-sufficiency is confronted with the need for divine assistance.[52] For Michalson, God is necessary; for Fackenheim, moral regeneration must be a matter of personal decision. How can people make morally bad choices; and for that matter, how can they change their character, their personality, from evil to good? As I mentioned earlier, Michalson takes Kant to be providing a secular version of the problem of nature and grace. In this respect, Michalson finds in these issues a Kantian venue akin to what Fackenheim finds in Kant's arguments in the *Critique of Practical Reason*. But Fackenheim's essay on radical evil does not feature this dialectic to the same degree; in fact, in dealing with radical evil he minimizes the role of divine aid.

Overall, it is not obvious what Fackenheim's primary interest *is* in his treatment of Kant on radical evil. In later writings, to be sure, Fackenheim will distinguish what Kant means by radical evil from what he himself means when he finds such evil in the Nazi Holocaust, especially in the character and conduct of Hitler, Heydrich, Himmler, and others. He will, that is, use Kant to help him identify what is extreme and demonic in such agents.[53] But in this early paper, Fackenheim pays no special attention to Kant's dismissal of the possibility of a demonic personality, nor does he feature Kant's role in the tension in religion between human autonomy and divine grace. Rather, if there is a thematic core to Fackenheim's account, it is the necessity Kant feels to clarify the metaphysical nature of freedom and its relationship to that self-determining mode of freedom he calls autonomy. For this reason, Fackenheim raises no problems for Kant's account; he is satisfied to show that Kant's intent is to show how basic freedom is to Kant's account and how committed Kant is to the twofold nature of finite, embodied human existence. He does not question the coherence or seriousness of Kant's account either of the grounds of moral evil and what makes it radical, or of the solution to the problem of moral regeneration and development. Fackenheim is more interested in how Kant understands human existence and what his conception requires for an account of moral defectiveness and moral advance. For him, it is sufficient to have shown how it is all grounded in a very strong commitment to freedom.[54]

Kantian Autonomy and Revealed Morality

In the mid-1960s, in "The Revealed Morality of Judaism and Modern Thought: A Confrontation with Kant," Fackenheim takes up Kantian moral philosophy once again, but this time his aim is not primarily expository. Rather, his purpose is critical and constructive, for he considers what is surely one of the most challenging difficulties that Kant's moral philosophy poses for religions like Judaism, which incorporate a revealed morality, most prominently in a divine command theory.[55] In this essay, he poses an important dilemma: Judaism is either a revealed religion or a moral faith, but it cannot be both. If Jewish morality is revealed, with its authority grounded in divine command, then Judaism must reject the Kantian requirement that all moral principles be grounded autonomously; but then it risks not being a morality at all. Or if the Kantian account is true, with the implication that human existence is essentially rational and autonomous, then Judaism must abandon its distinctive moral vocation – that is, morality can play no essential role in the Jewish enterprise. At best, it can be something that Jews share with all free, rational beings. In short, in this paper, unlike his earlier ones on Kant, Fackenheim is concerned specifically with the importance of Kantian philosophy for Jewish self-understanding. The result, to the degree that he succeeds, is a philosophically articulate interpretation of Judaism and a corrective to the Kantian claims about the grounds of morality.

In another paper, "The Dilemma of Liberal Judaism," published five years earlier, Fackenheim explores the larger terrain on which this conundrum about Kantian autonomy and revealed morality is situated. He argues that liberal Judaism faces a series of perplexities as it attempts to be both seriously Jewish and responsibly modern and liberal – that is, as it seeks to respect the primacy of the past as well as that of the present, the primacy of the individual as well as that of the community, and the pre-eminence of God alongside the central role of the human individual.[56] If we place Kant within these dichotomies, he seems to privilege human rational agency, the primacy of the individual and his autonomy, and the present over all the resources of the past. But if Kant is right, if Judaism is rooted in the past, in the priority of tradition and community, and in a commitment to divine power and divine authority, Judaism turns out to be at best a quaint anachronism or at worst utterly false.

Fackenheim begins with a brief and largely uncontroversial summary of Kant's moral philosophy as presented in the *Grundlegung* (1785). He focuses on autonomy, on the Kantian claim that the moral law is authoritative, universally obligatory, and binding as moral precisely because it is self-imposed by each and every free rational agent.[57] Divine command theories ground the authority of moral principles in divine legislation and ultimately in God's characteristics, His power and authority. Hence, the only sense that one can make of such theories is if we take the expression "divine commands" to refer to the principles endorsed by the rational will. Otherwise, the believer faces what Fackenheim calls a "grave dilemma":

> Either [the believer] concedes that the will can and must impose the God-given law upon itself; but then its God-givenness becomes irrelevant in the process of self-imposition and appropriation; or else he insists that the God-givenness of the law does not and cannot at any point become irrelevant; but then the will cannot impose the law on itself – it can only submit to it for such non-moral reasons as trust in divine promises or fear of divine threats.[58]

He points out, furthermore, that Kant faces the dilemma but does not succumb to it. Rather he recommends the choice of a rational religion or what he calls a "moral theology," in which religion is subordinated to the moral law.

Suppose, then, we turn to Judaism in the light of this Kantian problem. What do we find? The key to Fackenheim's response is his claim that we find in Judaism an understanding of morality that is neither exclusively heteronomous nor exclusively autonomous, to use the Kantian terminology. Rather, the matrix or framework for morality within Judaism incorporates a dialectical interrelation of the individual and the divine; only when that dialectical interrelation is properly understood does one comprehend the sense in which there is and can be Jewish moral experience.[59] Here is a sketch of Fackenheim's description.

First, as we noted in chapter 1, Fackenheim distinguishes between the "pristine moment revelation," where the divine calls out to the human and the human receives that call, and the subsequent development of the revealed morality where "the revelation has become a system of specified laws and commandments."[60] The pristine moment or the primordial experience involves a divine presence that calls everything into question; it is a command as challenge. It also incorporates a free human reception. Both are absolute and unconditional, in the sense that the divine calls everything into question while the human freedom is called upon to accept or reject the "divine commanding Presence as a whole and for its own sake." Fackenheim focuses on the human side of this event, the free receptivity. It is not wholly autonomous, for although it is free, it requires the divine presence and the challenge if it is going to be a free acceptance or rejection of that challenge; but neither is it wholly heteronomous, for while it requires the divine presence, it is very much a choice, and in choosing to accept, the human will makes the divine will its own. That is, what Fackenheim is describing is a moment of relatedness between two radically distinct agents, one dominant and one subordinate, and the way in which the two agents act and respond to each other. But since Fackenheim is concerned with Kant's claim about our essential autonomy, he focuses on the human side of the event, asking how it is possible that a finite human being, encountered by the infinite, can confirm the relationship and yet survive its finitude. His way of asking this question, which Judaism asks but philosophy must answer, is this: If the human recipient of the divine presence must be capable of choosing for or against the divine presence, and if, when it accepts that presence and its challenge, it does so by bridging the gap and making the divine will its own, how is this possible? If the gap is a gap and a radical one, how can man not simply submit but rather, from his side, bridge it? How can the human act out of love for God's sake?[61] The issue, we might appreciate, has a familiarity about it. Fackenheim has read Hegel's early writings where he charges Judaism with taking God to be a ruler or king and human subjects to be slaves, and he has also read Hegel's famous account of the master–slave relationship in the *Phenomenology* where Hegel exposes the subtle dialectic of their relationship.[62] Fackenheim knows that a philosophical analysis can show that what appears at first glance to be a wholly heteronomous relationship is not that at all. Viewed with care, the relationship becomes dialectical; the slave, it will turn out, is a genuine subject, a free being, and not a slave.

For the philosopher to answer the question about human independence – or human dignity, as it were – Fackenheim suggests he turn to the developed system of morality and religious law. We may not be able to see that the religious subject may not be free in the immediate encounter with God, but we can surely see that he is free when that divine revelation recedes into the past and may seem to become irrelevant. For when the philosopher does turn to the system of law, the question arises whether the divine presence has in fact become irrelevant. After all, once the individual confronts the system of moral principles or religious law, "new and revealing immediacy is either false or superfluous."[63] The philosopher wants to understand how the human can remain free in the encounter with the divine Presence; Fackenheim's point is that perhaps human freedom is overwhelmed, or at least obscured, by the immediacy of the encounter. If we turn instead to the system of law that stands between the divine and the human, we may better understand the human being's status vis-à-vis the divine. But if the philosopher operates according to Kantian principles, he must confront the system of laws as either autonomous or heteronomous. There is no third alternative. Either one obeys them for *their* sake or for the sake of *their divine lawgiver*; that is, the laws are either autonomous and moral or heteronomous and revealed; they cannot be both:

> Kant holds that, mediating between man and God, moral law rules out or renders irrelevant an immediate divine commanding Presence. Judaism affirms that, despite the mediating function of the revealed moral law, the Divine is still present in commanding immediacy. The Kantian premise is that moral law is a *bar* between man and its divine Giver. The premise of Judaism is that it is a *bridge*.[64]

Why is this so? Why does Judaism not assume that one is related either to the moral law or to God but not both? Is there an assumption that Kant makes but that Judaism denies? Fackenheim's answer is very important to his argument; in fact, arguably it is the central step in the essay and the fundamental insight that he brings to the encounter between Judaism and Kant. His answer is that

> for Kant, all morality, including religious morality, demands a two-term relationship between man and his human neighbor. The revealed morality of Judaism demands a three-term relationship, nothing less than a relationship involving man, his human neighbor, and God Himself ... Micah's celebrated summary of the commandments does more than list three commandments that exist side by side. It states an internally related whole. For there is no humble walking before God unless it manifests itself in justice and mercy to the human neighbor. And there can be only fragmentary justice and mercy unless they culminate in humility before God. Here lies the heart and core of Jewish morality.[65]

With this claim, Fackenheim argues, Judaism responds to the Kantian challenge with its own conception of morality as involving the moral agent with others and with God, at once.

Fackenheim had begun by asking how morality in Judaism can be divinely revealed yet autonomous. He started with the pristine moment of revelation, and he found, even there, that there was a possibility of free human appropriation, as he calls it. He then turned to the system of law that followed that moment. It is not altogether clear what his motives were for such a move. Perhaps he worried whether in such a situation, with the law in place, the divine Presence would still be relevant; or perhaps he worried that once the divine Presence was recovered, there would be some doubt whether the human response was still free. In either case, he argued that the result is a puzzle for Judaism: Kant had taken the law to be a bar between man and God; Judaism does not. For the latter, the law is a bridge between the two. How is this possible? Fackenheim puts the question this way:

> How can man presume to participate in a three-term relationship which involves not only his human neighbor but also God Himself? How can he – as he must, in order to participate in such a relationship – act out of love for the sake of God, when God is God while man is only man?[66]

Fackenheim calls this a Kantian question: "What is the condition of the possibility of such action?" To use Kant's more technical expression, it is a transcendental question. Supposing that Jewish morality exists and that there are Jewish moral agents, and supposing that this three-term relationship is essential to it, what must occur for this to be possible?

The route that Fackenheim takes to answer this question leads him to his most important Jewish predecessors, Martin Buber and especially Franz Rosenzweig. In the text Fackenheim never refers to Buber or Rosenzweig; rather, he cites midrashic texts. But the reading of those texts and his argument based on them clearly are strongly influenced by these predecessors, primarily by Rosenzweig. Before we look at that argument, however, I want to reflect for a moment on Fackenheim's answer to the question about what distinguishes Jewish moral thinking from Kantian ethics and what accounts for the fact that in Judaism the law is a bridge and not a bar between God and man.

Here I think Fackenheim has not understood completely or deeply enough the full significance of his answer. To begin, in answering the question, Fackenheim is in fact making two claims and not just one. The context for the question is the "developed system of law" in Judaism that follows the pristine religious moments and, by implication, the relationship between the individual and the moral law in Kantian ethics. In short, Fackenheim is examining the relation between the individual and obligations. In this regard, Kant and Judaism rely upon different assumptions. But assumptions about what? Fackenheim's words are that Kantian morality "demands a two-term relationship between a man and his human neighbor" and that "the revealed morality of Judaism demands a three-term relationship ... involving man, his human neighbor, and God Himself." That is, the role of moral and religious law, Fackenheim says, "demands" or "involves" what I will call interpersonal relationships. This is Fackenheim's first claim; his second is that Kant and Judaism differ regarding the scope of the relationships: for Judaism, they are three-term, for Kant, two-term. Let us say that for Kant they are interhuman, while for Judaism they are both interhuman and divine–human. In the course of his analysis, Fackenheim focuses all his attention on the difference in scope: in a sense, for Judaism the relationships are both/and, while for Kant they are either/or. He simply takes for granted that the role of obligations or principles in our ethical lives either incorporates or relies upon interhuman relationships. But arguably this step, from *principles* or *law* to *relationships*, is the more important of the two features in Fackenheim's claim. It may or may not be what distinguishes Judaism from Kantian moral philosophy, but it may be the more significant for our understanding of morality and hence our understanding of that difference.

We can understand Fackenheim in a slightly different way. Law in Judaism is not a free-standing entity that links or separates other free-standing entities. Rather, human existence and moral existence are intrinsically relational. They involve persons engaged with other persons, both embedded in a context or situation. But what is the scope of the relations that law expresses? In order to be law – that is, to be binding upon agents in relation – law in Judaism must express both the relations between persons and their relations to God. To use Charles Taylor's terminology, the moral source that grounds moral–legal relationships is always implicit in every moral encounter.

It is at least a controversial claim that all moral principles are interpersonal, and I doubt that that is what Fackenheim means. Indeed, trying to determine what he means would be sheer speculation. A more interesting approach is to notice that the theme of Fackenheim's essay – the conflict between divine command theories and Kantian autonomy – is about the ground of moral normativity. What gives moral obligations their normative force? In virtue of what feature or characteristic do such obligations make a claim upon us and count as moral reasons for us? For Kant, the answer concerns the way in which moral obligations are related to our capacity for rational self-determination; they have a certain form as a result of being expressive of such rationality. For Judaism, conceived traditionally as a revealed religion, the answer concerns the fact that such obligations are commands made by an authoritative ruler and legislator, God; they express His will – that is, what He wants human beings to do. One might argue, then, that the crucial shift in Fackenheim's essay comes when he directs the discussion away from talking about moral obligations as principles or imperatives, with the implication that the central question is what feature of them gives them normative force, towards talking about relationships within which claims arise for the agents involved in them. To be sure, there have been recent attempts to argue that even within a Kantian scheme or one similar to it, there are some obligations that arise and receive their authority from interpersonal relations; in such cases, the normativity derives from the interpersonal roles people play with respect to one another.[67] But Fackenheim does not merely identify some among our obligations as involving interpersonal relationships and perhaps even as deriving their normativity from these relationships. What he seems to be doing is something else, something more radical, more extreme.

I think that Fackenheim has Buber and Rosenzweig in mind, but the figure who has done the most with the greatest seriousness and philosophical sophistication to argue that morality, politics, and law arise out of interpersonal relationships is Emmanuel Levinas. Without launching into a digression on Levinas, suffice it to say that for him, not only these venues, but also indeed all human experiences, are grounded in interpersonal or social relationships and that these relationships are fundamentally ethical in character. What this means, as we reflect upon Fackenheim's move in this paper, is that our ordinary lives, with all the principles or policies or laws we use to negotiate them, must be understood and lived as expressions of the fundamentally ethical character of our interpersonal relationships. Furthermore, this relatedness is where the normative force of our principles and laws come from. It is also where the primary content comes from – our responsibilities to others for care, acceptance, attention, justice, and so forth. And finally, it is the ultimate truth, so to speak, of all our decisions and actions. That is, even when we perform an act of following a principle or doing our duty, at its root such an action is a matter of responding to particular other persons and taking upon ourselves responsibility for them, their needs, and their interests. For Levinas, rules and principles are often obstacles to reaching out to other persons, but they need not be. And in fact, the ethical content of following a rule lies in the way in which the act responds to the needs of others.

When Fackenheim claims that the individual's response to his obligations, his acting on principle or not, "demands" or requires certain interpersonal relationships, I take him to be making this Levinasian point.[68] He means that the ethical is in fact the claims and responses of people as they engage with one another. What distinguishes the Jewish way of understanding what takes place in such interpersonal encounters, however, from the Kantian way of understanding them, is that for Judaism, every interhuman encounter occurs together with a divine–human encounter. Levinas and Fackenheim would disagree on this matter. For Levinas, of course, there is no divine–human encounter other than the interhuman one. Divinity and transcendence are within the interhuman or face-to-face encounter.[69] But we can set this important difference aside. What Fackenheim and Levinas share is a conviction that morality, politics, and law are not at their deepest level about principles; they are about interpersonal relationships and the encounters that constitute them. At some level, of course, Fackenheim knows this. He understands the dialogical element in Buber and in Rosenzweig to involve interpersonal encounters and he takes the primacy of the mutual involvement with one another of the dialogical partners to require their independence, their distinctiveness. But in this essay, where his argument is about what distinguishes Kant from Judaism, he chooses to subordinate this issue to the one of scope, to the involvement of God within human affairs, as if that is the most important way in which the two differ. One might argue, however, that Fackenheim should have paid more attention to the primacy of relationship, for it is a distinction of Judaism that it knows this deeper truth about the ethical in a way that modern moral philosophy does not or at least does not typically acknowledge.

How can man act towards his neighbour with love both for his neighbour's sake and for God's sake as well? And how can he do so in response to a claim that is unconditional and yet with a freedom that is also unconditional? Fackenheim's answer is this:

> Man can appropriate divine commandments if they are handed over for human appropriation. He can live by the Torah in the love and for the sake of God, if the Torah itself is a gift of divine love, making such a life a human possibility. He can participate in a three-term relationship which involves God Himself if God, Who in His power does not need man, in His love nevertheless chooses to need him ... The Torah manifests love in the very act of manifesting commandment ... In Judaism the primordial manifestation of divine love is not subsequent to but *in* the commandments; primordial human joy is not in a future subsequent to the life of the commandments but in that life itself.[70]

In the same event, then, God "singles out" and calls upon the individual; God dominates the individual. But He also gives the individual the freedom to receive that call and to respond. The infinite power of the divine, as divine and as commanding, overwhelms the human and yet elevates it at the same time. The commandments are given in love; they give meaning and direction to human life and thus are an act of love, of grace; and the response to receiving this fixing and confirmation of meaning is to share that love with others. In *To Mend the World*, recalling this "neo-orthodox" account, Fackenheim formulates it this way: "a Grace that gives commandments also gives the freedom to obey them."[71] By "neo-orthodox" Fackenheim means Rosenzweig.[72]

What, then, does Fackenheim conclude? He concludes that Kant does not so much refute the revealed morality of Judaism as reject its terms, and in so doing Kant is a secular version of a long-standing Christian, Pauline attitude towards the law. When the law is treated as an obstacle between God and man, it must be rejected in favour of some mediation. But on Fackenheim's reading, this is to misunderstand the role of the commandments in Judaism. Martin Buber had a wholly negative view of Jewish law, and in this respect he accepted the dichotomy that underlies the Kantian critique but also chose against it. Rosenzweig, on the other hand, objected to this denigration of the law. In 1923, in his famous open letter to Buber, *Die Bauleute* (The Builders), he argued that within Jewish life, law (*Gesetz*) must be transformed into commandment (*Gebot*), that is, "it must regain that living reality [ordinariness]," which Rosenzweig calls "deed" and which means the living relationship that lies behind the formula.[73] Fackenheim's attempt to defend the character of Jewish ethics as both moral and revealed is in the spirit of Rosenzweig's critique of Buber.

The essay is more than a defence of Judaism against a possible Kantian challenge; it is also a foray into the general territory of what Fackenheim will later call "encounters between Judaism and modern philosophy." Recall his claim that Kant's inability to appreciate Jewish revealed morality in its distinctiveness is part of a tradition that begins with Paul and hence that bespeaks a bias against Judaism in the tradition of Western philosophy. How deep is this bias against Judaism? If Western philosophy were more honest about its own limitations, would there be, one might ask, something for Western philosophy to learn from Judaism?

Kant and Judaism after Auschwitz: First Stage

Encounters between Judaism and Modern Philosophy was published in 1973. Its second chapter, "Abraham and the Kantians: Moral Duties and Divine Commandments," includes as its nucleus the essay we have been examining. But Fackenheim does not simply appropriate the lesson of the earlier essay; he deepens it in several ways. The new essay's innovations are several. First, Fackenheim focuses the treatment of Kant by asking how Kant would and did respond to God's call for Abraham to sacrifice his son Isaac in the famous passage from Genesis 22 (that near-sacrifice is designated in the Jewish tradition as the Akedat Yitzhak, i.e., the Binding of Isaac). Second, he contrasts Kant's response with Kierkegaard's influential account in *Fear and Trembling*, taking Kierkegaard to share Kant's basic assumptions but to be responding in a contrasting way: he is an anti-Kantian Kantian. Third, Fackenheim, relying on his account of the interpretive recovery of the past in the first chapter of *God's Presence in History*, explores the challenges of Kant and Kierkegaard and how the Akedah has been and can be recovered by later Jewish interpreters. Finally, Fackenheim asks how, specifically, the lessons of the Akedah can be recovered in a post-Holocaust present. In this essay, then, he addresses issues that are much deeper and richer than Jewish ethics. He also deals with them with much greater nuance regarding history and interpretation and in the context of the thought that Nazism and the death camps have radicalized how any recovery of the Jewish past can be conducted. If we want to examine whether the Holocaust altered Fackenheim's engagement with Kant, we must start here.

To begin, Fackenheim has several reasons for focusing his discussion of Kantian moral philosophy on the Akedah. In this particular episode, the conflict between moral principle and divine command (autonomy and heteronomy) is central; moreover, the way in which that conflict is resolved receives divergent judgments from Kant, Kierkegaard, and the Jewish tradition. Also, the event features a figure, Abraham, who would become a paradigm for Jewish faith and for the covenantal relationship with God, and whose obedience would be interpreted later in the tradition as especially meritorious. Furthermore, the event raises the question of what role sacrifice and self-sacrifice play in Judaism – that is, it focuses our attention on its moral content and not simply on its form. As we shall see, the exposure of Judaism and philosophy to the Holocaust raises serious moral problems; Fackenheim's attention shifts from the possibility of revelation and even the relationship between revelation and morality to the content of moral obligation and the special role of human dignity and worth. For a host of reasons, then, Fackenheim's choice of Abraham and the Akedah is significant.

Fackenheim contrasts Kant and his criticism of Abraham with Kierkegaard and his praise of him as a "knight of faith." In the *Conflict of the Faculties*, Kant argues that any divine voice that would call upon Abraham to sacrifice his only son must be false, and that Abraham, in obeying such a voice, is "morally obtuse" if not worse.[74] In short, Abraham should have tested the voice against universal moral principles, and had he done so, he would have found it wanting.[75] Kierkegaard, by contrast, argues that Abraham made the right choice, in that he teleologically suspended the ethical in favour of the immediacy of the divine command. As Fackenheim puts it, Kierkegaard's Abraham separates himself from the community of humankind by making the "existential decision" without any support from the "mediation of universal, ethical standards." He is utterly alone, "and the loneliness is terrifying because the command is not merely extra-ethical but contrary to the ethical."[76] Kant and Kierkegaard, then, can be contrasted and indeed *should* be, for Kierkegaard is, as Fackenheim puts it, an "anti-Kantian Kantian." Basically, they share a common view of the ethical as universal, and they ignore history and place Abraham above it. Where they differ is that for Kant, the universal takes priority, whereas for Kierkegaard, the divine–human relationship takes precedence.

Fackenheim, following Buber in a famous paper, argues that Judaism must reject Kierkegaard's Abraham, for his isolation flies in the face of the Torah and evades the fact that the divine–human relationship must take place alongside the interpersonal or social one.[77] This moves Fackenheim in the direction of Kant, but here, he argues, the covenantal relationship and its social implications introduce their own worries. As one turns to Kant, one wonders whether one can do one's own duty and follow the moral law, when it is autonomous and the expression of self-legislating reason, and at the same time "come into relation with God." It is at this point that Fackenheim introduces his earlier paper.

Fackenheim's earlier judgment was that Kantian ethics was too narrow. Wedding the moral law to autonomy, it left no room for revealed morality. We now learn that Kierkegaard is also inadequate; he fails to appreciate the social character of the life of faith. Yet both, and Judaism too, grant the Akedah a certain prominence. As Fackenheim puts it,

> it is by condemning Abraham that Kant makes every divine-human relation one that is essentially an interhuman moral relation. It is by praising him that Kierkegaard exposes every moral relation to the threat of a teleological suspension religious in nature. And if it has thus far appeared that the Midrash avoids this fatal alternative by means of the Torah – a three-term relation in which God, man, and fellowman are all immediately involved – we must now face the rabbinic view that the Torah itself was given on account of the merit of Abraham's act at Mount Moriah.[78]

What Fackenheim means is that the Akedah is the site, the location, for two major conflicts or tensions that Judaism must confront. One is between religion and ethics, the other between sacrifice and religion. Religion – Judaism – cannot be serious if it does not deal with sacrifice, and it is not responsible if cannot reconcile itself with ethics. If the conception of Judaism as a three-term relationship served to show the inadequacies of Kantian ethics, can it survive a genuine attempt to recover the Akedah today?[79]

Fackenheim points out that the Akedah is a "pristine commanding divine Presence" and that it therefore calls all standards into question, even if it is in its content "anti-moral." In what sense can such a moment register in the later developed life of Judaism and, in particular, in the system of "revealed morality of Judaism?" Does the Akedah, because of its content, give the lie to any Jewish recovery of it? Does it leave Judaism and its three-term morality in shambles? This is the question Fackenheim now seeks to answer. He initiates that answer by noting that the midrash takes Micah's formulation – which, he had argued, is an expression of the three-term morality – to be aimed at Mesha, the king of Moab, who actually sacrificed his son, and at Isaac, who accepted the act as if it had been done. That is, the midrash holds together the three-term morality of Judaism and the rejection of child sacrifice. But it would be baffling if the Akedah were to be understood as a divine rejection of precisely what was being commanded. Surely, Fackenheim argues, a modern Jew would have to side with Kant and to "reject the voice as spurious."[80]

The next section of the essay is titled "On Human Sacrifice, Or the Akedah as Perpetually Reenacted and Superseded Past." What dialectic does Fackenheim have in mind here? He admits that a Jew today would on moral grounds side with Kant and reject any contemporary recovery of the Akedah and yet on Jewish grounds would side with the Torah and revere Abraham. How is this possible?[81] How can the Akedah be re-enacted but also superseded?

Earlier, in 1965, Fackenheim's concern had been with Kantian autonomy as a formal aspect of morality, which conflicted with Judaism, which seeks to respect both human freedom and divine power. Now Fackenheim's concern is with the content of the moral imperative, so he calls attention to the formulation of the categorical imperative that involves respecting humanity as an end. Turning to Kant, he argues that for him the relationship with God is mediated by the moral universal, which in this case Kant takes to be the duty against murder. But, Fackenheim suggests, perhaps it is not murder but rather sacrifice that should be counted as the relevant universal, and if it is, he asks, might Kant's judgment be otherwise? His answer is "no," for religious sacrifice, as well as moral sacrifice, involves treating a person simply as a means; for Kant, it is obvious that religious sacrifice must be rejected – both the sacrifice of another, as in the Akedah, and even the sacrifice of oneself, as in martyrdom.

Kierkegaard, on the other hand, reveres sacrifice and wants to keep its possibility alive; for him, there is no higher commitment than the one of sacrificing for God. Hence, Kant shares the Torah's rejection of child sacrifice but not the Torah's respect for Abraham, while Kierkegaard shares the Torah's respect for Abraham but not its rejection of child sacrifice.[82] With these alternatives in mind, then, the Jewish re-enactment of the Akedah is distinctive, for it respects the universal and the community and yet at the same time holds to the three-term morality of Judaism. "The Midrash," Fackenheim argues, "connects the *Akedah* with the Micah passage that places all members of the covenant – and in the end, all men – into a three-term relation in which God, man, and fellowman are all involved."[83] What Fackenheim here emphasizes is that while Kant focuses on our relationships with our neighbours and Kierkegaard on Abraham's relationship with God, Judaism recalls Abraham both for his fidelity to God and for the merit that results in God's "eschatological concern for all the nations and his immediate concern for future Jewish generations."[84]

What does Kant's response mean to Judaism? Fackenheim is unqualified in his conviction that a modern Jew would agree with Kant that the moral law and humanity have intrinsic value. At the same time, however, "they disagree in that the one accepts, and the other rejects, pristine moments of divine Presence in which every content and all standards are called into question. Having rejected these latter, Kant can hold fast to the intrinsic value of humanity, for it is ultimate and unchallengeable. But how can Jewish morality hold fast to such value when it accepts pristine moments of divine Presence, in which all content and all standards are called into question?"[85] The question that Kant raises for Judaism is not whether the moral law and humanity have intrinsic value: there is no question that man has been created in the image of God. The issue is whether this is true absolutely, or whether it is true "only relatively, contingent as it is on an extraneous divine source."[86] This dilemma has been crystallized by the modern challenges to divine command theories of morality, among which the Kantian challenge is pre-eminent. Fackenheim takes the Akedah to express this dilemma in its own way: "How can [the Jewish tradition] both abhor child sacrifice and exalt the *Akedah*, never so much as raising the question of whether Abraham was not, after all, a would-be murderer and 'idolater'?" This question, implicitly, is about how the commitment to the intrinsic value of humanity and hence the abhorrence of murder and child sacrifice can also be a commitment to the determinative character of divine revelation.

Fackenheim's answer resorts to time – that is, to the temporality of human existence and hence the temporality or historical situatedness involved in returning to the Akedah, grasping it, and recovering it. When the Jew hears the story of Abraham, he listens to the Torah, but he does so today as a Jew who possesses the Torah only as a member of the covenantal community, and this means only "on account of Abraham's merit. In short, the *Akedah* is present for [the Jew today] as a past, perpetually reenacted, and superseded."[87] That is, one dimension of the dialectic between the Jew of today and the Akedah is that the Jew is a Jew, a member of the covenantal community, only on account of Abraham's action then. But what is it for the Jew today "to receive the Torah on account of Abraham's merit"? It is, Fackenheim says, "first, to have called all things into question in the sight of Divinity, the intrinsic value of humanity included; second, it is to accept that some things are in question no longer; and third, it is to receive, in surprise as well as gratitude, the value of humanity as a gift that Divinity might have withheld and that is yet given forever."[88] In short, the Jew of today is the recipient of two features of the original Akedah: the value of humanity that it questions and then endorses, and the encounter with the divine Presence in the pristine moment that calls everything into question and then endorses what is confirmed thereafter. That is, the narrative and hermeneutical quality of the response to the episode results in a present re-enactment of the surprise that characterizes the last stage in that narrative. The value of humanity is not given once and for all; it is given, put at risk, and then endorsed in the face of that risk. The commitment to the pre-eminence of human worth is not immune to history; rather, it is historical and contingent through and through.

Fackenheim then applies this general framework, and Judaism's difference from Kant, to the Akedah in a post-Holocaust present. In this context the issue is not child sacrifice but a different mode of sacrifice: martyrdom.[89] Here, in the case of religious self-sacrifice, Kant is no help. In Judaism, for many commentators, martyrdom as an act of sanctifying God's name is the highest stage of piety, but all the same, there is a caveat when apostasy might serve a significant purpose, one being Jewish survival. Fackenheim asks if today there is such a higher purpose that is served by Jewish life and the choice against self-sacrifice. Is Jewish survival more worthy than martyrdom?[90] During the Holocaust, there was no choice. But for Jews, now, there is, and it is the choice of how to respond. Fackenheim concludes the essay by indicating what one learns from reflecting on Jewish martyrdom in antiquity and in the

Middle Ages: that in the face of threat, "countless [Jews] ... refused to abandon their covenantal post." In those periods, that might have meant self-sacrifice. But "after the martyrdom of Auschwitz, forever unfathomable and without equal anywhere, [it means that] Jewish life is more sacred than Jewish death, even if it is for sanctification of the divine name."[91]

How might we summarize what Fackenheim is saying here about Kant's relevance to contemporary Jewish philosophy and thought? First, as he had shown in the earlier essay, Kantian moral theory presupposes a two-term relationship between persons and makes no room for the three-term relationship of Judaism. Furthermore, as I pointed out, Kant does not, as Judaism does, take moral experience to be fundamentally interpersonal. Second, Kant and Judaism may share a commitment to the intrinsic value of humanity, but for Kant this is a necessary feature of rational agency and hence timeless, while for Judaism it is a historical, contingent outcome of the complex interplay among God, the Jewish people, and history. Finally, for this reason, Jewish moral thinking today is historically complex. The Jewish moral philosopher today comes to grips with the present by means of a complex, dialectical reflection on the past and the present, and for this reason, Fackenheim claims, Judaism leaves Kant behind. Or so Fackenheim seemed to be saying in 1973, when this account was published. During the next decade, however, Fackenheim would rethink this judgment. If the theological implications of Kantian moral theory and the centrality of autonomy were the core of his encounter with Kant in the period through the mid-1960s, Fackenheim's turn to the Holocaust led him to highlight the moral content of Kant's moral law. By the time he wrote *To Mend the World*, it is this core – the intrinsic value of humanity – that would emerge in particularly important ways.

Kant and Judaism after Auschwitz: Second Stage

As we have seen, in the chapter "Abraham and the Kantians," Fackenheim *begins* to consider what features of Kant's thinking about morality and religion can be recovered for Judaism in a post-Holocaust present. That question becomes more serious and is more developed in Fackenheim's greatest work, *To Mend the World*. In this context, I think that Kant is relevant for Fackenheim in two respects. One concerns the evil of the Nazi criminality and how one ought to understand it; here, Kant is a kind of background and unmentioned presence. As part of his analysis of the evil of Nazism, Fackenheim considers Arendt's expression "the banality of evil" and its application to Eichmann, and he also examines reflectively the evil of perpetrators of various kinds, eventually considering Hitler himself. Kant had said that there is no such thing as "diabolical evil." But what of Himmler, Goebels, Heydrich, and Hitler? Was their evil not demonic? And if so, does this compromise Kant's doctrine of radical evil? Second, when Fackenheim turns to the question of what a genuine or authentic post-Holocaust philosophy would be like, he uses as an example Kurt Huber, whose final testament in defence of the White Rose has Kantian and Fichtean overtones. Here the presence of Kant is on the surface, so to speak; it is explicit. What Fackenheim finds in Huber is the importance of the content, rather than the form, of the Kantian moral law; that is, it is respect for human dignity and worth that becomes prominent. We must discuss both these issues in order to consider, for Fackenheim, those features of Kantian moral philosophy that one might recover today.[92]

Fackenheim's analysis of the Holocaust's perpetrators and victims, of their understandings and motivations, in To Mend the World is complex and subtle, and it is far beyond my purposes here to consider it in detail.[93] Since I am interested in what Kant means for Fackenheim in this post-Holocaust context, let me focus on what Fackenheim says about radical evil and especially on his understanding of Hannah Arendt's expression the "banality of evil." In The Origins of Totalitarianism, where Arendt uses the expression "radical" or absolute evil and where she argues that such evil, in the Nazi death camps and Stalinist labour camps, was unprecedented, she mentions that such a notion of evil is beyond the understanding of the Western religious and philosophical traditions. She explicitly mentions Kant as someone who fails to grasp the meaning of this kind of evil. Fackenheim would seem to agree, since his analysis supports Arendt's earlier view as expressed in The Origins of Totalitarianism. In short, there is good reason to consider Arendt's views in the light of Kant's, and the same goes for Fackenheim's treatment in To Mend the World and later essays.

Fackenheim does not seem to be familiar with the vast literature on Arendt's views about evil; nor does he seem to have been familiar with the extensive literature on Kant on radical evil.[94] Like other commentators, however, he does seem to have Kant in mind as he examines the evil of Auschwitz and the Nazi death camps and as he evaluates Arendt's famous claims in the course of his own analysis. It will be helpful, given these matters, to begin by considering how Henry Allison compares Kant and Arendt and their views about radical evil.

Allison does something that Fackenheim does not do in *To Mend the World* or even, in any detail, in his early paper, which we have already discussed. That is, he seeks to clarify what Kant takes moral evil to be, as a type of choice, and hence what its motivational structure is. As we have seen, for Kant, moral evil must be grounded in the will, in free choice; it must also involve both natural inclinations and the moral law or non-moral and moral incentives. "Evil must be rooted in a free choice against the law (a kind of inner voting in favor of inclination), which recognizes and respects the authority of the law even while contravening it. At its maximum, evil, so construed, takes the form of wickedness [*Bosartigkeit*], which rather than choosing evil for its own sake intentionally subordinates moral considerations to those of self-love."[95] In short, moral evil, which is radical, is a matter of the will taking upon itself a pattern or program to order in a certain way the moral and non-moral incentives it has, and that order involves subordinating the moral to the non-moral incentives (cf. *Religion* 6:36).[96] According to Kant, then, there is no wholly diabolical thing (*Religion* 6:35), no person who pays no attention to moral considerations and who in fact "defiantly rejects the moral law."

Allison, moreover, seeks to defend Kant against the charge that this denial of absolute or demonic evil flies in the face of psychological realities as exemplified by historical figures such as Napoleon and Hitler and fictional characters like Ahab and others testified to by Kierkegaard, Nietzsche, and Dostoevsky. To begin, Allison cites Allen Wood's point that Kant's account is an a priori account aimed at showing why moral evil, even of the most extreme kind, is blameworthy and culpable. If it were not grounded in the choice against the good, against moral considerations, the agent would not be making a choice between good and evil and hence could not be held accountable but would be a kind of non-person or beast, but not an immoral agent.[97] But even if this is correct, it is to say that there is a consistency to Kant's overall account; it does not yet show that the account as a whole is empirically responsible and historically applicable.

Here, as Allison points out, "the Kantian account begins to make contact with Arendt's portrait of Eichmann."[98] Drawing on Sharon Anderson-Gold's work, Allison points out that Kant does recognize "devilish vices," included among which are envy, ingratitude, and joy in the misfortunes of others (*Religion* 6:27). Kant takes these vices to arise from the disposition to prefer self-love and natural inclinations over the moral law, and they do so in the social context, when persons incline towards competition with others in a way that can result in an attitude of hateful superiority towards others, and worse.[99] Allison calls this the "social conditioning of vice."[100] Without pursuing the details of this social view of how extreme moral evil arises, it is sufficient to see that Kant does have an account and that it is intended to deal with various degrees of evil, including very extreme ones. This is the point of Kant's third and most severe degree of evil, which is wickedness or depravity; here we have people who defiantly and regularly choose against the moral law. But this is not a "diabolical being" or what Jaspers calls in a letter to Arendt a person of "satanic greatness."[101] Jaspers is here calling attention to what Kant wants to avoid – and Arendt after him – which is, the romanticizing or aestheticizing of evil personalities.[102]

Furthermore, as Allison emphasizes, Kant recognizes in such evil an element of self-deception (cf. *Religion* 6:38).[103] To evade responsibility, we tell ourselves that our disposition to serve the interests of self-love over moral considerations is bad luck on our part, at most, and not something we can do anything about. Kant calls this "throwing dust in our own eyes" and "unworthiness." What Allison now argues is that a kind of self-deception is also involved in Eichmann's admissions and that this, added to his inability to imagine himself in the position of those he deported, contributes to the ordinariness of his criminality, of his evil. And this – his *normality* – is central to Arendt's account of him. In short, Allison concludes that Kant's account of moral evil may not describe Eichmann with precision, but it bears significant similarities to Arendt's description of him as thoughtless and of his evil as ordinary and banal.[104] Eichmann had motives for what he did, but they were not "monstrous evil intentions" or motives.[105] For neither Kant nor Arendt is this diabolical evil of an absolute kind.[106]

Before I turn to Fackenheim, there is a further ingredient I want to introduce. In his discussion of Arendt, Richard Bernstein distinguishes between Arendt's account of the evil of Nazism and the camps and the motivations of the criminals.[107] In *The Origins of Totalitarianism* Arendt addresses both issues; in *Eichmann in Jerusalem* she focuses on the latter. Kant's account of moral evil is solely concerned with the evil of the will, that is, with evil decision or choice; he is not concerned at all with the outcome – with the result for the victims, so to speak. For Kant, good and evil are not about states of affairs in the world; they are about intention, choice, and character. What, then, does Arendt say about the evil of the death camps?

According to Bernstein, Arendt distinguishes three "thought-trains" that characterize the evil of the camps: "superfluousness, the elimination of predictability and spontaneity, and how omnipotence threatens plurality."[108] Arendt's understanding of evil as radical is a real departure from Kant's, and what she has in mind as the primary product of the camps for human beings is an evil that is much deeper than anything Kant considers. Arendt describes the death camps as laboratories in which human nature was the subject of experimentation. They operated processes that stripped away layers of human dignity, status, and individuality, until beings were left that were wholly replaceable by all similar beings; these were beings whose juridical, moral, and psychological distinctiveness no longer existed. In Arendt's mind, there was a train of thought that linked assembly lines in factories to the pointless labour and ultimate liquidation of the death camps. Nothing distinguished one person from another; all that might have made them distinctive was superfluous – redundant, meaningless, pointless. Each and every person was thus dispensable and replaceable. Moreover, to create such beings, in whom genuine "plurality" had been eradicated, the camps "destroy[ed] [each victim's] spontaneity." With this anti-Kantian vocabulary, Arendt contends that the ideal product of the camps was a non-human human – a being who, though human, could not initiate thought or action, who had no spark of freedom or autonomy left.[109] In short, "Arendt does not disagree with Kant that spontaneity is a necessary condition for the very possibility of a rational human life. Where she differs from him is in thinking that even this apparently *transcendental* condition of a human life *can* be eliminated *empirically*, by totalitarian means. This ... stands at the heart of her understanding of radical evil."[110]

There is a tendency in recent accounts to take Kant and Arendt to be similar at least in the sense that both reject absolute or demonic evil; both want to avoid giving evil, even extreme evil, a kind of satanic greatness, to mythologize it. To be sure, Arendt does think that ordinary or banal evil is a modern phenomenon, but in terms of motives, she and Kant seem similar. The evil of the outcomes is another story: Kant is not concerned at all with the results of evil actions. But otherwise their accounts are similar. Fackenheim has a very different view of things.[111] He is historical, as Arendt is, but he also believes that while we can never fully and ultimately explain why the Nazis did what they did, even if we can understand the motives of some, the evil is unqualified, deep, and distinctively horrific; it leaves thought in shambles and registers in direct and unqualified opposition. Let us see what Kant and Arendt mean to his analysis.

For Fackenheim, the Holocaust manifests absolute evil. Often, to characterize it, he says that it is "evil for evil's sake." This phrase has been widely employed by commentators, but it is not always clear what is meant by it. The phrase is subject to two sorts of ambiguities. The first concerns the word "evil." That word can refer to a type of action or a type of result, that is, it can refer to an act of violence or hatred or malice or sadism, for example, or it can refer to a state or condition of physical harm or pain or subhumanity. "To do evil for evil's sake" could mean "to perform an evil act because it is an evil act," relishing the act itself and its violence or its malevolent intensity or powerfulness.[112] Or it could mean "to produce an evil result because it is an evil result," being fully invested in producing pain or suffering or the state of being subhuman. But many commentators argue that neither of these seem to be what Kant had in mind by the phrase. When commentators use Kant's account as the context for identifying such demonic evil, their point is that while Kant takes us all to have moral and non-moral incentives, a demon would not have moral incentives at all or, if he did, he would freely relish the choice against them, the rejection of them by always subordinating them to some other consideration. How depraved can we be, according to Kant, and still be free and responsible agents? We have to know that the rational and right thing to do is to obey the moral law, but the depraved person chooses not to do so, for other reasons. But what the depraved person cannot do, they argue, is reject utterly the attraction of the moral law or to disobey it for no reason other than it is that law; he or she cannot hate the moral law because it is moral. This is John Silber's view. Silber gives, as an example of the evil of which Kant cannot conceive, the evil of Milton's Satan. He is a being of "solitary, defiant rage, consumed by everything God-like save God-like power."[113] Silber speaks of this evil as a "free rejection of the moral law," but it may be that it requires more. It requires a kind of fascination, unconditional indulgence and captivation, with destruction, annihilation, pain, suffering, and such, yet of a kind that is freely accepted and performed; it is wilful, knowing, and intentional. But while commentators like Silber, Bernstein, and others interpret Kant this way, not all agree. Allen Wood and David Sussman, for example, argue that Kant's account of "devilish vices" includes just these possibilities, of "the knowing choice of an evil end for its own sake."[114]

If we turn to Fackenheim and especially to the account of evil in *To Mend the World*, where does Fackenheim stand on these matters? Does he find some truth in Arendt's account? Does he think that Arendt and

Kant both fail to appreciate absolute evil? How does he understand the evil of the Führer himself and that of his closest associates – Speer, Heydrich, Himmler, and others? Does he take them to be acting freely and responsibly? Or are they agents of a different sort, even if their evil can be understood in terms of the outcomes of their actions and those of the Nazi bureaucracy?

Sections 8 and 9 of Chapter IV of *To Mend the World* are the core of the work. In them, Fackenheim gives a descriptive and analytical account of resistance during the Holocaust, a resistance that becomes the condition of possibility for a response to the evils of Nazism. In the course of his account in these pages, Fackenheim turns to what he calls "the assault in its own extremity – the Nazi 'logic of destruction.'"[115] He asks what it is that Nazism did and why it was done. In short, he presses thought to comprehend the Nazi evil, the horrors. In the end, it will not succeed. Indeed, part of what Fackenheim means by calling the Nazi atrocities "unique" is that detailed and precise reflection on what occurred in the camps and elsewhere in the Nazi world stymies our analytical and explanatory skills; thought arrives at a standstill.[116] But out of such an aporia arises a resisting thought that becomes a resisting action; as Fackenheim puts it, even if explanation and understanding are impossible, response is necessary. In short, to make sense of what resistance to the Nazi evil is and how it arises, Fackenheim must first attempt to understand that evil. It is this attempt we need to consider in order to see what, in the course of that attempt, he gets from Kant and Arendt and what he means by taking the ultimate stage of this inquiry to be absolute or radical evil.

Fackenheim's encounter with the Nazi agency occurs in three stages. He begins his first important discussion with this caveat:

The sadists, perverts, madmen – the kind that may be found anywhere and at any time – were least in significance … More significant were the ordinary men and women who performed their new, extraordinary jobs in much the same manner in which they had once performed – and would soon perform again – their ordinary jobs. However, most significant of all – indeed, setting the tone – were the idealists: these were much like other idealists, except that their ideals were torture and murder. (They did not just "use" torture, but "worshipped" it.) On their part, these idealists were subdivided into those who practiced the ideals and those who provided the theory. And the theory and the practice, in the last analysis, had their "reality" and "law" in the Führer himself.[117]

Fackenheim continues by providing short descriptions of several members of the last two groups, the "practitioners and the philosophers," from Rudolf Hoess and Johann von Leers to Himmler and Hitler himself. In the course of these descriptions, he identifies what he takes to be the central aims of Nazism: "one was the annihilation of the Jewish people," and "the other was the conquest of *Lebensraum* and of lesser races by the master race, all this with an ultimate (if vague) view to world conquest."[118] But in the end, he argues, the first aim was dominant; the latter – the totalitarian desire for expansiveness – dissolved into a kind of nihilism or an impulse to self-destruction. In short, the highest level of Nazi intentionality was aimed at domination and destruction. This is Fackenheim's first conclusion.

In the second stage of his analysis, Fackenheim turns to what he calls, after Jean Améry, the Nazi "logic of destruction." Fackenheim gives a developmental account of how such a logic emerged, and that account's central theme is that it ultimately aimed at "their victims' self-destruction." To confirm that this was the Nazis' primary aim, Fackenheim elaborates on what Terence Des Pres called the strategy of "excremental assault," which "was *designed* to produce in the victim a 'self-disgust' to the point of wanting death or even committing suicide." Fackenheim concludes that "the Nazi logic of destruction was aimed, ultimately, at the victims' *self*-destruction."[119] Moreover, since the primary and paradigmatic victims were Jews, this project was aimed at them. "From the Nazi point of view, the ideal 'solution' of the 'Jewish problem' was wholesale Jewish suicide, but only if preceded and motivated by Jewish self-loathing, or wholesale Jewish self-loathing, but only if it was extreme enough to lead to Jewish suicide."[120] But if the Jews would not commit suicide, the next best thing was to drive them into death. The Nazi perpetrators did this in a number of ways, often by making Jews destroy one another through forms of forced complicity that always ultimately ended in death.

In these first two stages of Fackenheim's analysis of the Nazis' evil agency, his focus is on their idealistic leadership – the theorists and practitioners, as he calls them. These agents were motivated by aims or goals that Fackenheim now tries to articulate: domination, dehumanization, and destruction, aimed at Jews and then at all non-Aryans (i.e., honorary Jews). I think there are implicit Kantian undertones to this account; correctly or not, Fackenheim no doubt took such evil agency to exemplify the demonic that Kant's account does not touch. But all of this is preparation for Fackenheim's third stage, his most developed account of the evil of the perpetrators and the one where he engages with Arendt and her understanding of the functionaries and ordinary citizens who were complicit in or contributed to the atrocities.

To consider whether thought can comprehend the Holocaust, Fackenheim asks whether historical or psychological inquiry can understand why they did it. In other words, he asks, among various questions, whether these disciplines can understand or explain the motivations of the perpetrators and hence tell us why they performed the evil acts they performed. He contends that all such explanations fail. In the course of his dialectical argument, for example, he notes that some historians point to the role that anti-Semitism played in the Nazi state, as if it were a means to the survival of that state, but then he notes that in the end that will not do, since "the 'extermination' of the Jewish people became an end more ultimate than the Third Reich's very survival." Referring to the important German historian Karl Bracher, Fackenheim then notes that at this point even he lapses into "medical metaphors." Bracher refers to the "biologistic insanity of Nazi ideology" – but, Fackenheim says, "'insanity' explains nothing."[121] It certainly fails to clarify in what sense Hitler, his immediate leadership cadre, and then the German people acted with evil intent and did so voluntarily.[122]

Fackenheim argues that thought – explanation and understanding – reaches an impasse when it cannot understand the individual agent and his actions and when it cannot understand the whole, the totality of the Nazi bureaucracy and the German people and state, when it is thrown from one to the other and finally realizes that to cope, it must be a resisting thought and finally a resisting action, an opposition to the evil. But in order to clarify this movement of thought, he turns to individuals – to Hoess, Himmler, and Hitler and then to all the others, the functionaries and then all those who were complicit, ordinary citizens of the Reich. What does he say about these perpetrators and philosophical attempts to understand them?

First, he points out that one cannot resort to a concept of the demonic-in-general in order to try to understand any of the agents or perpetrators. To be responsible, one must rely upon evidence and testimony in order to try to grasp exactly what they did and why in each individual case. With one wave of the hand, then, Fackenheim sets aside Kant, whom he thinks never had such a notion even if he did discuss radical evil, and Schelling, who did recognize an evil that could not be comprehended within the system of absolute idealism.[123] Neither had to deal with an event like the Holocaust and hence with what it accomplished

– the domination of humanity, the instilling of self-loathing, and, finally, destruction and annihilation. His point is that if philosophy wants to cope with the utter particularity of this event, it cannot simply assume at the start that it understands what the most extreme evil is. He calls this escapism, and it would lead the philosopher to find it in one agent or in the whole people, or in one kind of motivation or another. Indeed, it might not have seen these aims as possible at all, and it certainly would not have seen how any whole, any system or state, could be moved by them at every level.

Second, while Fackenheim does admit the relevance of Arendt's notion of the "banality of evil," he argues that that relevance is limited.[124] He remarks at one point that Arendt's argument is "untenable" and at another that the "doctrine of the banality of evil is only half a thought and half the truth."[125] What I think Fackenheim means is that the doctrine of the banality of evil is part of a larger, inadequate argument and that by itself the doctrine is only partly true. Fackenheim's larger argument is this: The philosophical challenge regarding the "inexhaustible, groundless evil of the Holocaust" is how to assign it appropriately to the rulers and the jobholders. What one wants, he implies, is to avoid two extremes: first, to belittle the evil while at the same time holding on to the humanity of the agents, and second, not to make of them monsters or mere puppets. His argument is that this dilemma or enigma "has given rise to the doctrine ... of the banality of evil." According to Arendt, it can be demonstrated that all of the agents – from Eichmann to Himmler and even to Hitler – were nobodies who wanted to be somebodies; they were all banal, common, trite, and ordinary.[126] Hence, the "extreme" evil of the Holocaust world, if it did not lie in the agents, must have been found in their deeds. But we can connect the agents with the deeds only by situating both in a vast, dynamic, totalitarian system that in a sense escalated by itself. Fackenheim takes this way in which the agents and their deeds are tied together by the mediation of the system to be what Arendt means by the evil being "'thought-defying,' in the sense that thought, 'trying to reach some depth,' is 'frustrated because there is nothing.'"[127]

This is an intriguing reading of Arendt. I think that ideally one would have to clarify some of its features and in particular what Fackenheim thinks Arendt means by "thoughtlessness" and "thought-defying."[128] But for our purposes, it is sufficient to see that for Fackenheim the problem is the way in which Arendt argues that the evil of the deeds is connected to the agents by means of the *mediation of the system*. To put this somewhat differently, for Arendt, the actions (i.e., reducing the humanity of the victims, and so forth) were evil, while the agents' motives were not directed at evil outcomes. What connected the two was the totalitarian system. Fackenheim says that this argument is reasonable but "untenable," because there is reason to think that perpetrators like Himmler and Eichmann knew what they were doing and relished it. Hence, as Fackenheim argues,

> just as the "totalitarian" system produced the rulers and operators, so the rulers and operators produced the system. In however varying degrees, those manipulated let themselves be manipulated; those obeying ever-escalating orders chose to obey without limits; those surrendering in a blind idealism made a commitment to blindness. Not only Eichmann but everyone was more than a cog in the wheel.

With this Kantian move, Fackenheim refuses to let the banal agents off the hook.[129] To be sure, the agents were not wholly free, but neither were they wholly compelled.[130] They were both, and this fact, when placed in the context of the horrific atrocities of the Nazi regime and the death camps, "chills the marrow and numbs the mind ... [and] also haunts it." For our purposes, the central point is that Fackenheim does not think that the evil outcomes, the deeds and the system, were unintended by at least some of the agents; even the most ordinary were not simply "conditioned."[131] He maintains that some of them were evil in this radical and intentional way. Moreover, even the banal agents were responsible for what they did and for the whole they contributed to creating.[132]

In sum, Fackenheim's analysis of the evil of the Nazi world – "inexhaustible" and "groundless" – has Kant, Schelling, and Arendt as its chief background figures. Kant took moral evil to be about what we do and what our motives are for doing it. Fackenheim follows Arendt in appreciating the role of the system or the bureaucratic whole in which the actions take place. He also focuses on the single case of Rudolf Hoess in order to allow its distinctiveness to emerge. He takes Kant to reject demonic or absolute evil, what he calls "groundless" evil, evil for no reason other than it is evil. Like Kant, he takes even evil actions to be voluntary, even if the degree of freedom one has varies with the system or determining context in which one chooses and acts.

If we look back on Fackenheim's treatment and interpretation of Kant, we see that during his early period he emphasized the role of Kantian autonomy, its challenge to Judaism, and how Kant's account of morality and religion invites and yet excludes the covenantal, dialectical Jewish view. Basically, the very form of Kantian morality poses problems for Judaism and fails to accommodate it. Yet when Fackenheim turns to the Holocaust, various other dimensions of Kant become important to him. One is the Kantian commitment to the intrinsic value of humanity; another is the Kantian commitment to the timelessness or permanence of that value and the way in which for Kant moral normativity is grounded in rationality. The latter differs from Judaism's belief that norms, religious and moral, acquire their normative force from moments of divine–human encounter, the relationship those encounters establish, and the subsequent interpretation of them, and also from the ongoing historical character of those encounters and their interpretations. Finally, the Holocaust calls upon Jews, as others, to oppose the evil assault, groundless and inexhaustible, on the divine image and the value of humanity, and hence to recover a central Kantian commitment but to do so in the context of a Jewish historical hermeneutic. As we turn, now, to Fackenheim's discussion of Kurt Huber and post-Holocaust philosophy, it is these latter themes that emerge as most pressing.

Kant and Judaism after Auschwitz: Final Stage

In Section 12 of Chapter IV of *To Mend the World*, "On Philosophy after the Holocaust," Fackenheim challenges Leo Strauss's claim that the way to confront the "low" of Nazism and its atrocities is "in the light of the high." Rather, the Nazi evil reveals itself "to the extent to which it reveals itself at all, only ... to a thinking confronting it, shattered by it, and saved from total destruction only if it opposes its horror with a sense of horror of its own."[133] That is, the only way to seek to recover the value of the past, respect for humanity and for the good, is hermeneutically, by situating oneself on this side of the horrors, by taking them seriously for what they threaten to destroy, and by means of an "act of recovery" to bridge the abyss, if only in a fragmentary way, through an act of *tikkun* or repair. But as we turn to philosophy, Fackenheim claims, based on his earlier argument in *To Mend the World*, that "a philosophical *Tikkun* is possible *after* the Holocaust because a philosophical *Tikkun* already took place, however fragmentarily, during the Holocaust itself."[134] As Fackenheim sees it, both the content and the possibility of a responsible philosophical future depend upon locating a single such case and articulating its character. It is here that he turns to the testimony and conduct of Kurt Huber, spokesman for and mentor to the White Rose and a professor of philosophy.[135]

In Huber's testimony and actions Fackenheim finds a kind of philosophical heroism. He contrasts this philosophical heroism with the philosophical weakness of Heidegger, and since Huber, an obscure philosophy professor, represents the Kantian tradition, what Fackenheim sees here is in effect a post-Holocaust re-enactment of the famous Davos confrontation between the new and old representatives of Cohen's Marburg tradition, between Heidegger and Ernst Cassirer.[136] But whereas even someone as sympathetic to Cohen as Franz Rosenzweig could side with Heidegger in that 1929 encounter, Fackenheim now, recognizing that the new philosophy is certainly to be preferred over the old, sides at this one moment with Huber, the representative of Kant, liberal morality, and the Enlightenment. As Fackenheim puts it, the Kantian–Fichtean philosophy is outmoded and outlandish, except for this one moment of truth. That truth, however, concerns Kantianism not as a mode of philosophical thinking but rather as a commitment to moral value, to the ultimate value of human dignity and worth.

Huber's "Final Statement of the Accused" before the court ended with words that Fackenheim, following Huber, took to be from J.G. Fichte:

And act thou shalt as though
The destiny of all things German
Depended on you and your lonely acting
And the responsibility were yours.[137]

As Fackenheim points out, Kant's first formulation of the categorical imperative identified as one's moral duty a prohibition against any action that could not in similar circumstances be universally performed by all persons; Fichte singled out duties for Germans alone.[138] In general, Fackenheim argues, both ideals are surpassed by the new philosophy, which entails an existential and hermeneutically situated understanding of the experience of human beings in the world. But the latter – a development from the thinking of Heidegger and Sartre – takes human existence to be responsive to a single imperative, "Be authentic," which is empty and unrestricted and thus without resources to oppose unconditionally the evils of Nazism. Fackenheim, in a footnote, quotes from Hans Jonas, who in a personal anecdote admitted that after the atrocities, upon his return to Germany, he chose to withhold himself from his old teacher Heidegger and also to visit another professor, one for whom Kant had provided strength and courage during the dark years. Fackenheim wonders if a return to Kant is not possible and necessary; but at the same time, he recalls Eichmann's use of Kant's categorical imperative during his trial and wonders if such a return is to be rejected. Perhaps the formality of the Kantian moral law is no more acceptable a response to Nazism than the abstractness of Heideggerian authenticity. That is, even if we should turn from Heidegger to Kant, the evidence regarding Kant's service in a post-Holocaust world is conflicting. Ultimately, where do we stand with respect to Kant?[139]

Fackenheim summarizes Kant's moral theory – in particular, his conception of the categorical imperative – and then asks how we should understand Eichmann and Huber in terms of that summary.[140] The summary includes three claims: "(1) It is morally necessary to do duty for duty's sake. (2) It is morally necessary so to act that the 'maxim' of one's acting could become, through one's will, universal law. (3) It is morally necessary to treat humanity, whether in one's own person or in that of another, never as a means only, always as an end as well."[141] Fackenheim offers no interpretation of this summary, but let me offer one here. Kant, as Fackenheim understands him, takes morality to involve obligations to act that are expressions of rational agency and that apply to all rational beings in similar circumstances. These obligations ought to be subject to a rational agent's commitment insofar as they are rational and autonomous and not insofar as they have a desired outcome or consequence. In committing oneself to such obligations, moreover, a rational agent never treats either himself or another only as a means or instrument to accomplish certain goals. To some degree, that is, the act determined by the obligation involves respect for the agent's and the other's dignity and worth, that is, their status as rational agents. In short, Kant's conception of morality is marked by the autonomy, rationality, and humanity of moral obligations.

Did Eichmann's appeal to the categorical imperative during his trial show that he understood Kant correctly, in these terms? At least minimally, Fackenheim argues, Eichmann's appeal suited the first two of his conditions, even if Nazism did place extreme restrictions on who counted as rational agents and hence on who would be counted among those to whom the law should universally apply. But the real difference concerned the third condition – that is, the way in which moral law respects the humanity of all. "That human personality is an end in itself is the heart and soul of Kant's categorical imperative."[142] This is tantamount to the ultimacy of respect for human dignity and worth. In fact, Fackenheim's first two features of Kant's moral theory are formal ones, whereas this one – that moral obligations always incorporate respect for human dignity – is substantive. Here is where Eichmann's appeal was an utter distortion, for the Nazi regime was committed to eradicating such respect with regard to both the victims and the perpetrators. Moreover, as Fackenheim argues, it succeeded, and in succeeding, the Nazi empire destroyed the empirical basis on which such Kantian respect was based. With the Holocaust, "the reality that is the object of the belief [in humanity's ultimate worth] was itself systematically annihilated."[143] Hence, even as Eichmann invoked Kant's moral theory, he represented a world in which it had been utterly refuted.

Is it, then, impossible to recover Kant after the death camps? Or is it, in the light of this refutation, a necessity? Here Fackenheim turns to Huber and his final statement. What, as he puts it, was Huber doing in invoking Fichte and Kant? Fackenheim turns to the Idea of Humanity itself, that is, to the respect for human dignity that Nazism was in the process of destroying, and he asks what relation that Idea had with respect to Huber's act. First, Huber, like the students of the White Rose, acted in defiance of the regime and hence in opposition to the forces of evil massed against it. Second, Huber was emboldened by the Idea in his resolve, and yet at the same time, he gave support to the Idea *through* his resolve.

> If Huber, in contemplating the great but fearful deed, was irresolute – and what reflective man would not have been? – then it was the Idea that strengthened his resolve. And if the Idea was weak – abandoned, betrayed, assailed, and mocked on all sides – then it was just this weakness that so intensified his resolve as to make him act (if act he must) without regard to consequences, and – except only for a few comrades – alone. Thus he gave strength to the Idea even as, in turn, he was given strength by it … In acting in behalf of Kant's Idea of Humanity, he mended that Idea – it was broken – for he recreated the matrix or *Boden* of it in actual humanity, even if only in his own person.[144]

Hence, Huber's action and his advocacy of the Idea of Humanity, of Kant, was a recovery of that idea, both an appropriation of it and a revitalization of it, at once. In Fackenheim's terminology, it was a *tikkun* (mending or repair).

But a *tikkun* is a mending of something, and we need to ask of what. In one sense, the mending here is of the Idea of Humanity itself, of the moral ideal or aspiration that all our moral actions represent, a respect for the dignity and worth of persons. A mending of that Idea, Huber's action, then, is also the ground of the possibility of any subsequent mending of that Idea. Such mending, of course, must admit that the Idea of Humanity can be destroyed, but it also affirms that such destruction must be opposed and the Idea revived. In a sense, of course, this is no longer Platonism and hence no longer Kantianism; it is a historically sensitive acknowledgment of the possibilities of real evil and of the need for real goodness. Nonetheless, this *tikkun* is also a mending of Kant's philosophy, for it involves the necessity of recovering a Kantian ideal and hence a commitment to keeping alive a respect for human dignity, even at the most threatening of times. But this feature of Platonism and Kantianism, its commitment to the good as an ideal, is essential to philosophy, at least as Fackenheim sees it. For what he now argues is that "this *Tikkun* [through Huber's action], then and there, created the possibility and necessity of a post-Holocaust philosophy, here and now."[145] We have returned here to the theme of chapter 3, Fackenheim's concept of post-Holocaust philosophy. For Fackenheim it involves returning to the tradition of philosophy but with a keen awareness of the current historical context and all that separates it from that tradition. In short, whatever a genuine post-Holocaust philosophy will be, it will involve "a new reading of the old great texts of Western philosophy," Kant's included, which will provide "new, unexpected evidence confirming the belief in their inexhaustibility."[146]

Here too, as before, we see that what Fackenheim finds enduring about the Kantian legacy is its attention to the ultimacy of respect for human worth and dignity. He takes this commitment to be, after the Holocaust, vulnerable but still inspiring and hence justified. It is indeed that feature of Kant's moral philosophy that deserves our attention today, just as it did his commitment then. In his own way, therefore, Fackenheim seeks to take seriously the hermeneutical and historical character of human existence, a central feature of the Heideggerian teaching, but at the same time to eulogize the moral legacy of the Kantian tradition, its respect for human dignity and worth. In short, a genuine post-Holocaust philosophy ought to seek to repair, to the degree possible, the ultimacy of human worth, in a world where that ideal has been damaged and even destroyed, but to do so in the context of a historically shaped human existence that needs and demands such a repair. If this is Platonism, it is a highly relativized, historicized Platonism indeed.

For Fackenheim, in these later years, then, what endures of Kant's moral faith is its moral tenacity, its commitment to human dignity, and its ultimacy, and no longer, as it once had been, his allegiance to faith and the role of God in the context of the priority of autonomous self-hood. Morality and history have replaced faith and reason as the conceptual poles of Fackenheim's world, and his engagements with Kant show how this is so.

5

The Hegelian Dimension
in Fackenheim's Thought

Late in life, in two documents, Fackenheim recalled his earliest encounters with Hegel's philosophy. The first came on a Saturday night in 1937 or 1938, at the home of Arnold Metzger, a former assistant of Edmund Husserl who was teaching at the *Hochschule* and who had invited a group of promising students to study together.[1] There he was introduced to the Preface of Hegel's *Phenomenology*, and while he understood little of what was said, he came away, he says, "thinking that if I ever am to understand philosophy, I must understand the *Phaenomenologie* for, as Metzger put it, in that work *nothing* mattered, *ultimately*, except the 'presence' or 'absence' of Hegel's 'Absolute.'"[2]

I recall Fackenheim telling me that in Aberdeen, where he had fled from Berlin, during the year he spent studying philosophy before he was sent to the Isle of Man and then sailed to Canada, he spent time on his own studying Hegel. But in the lecture just cited, he says that his second encounter with Hegel came later, in 1952 or so, when he approached F.H. Anderson, Chair of the Philosophy Department at the University of Toronto, asking that he be allowed to teach a graduate course on Fichte, Schelling, and Hegel.[3] From that year until 1967, when he published *The Religious Dimension in Hegel's Thought*, Fackenheim pored over the *Phenomenology* and the rest of the Hegelian system, which would become the matrix or the foundation for all of his subsequent thinking, both philosophical and Jewish.

In this chapter I consider in a brief way the role that Hegel played for Fackenheim and what Hegel meant to him. I will look first at his Hegel book and his articles on Hegel from that period.[4] I will then examine the chapter "Moses and the Hegelians" in *Encounters between Judaism and Modern Philosophy*, as well as two essays from *The Jewish Return into*

History.[5] Here the encounter between Hegel and Judaism takes centre stage. Finally, we shall look at "The Shibboleth of Revelation," Chapter III of *To Mend the World*, which is Fackenheim's last important engagement with Hegel and his most extended effort to expose Hegel's thought to the Holocaust.

Fackenheim on Hegel: Religion and German Idealism

There are various indications in Fackenheim's early writings, from the late 1940s through the 1960s, that Hegel was gradually influencing the way he did philosophy and the way he understood religion. While his understanding of the role of contradictions and paradoxes in human existence and historical agency could have come to him from his reading of Kierkegaard, it is very likely that beginning in his year at Aberdeen and certainly once he started to teach Hegel in the early 1950s, the centrality for him of polarities and their dialectical relationships was the result of his reading Hegel. Also, his understanding of God as the Absolute – that is, the unconditional Ground of all being, or the Infinite – is most likely something he inherited from German Idealism – from Fichte, Schelling, and Hegel. But the best evidence we have that Hegel became his central philosophical interlocutor is surely the decade-long examination of Hegel that led to the publication of *The Religious Dimension in Hegel's Thought* in 1967.

The central task of that book is to show how for Hegel "the actual existence of religious life ... [is] an indispensable condition ... of his philosophy as a whole."[6] He largely ignores art, history, politics, and much else to focus on this one theme: the relation between Hegel's system and religious life. In short, the book is about philosophical thought and religious life, and hence, in its own way, it is for Fackenheim a centrally important attempt to understand how history and thought are related to each other in modern philosophy. As we shall see, Hegel's accomplishment requires that he view Christianity in a certain way and also results in him failing to appreciate the continued vitality and historical significance of Judaism as an ongoing religious reality. But more about that later.

In Chapter One of *The Religious Dimension*, Fackenheim summarizes how Hegel accomplishes this task. He begins by proposing that "not only Hegel's but all philosophy is a rise of thought to absoluteness or divinity."[7] That is, philosophical thought seeks an unconditional ground; it seeks to explain everything, including the most fundamental things, in an ultimate and unqualified way; it seeks complete and per-fect understanding.[8] In daily life and even in the special sciences, we seek explanations, but philosophy strives for comprehensiveness and for ultimacy when it comes to such explanations. In religious terms, such an ultimate and absolute ground is what we mean by divinity. Hence, in Plato the Forms are divine, and in Aristotle the unmoved movers are divine. At the same time, this "rise to absoluteness" can be accomplished either with or without a kind of receptivity or openness to the concrete and contingent world. Once again, in religious terms, philosophy can be Gnostic or not; it can respond positively or nega-tively to the everyday world. In Plato's case, for example, the complete-ness and comprehensiveness of the domain of Forms is achieved only at the cost of seeing the world of change and of inadequacy as a world of mere images or imitations. Only if the everyday world of becoming, the domain of sense perception and of change and instability, is denigrated can Plato promote the Forms to the pre-eminent status of pure being.

As Fackenheim points out, however, the relationship between philo-sophical thought and the concrete world is itself a historical one. In antiquity, philosophy could achieve the status of divinity, of a "view from nowhere," only because the world was demeaned and considered inadequate or deficient. In the Middle Ages, once Christianity had come on the scene and the divine was seen to have revealed itself in the world in the person of Jesus as the divine presence in the world, phi-losophy could attain absoluteness but only with the sacrifice of the hu-man. That is, the ancient heroic attitude towards subjectivity had to become the submissiveness of the servant of God. For philosophy to attain absoluteness but in a way that respected and did not offend against human subjectivity, a modern world was needed in which the subject became autonomous and the divine entered the world not through the hierarchy of the Church but directly into the heart of every believer. As Fackenheim puts it, in the modern Protestant world, "the realities manifest in modern Protestant faith and modern secular life are not two realities; they are two aspects of *one* Reality which are al-ready implicitly united. And the philosophy which *recognizes* the one Reality in these two aspects makes the implicit explicit."[9] It rises to di-vinity and yet respects and stays with the world, both at once. This is the accomplishment of the Hegelian system: divine power is what it is, and human freedom confronts it; the two are two but also one.

At the centre of this account, moreover, is the fact that the relation-ship between the divine and the world, between thought as absolute and the world as contingent, is itself historical. That relationship under-goes changes, and events occur in the world that express their unity, while others occur that forbid it. As Fackenheim puts it, "no wisdom is required today for the insight that the Hegelian synthesis, if ever a gen-uine possibility, has broken down beyond all possible recovery."[10] Spe-cifically, he refers to colonialism, Hiroshima and Nagasaki, and most significant of all, Auschwitz, "a depravity unequaled in all history." In our day, no comprehensive philosophical understanding, no complete system, is possible. Moreover, Fackenheim claims that even though he is "a Jew committed to Judaism," the Hegelian synthesis is beyond ev-eryone's belief – "Christian, post-Christian, or non-Christian." And not only is the Hegelian synthesis beyond any of us; it would be beyond Hegel himself: "it is entirely safe to say that Hegel, were he alive today, would not be a Hegelian."[11]

These are the broad strokes with which Fackenheim paints his picture of Hegel, modernity, and history. *The Religious Dimension* fills in the pic-ture, and while we need not (and cannot) survey all of its details, there are some points worth considering in order to appreciate what Hegel meant to Fackenheim. One point, which he reiterates again and again, is that the Hegelian system is about standpoints, in particular the finite standpoints within the world and the infinite standpoint of a philoso-phy that comprehends all the partial ones and rises to comprehensive-ness and completeness.[12] The notion of a standpoint – or perspective or point of view – is important in modern philosophy and especially in twentieth-century philosophy.[13] Hegel appropriated it from Kant, who had distinguished between the philosopher's (also the scientist's) de-tached point of view, the standpoint of the observer, and the practical agent's engaged point of view, that of a participant. For Hegel, there is only one unconditionally detached point of view, that of Science or ab-solute knowledge or philosophy. All other points of view are finite – that is, limited by perspective, partiality, and such. And this applies to insti-tutions as well as to individual agents – and also to programs, policies, and indeed everything in the world and in history. Given this distinc-tion, Fackenheim can describe the Hegelian system as involving a two-stage process of describing a worldly phenomenon – say, religious life – in its own terms and from its own finite points of view, then returning to it in order to grasp it from the infinite standpoint of philosophical knowledge.[14] Moreover, as he points out, with regard to religion Hegel engages only in the second task, that of presenting an account of religion as philosophically comprehended. What Fackenheim will fill in is the first task, the description of religion – in particular, Christianity – on its own terms, as yet uncomprehended philosophically.

This talk of standpoints, of course, is but another way of stating the crucial relationship in Hegel's thought between philosophical thinking, on the one hand, and history and worldly experience (or life), on the other. Hegel cannot do without either. For him, there is no form without content, no dialectical relationship of ideas without a dialectical relationship of events and realities. But in contrast to Berkeley or Schelling, he sees the two as not ultimately eliding; if there is an identity, it is an identity with difference. Fackenheim is fond of quoting Hegel's early statement that "life is the union of union and nonunion." Here, as one commentator puts it, is the future system in a nutshell.[15] This relationship between philosophical thought and historical existence is extremely important to Fackenheim and continues to be so, even when the comprehensiveness and generality of philosophy (including Hegelian philosophy) are exposed to the atrocities of Auschwitz and the evils of Nazism.

As I have indicated, the central theme of *The Religious Dimension* is the relationship between religion and philosophy. That theme first arises in Fackenheim's discussion of the *Phenomenology*. After examining selfhood, individual and social, Hegel turns to religion.[16] That is, once the self has emerged as a process of self-constitution, it must turn to "confront a divine *presence*, in and for human subjects, and hence *permeating* their individual and social worlds." He turns, that is, to "the standpoint of religious faith [which] bears witness to a human relation to nothing less than the Divine."[17] But insofar as the self encounters the Divine, it might seem that its selfhood is not active and self-constituting but rather passive and constituted by this Divine Other. Religion comes on the scene, that is, as a challenge to the definition of selfhood thus far articulated.[18] This is how Fackenheim explains the point of Hegel's introducing religion as a stage in the self-revelation of Spirit.[19] And to clarify how Hegel accomplishes this encounter between self-active subjectivity and Divine presence, he notes that Hegel must show how the subjective is both receptive and active and how this occurs in actual, concrete religious life and is then comprehended by philosophical thought.

Human subjectivity or selfhood stands between nature and Divinity. It is beyond the one: human beings are more than animals. But before the other it is wholly overwhelmed. Still, even in this being overwhelmed, the subject recognizes itself: "the self recognizes itself as dissolving in the very moment of being dissolved, and it recognizes the divine Infinity which does the dissolving." That is, the self confronts the Divine and is overwhelmed by it, but its recognition of its being overwhelmed is a "free act of self-surrender." Hence, this encounter involves a "gaining-of-self event as it is a loss of it."[20] As we have seen in his treatment of revelation in Judaism, Fackenheim takes this moment of self-acknowledgment to be fundamental to all divine–human encounters. But here Hegel proposes it first as an abstract or structural articulation, which he then goes on – in only vague terms – to exemplify in the historical development of religions from "religions of light" to "religions of art" and finally to Christianity. Since this historical account is carried out in much greater detail and with greater richness in Hegel's *Lectures on the Philosophy of Religion*, we shall say something about it later. The crucial point is that for Hegel, what distinguishes Christianity is that it alone – on his view – accomplishes the synthesis of human self-activity with a fully genuine receptivity and surrender to the Divine. It accomplishes this by representing in ritual and practice that "finite spirit ... is a phase of the self-realization of divine Spirit."[21]

With this step, as Fackenheim argues, something momentous has occurred. Hegel has as his ideal the realization of the system of philosophy in history, but he is committed to the thought that such a realization can only occur if the times are ripe for it. That is, comprehensive philosophical knowledge is possible only if what it comprehends is already real in history. For this to occur, history must be more than human; it must be divine–human, and this means that "Hegelian thought presupposes the prior existence of religious (more precisely, Christian) life." Moreover, that thought, the comprehensive system, must "accept the faith of that life as – in some sense – true."[22] But Fackenheim points out that this is not enough: thought must not take religion to be true from a finite point of view. In order to be the comprehensive philosophical system, such thought must do so from an *infinite* point of view. That is, somehow the religious self must become the philosophical self, and what lies between the two Fackenheim calls a "veritable gulf."

Hegel finds the bridge in what Fackenheim calls a "post-Kantian moral life ... in which ideal universality and contingent particularity are inextricably intertwined."[23] This is realized, as Fackenheim reads Hegel, in a "community of conscientious persons, united through mutual recognition."[24] But, as he argues, this moral community is also a religious one and indeed must be, for in recognizing the moral ideal, it looks to a divinity within. That is, "in modern moral self-activity ... Spirit is *certain* of itself."[25] But this reconciliation of moral reason and religious truth in a philosophical system can occur only if it already exists in reality, that is, only if it already is "actual in modern life." And once it is realized in actual life, the last step is its realization in Spirit, as the self-activity of Spirit. Fackenheim refers to this final step as the ultimate divine self-activity: "the human self which has risen to this selfhood has risen to the absolute standpoint. And what it is and does is in the final philosophical thinking – Hegelian 'science.'"[26] Ultimately, that is, finite spirit becomes infinite Spirit but in such a way that the two struggle with each other, for "in producing a simple union, the Notion [cannot] ignore or deny the contingent realities of human existence which are shot through with finitude, conflict, and nonunion."[27]

In Chapter Four, Fackenheim explores the central problem of the Hegelian system and the notion of the "Hegelian middle." He would admit later that it was this problem and this notion that caused him the greatest difficulty, and later in the book and in his career, when he refers to a crisis in the Hegelian system, he uses this notion, of the Hegelian middle, to characterize that crisis. What is the basic problem of the Hegelian middle? And what is its solution? What is the "central problem … of the Hegelian system"? Fackenheim formulates it in terms of a dilemma or in terms of polarities that must be united even though they pull apart. Take Reason and the actual world: if Reason is all-encompassing, how can it recognize a world outside itself? But if the "contingent and frag-mented" world is to be taken seriously, how can it be essentially ratio-nal? Or, can an "absolute and therefore all-comprehensive philosophic thought" be saved only if we give up "the contingent world of human experience"? Or can we save the latter only at the price of "reducing philosophic thought itself to finiteness"? That is, is the choice between "a pluralistic openness as hospitable to the varieties of contingent expe-rience as any empiricism" and a "monistic completeness more radical in its claims to comprehensiveness than any other speculative rational-ism"?[28] Or, alternatively, is it between "the contingency which perme-ates human life" and the "necessity achieved in philosophic thought"? Fackenheim gives all of these formulations, and he suggests there are more. In all cases, the problem is that while it appears that each polarity forces a choice and hence poses a dilemma, the Hegelian system refuses the choice and the dilemma and instead, as he puts it, "dwells in the middle." That is, Hegel's system attempts to mediate all the tensions and articulate a coherent whole. The central question of Fackenheim's Chapter Four is how it can do so.

Fackenheim rejects both a Platonist reading of Hegel and a material-ist reading.[29] The three components of the Hegelian system – logical Idea, Nature, and Spirit – must be reconciled. One cannot choose the Idea [metaphysics] and assimilate the worlds of nature and spirit to it or denigrate them; nor can one choose the worlds of nature and spirit and treat the Idea as epiphenomenon. Rather, one must carry out three arguments, in such a way that each of the three is shown to mediate between the other two, and as a consequence of which all three are seen to form a whole, a unity. It is in this sense that Hegel "dwells in the middle" and reconciles the dilemmas that face him.[30]

According to Fackenheim, the Hegelian middle "combines a pluralis-tic openness as hospitable to the varieties of contingent experience as any empiricism with a monistic comprehensiveness more radical in its claims than any other speculative rationalism."[31] But to accomplish this task, it relies upon a "crucial assumption": that "*Nature, and hence the whole contingent but actual world, is* doubly *overreached, by Spirit and Idea.* Spirit overreaches the actual world by raising Nature above naturalness and Spirit above finiteness. The Idea overreaches it by self-externalization in Nature and return-to-self through finite spirit." The middle is philo-sophic thought, which is the "*identity of Idea and Spirit*," and it cannot occur without such double overreaching (or sublation, *Aufhebung*). Or, to put it otherwise, the Idea externalizes itself in Nature and returns to itself through it and through finite spirit, and Spirit becomes infinite Thought only after moving beyond the finite real in Nature and finite spirit. And, as he says, the result is not a once-and-for-all outcome. It is the "process – its perpetual reenactment," and *that* takes place in the human life of the thinker.[32]

Fackenheim contends that demonstrating this assumption is the "de-cisive" task facing the Hegelian system.[33] But there is no external dem-onstration of it, no standard that it must meet that is outside it. Rather, if there is a demonstration, it must come from within, and it must take the form of each overreaching confirming the other: the one the over-reaching of the actual world by Spirit, and the other the overreaching of the actual world by the Idea.[34] That is, the demonstration comes when in fact absolute science arises and only when absolute Spirit is realized in the world. As Fackenheim puts it, the two overreachings grow into an identity in philosophical thought only once they are a "reality al-ready *present in life* before philosophy comes upon the scene to *convert it into thought*." Or, in other words, only when "philosophy shows itself to be a conversion which life itself requires."[35] Fackenheim explicates or illuminates this fact by pointing to how Christian modernity overreaches or sublates the pagan ancient world – that is, he shows how this demonstration has a religious and historical character. In pagan antiquity, philosophy could acknowledge the centrality of the Idea, of the Infinite and the Necessary, provided that it also denigrated the concrete world, the domain of the finite and the limited. With Christianity, however, the Infinite became present in the finite, and, as he puts it, "the modern world ... has long been Christian."[36] Hence, we have a historical epoch characterized by an overcoming of the pagan separation between nature and spirit but one that does so while at the same time living with their "discord," the tension between them. And this epoch is the "decisive condition without which modern philosophy could not break through the limits of ancient philosophy, in order to overreach in thought the contingencies of the actual world already overreached in life."[37]

What Fackenheim has shown, then, is that "the problem of the Hegelian middle thus turns into the problem of the relation between religious life and philosophic thought." Ultimately, that is, the final mediation of the tension between the finite and the infinite in the Hegelian system – a mediation carried out by various overreachings – can occur only insofar as it has already been actual in life as modern Christian society. Or, in other words, the Hegelian system that is the final realization of philosophic thought is in effect the true content of Christianity in its true form. This conclusion conflates two outcomes: first, that philosophical thinking of the most comprehensive and systematic kind occurs as the ultimate realization of a historical form of life only once that form of life has become actual; and second, that Christianity is that form of life, so that true philosophy is nothing other than Christianity in perfect form.[38] Fackenheim quotes Hegel: "Religion can exist without philosophy. But philosophy cannot exist without religion. For it encompasses religion."[39]

Fackenheim proceeds to explore in two steps how this occurs. First, he sets out to examine religion on its own terms, that is, as "religious self-understanding." Second, he examines "what occurs when religious life is transfigured by philosophic thought."[40] The first task – a challenging one, since Hegel himself never takes it on – is to offer a representational account of religion on its own terms, prior to its being refashioned from a philosophical point of view. This is what Fackenheim does in Chapter Five of *The Religious Dimension*.

The first thing he does is articulate provisionally what Hegel takes "religion" to mean.[41] After contrasting religion with magic and with later phenomena such as deism, Fackenheim concludes that for Hegel, "genuine religion is a relation of the human to a Divinity *other* than human and *higher* than human, and it is a relation in which *man's very being is involved.*" Human being is involved through feeling at least; that is, the God one worships must be my God and not simply some God-concept. But this feeling must involve an attitude that has some content, and that content – the characteristics of the divine in virtue of which or towards which one has this feeling – is articulated in "religious representation" (*Vorstellung*). This nexus between the religious believer and God is a mutual interdependence: feeling and representation are "bound up" with each other. God is not the object of a subjective state in any empirical sense – for example, the object of observation and belief. Rather, the finite subject is intimately engaged with the Divine in a representational-emotional way, so to speak.

And the content of the representation unites in what Fackenheim calls the religious symbol, which is itself finite and yet which points beyond to the Infinite, "relating them and keeping them apart." Furthermore, this relationship must be made concrete and "serious" in a way that preserves its representational content and yet infuses religious life:

> The relation *between* the Divine and the human must preserve its tension even while it does its relating, and it can do so only by *acting it out*, in a labor which so thoroughly permeates the whole length and breadth of existence as to cause it, not merely to *feel* transformed but actually to *be* transformed. This labor is *religious cult.*[42]

Cult is what we might call "religious practice" or the "rituals of religious life." Without it, religious representation is merely an idea or a notion; it is not yet realized or concretized. "The life of cult acts out the clash and apartness of the Divine and the human in the divine-human relationship in all its undiminished reality, and it *transfigures* that relation so as *actually* to unite them."[43] The cult and the feeling must occur together; one without the other is deficient, the former a bare formality or ritual and the latter a mere subjective fancy.

The totality of religious existence thus requires both, and this totality is what Fackenheim calls "faith." "*Every genuine religion, then, is a totality of existence in which the inwardness of pure feeling is united with outward action and overt occurrence, through a representational meaning which permeates both.*" It is not surprising that we have here an understanding of faith that refers to the totality of human existence and not either to a mere feeling or belief or to the formal rigour of religious practice and law.[44] This is the kind of account of religion that religious life would have of itself – although brought to a level of reflective self-understanding; it is religion from its own point of view, from the *engaged* point of view. "Faith is the total inward-outward life of finite man in his relation to the divine Infinity."[45]

Two features of this account are worth a moment of consideration. One is Fackenheim's clarification of Hegel's notion of religious *Vorstellung* (representation), which provides the meaningful content of religious attitudes and practices. The second is what Fackenheim has to say about the precise status of this account of religion and faith and especially about the standpoint from which it is framed.

Fackenheim formulates five claims that Hegel makes about representation:

1 "Religious *Vorstellung* refers to the Infinite, in contrast with the merely finite 'picture' (*Bild*)."
2 "Religious *Vorstellung* refers to the Infinite in a finite way … above all by taking the Infinite referred to as external to the human person who does the referring."
3 "… the represented is accepted by the representing person, at least to begin with, as *given*."
4 "Even while it remains *Vorstellung*, however, *Vorstellung* is capable of expressing its own fundamental inadequacy, i.e., the inadequacy of finitely referring to the Infinite; and when it assumes such an expression, it becomes dialectical."
5 "Even though to begin with the represented is accepted as given, both the represented and the representation itself are in every genuine religion part of a spiritual God-man relation in which mere external givenness is transcended."[46]

What Fackenheim takes Hegel to mean, I think, is that religious experience and practice, insofar as they involve the participant's involvement, have a meaning for that participant, and that the meaning is present in the way an Infinite is given representationally, which in religious representation is God, characterized in some way or other. Hence, as we shall see in our discussion of midrash in Judaism, Fackenheim takes midrash to function in rabbinic Judaism as the symbolic, literary vehicle for representing dialectically the features of the divine–human relationship that are referred to in Jewish experience and practice. In short, this Hegelian account of religious representation provides Fackenheim with the framework for his reflective account of what midrash is and what it provides theologically for classic Judaism.[47]

Second, Fackenheim considers the standpoint from which the above account is given. That standpoint is not the Hegelian system or absolute knowledge – that is, comprehensive philosophic thought – nor is it the perspective of a "detached observer," for the latter cannot grasp the divine–human relation in all its actuality. At one point, he admits that the account is provisional and its status problematic.[48] Hegel's answer to this problem is an account of the history of religious life that includes all particular religions and yet culminates in the situation of a religion that is particular but also comprehensive; this is modern Christian society. In one sense, this history will not redeem his account of religion as representational, but in another sense, it will. It will not since that account is still a general one; but it will insofar as its generality will be shown to apply in particular to Christianity and in virtue of that to all the religions that preceded it and that it overreaches or sublates. For our purposes, however, we can skip over Fackenheim's careful and detailed history and account of Christianity. Its gist is that human existence involves recognizing the world as created and that one has the capacity for good and for evil, and hence the need for redemption.

Ultimately, Christianity best shows what that redemption is and how one receives it. "This redemption is the all-comprehensive reconciliation of the Divine in the extremity of its transcendent infinity with the human in the total concreteness of his worldly and human finitude."[49] That is, the redemptive event – in Christianity, the incarnation and then the death of Christ – must retain the character of the extremes and yet reconcile them into a unity; or, as Fackenheim puts it, "the Divine must *enter into* the human world, and yet it must preserve both the humanity of the human and its own divinity."[50] This paradox is recognized as one and then endured through divine action, and that action is the resurrection, where human death is recognized for what it is and is then overcome. "In this death of death, man is at once recognized in his humanity and redeemed from his self-alienation from God."[51] Moreover, this event is not only in the past; it is continually re-enacted in the present through cult and practice; it is in this way a remembered reality and not a past relic.[52]

How does philosophy attain absoluteness and comprehensiveness? How does faith become philosophy? How does the representational content of Christianity receive its true form in speculative thought? These are the questions that Fackenheim addresses in Chapter Six of *The Religious Dimension*. In his words, Hegel must show how philosophy does not demythologize religious content but rather *trans*mythologize it.[53] He summarizes the accomplishment this way:

> The final philosophy presupposes the final religion: unless the absolute content were present in Christian life, philosophical thought could not, in its own right, hope to attain it. But in attaining that content it transfigures its form: for whereas the Christian (and indeed every) religion is a divine-human relation the final (and indeed every) philosophy is a oneness of thought with Divinity. The final philosophy produces peace with the final religion, in that it rises in thought to the divine side of that divine-human relation at whose human side the final religion remains; and having so risen, by reenacting that relation in thought.[54]

In short, the final philosophy – Hegel's system – takes up religious content from a philosophical or divine point of view. It grasps the content of Christian representation from the divine side of the religious (divine–human) relation but does not, in so doing, dissipate or destroy the human side – that is, the representational way in which it occurs in Christian life.[55] And the two excesses that Hegel seeks to avoid are a "speculative pantheism," on the one hand, and an "atheistic humanism," on the other – that is, philosophical views that assimilate the finite to the Infinite or vice versa.[56]

Fackenheim sketches the movement of philosophical thought as it reflects upon Greek religion to Judaism and then to Christianity and describes its culmination with a reflective articulation of the role of love in Christianity and its double activity between the human and the divine. His conclusion is that the true philosophy achieves this:

> A thought which *recognizes* the divine Love of Christian faith forever *begins as* faith, humanly receptive of the divine gift; forever *rises above* such human receptivity, by reenacting the divine gift to the human other as a divine self-othering; and forever *reinstates* human faith as a phase in its own rise above humanity. Only a thought of this kind can be divine and yet a possibility for thinkers who are, and remain, human.[57]

Here we have a statement of how faith becomes philosophy, of how the thought of finite humanity can rise to the level of the divine and yet remain human. As Fackenheim puts it, it is Hegel's intention that such philosophical thought not dissipate faith or turn it into a mere appearance, for only then can the philosophy be saved as well. Or, in other words, philosophy must overreach or sublate all finite points of view and not destroy them; this is a central feature of the Hegelian system.[58] If faith were destroyed, philosophy would be impossible.

The actuality of faith is a form of ethical life (*Sittlichkeit*) that combines Protestant freedom with "free" modern, secular, political society. This is the "ultimate revelation of Reason in modern life."[59] Fackenheim clarifies this relationship as the mature Hegel sees it: philosophy is not a motor of change or a revolutionary program; rather, it is a reflective comprehension of what is already actual in life.

> But Hegel's mature thought has turned sharply from this early conception of a new religion to be produced by philosophy. The "grey in grey" of philosophy cannot rejuvenate but only comprehend a "shape of life." It reenacts the old religion in thought; it can produce no new religion to replace the old. It is not the cock which heralds a new morning but rather – in one of Hegel's most celebrated passages – the "owl of Minerva [which] rises to flight with the coming of the dusk."[60]

This famous passage from Hegel's *Philosophy of Right* articulates a theme that is central to Fackenheim's reading of Hegel. But the thesis is not true of all cultures or epochs; it does not promise philosophical comprehension of any and all ways of life. Only a particular culture and age can be ripe for philosophical articulation; only one can be unified and perfectly coherent. "His own philosophy is in principle the final philosophy, comprehensive of the civilization which – by virtue of its religious and secular aspects, both endowed with a dimension of infinity – is itself in principle complete."[61] That civilization is both unified and diverse, and it is in need of only that philosophical comprehension to bring it to actual completion. And *that* is what, Hegel thought, his own system provided.

The result, as Fackenheim indicates, is a confidence that Hegel has about the modern world, a faith in modern Protestant Christianity and in modern society. But this means not only that he has confidence in both separately; he also has faith in both together, in an "actual – and in principle, final – secular-Protestant synthesis in modern life."[62] And even though this has a conservative sound to it, Fackenheim argues that in fact it is a dynamic synthesis and one that "keeps what it has permanently united, at the same time, in permanent creative tension."[63] The upshot, then, is a world that is complete in principle but that is open to continual reform to meet new exigencies.

But this internal connection in Hegel between philosophy and history, between thought and the actuality of life, suggests a problem, and it is one that Fackenheim perhaps had his eye on all along.[64] "What if Hegel's appraisal of his own age, and hence of all history, were radically mistaken? Or what if epoch-making events were to occur which destroyed all grounds of the Hegelian estimate, either of modern secular freedom, or of modern Protestant faith, or of the inner bond between them?"[65] The answer is obvious to Fackenheim: this would fragment the Hegelian middle and leave in shambles the system and its attempt to unite faith and philosophy. Moreover, this situation is no longer a mere possibility: "such are the crises which have befallen the Christian West in the last half century that it may safely be said that, were he alive today, so realistic a philosopher as Hegel would not be a Hegelian."[66] Fackenheim has worked hard not to give Hegel's system a one-sided reading, and the result is comprehensive, balanced, dialectically subtle, and deep. But as a consequence of that effort, he has exposed a very serious vulnerability indeed – what he refers to as "a realistic self-exposure to the contingencies of the actual world."[67] What if an event occurred that could not be encompassed by a rational synthesis of the free secular world and Protestant faith? The answer: its philosophical comprehension would be prevented; wholeness or unity would be blocked. In other words, as Hegel would have addressed it, the problem is whether in fact the "modern bourgeois Protestant world" is "indestructible."[68]

Since "the modern bourgeois Protestant world" is a synthesis of the "faith of a community which bears witness to the indwelling Kingdom of God" and "free modern rationality" in various manifestations – for example, in science, morality, and politics – the question is whether features of our world are obstacles to one or the other or prevent their mutual interrelation.[69] Fackenheim refers to the world wars that have "destroyed Europe's spiritual hegemony," the emergence of "philosophical, sociological, and psychological skepticism," and the way in which advances in "science and scientific technology" have inspired "self-confidence" that is, however, "since Auschwitz and Hiroshima … mixed with terror."[70] The importance of Hegel in this situation cannot be overestimated, for without him there is an ever-present temptation to avoid the secular–religious predicament in favour of either some form of scientism or narrow empiricism, on the one hand, or a reactionary neo-orthodoxy, on the other. One simply refuses to take religion seriously, while the other minimizes any responsible attention to human freedom.[71] Since Hegel's was the last great attempt to hold both the religious and the secular in place, it is important not to avoid him in order to cope with contemporary realities. Fackenheim's conclusion, for philosophic thought, is that a genuine encounter with Hegel ought to bring us today to a responsible realism about the Hegelian middle and the impossibility of occupying it. Yet the extremes are to be avoided. Hence, philosophic thought today ought to

> grope for what may be called a fragmented middle. This is not to suggest a revivial of Hegelian philosophy. But it is to suggest that philosophic thought, however rooted in existential commitments, craves a comprehensiveness which transcends them. To be sure, this craving can no longer expect, or even seek, more than fragmentary satisfaction. Yet it is not doomed to total frustration, and it is unvanquishable.[72]

The comprehensiveness of which Fackenheim speaks here is a synthesis of faith and philosophy, of the religious and the secular. It refers to the finite and the infinite and their interrelation. The desire to unite them is insatiable, Fackenheim says.[73] Hegel has taught us this truth. But reality – our world – makes it impossible to accomplish that unity. The fragmented middle that we might hope to occupy is a place from which the poles remain, and although they are interrelated in some ways, they also remain in tension and forbid complete coordination. If we think ahead, we can imagine why Fackenheim takes Judaism and not Christianity to best represent such a position, and why the self-exposure to the Nazi horrors and the evil of the death camps counts as an epoch-making event that forces upon us the limitations of fragmentary recovery and response.

Fackenheim already saw the problem in 1970. In "Hegel on the Actuality of the Rational and the Rationality of the Actual," he concludes by asking: "Can the historical conditions producing the actuality of the Rational (and hence the rationality of the Actual) pass away?" In that essay, he had argued that the conditions are religious and secular. The Hegelian claim is that philosophy unites "Christian religious and modern secular optimism," but can this optimism cope with "eruptions of demonic evil in the world which produce genocidal industries with by-products including human skin made into lamp-shades, human hair used for pillows, human bones turned into fertilizer"?[74] That is, "any inquiry into [the truth of Hegel's philosophy] must confront its claims with the gas chambers of Auschwitz."[75] For these events are not "world-historically insignificant evils to be disposed of as relapses into tribalism or barbarism." Rather, they are evils of a different order, and their character puts into question the very possibility of occupying the Hegelian middle, of realizing the mediation and synthesis of faith and philosophy that is the goal of philosophy as Hegel understood it. Auschwitz and the events it represents are actual and rational, but their actuality cannot be rational and their rationality cannot be actual.

The research and writing that resulted in *The Religious Dimension in Hegel's Thought* provided Fackenheim with philosophical tools of a different order. With them, he deepened his understanding of the relationship between revelation and reason, faith and philosophy, the religious and the secular. Furthermore, in working out the subtle nuances of Hegelian thought – in the *Phenomenology* and then in the system as a whole – he honed his skills as a dialectical thinker and acquired a rich repertoire of particular arguments and concrete motifs that he would employ in his writings from *God's Presence in History* to the very end of his life. In short, he became a deeply dialectical philosopher, whose style of argument and whose content of thought revolved around identifying manifestations of the secular–religious polarity and articulating the dialectical relationships between its poles. We have already said enough about *God's Presence in History* for us to appreciate how Fackenheim's work on Hegel infuses that book. This is obvious in the first chapter, with its account of revelation and the divine–human relationship. It is also explicit in his overview of the Midrashic framework, which is heavily indebted to Hegel's notion of religious *Vorstellung* (representation). But these are only two of many ways in which Hegel influenced his thinking. To see this best, I suggest we turn from *God's Presence in History* to his work of the 1970s and especially to *Encounters between Judaism and Modern Philosophy*.

Hegel in Fackenheim's Writings of the 1970s

The first three chapters of *Encounters between Judaism and Modern Philosophy* follow the arc from what Fackenheim took to be the weakest encounter to the strongest or deepest. He begins by asking how modern empiricism or logical positivism (and its heir, analytic philosophy) treats Judaism; he then turns to Kantian moral philosophy. But it is in the third chapter, "Moses and the Hegelians," that he deals with the encounter that he takes to be the most challenging to Judaism as well as the most revealing about what modern philosophy has learned from Judaism and where its openness to Judaism has been most sharply limited.[76] That is, by asking how Hegel and those who responded to Hegel deal with Judaism and what the limitations are of their treatments, we learn the most about what Judaism has to teach modern philosophy.

We shall see that several important insights emerge from Fackenheim's examination of Judaism and the Hegelian tradition. One concerns the covenantal relationship that is at the centre of Judaism and the divine–human relationship that characterizes it. Hegel takes such a relationship to be superseded in Christianity, with the implication that Judaism is an anachronism: history has passed it by. But a Jewish self-understanding recognizes such a relationship as essential to Judaism and hence as a testimony against the Hegelian synthesis. A second insight is that for Judaism, messianism is about a divine redemption yet to come, while for Hegel, a central feature of Christianity and the philosophy that comprehends it is that redemption has already occurred.[77] A third involves the role of the state in history and the acknowledgment that in the State of Israel, Judaism has re-entered history for political and redemptive purposes. Finally, not only do core Jewish ideas disrupt the Hegelian system; but also, Jewish reality and in particular the evil perpetrated against it, the evil of Auschwitz, constitute an impasse to Hegelian mediations as well as to the ultimate synthesis that is true philosophy. As we find our way through Fackenheim's rich account of Hegel, the Hegelians, and Judaism, we ought to keep our eye on these themes and what they mean to Fackenheim's own thinking.

Fackenheim contends – and this argument is central to his Hegel book – that Hegel's philosophy takes history seriously in a way that other philosophical thinking does not. But this means that Hegel's synthesis of all partial truths and of all finite standpoints into an infinite standpoint and into a comprehensive philosophical thought, "absolute, all-comprehensive Truth," must do justice to Judaism, and in so doing, it finds a non-absolute place for it and thus threatens Judaism. But this synthesis also can be threatened by Judaism, that is, by "a conscious self-exposure on Hegel's part ... to actual Jewish religious realities [that might very well call] into question, not some minor aspects of his thought, but nothing less than his system as a whole."[78] The central feature of Judaism that Fackenheim points to is the "ultimate incommensurability" of God and man, the divine and the human. To Jewish experience, that distinction or separateness is absolute and unconditional, and yet the two are dialectically interrelated. But this Jewish self-understanding is itself historical and hence must either reject any possibility of historical change or accept it and risk total immersion in history, with the result that all of Judaism becomes negotiable and relative. "What if," he asks, "in point of historical fact, Hegel's external mediations of Jewish history with the periods of world history were matched by *internal* Jewish *self*-mediations *in response* to the epoch-making changes which are cited by Hegel against it?" As Fackenheim points out, "this question has never been asked."[79] Yet when it is, the outcomes are momentous, for it might be that Judaism holds fast to certain truths in the face of all history and in so doing poses a serious challenge to the Hegelian system itself. Fackenheim frames this possibility with two rhetorical questions:

> What if *some* distinctions – between God and man, and between the one true God and all the false – were in fact as absolute as they are held to be by the Jewish religious self-understanding? Or, to put it more cautiously, what if the Jewish religious self-understanding has been able to hold fast to these distinctions in response to three thousand years of world-historical change rather than at the price of withdrawal from it?[80]

This is the project that Fackenheim sets for himself – to explore Hegel's account of Judaism and his response to Jewish history and then to ask how Judaism itself responds to its own history in order to confront Hegel with that self-understanding.

Fackenheim first reviews Hegel's mature account of Judaism as a "religion of sublimity." "Judaism appears as the stern, stubborn, incorruptible witness to divine-human nonunion."[81] God is not irrelevant to the human; neither is the divine simply assimilated to the human or vice versa. This view is a later manifestation of Hegel's early view – similar to Kant's – that in Judaism, God is a stern lawgiver, a monarch, while the human is wholly subservient. For the mature Hegel, the central mediating device in Judaism is the cult or later the law, the Halakhah, a view that is affirmed of Judaism by Fackenheim as well as by Hegel. Centrally, then, Judaism is about a divine power that is responsible for nature and for human conduct. God is benevolent; human beings honour God through worship and obedience. Furthermore,

Judaism's commitment to the one God but also its sense of particularity as God's elect exhibit what Hegel calls an "admirable" fidelity.[82] For Hegel, this structure is Judaism's metaphysical notion; the actuality of this notion rests in Jewish cult, "obedience to a God-given law in the fear of the Lord."[83] This understanding of Judaism shows that Hegel does seek to do it justice; his philosophical comprehension of Judaism as "the living relation between a God who is Lord of Creation and one singular human family" shows a genuine seriousness on Hegel's part.[84]

But just because Hegel is serious about Judaism and does some justice to it does not mean he is completely fair and responsible in his understanding of it. He takes Jewish particularism (or parochialism) to be excessive and fails utterly to appreciate the prophetic acknowledgment of God's role among the nations. He also still believes that the Jewish God is worshipped only in fear and hence is only Lord, that "biblical Judaism implies, for man, a stance of frozen and passive obedience [and] for God, a stance of frozen and commanding otherness"; and this one-sided view neglects the rabbinic view that God is worshipped in love as well as fear and that the law is freely interpreted to the degree that even God can be challenged by rabbinic judgments.[85] Most of all, however, Hegel "mentions the concept of covenant but can make nothing of it," and even more remarkably, he completely omits so much as a comment on messianism.[86]

But system is one thing, history another. Fackenheim's strategy is twofold: to consider first how Hegel understands the Jewish response to the Greek West and then to examine how Judaism understood its own response to the confrontation. "What if every Hegelian mediation of Jewish history with an epoch in world history were matched, unrecognized by Hegel, by a Jewish self-mediation?"[87] What Fackenheim sets out to accomplish, then, is this project step by step, beginning with antiquity, moving to Christianity, through the modern period, and then to the contemporary world. We can pass over the details of this narrative, except to notice that for Judaism the rabbinic response to Christianity involves two central ideas: a "divine-Jewish covenant," and "the messianic expectation."[88] For Hegel, these two doctrines are "marginal to the inner core of Judaism," but rabbinic Judaism would never have thought so. "Had Hegel's thought permitted rabbinic Judaism to speak with its own voice these two doctrines would necessarily have moved from the margin to the center."[89] That Judaism clings to these doctrines in the Middle Ages and in so doing stands opposed to the latter's otherworldliness, even Hegel sees, if Fackenheim is correct. That is,

Judaism "longs, however painfully and vainly, for a salvation that is not in heaven but rather on earth," and in so doing, it is "the witness par excellence to the 'untruth' of that world-historical epoch."[90] But if Judaism might seem to hold its own in Hegel's understanding of the Middle Ages, it does not continue to do so when Hegel turns to the modern world. Here "the medieval untruth vanishes and the Jewish testimony is superseded." The unity of divine and human realizes its most complete form in a society that is then realized in thought by the Hegelian system itself, and with that event "the religious truth of Judaism is both absorbed and, as such, superseded."[91]

When Fackenheim turns to "Jewish responses to [the modern world]," he finds an array of them, but "we cannot find," he adds, "self-exposed, self-mediating, yet normatively Jewish responses of the kind discovered earlier in this discourse … Not until the twentieth century did responses of this sort come upon the historical scene," but by then Hegel's modern world "lay in ruins."[92] He recalls, for example, the failures of the *Verein für Cultur und Wissenschaft der Juden* in the nineteenth century and then what he calls the "holding operations" of Abraham Geiger and Samson Raphael Hirsch.[93] He counts them among those "realistic, steadfast, or self-respecting Jews," who were committed to "defend[ing] their Jewish substance by whatever means they could."[94] More self-exposed, less apologetic responses occurred in the early decades of the twentieth century – before and after the First World War. Fackenheim remarks especially on the work of Hermann Cohen, Franz Rosenzweig, and Martin Buber. He focuses on the first two, who recover for Judaism in the face of Hegel respectively the idea of messianism and the centrality of the divine–human encounter. But each pays a price, Cohen by taking God to be exclusively an idea and by sacrificing Jewish ritual, Rosenzweig by clinging to Jewish actuality at the price of making it ahistorical.[95] In short, while we find a genuine self-exposure of Judaism to the modern world and to Hegel's understanding of it, we still do not find an uncompromising mediation.

Fackenheim then turns to the spiritual decay of the West, and he asks how those who came after Hegel, especially his left-wing followers, responded to it and to Judaism as well. These left-wing Hegelians correct the master on one point. If, for Hegel, philosophic thought can provide ultimate reconciliation because that reconciliation of the divine and the human has already been realized in the "bourgeois Protestant world," these left-wing critics argue that Hegel is mistaken in one crucial respect:

In its secular aspect, that world is free in idea only, not yet in concrete reality. In its religious aspect it is true and ultimate insofar as it remains religious. Taken as a whole, it calls for one final revolution, whose negative aspect is to destroy the Christian-Protestant God (and *ipso facto* all possible gods), while its positive aspect is, for the first time in all of history, to produce an "existence" that, both *absolutely* free and *concretely* human, has been all along the unrecognized and unrealized "human essence."[96]

That is, it is genuinely necessary to transform society into a secular venue for free human activity, and this requires in turn that philosophy become not a subsequent comprehension of this reality but a prior force on its behalf. In this way, the Hegelian "owl of Minerva" would become the "cock" that announces and even "*helps produce* a new day."[97] This is the core idea in the writings of Karl Marx, Arnold Ruge, Ludwig Feuerbach, Bruno Bauer, and later Ernst Bloch, all of whom, Fackenheim shows, think too little of Judaism and fail completely to do it any justice. The critical factor for them, as it is for Hegel, is that they do not and perhaps *can*not appreciate what the covenant means for Jewish existence. "Any genuinely contemporary Jewish religious existence would serve to show that all forms of Hegelianism, Hegel's own included, dispose too cheaply of the otherness of the Divine."[98]

When Fackenheim finally turns to the contemporary situation, he asks: "Would Hegel today be a Hegelian?"[99] To be sure, one can imagine Hegel surveying contemporary Jewish experience and finding a way to assimilate it to his system – that is, a way to treat the Jewish experience of the divine–human encounter as still harbouring unfree humanity and an overwhelming divine dominance. But might it be that "radical, normative, self-mediating" responses to Hegel's modern world can be found in Jewish existence? And could there be historical events that reconfigure the modern world in ways that prohibit Hegelian mediations? Fackenheim clarifies what needs to be examined: Jews' self-understanding of their historical reality, and the Hegelian philosophical comprehension that claims to reconcile all conflicts in finite understandings and to be world-historical. "Have events been such as to affect the claims of both Judaism and Hegelianism deeply enough to require a *transformation* of the encounter between them?"[100]

As Fackenheim moves forward, his first claim – and a momentous one it is – is that events have occurred that belie the Hegelian contention that its standpoint is world-historical and that its account is "the totality of all points of view."[101] Not philosophy or thought but rather reality or history makes such synthesis or mediation impossible today, if indeed it was ever possible. What Hegel had argued, Fackenheim clarifies, is that his thought articulates in a "dialectically interwoven whole" the relationship between "modern secular freedom and modern Protestant faith" – a relationship that was already implicit in the bourgeois Protestant world. In this way, divine–human history is shown to respect the identity between the divine and the human and their difference. What Fackenheim now argues is that events have occurred that "render this identity problematic."[102] As he shows, neither the decay associated with rampant technology nor "contemporary spiritual corruption" poses such a threat. But rampant technology and corrupt or outdated forms of spirit are one thing; "radical anti-Spirit" is another. With this expression, Fackenheim calls attention to the Nazi atrocities and to Auschwitz. These horrific events were not a "lapse into 'unfree' spirit" or a "work of unspiritual, fragmenting 'Understanding.'" Rather, "at work was an all-too-spiritual anti-Spirit that affirmed the modern identity of the divine nature and the human in an unprecedented, enthusiastic, self-sacrificing celebration of hatred, degradation, and murder."[103] In short, Hegelian thought would be shattered today if it were called upon to face and to comprehend the Holocaust.[104] Hegel's philosophy could not survive an idolatrous identification of the divine and the human, nor could it survive a world in which "universal mediation" had not occurred.[105]

The remainder of Fackenheim's discussion of a post-Hegelian Hegelianism begins with the recognition that since the divine–human identity has failed to be realized, philosophy must recognize and accept a religious–secular reality that is dialectical and yet unmediated. He quotes Martin Buber's famous reflection on the religious antinomy from *I and Thou*, in which both human freedom and divine Grace are present.[106] This "Jewish antinomy is … an unequivocal testimony against any such [Hegelian] identity." But

> for Hegel to concede that the divine-*Jewish* relation is not harsh but rather a covenantal mutuality would have meant nothing less than to concede that the Divine is and remains other than the human even in a dialectical togetherness of Grace and freedom; that therefore the Christian no less than the Jewish religion remains with this otherness; that there is not and cannot be an "absolute religion" in Hegel's sense of the term; and that a philosophical Thought at once human and divine – that is, Hegel's Notion – is impossible.[107]

Once Hegel's Notion is shattered, Judaism presents itself for what it is; it is "liberated," as Fackenheim puts it. Or, alternatively, philosophy is liberated to confront and grasp Jewish existence honestly, for Buber's dialectical understanding of the I–Thou relation between the divine and the human is, as we have seen in an earlier chapter, a way of understanding what is already present in the midrash representationally – or so Fackenheim argues.[108] So the first result for post-Hegelian philosophy and its encounter with Judaism is to take seriously the covenantal mutuality at the heart of Jewish existence. The second is to acknowledge the messianic dimension of that relationship.

In Hegelian terms, the messianic confidence must be as "doubly representational" as the covenantal relationship. "The Jewish Messianic expectation is a dialectical togetherness of working and waiting, of action and prayer."[109] But how, Fackenheim asks, can it confront contemporary history and survive? What kind of confidence can the Jew have after Auschwitz? Earlier, Fackenheim had exposed Hegel's philosophy to the Holocaust and found it to be "threatened merely with intellectual fragmentation"; now he exposes Judaism to it and contends that it is "threatened with existential despair."[110] He draws on the same thinking that he had articulated in "Jewish Faith and the Holocaust" and in *God's Presence in History*. In fact, as we will very soon see, his argument in those texts follows naturally from the breakdown of the Hegelian system and uses its terms – those of secularity and religiosity – to describe the contours of authentic Jewish response.

Finding himself unable to provide an intellectual response to the Holocaust, Fackenheim turns to the lives of ordinary Jews who survived it. As we have seen elsewhere, this is what he calls "thought going to school with life." In these lives he finds a "radical, normative Jewish response," one that does not seek to mediate the horror and the atrocity, which such radical evil will not allow, but instead faces it with an "uncompromising opposition." "Every Jewish survivor by his mere decision to remain a Jew [realizes] such a radical opposition," he says, and "by virtue of [that decision], the survivor has become the paradigm of the whole Jewish people."[111] In short, those who survived – at least some of them – confronted the evil that assaulted them and did so with an awareness of its character and with a will to resist it and to oppose it. For Fackenheim, such lucid and intentional opposition in response to the horror and the atrocity becomes a model of how others should live after these events. That is, instead of a mediated response that "domesticates" the evil by finding a rational place for it, a meaning or purpose, he finds an unmediated, direct response and the only kind that is appropriate to it as evil: that is, opposition.

Moreover, if all life must negotiate the relationship between the religious and the secular, then such acts of opposition to evil do so in a special way, a dialectically interactive way. That is, in opposing the forces of evil, the survivor's actions exemplify the religious and the secular in a precise way. Fackenheim describes this secular–religious dialectic as follows:

> Only by virtue of a radical "secular" self-reliance that acts as though the God who once saved could save no more can even the most "religious" survivor hold fast either to the Sinaitic past or to the Messianic future. And only by virtue of a radical "religious" memory and hope can even the most "secularist" survivor rally either the courage or the motivation to decide to remain a Jew, when every natural impulse tempts him to seek forgetfulness and even bare safety elsewhere … After Auschwitz, the religious Jew still submits to the commanding Voice of Sinai, which bids him witness to the one true God. He is now joined, however, by the secular Jew, who, by the sheer act of remaining a Jew, submits to a commanding Voice heard from Auschwitz that bids him testify *that some gods are false.* No Jew can be and remain a Jew without ipso facto testifying that idolatry is real in the modern world.[112]

Fackenheim here wants us to agree that secular self-reliance and religious commitment are inseparable in a genuine oppositional or resisting response to the Nazi assault and thereafter to those acts of dehumanization and terror that are its legacy. This appeal may not convince everyone. But it does resemble a Hegelian reading of concrete events, for it resists treating any genuine actions as exemplifying an extreme. Rather, it locates in the act or response dimensions of both poles, the secular and the religious, in this case the self-reliance of secularity and the kind of commitment that supersedes normal reasons in favour of a transcendent confidence. That is, in the genuine response to the Nazi horrors one finds some degree of self-sufficiency and some degree of other-grounded motivation or will, a degree of activity and one of receptivity.

Fackenheim adds to this result one last dimension: he associates this religious–secular combination with the State of Israel. In this way, as one finds most clearly in "The Holocaust and the State of Israel: Their Relation," and in other essays on Israel in *The Jewish Return into History,* he claims that what is meaningful about the relation between the death camps and the rebirth of the Jewish state is not any causal or explanatory connection.[113] It is instead the fact that Israel is a paradigm of authentic response to Auschwitz, which means that Israel ought to be understood as an act of opposition to the forces of evil that Nazism realized then and that continue to be realized in genocidal and other actions in subsequent history, acts of dehumanization and humiliation. As Fackenheim puts it:

> This commingling of religiosity and secularity has found historical embodiment in the rebirth of a Jewish state ... After the Holocaust, the Israeli nation has become collectively what the survivor is individually. Except only for those who never became part of the modern world, all religious Israelis are willing, if required, to take up "secular" arms in defense of the state. And except for those who cannot extricate themselves from ideologies that do Jewish history no justice, all secular Israelis have the "religious" wish that the state be Jewish.[114]

Once again, this reading of Israeli action may be, or may seem now, unrealistic, if not a serious distortion. But for our purposes, whether it holds up today is not the issue. What is most significant is that Fackenheim's imaginative reflection on what Hegel would say if he were to be reborn into our world shows how a central matrix for his conception of the mediation of the Notion – that is, the relation between the secular and the religious – might very well be employed by such a Hegel to understand what the rebirth of the State of Israel means and how that meaning is connected to the destructiveness that has been aimed at Jews and Judaism in the twentieth century. For Hegel, secularity is about freedom and self-reliant action, whereas religiosity is about dependency, submission, and receptivity. Both are aspects of human existence; to some degree and in some ways we are both independent and dependent beings. What Fackenheim shows is that this fundamental framework for understanding all human existence can still be employed in a Hegelian way to characterize the unmediated opposition to radical evil that is, for Fackenheim, the orienting situation of modern Judaism and modern philosophy.

Encounters between Judaism and Modern Philosophy was published in 1973 at a moment, for Fackenheim, when his thinking about the centrality of the Holocaust and the need for a response to it had crystallized and had been linked, in his mind, with the rebirth and continued defence of the State of Israel.[115] It also marks the first venue in which these reflections and his examination of Hegel's philosophy intersect in an important way. Hegel is, in his mind, the epitome of modern philosophy; his thought is the place where faith and reason, religion and philosophy, are brought to their most systematic and comprehensive synthesis. Every subsequent encounter with the question of religion's relationship to reason – to philosophy, politics, ethics, and more – takes place against the background of the Hegelian achievement. In Fackenheim's next major step towards understanding what can and should be recovered from the past in a post-Holocaust world, his magnum opus *To Mend the World*, Hegel does find a place, and the Hegelian influence on Fackenheim's thinking continues to be a powerful one. But while the focus of Fackenheim's thinking is changing, it does include a role for Hegel in that thinking. We need to look at this important discussion in order to see how.

The Role of Hegel in *To Mend the World*

When Fackenheim first turns to the Holocaust, in 1966 and during the half-dozen years thereafter, his focus is on Judaism and to a degree on Christianity. He asks how Jews and Christians have responded to that event and how they *should* respond to it. But at the same time, as a philosopher, he is always plagued by the worry that philosophy – the tradition of Western philosophy – may not be able to respond to Auschwitz. In a sense, *Encounters between Judaism and Modern Philosophy* is about whether Western philosophy has done justice to Judaism or has a bias against it, and it is about what Judaism might contribute to philosophy if the latter exposed itself honestly to the reality of Jewish existence. But the book is also about how the Western philosophical tradition – including empiricism, positivism, and even analytic philosophy, Kantian moral philosophy, Kierkegaard, Hegel and the Hegelians, Sartre, and Heidegger – has responded and perhaps should respond to the unprecedented and radically evil Nazi assault on humanity. In carrying out this assessment, Fackenheim's greatest effort is given over to considering Hegel and the Hegelian tradition; after all, he had recently completed a decade of serious thinking about the Hegelian system. But we should not forget that the encounter with Hegel is, for him, one of many. This is also true of *To Mend the World*. Hegel is important. Arguably, however, he is not the central figure whom Fackenheim engages in the book; that may be Spinoza or Rosenzweig or Heidegger or all of them. Still, he is an important interlocutor, and not just because he must be taken seriously if one wants to understand what an "epoch-making event" is and how it is possible, after such an event, to go on with honesty and seriousness. He is also important because much about the way Fackenheim thinks as a philosopher, much about how he reasons and examines and analyses, is Hegelian in style and spirit. There is much to be learned from *To Mend the World*.

In the second chapter of *God's Presence in History*, Fackenheim deals with nineteenth-century challenges to the very idea of revelation. But arguably the greatest challenge to revelation for Judaism comes not from outside the religious sphere, from critics such as Feuerbach, Marx, Nietzsche, and Freud, but rather from *inside* that sphere, from one who might take the divine–human relation to be superseded by a divine–human identity. This would be someone like Hegel. Let us see if that is how Fackenheim views it. In the third chapter of *To Mend the World*, "The Shibboleth of Revelation: From Spinoza beyond Hegel," Spinoza represents the naturalist challenge to revelation, Hegel the Christian one. But what lies beyond Hegel?

Fackenheim frames his discussion in Chapter III in just this way: Spinoza's naturalism threatens to reject all revelation, for after all it denies that the divine is transcendent, and hence Spinoza has contributed to the separation between secular Jews and religious Jews. Hegel's significance for Judaism differs. As Fackenheim puts it, "Hegel, in contrast, draws this God *into* the fatal circle. No escape is left."[116] That is, Hegel identifies the divine with the human. Fackenheim then indicates that his argument in *To Mend the World* begins where his Hegel book and *Encounters* had left off, by assuming that "Hegel's philosophy fails respecting its highest objective," which I take to mean that it fails to supersede Judaism honestly by comprehending the divine–human encounter or revelation and then establishing the identity of the two.[117] But in failing, as Fackenheim has shown, Hegel's philosophy does not leave us without resources – that is, its failed mediation leaves behind fragmentary efforts at mediation.

His aim is to answer two questions. "One is: How does revelation function as the shibboleth in Jewish modernity?[118] The other is: What can be made of the claim that this conflict between the religious Jewish affirmation of revelation and its secularist Jewish denial is mediated at a standpoint higher than both?" We might put Fackenheim's problem in different terms: Is revelation still today the core feature of Judaism that separates traditional believers from secularist critics? In one of his earliest writings on the Holocaust, Fackenheim had said that after the Holocaust, Jews are distinguished not into believers and non-believers but rather into those who take Auschwitz seriously and those who do not. As we have just seen, Fackenheim in his discussion of Hegel in *Encounters* showed how post-Holocaust Jewish response is characterized by a commingling of the secular and the religious. Is his chapter of *To Mend the World* an effort to elaborate on these claims?

First, what does Hegel think of Spinoza, and how does he think Judaism and Spinoza are related? If we tend to think that what separates Spinoza from Judaism is the belief in a transcendent God and in revelation, and hence if we take them to be in conflict, how does Hegel view their relationship? Fackenheim answers: Judaism clings to its particularity, whereas Spinoza is committed to universality. That is, the Jew submits himself totally to the divine Lord, who is Lord of all creation to be sure, but who has chosen this particular people. Spinoza abandons the particularity of this people in favour of a "universal faith of all humankind" and thus becomes, as Fackenheim puts it, a "man-in-general."[119] Judaism and Spinoza, then, are in conflict, but for Hegel it is a conflict that can be superseded only by a mediating activity that respects both but leaves them behind. The standpoint from which such a mediation can be conducted is Hegel's standpoint, one that will do justice to both Judaism and Spinoza and yet arrive at a "union of union and nonunion." Hegel respects the finitude and the subordination characteristic of Jewish particularity and Jewish subservience, but at the same time he seeks to deepen the infinitude of substance and its ultimate unity. That is, he can mediate the conflict between Judaism and Spinoza because he takes that mediation to exist already in Christianity. But this means, as Fackenheim argues, that Hegel understands Christianity as not rejecting revelation but as *realizing* it, and hence he takes his own philosophy to be expanding its scope and actualizing what revelation anticipates. Fackenheim understands that Hegel does not reject revelation; as Rosenzweig saw, Hegel's "philosophy ... consummates what is promised by revelation."[120]

Spinoza rejects revelation and leaves it behind. Hegel appropriates and transfigures it. That is the difference between the two in a nutshell. Fackenheim says that Hegel's acceptance of the revealed Christian truth forces him to confront the central problem of his whole philosophy. Hegel faces this dilemma: either he sides with Spinoza or he sides with Christianity:

If the divine incursion into the Christ, *passively accepted* by Christian faith, *remains* as accepted by Hegel's philosophy, then this latter surely falls philosophically far short of Spinoza's self-active rise to eternity; it may indeed, by the highest modern philosophical standards, destroy itself as philosophy altogether. Yet if it emulates or surpasses Spinoza's self-active rise to eternity, then it surely retroactively negates that revelation itself. This dilemma must seem inescapable unless, in its self-active ascent to the Divine, philosophy *transfigures* and thus *preserves* the Christian "content" instead of destroying it: and unless, moreover, it not only *ascends* to divinity *above* time but also *reinstates* the divine descent *into* it.[121]

Let me simplify the problem. Spinoza's monism and his system aspire to know the totality of nature from an impersonal, absolute point of view; Fackenheim, after Hegel, refers to this as a "self-active rise to eternity." It is the mind's freeing itself of partial and relative understanding in an effort to attain the unconditional perspective of "eternity." If Hegel accepts the Christian understanding of revelation as God's presence in Jesus as the Christ – since the Christian claim, which is not known by reason but is passively accepted on faith, is about the presence of a transcendent God in finite humanity – then Hegel's philosophy ceases to be philosophy and fails to attain the point of view that Spinoza aspires to occupy and takes to be the highest form of knowledge. Somehow, Hegel must accept the Spinozist conception of the highest form of knowledge, but he must do so without "destroying" the truth of the incarnation – that is, what *makes* it revelation; rather, he must "transfigure" it. He must find a way between philosophical naturalism, on the one hand, and Christian fideism, on the other.

If we compare this problem and the way Fackenheim formulates it with his defence of revelation in the second chapter of *God's Presence in History*, we see that his study of Hegel has transformed his approach to the problem. The early Fackenheim takes the naturalist or empiricist challenge to revelation to be the central problem for reclaiming faith; his chief interlocutors are those, such as Feuerbach, Marx, Nietzsche, and Freud (whom he never really discusses), whose naturalist assumptions rule out transcendent incursions from the beginning. In the late 1970s, however, having investigated so thoroughly the relation between religion and philosophy in Hegel's thought, he sees that the naturalist challenge is not as serious as the Hegelian one. Naturalists and empiricists make no allowance for the absolute or infinite; Hegel does. Hegel does not refute revelation; he assimilates it and finds a place for it within his system. Philosophically, then, his challenge is more serious, for if Hegel is right, then revelation can be understood as one dimension of the divine–human relationship. Or, to put it otherwise, revelation is rational, just as all actuality is rational. Moreover, it does not rule out human freedom; that freedom is an expression of it. If such is the case, then Christianity does not simply reject Judaism; it swallows it up.

Fackenheim discovers the key that unlocks the puzzle of how Hegel's interpretation of Christianity exposes the mediation between Spinoza and Judaism – that is, how it takes revelation seriously but at the same time rises to an absolute standpoint that synthesizes the religious and the secular. From within Christianity, the incarnation is viewed as a divine incursion. From the finite human side, that is, it is "passively received" from a transcendent other. But "Hegel's philosophy rises in thought from the human to the divine side of the Christian union of union and nonunion."[122] This does not simply mean that philosophy views this incursion from God's side as an act of Grace from the perspective of the giver. Philosophy, after all, is not simply a different perspective; it is one that sees more deeply into what is taken, in life, only representationally. As Fackenheim puts it, Hegel's philosophy, in "philosophically re-enacting" this ultimate incursion, is "a divine self-othering in man and world."[123] The philosopher realizes that the incursion represents what in reality is the manifestation of Spirit or God in man and world. It also is itself such a manifestation in its highest form, yet at the same time, it "reinstates" modern secular–religious life in all its complexity and "with all its diversities." In short, by depicting the reality behind the modern religious–secular world, the Protestant bourgeois world, as a "divine self-othering," Hegel's philosophy succeeds in identifying the unity of that world while at the same time respecting its diversity.

In this way, then, the Hegelian philosophy "consummates" what was "promised by revelation," as Rosenzweig put it. Revelation was about separation; philosophy is about a unity that respects separation – between the absolute and the conditioned, between the divine and the human and worldly. Moreover, this way of understanding what Hegel achieves shows how he can mediate between Judaism and Spinoza. As Fackenheim points out, Hegel may find more value in Spinoza and may be more inclined to leave Judaism behind, but in truth his commitment to Christianity and to modernity indicates that he finds some truth in each. We need not repeat Fackenheim's examination of how Hegel mediates between Spinoza and Judaism. The crucial point, I think, is that for Hegel, revelation is not an ultimate obstacle between the two and something that prevents us from taking both seriously. Rather, Hegel finds a way to "transfigure" Judaism, Spinoza, and revelation in a new synthesis.[124]

But, as Fackenheim has argued elsewhere and only repeats here, the Hegelian mediation fails. It re-enacts and requires a modern world in which are united an "unconquerable Christian faith" and "a boundless secular self-confidence." But the world today, Fackenheim reminds us, is rife with fissures and fragmentations. For many, Hegel is dead and the age of totalizing systems has ended; for some, the only responsible option is to return to earlier epochs, older ideas, or older principles; for others, the failure of the Hegelian synthesis should leave us only with differences, pieces, wreckage. Fackenheim disagrees with all this. Our age, he argues, ought to appreciate that Hegel's failure has left "dialectical traces." Hegel's system has not been a total failure or loss, for what it attempted – not to choose between revelation and reason but rather to find some reconciliation between them – was valuable and even "necessary." The failure need not throw us back on the alternatives; perhaps it has left "dialectical results" of value to us.[125] If there are separate fragments, they may exhibit subtle and valuable interrelations. In the chapter, Fackenheim turns to these: first to the fragments of left- and right-wing responses to Hegel, then foremost of all to Marx and Kierkegaard, then back to what he calls the "broken middle."

Basically, Kierkegaard clings to the religious while abdicating any interest in history, whereas Marx rejects religion altogether and totalizes his commitment to history and its importance. It follows that Kierkegaard's appreciation of history and Marx's of religion are surely one-sided and inadequate.[126] This then is our situation, one in which old biases return in new ways in the wake of the Hegelian failure. Fackenheim describes the situation as a "post-Hegelian broken middle" and as "mark[ing] the end of Constantinianism." He uses this expression to refer to "the theopolitical praxis of two beliefs: that the Christian revealed truth is the complete revealed truth; and that truth itself is not divided into 'religious' and 'secular' but rather is one and indivisible."[127] That is, Constantinianism is about comprehensiveness, authority, dominion, and even domination. Insofar as Hegel's philosophy claims to separate and at the same time unify the religious and the secular, it fulfils the Constantinian tendency. To be sure, Hegel's system seeks to demonstrate its comprehensiveness and to do justice to all those who oppose it, but it does have an imperialistic aspect, for the justice it serves is judged by its own standards. It is hard, Fackenheim might claim, to imagine a more extreme form of "domination" but, if Fackenheim is right, not to recognize its failure.[128]

In the wake of such a breakdown, what is left is a move towards the middle but now a middle that shows an openness to dialogue. Fackenheim illustrates this by pointing out how a post-Constantinian Kierkegaard should be open to historical and worldly different decisions, while a post-Constantinian Marx should be open to quasi-religious, if not actually religious, demands and "surprises." This, he argues, is where we find ourselves after the failure of Hegelian philosophy. It is not, he says, a concrete situation or condition; rather, it is a situation that involves "the convictions, religious and secular, that are honestly possible – and that are accompanied by the faith that, however fragmentarily and precariously, they can prevail."[129] This latter is the hope that one can bring to this situation, a hope that no matter what the inadequacies and what the corruption or threat, something can be done. Fackenheim uses the Hegelian notion of "overcoming" here, arguing that for Hegel the overcoming would be comprehensive and complete, while for us it is "limited and fragmentary." But, he claims, we do confront the world in this spirit and with this hope, that even the humanly orchestrated forces that threaten to destroy us can be confronted and opposed, even if not overcome.

It is at this point that Fackenheim introduces the Holocaust as "the event that cannot be overcome." The testimonies he uses to characterize this feature come from the journalist and philosopher Jean Améry and the novelist Primo Levi.[130] The conclusion he arrives at is familiar: for people in a post-Holocaust world, "where the Holocaust is there is no overcoming; and where there is an overcoming the Holocaust is not."[131] He then calls upon Améry and Buber to show that this result holds as well for the post-Holocaust Jewish people, "heir to the most unequivocally singled-out victims."

But at this point in *To Mend the World*, exposure to the Holocaust is premature. Fackenheim sets it aside – we have discussed his central engagement with it elsewhere, and the very notion of an epoch-making event in chapter 4[132] – and returns to the central issue of the current exploration: revelation and the challenges to it, and the Hegelian synthesis and its failure. But now he looks at what this situation means for Jewish modernity, as he calls it, and in particular what role Rosenzweig and Zionism play in such an encounter between the Hegelian collapse and Jewish life.

I have discussed this section of Chapter III in another chapter, so there is no need to trace its argument in detail.[133] Rather, what we want to appreciate is the special role that Hegel's thought plays in it.[134] Fackenheim reviews what he has accomplished thus far: he has shown how Hegel views Jewish existence and Spinoza's "acosmism" and at what cost.[135] But Fackenheim has carried out this mediation from the standpoint of philosophy on the assumption that Hegel's system had attained the comprehensiveness it sought. If it has failed, however, as Fackenheim has argued, then what remains are the fragments of a broken middle, and all kinds of "dialogical openness." In this situation, Judaism and Spinozism can now speak for themselves and to each other in a new way. With this preamble, Fackenheim then provides a summary of the Hegelian mediation, of what Hegel took philosophy to have accomplished. His summary examines the nature of religious life as a representation of the divine–human relationship; how philosophy expresses that same content in different form; the special role of Christianity; and, finally, the way in which Hegelian philosophy reformulates the Christian teaching in its own, mediating, terms.

Modern Jewish existence does not accept the identity of the divine and the human, the religious and the secular; and after having its middle "broken," a post-Hegelian Hegel would see this. Fackenheim points out that Judaism is "doubly-representational, and this despite the fact that the 'double activity' is not 'one' but two."[136] What he means is that Judaism takes the divine–human relationship to be dialectical and one of mutual interdependence, even though it does not take this relationship to result in identity; rather, it holds firm to the separation of the divine and the human. That is, Jewish existence is committed to "the incommensurability within Judaism of a divine Presence that is and remains infinite and universal to a humanity that remains unyieldingly finite and particular," and yet it also appreciates "a divine-human moving-toward-each-other."[137] God is infinite and overwhelmingly powerful, and the particular Jew is dependent and obedient; at the same time, God is loving and benevolent, and the Jew is free and committed to accept God's will as his own. This teaching of classic Jewish self-understanding, represented by midrashic texts, is appropriated by Franz Rosenzweig, Fackenheim argues, but not without a cost. In this respect Rosenzweig is a modern Jew and also a post-Hegelian.

Rosenzweig affirms as the core of Jewish experience the continued possibility of the divine–human relationship in a way that always anticipates eternity. "Hence," as Fackenheim says, "the 'old' is not overcome by the 'new' but rather forever renewed." On Rosenzweig's reading, there is no real history for Judaism. The ideal for any given moment is not to surpass the past or exceed it; rather, it is to "return" to a past that is ever-present, as it were. For this reason, Fackenheim identifies as central to Rosenzweig's conception of Judaism the concept of *Teshuvah* (return), and

> the core [of *Teshuvah* of whatever kind] is a divine-human turning-toward-each-other, despite and indeed because of their persistent and unmitigated incommensurability. This, as the above-cited Midrash illustrates, is the central experience of Sinai. It is also the experience of countless generations that, alienated from the God of Sinai, found themselves ever turning, and ever being turned, back to Him.[138]

As I indicated in an earlier chapter, this use of midrash and then Rosenzweig underlines how central revelation as a divine–human event is for Judaism and for Fackenheim after Hegel's failure.

For Rosenzweig, as Fackenheim points out, the cost of such an affirmation is a one-sided fideism and an inadequate appreciation of history and worldliness.[139] To rectify this, Fackenheim recommends – after the Hegelian broken middle – a move towards the centre, which means a confrontation with Jewish secularism, and the form of it he finds undeniable is "Zionism and its result, the state of Israel."[140] In short, as we saw in *Encounters*, Fackenheim finds in Zionism and in Israel a commingling of the religious and the secular, a combination that will later emerge as the way in which a post-Hegelian Jewish existence that is also genuinely post-Holocaust can find the confidence and the sense of purpose to oppose unconditionally the "demons of Auschwitz." For now, however, Fackenheim's turn to Zionism and Israel is framed in terms independent of the Holocaust. He focuses on Zionism's "confident, self-active self-reliance" and its commitment to a "secular-democratic state."[141] But he also must defend the religious dimension of Zionism, and this, he admits, is harder to do. "If Zionism were nothing but an escape from persecution, or a flight from economic abnormality, or a variant of economic nationalism, or a Jewish contribution to the [Marxist] Revolution, the Zionist impulse should have led to Uganda or Argentina, Biro Bidjan or Moscow."[142] The result of this combination of the old adherence to revelation, of "a modern-religious *Teshuva* to the old God," and "a modern-secular *Teshuva* to the old land," is the "location" of "future Jewish thought."[143]

I do not think that Fackenheim is arguing that Zionism and the State of Israel are the only sites where future Jewish thought can find a home. Rather, as we found earlier, Zionism and support of the Jewish state are paradigmatic of what a genuine modern Jewish thought must involve. Any such Jewish thought must live with Hegel's failures, which means that it must take the religious and the secular to be separate and yet also incorporate both in their interrelationship. It needs to find in Judaism a "religious inspiration" and "secular self-activity." The extremes must be coordinated, while they may very well be pulled asunder, he notes, and it may be that as time goes on they will be pulled ever farther asunder. But in Zionism and the commitment to the Jewish state, "the Jewish shibboleth of revelation assume[d] a modern form that was both unambiguous and inescapable."[144]

This conclusion brings us to the end of Chapter III of *To Mend the World*. In it, Fackenheim has shown how Hegel challenges modernity and Jewish modernity and how the failure of Hegel's system requires a response from all people and especially from Jews and Judaism. But the encounter with modernity is one thing, the encounter with Auschwitz another. For here we have an epoch-making event that threatens the Hegelian synthesis or mediation in a new way. Moreover, for his purposes, Fackenheim sees that his most formidable interlocutor at this point is no longer Hegel; it is Heidegger. And at least part of the reason for this change of opponent is that Heidegger's conception of human existence is so uncompromisingly historical, situated, and temporal. But for our purposes, we need not go further. We have done enough to illuminate the very central role that Hegel plays for Fackenheim in this crucial period of his career. Hegel becomes for him the greatest hope of philosophy; he sets the highest standard, and his failure is the background, the context for any Jewish thought of the future.

Last Thoughts: Fackenheim's Latest Reflections on Hegel

I began this chapter by calling attention to Fackenheim's late recollection of his earliest encounters with Hegel, in Berlin and then in Toronto. In the 2001 lecture "Hegel and 'The Jewish Problem'" and in his memoirs, *An Epitaph for German Judaism*, he returns to Hegel.[145] We have looked at his three most systematic encounters – in his Hegel book, in

Encounters, and in *To Mend the World* – but we would be remiss if we did not take a moment to consider his very late thoughts.

We might characterize a certain strand of Fackenheim's philosophical development this way. In his early period the main challenge to religious belief and religious thought is naturalism. That is, if we take human existence to involve a relationship between finite existence and the absolute, the main challenge is a materialism or naturalism that reduces the absolute to finite, concrete terms. This is how Fackenheim sees the problem in an essay such as "On the Eclipse of God" and in the second chapter of *God's Presence in History*. However, once he comes fully to appreciate the systematic and historical character of Hegel's thought, he realizes that it raises a more serious problem for religion and specifically for Judaism: it assimilates the divine–human relationship into a whole in which this relationship's identity and its respect for diversity both play a role. That is, Hegel's philosophy is Christian, modern, and also comprehensive. It rules out Judaism not because it is false but rather because it is anachronistic or overcome. This is the stage we see portrayed in Chapter III of *To Mend the World* and also described in "Moses and the Hegelians" in *Encounters*. Furthermore, this replacement of naturalism with Hegelian Idealism as the primary challenge to Jewish modernity illuminates, for various reasons, the encounter with the radical evil of Auschwitz in a deeper way than by reducing Auschwitz to barbarism or to rampant technology and rationality. So Fackenheim believes. In *To Mend the World*, moreover, Heidegger becomes Fackenheim's chief interlocutor regarding the encounter with Auschwitz because his thought appropriates the finite point of view left behind by the Hegelian failure while nonetheless failing to appreciate the "evil" of Auschwitz for what it is. But to a great degree, even though Heidegger becomes a central figure, the terms that Fackenheim employs to carry out this final step are Hegelian ones. What Fackenheim needs to do is understand how Judaism, Christianity, and philosophy – the major players in his Hegelian and post-Hegelian drama – take on new shapes in a post-Holocaust world, shapes dictated by finitude, the religious–secular dialectic, and a hermeneutical opposition to evil. This is the primary task of *To Mend the World*, and it is, to a great degree, carried out in the shadow and failure of Hegel's system. It is as if we were left with the *Phenomenology of Spirit* with its finite points of view but without absolute consciousness and absolute science and with a central threat – the reality of an unassimilable historical evil.

In the lecture of 2001, Fackenheim returns to his central concerns: How does Hegel interpret Jewish existence? And what role does Judaism play in *Weltgeschichte* (world-history, i.e., in world-historical terms)? If world-history has come to an end, Hegel notwithstanding, what becomes of "the Jewish problem?"[146] For Hegel, world-history is the history of Spirit; it is the history of the Divine in the human and not a history of God and man in the world. In such a story, Christianity is "absolute" and penultimate; all that it needs to arrive at its culmination is Hegel's systematic comprehension of it. Indeed, that system is the "true theodicy," as Fackenheim quotes Hegel, "the justification of God in history." Moreover, as he says, this is the "end ... not of *Geschichte*, that is, the social-political, but of *Weltgeschichte*, that is, the theo-political."[147]

But Fackenheim now asks how well Hegel understood his own *Zeitgeist* and his own concrete historical period.[148] His real attention, however, is not on Hegel's Germany and Europe but rather on our own world and the Holocaust that casts its shadow over it. He calls attention especially to the relation between Hegel in his own time and Heidegger in his. As I understand his comments, he wants us to appreciate that Heidegger returned to a kind of naturalism and could not, as Hegel did, appreciate that human existence is an engagement between the divine and the human, the absolute and the conditioned. What makes Hegel an important background figure is that for him, if not for Heidegger, "'Auschwitz' would have been *an assault on both*, God and man, extreme enough to cause his 'theodicy' to lie in shambles."[149] Moreover, the Holocaust "began and ended with attacks on Jews and, with it, on the God of Abraham, Isaac, and Jacob."[150] And what is the worst that Hegel can imagine? The death of God so that all is left to humanity? But this is not the worst that has occurred – at Auschwitz "evil was commanded" and not simply permitted. Here, then, "the Jewish problem" threatens the Hegelian system as a whole.

Fackenheim concludes his lecture with a brief section titled "For Recovery, Back to Hegel and Heine." Hegel had been open to Judaism, and his systematic impulse required doing justice to it. Today, in a time post-Hegel and post-Holocaust, what recovery is possible? Fackenheim calls attention to the Jewish intellectuals of the early nineteenth century who founded the *Verein für Cultur und Wissenschaft der Juden* and who were "devoted to Jewish Renewal in a truly modern time, not merely abstractly but historically."[151] They committed themselves to remaining Jews and not to convert to Christianity, but all save one did in fact convert. Indeed, the two of them with Hegelian connections – Eduard Gans and Heinrich Heine – did so; neither found it possible to be modern and to remain a Jew. Fackenheim notes that Heinrich Graetz would ascribe their failure to their Hegelian ideas. Another, Leopold Zunz, remained a Jew, but renewal for him came in the form of a *Wissenschaft* that Fackenheim judges to have become increasingly weak as a ground for Jewish life. Fackenheim ends the essay by wondering if "the grandchildren of the perpetrators and those of the victims" might not "find the recovery they need" in Hegel and Heine, rather than in the thinkers and poets of our own day.

What recovery would they find in Hegel? Germans might find the hope for reconciliation and a will to be open to Jews and to do justice to Judaism. Jews might find in him a worthy failure to deal with them and with world history, with evil. But what of Heine? Fackenheim quotes in German the last stanza of the poem "On Edom":

> And all the tears are flowing
> To the south, in silent union (*Verein*),
> They all flow and pour out
> Into the Jordan.[152]

He takes this to be a reference to Israel, to the wailing and crying of Jews – old and young, living and dead – whose tears "flow" southward, to the Jordan, to Israel. In short, could it be that Fackenheim is suggesting here that while Hegel points to a Jewish reaffirmation of the centrality of the covenant – the divine–human relationship, Heine points to the role of Zionism and the Jewish state as paradigmatic of Jewish renewal in a post-Holocaust modernity? These are the twin pillars of a future Judaism and of future Jewish thought. And both, in their own ways, as we have seen, are related to the Hegelian legacy that Fackenheim takes to be the matrix of his mature thinking. I have tried to show in this chapter how this is so.

6
Politics, Messianism, and the State of Israel: Fackenheim's Early Post-Holocaust Thoughts about Zionism

If Judaism is a way of life, the beliefs that frame it and the norms that guide it must take up what the Jew understands Judaism to be. We have already discussed the concept that for Fackenheim is central to that understanding, and how Judaism arises out of the divine–human relationship. That concept is revelation. At any given moment, moreover, Jews are called upon to act, and their actions not only are shaped and perhaps dictated by norms, however they are conceived, but also are placed in a philosophy of history. The concept that best reveals that philosophy is redemption, and in the twentieth century, ultimate redemption is primarily associated with the idea of messianism.[1] At a crucial moment, Fackenheim links this idea with a conception of the role of the State of Israel and ties both to post-Holocaust Jewish existence overall. In this chapter I want to say something about this cluster of themes as they arise in Fackenheim's writing and thinking primarily in the early 1970s.

Fackenheim's Zionism

From the Six Day War in 1967 until his death in 2003, Fackenheim wrote a great deal about Israel and Zionism.[2] After he made aliyah in 1982, the political situation in Israel became almost an obsession with him. He came to think of Zionism and of Israel itself as exemplifying authentic Jewish responses to the Holocaust; he also came to believe that a commitment to Israel's security and survival was at the core of any serious and responsible Judaism. But for the moment I want to restrict myself and to focus on Fackenheim's writings about Zionism prior to 1967 and then his earliest writings about the State of Israel after the war, during the early 1970s. We need to keep in mind that Fackenheim was not a political theorist or commentator; he was a philosopher and a theologian, and it was philosophical and theological reasons that led him to take Israel and Zionism seriously, after the Six Day War, in ways that he had not done prior to those events and to his engagement with the Holocaust. Although Fackenheim was a political realist, in a sense, especially in the late 1960s and early 1970s he was primarily an idealist of a sort. In those early post-1967 years, he had a way of placing the Jewish state within his newly developing understanding of Jewish existence, and it differed from his youthful anti-Zionism and the by-and-large neglect of Israel in his thinking during the postwar period.

If the State of Israel is virtually everywhere in later books like *To Mend the World* and *What Is Judaism?*, it is virtually absent from Fackenheim's early writings. One of the rare moments when he does touch upon Israel and Zionism in his early period is in a review of Martin Buber's *Israel and Palestine: The History of an Idea*, published in 1954 in the *Jewish Quarterly Review*.[3] His way of treating Buber's book shows how detached he was personally from the concrete urgencies of Zionism and the Jewish state in 1954, a short six years after its re-establishment and the war that secured it. Most of Fackenheim's review concerns the kind of work Buber has written, an exploration of the way that the idea of the physical rootedness of Judaism in a particular place must be responsive to the history of that idea in Jewish texts and in the Jewish past. Moreover, when he does turn to the content of the book – which, in his words, concerns the way in which God, the people of Israel, and the land of Israel form a unity in Jewish belief and Jewish life – he notes that Buber emphasizes the land of Israel, the way that Judaism and the Jewish people must be rooted in the land. That is, Buber emphasizes the land of Israel precisely *because* he is carrying out a polemic against "idealism and conventional liberalism." For as Fackenheim points out, idealism has argued that in the course of history, Judaism as a natural religion had been replaced by Judaism as a spiritual faith, and liberalism has come to treat "the dispersion of Israel, far from being *Galuth*, as a providential act of history which, by depriving Israel of its 'narrow' nationalistic basis, raised it to a higher and more universal level." Both idealists and liberals, then, have tended to be anti-Zionist, and hence it makes sense that Buber would oppose them. But, as Fackenheim notes, this does not mean that Buber bought into the nationalistic view of Zionism; his view of Judaism was too "spiritual" for that – we would say that it was too grounded in revelation, faith, covenant, and the religious character of Judaism. Fackenheim points to the fact that Buber was "never willing to sell his spiritual birthright for a mess of nationalist pottage." Hence, for Buber, "the idea of Israel *and* Palestine is essentially the idea that spiritual existence requires roots; that spirit requires nature and is a mere empty abstraction without it." On the one hand, then, Jewish faith demands a place in which to realize itself, but on the other, Zionism cannot afford to be a secular defence against persecution or a feat of normalization. Rather, as Fackenheim puts it, "'Israel and Palestine' is a search for and encounter with God, by a concrete people in a concrete land; or, if not that, it is at least the concrete longing for such an existence."

This all seems rather balanced as a view about Zionism, and one could easily take Fackenheim himself to be a partisan, except for how he ends the review. When it comes to registering his judgment on the book, he lauds Buber for the "true idea" that is its core. But he wonders if Buber's polemical emphasis is right for the postwar period, marked as it is by "naturalism, nationalism, and pragmatic hard-headedness," what we would call a kind of acquisitive, materialistic, and utilitarian mentality. Modern Judaism is not endangered by a lack of appreciation for worldly possessions and nature. If it is "endangered by rootless spirituality," which is Buber's worry, "it is certainly no less endangered by the idolatry of the roots," which is Fackenheim's.

Fackenheim's rare public comment on Israel had some peculiar features. Because it took up a book written by Buber, who was not an advocate of a Jewish state but who was deeply committed to the renewal of Judaism in a particular land, Fackenheim might be excused from neglecting to talk about a Jewish state.[4] That, after all, especially in 1954, was clearly his choice. Furthermore, his own agenda, unlike Buber's, reflected his view that the modern Jew had become utterly secularized and alienated from the notions of revelation and faith and that *this* – and not a rootedness in concreteness – was the most serious threat to Jewish existence. Still, he did apparently accept the view, which he found in Buber, that a genuine Zionism should combine the spiritual and the natural; it should be about Jewish existence rooted in the world. That is, Zionism should be both spiritual and natural or, as he would later put it, religious and secular. Or, perhaps more accurately, Fackenheim thought that Judaism should be both. He showed no special affection for the land of Israel as the *sitz-im-leben* of Jewish existence.

By 1970 things had clearly changed for Fackenheim. In July of that year, at a study circle convened by President Zalman Shazar in Jerusalem, Fackenheim gave what I think was his first important statement about the State of Israel: "From Bergen-Belsen to Jerusalem," published in 1975 and reprinted in *The Jewish Return into History* in 1978. It was followed in 1974 by two very important papers, "Israel and the Diaspora: Political Contingencies and Moral Necessities; or, The Shofar of Rabbi Yitzhak Finkler of Piotrkov" and "The Holocaust and the State of Israel: Their Relation" and then in 1977 by "Post-Holocaust Anti-Jewishness, Jewish Identity, and the Centrality of Israel: An Essay in the Philosophy of History."[5] By the 1970s, Fackenheim had come to be consumed by the role of the State of Israel in Jewish existence and by its relation to anti-Semitism, Jewish life in the diaspora, and the Holocaust. But before we turn to some of this, let us return to 1970 and ask what had changed in Fackenheim's thinking, in his life, and in the world.

Fackenheim had not visited Israel until 1968, when he was invited by the Israeli government. He had been, by his own admission, "brought up in an anti-Zionist tradition." As he remembered it, he had been taught that Jewish "religion" and Jewish "nationalism" are not the same. When in 1970 he recalled his upbringing, he did comment that he had given up those terms and the distinction, but that it was only in 1968, on his and his wife Rose's first visit to Israel, that he had come to realize and to be astonished by the way religiosity and secularity were intertwined in Israel, by and large in the secular Israeli Jew. Fackenheim's political engagement with Zionism was deeply influenced by the intensity and passion of Rose's commitment, but he found for that passionate commitment an intellectual justification. He might have been romanticizing what was surely an emotional experience, but his observation about the religious and the secular had an enormous influence on him nonetheless. He would associate this realization with the view he came to hold in those years, in the 1970s, about Israel. "Jerusalem, while no 'answer' to the Holocaust, is a response; and every Israeli lives that response. Israel is collectively what every survivor is individually; a No to the demons of Auschwitz, a Yes to Jewish survival and security – and thus a testimony to life against death *on behalf of all mankind*."[6] That is, in a sense Israel became for him an exemplification of (and an opportunity for) obedience to the 614th commandment. Given that the Holocaust had no purpose or meaning but that response to the Nazi atrocities was necessary, he came to view Israel as a mode of response and even, as the quote I just cited shows, a paradigmatic one. As he put it in *God's Presence in History*: "The Commanding Voice of Auschwitz singles Jews out; Jewish survival is a commandment which brooks no compromise. It was this Voice which was heard by the Jews of Israel in May and June 1967 when they refused to lie down and be slaughtered."[7]

One event, then, that facilitated the shift in Fackenheim's attitude towards the State of Israel was his visit to Israel. Another one, of course more important, was the Six Day War, together with Fackenheim's reflections on it, for that threat of extinction and the response to it provided a link in his mind to the threat of extinction during the Nazi years and the response to *that* threat. In a sense, he came to see the later response, by Israel and her soldiers in a war of survival, as a re-enactment by Israelis of the earlier response, by the Warsaw Ghetto fighters and others who resisted the Nazi assault and who gave their lives in defence of the survival of Judaism and the Jewish people. This, at least, was how he interpreted these events on the basis of testimony and reports that were conveyed to him – for example, in a letter by Harold Fisch of Bar Ilan University, which he would quote at the end of his famous essay of 1968, "Jewish Faith and the Holocaust: A Fragment."[8]

Fisch's letter reported a conversation he had had with a friend, a psychologist, about the war and the heroism of so many Israeli soldiers. Fisch had asked his friend what motivated their bravery, and his friend attributed it to their memories of the Holocaust and their commitment to ensuring that it would never happen again, that Jews and the Jewish people would survive. Fisch was incredulous, but his psychologist friend was confident that the Holocaust and the memory of the near-annihilation of the Jewish people had become a collective motivation for the soldiers, consciously or unconsciously. Fackenheim latched on to this link between the two events, and by 1970 he would regularly claim that after Auschwitz a commitment to Jewish survival was a religious commitment and not merely a human or physical one. It was in those days that he became fond of citing Milton Himmelfarb, who had responded to a sceptic who had been arguing that mere Jewish survival could not justify remaining Jewish with this reprimand: "After the Holocaust, let no one call Jewish survival 'mere.'" As Fackenheim translated this point into his own terms, "Jewish survival has become holy even for 'secularists' – and the holy is not negotiable."[9]

Here, then, we have the unity of spirit and nature that Fackenheim had once praised in Buber's vision of Zionism. Now, however, the unity was not one of faith and land or rootedness; it was one of survival and self-defence. That is, in order to see the soldiers during the Six Day War and later all Israelis, even secular ones, as representing a unity of religious purpose and self-reliant action, Fackenheim had come to treat survival itself as a spiritual goal, so to speak, as "holy," to use his words. He called this a "secular holiness."[10]

Even if one were to grant that Fackenheim has accurately observed something about Israelis and Israeli society, that the dedication to Israel's survival is intimately tied to the survival of Judaism and the Jewish people, it is almost immediately clear that a link with something deeper and more spiritual, to use Buber's vocabulary, is necessary. It is for this reason that Fackenheim finds it so appealing to treat the defence of Jewish survival and the survival of Israel as a spiritual or religious act. He seems to sense that need early. After all, when it comes to interpreting the content of his 614th commandment, he holds that one fragment of it is keeping Judaism alive by not despairing of God, even when it might be easy to do so, and that another is not to despair of the world as the place that is to become the kingdom of God. What this last fragment means is that in responding to the obligation that arises from Auschwitz, we must not give up thinking that the world is a meaningful place and that part of understanding God's relation to history and to humankind is to work for and hope for a world in which people live with one another in justice, humanity, and peace. That is, very early on in these post-Holocaust reflections, Fackenheim sees that the way to link the Holocaust with responsible resistance to it and with a genuine response to what obligations emerge is through the notion of messianism – that is, the belief that the world will become the kingdom of God. And if Israel is a paradigmatic response to Auschwitz, then one way of finding a religious purpose in the re-establishment and defence of the Jewish state is through the idea of messianism.[11]

This strategy – to show that the link between the Holocaust and the State of Israel is a recovery of the traditional idea of messianism but with a new sense – is most evident in Fackenheim's beautiful essay of 1974, "The Holocaust and the State of Israel: Their Relation." But in order to see how Fackenheim uses the idea of messianism as the bridge between the two events, we should look first at how he had understood the idea of messianism in Judaism prior to his encounter with Auschwitz. Messianism has been employed by religious Zionists and more recently by fanatically right-wing ideologues, especially those connected with the settlements and the recovery of the Temple Mount.[12] If Fackenheim wants to appropriate the vocabulary of Jewish messianism, it cannot be along such lines. We need to understand what he thinks the role of messianism is in Judaism. Fortunately, there is an essay from 1965 in which he provides just what we need: "Judaism and the Meaning of Life."[13]

Messianism and the Philosophy of History

Messianism is a feature of a philosophy of history. Fackenheim outlines his Jewish philosophy of history in several essays, using the concepts of creation, revelation, redemption, community, and history. His account looks like this. He reads traditional Jewish texts as adhering to the incomplete nature of human existence. Human beings are both animal and spirit; they are natural beings, mortal and finite, and yet also beings with a moral perspective on the value of life and its purposes. If the individual Jew were simply a natural being, life would have no meaning but only an end, and if he were simply a spiritual being, then the evil and suffering in history "would be a mere temporary accident." But in man these twin poles, the natural and the spiritual, so to speak, are always in tension. This is what creation means and why, if human existence is to be redeemed, it must be complemented by a doctrine of redemption. There must be a hope that ultimately these contradictions and tensions will be resolved. Man will not cease to be an animal or cease to have spirit; both sides of human existence will be redeemed. As Fackenheim puts it, "the creator of all is also the redeemer of all."[14]

In a sense, then, the human problem is established and resolved by the combination of creation and redemption. "God will redeem man, but not by making him either less or more than human ... God redeems man by preserving the contradictory elements that constitute his humanity, yet by transforming them in such a way as to take the sting out of the contradiction." But the pair requires that the path of history, from creation to redemption, be meaningful, and this is the function of revelation. For revelation involves God's incursion into history at a particular moment, his singling out of the individual as a particular participant in this movement from contradiction to resolution. Fackenheim puts this by saying that without revelation, even a history with God would be made up of events and people all of whom are a "dead and sodden weight." Particular events and people take on significance only because they are called to respond to God's claim on them, and this means to play a role in the historical drama. Each and every human action can become a unique contribution in the process of redemption.[15]

For Fackenheim, revelation is an event of divine–human encounter in which the divine presence both obligates and enables man to respond, and one form of that response is the articulation of commandments. In Judaism, revelation establishes the relationship between God and the Jewish people, that is, the covenant, and the continued possibility of revelation for Jews confirms their covenantal existence, the claim on them to perform those commandments. Furthermore, the response involves the obligation to love one's neighbour, to care for others, which is one aspect of covenantal existence and also a contribution to the redemption of human existence and history. Hence, human action is meaningful insofar as it plays a role in bringing redemption, but if that redemption were solely up to man, then history would be a scene of despair. As Fackenheim puts it, "history is wholly in Divine hands even while man has a share in making it."[16]

The meaning of history, however, is only gradually and imperfectly disclosed to man; there are times when redemption is hard to fathom. Also, however, in the course of history, the meaning *itself* is fragmentary. "Past and present point not only to a finite future but to one which is absolute and all-consummating as well. Not until an eschatological dimension, a messianic belief, comes into view is the Jewish understanding of meaning in history complete." That is, only when the prophets came to see history as culminating in an epoch that was qualitatively different and one that required a divine accomplishment was the meaning of history fully understood. "Meaning in history, then, is fragmentary; and a merely historical future, no different in nature from the past, cannot complete it. Thus an eschatological future comes into view."[17] In short, man cannot consummate history. Human beings are limited and often cruel, sinful, confused, and more; if the redemption of history were solely in human hands, history would be the scene of tragedy. To complete human existence, history requires divine aid, and that is what the doctrine of the messianic age guarantees.

At one time, the goals of messianism were taken to be parochial and national; the messiah was to be an anointed king of a re-established state in the promised land. But as time went on, this limited view became universal and "all-encompassing." "All nations flow to Jerusalem; the Kingdom of God is forever established; and it extends over the whole earth."[18] Moreover, the coming of the messiah is doubly related to human conduct and the human response to revelation in every moment. Man must work for the coming of the messiah and yet wait for his arrival. He must work for it in order to appropriate it for history, and he must wait for it since he has no idea of when it will occur. "Men must act as though all depended on them; and wait and pray as though all depended on God." And part of what makes the coming of the messiah so unexpected is that no simple state of the world will signal the coming: "the Messiah will arrive when the world has become good enough to make his coming possible; or evil enough to make it necessary."

Hence, the messianic age is connected to history but at the same time oddly dissonant with it. The messianic goal is, paradoxically but necessarily, worthy of human aspiration and labour and yet beyond human realization. In Fackenheim's early writings, nonetheless, the doctrine of the messiah is the capstone of a Jewish philosophy of history.[19]

We might reformulate the import of this doctrine in this way. For the Jew, when it comes to the human condition and the aspiration to see its limitations resolved or rectified, the doctrine of the messianic is a kind of insurance. It brings confidence that even given human weakness, there is hope and confidence; history is not condemned to meaninglessness. We recall, moreover, that one fragment of the 614th commandment, as Fackenheim interpreted it, was that the Jew today, after Auschwitz, even in the face of that peak of horror and atrocity, must not "despair of the world as a place that will become the Kingdom of God." After Auschwitz, one must not abandon the ideal of redemption and hope for the future. And Israel is the paradigm of one who listens to that commandment and seeks to accomplish it. With a bit of tinkering, then, one could conclude that in the late 1960s – when he first visited Israel and felt its impact, when he saw and heard about the secular soldiers who felt under orders never again to succumb to the threat to Jewish survival – Fackenheim had begun to associate Israel with a messianic function, with the task of inspiring confidence that the world and   . history would not be be abandoned to the demonic, that there would continue to be hope, even in the face of human failure and radical evil.

The Holocaust and the State of Israel

This convergence of ideas is realized in the remarkable paper I mentioned earlier, "The Holocaust and the State of Israel: Their Relation." The paper has three parts. In the first, "Hope," Fackenheim considers the connection in Jewish belief between messianic expectations and "the ingathering of the exiles in a restored Jewish commonwealth." What he finds striking is the way that the re-established Jewish state, a present historical event, is linked with the concept of the messianic coming, which is an absolute end to history. In the second, "Catastrophe," he asks whether there is any explanatory connection between the Holocaust and the re-establishment of the Jewish state. He argues that there is not, but that they still must be linked, and that the only way to link them is to turn to the notion of response. In the third, "Response," he shows how forms of resistance during the Holocaust pointed towards the proposal that an affirmation of Israel is a paradigmatic response to Auschwitz; it is the way to recover hope in the midst of utter despair. In a sense, Fackenheim's paper is an attempt to understand the sense in which the State of Israel itself, a commitment to its survival, and an affirmation of its existence, is messianic. That is, in a world in which hope has been challenged to the limit, can it be recovered?

To put Fackenheim's argument in a slightly different way: He is asking in effect whether the State of Israel can be understood in messianic terms. Although religious Zionists have done so – some of them extremely right-wing and fanatical about the land's messianic role – Fackenheim notes that it is still remarkable that a present reality should have messianic implications.[20] But if it can, it is by claiming a link between a concrete historical event and an absolute non-historical expectation or commitment. What justifies such a link?, Fackenheim asks. And if the Holocaust does, then how? He rejects various ways that others have understood the connection between the Holocaust and the Jewish state – causal, explanatory, and so forth.[21] Instead he notes that the character of certain modes of resistance during the Holocaust pointed to the battle for statehood in Israel and re-emerged during it. This suggests that Israel itself is a *mode of resistance* and hence of response to Nazi purposes. Its refounding was not an absolute event but rather a historical one. It cannot guarantee hope forever. But in our time, given the extreme doubts we have about human capabilities and the chances of our world being redeemed from failure and atrocity, Israel goes some way towards reviving for Jews confidence and hope in redemption.[22] This, I think, is Fackenheim's argument. What is critical to it is the way in which his earlier understanding of messianism is here transformed or modified in an important way. Whereas in 1964, he had taken the doctrine of messianism to be a *permanent, absolute* guarantee that history would be redeemed, even if we could not count on human effort and abilities to accomplish that task, here in 1974 Fackenheim argues that for the doctrine of messianism to be recovered for the Jewish present, it must be *historicized*. This is part of what it means to say that after Auschwitz, Judaism has returned to history. The Jewish people have become more historical, political, and involved in the world, and Judaism, that is to say, the very ideas that are central to Jewish belief, has become historicized. There are no permanent, unconditional guarantees about the world's redemption; all we can hope for are temporary guarantees – some confidence and some hope, even if unqualified. In a sense, for Fackenheim after the late 1960s, Israel and the conduct it exemplifies have replaced God and divine agency in the messianic scheme of things.[23]

By 1974, then, not only had Fackenheim developed an emotional attachment to the State of Israel. Not only had he romanticized the way in which religious purpose and secular self-reliance had become intertwined in the lives of Israelis and indeed in the Jewish state itself. He had also come to see Jewish concepts and Jewish themes in a new way. In particular, he had come to understand what messianism means in Judaism in a way that enabled him to discern in what sense the State of Israel could be taken to be messianic.

I think we can be even more specific about how his understanding of traditional Jewish messianism had changed by 1974 if we look more closely at what he says about messianism in the first section of "The Holocaust and the State of Israel." The rabbis, he points out, understood that there was some connection between history and its messianic fulfilment, but they intentionally gave conflicting answers about what that connection was. To some, the end would come as a result of progress; to others, it would occur after catastrophe. To some, Israel would already have been freed from foreign domination; to others, Israel's impoverishment and despair would have been exceedingly great.[24] As a consequence, the link between history and the days of the messiah is precarious and filled with tension. But Fackenheim notes that even if the link between history and its fulfilment is precarious, there must *be* such a link, and this has given rise to the tension between historical concreteness and messianic absoluteness that is present everywhere. The tension can be endured only because the guarantee of future redemption is absolute, and with that absolute guarantee comes a secure hope that history will be redeemed. Clearly, then, Fackenheim is emphasizing that the guarantee or certainty that made hope absolute in antiquity and the Middle Ages, and that Fackenheim himself affirmed in 1964 as central to Judaism, he now believes is already mitigated or abandoned in the modern period. Liberals have converted it into a doctrine of progress, and Zionism first came on the scene as an effort at normalization only to realize that at its heart was the old messianic idea after all, but with a difference. That difference concerns the way in which, in Zionism, the secular is united with the religious.

What Fackenheim has in mind is that Zionism is no simple nationalist movement. It has always required human effort and courage and self-reliance, but at the same time, its accomplishments have been so remarkable that if the whole project were simply secular, political, and social, that could not account for them all. The re-establishment of the Jewish state involved the unification of a people scattered throughout the world and alienated by vast cultural differences; the creation of a living language from an ancient liturgical and textual one; the development of political, social, and military skills by a people among whom they were dormant at best; and the defence of the young nation against enemies on all sides under extraordinarily difficult circumstances. In the face of these tasks and challenges, the mere will to self-determination could not be enough to explain the success. That will had to have deeper roots, so to speak; more was needed to inspire confidence and hope. In Fackenheim's words, "only a will in touch with an absolute dimension could have come anywhere near solving these problems, and even those acting on this will may well be astonished by its accomplishments."[25] What Fackenheim finds in the State of Israel, then, is a paradigmatic combination of secular action and religious purpose, and that action expresses how the messianic dimension of Jewish experience has been realized in the age of Auschwitz. To put it differently, even in the shadow of the death camps, one can work towards redeeming history from all its failures; there is some hope for those who take on the task.

Messianism, Hegel, and the State of Israel

Traditionally, the messianic idea in Judaism is about divine promise and an absolute certainty in God's redeeming power. What leads Fackenheim to think that a new messianic idea must somehow combine the secular with the religious, realism with hope? As we have seen, at around this time, a few years after publishing his book on Hegel, Fackenheim returned to Hegel to examine how he viewed Judaism and what he might have gleaned from a deeper understanding of Jews and Jewish experience. In "Moses and the Hegelians," published in 1973 in *Encounters between Judaism and Modern Philosophy*, Fackenheim turns to the themes of messianism, secularity and the religious, and the State of Israel.[26] In these few pages, how does Fackenheim understand the relations among these themes and realities?

Today, would Hegel still be a Hegelian, or would Jewish realities lead him to revise his central affirmations? We have already considered what this question means and how important it is to Fackenheim.[27] He addresses it in the concluding pages of "Moses and the Hegelians," and he concludes that when faced with Judaism and the realities of Jewish existence, Hegel would have altered his system. The polarity with which Fackenheim works is the one between secular self-confidence and religious purpose. Hegel took these to be united in history and in thought, insofar as he saw the divine and the human to be one. But Judaism – for many reasons – and especially as a consequence of the horrific assault on Jewish body and soul that we call the Holocaust – shows that the vaunted Hegelian synthesis, the unity of the secular and the profane, lies in ruins. Yet the destruction is not total; the principle of universal mediation of all things, shattered in life and thought, leaves behind dialectical fragments.[28] Worldly secularism and pious fideisms confront each other, neither able to avoid the other. There is, in the modern world, both secular self-activity and religious receptivity, and in Judaism the two have always engaged each other in dialectical ways, in a "double activity" of human freedom and divine grace. Fackenheim cites a famous passage from Martin Buber's *I and Thou* where Buber describes precisely this double activity, this sense on the part of the religious Jew that his life is both wholly dependent on his own efforts but at the same time given over and disposed to God's claims upon him.[29] This Buberian formulation is at the heart of what in Judaism is known as the covenantal mutuality between God and the Jewish people, a view articulated again and again in the midrash. "Jewish religious existence is the togetherness of divine Grace and human freedom, the difference between the human and the Divine notwithstanding."[30] As Fackenheim puts it, the Hegelian unity has been abandoned, shattered, yet one can use a Hegelian way of thinking to articulate the Jewish existence that remains, thus "doing justice to the inner logic of Judaism."

The outcome of such an undertaking, which Fackenheim sketches, is a movement towards a notion of redemption, of a messianic future, that combines both features, the human freedom and the divine Grace, in dialectical ways. That is, Hegel's system rules out any messianic future, for it points to a unity already accomplished, but once one recognizes that the system lies in fragments and that Judaism joins them in dialectical mutuality, we see that Judaism does point ahead to a promised though as yet unfulfilled "reconciliation and redemption." Fackenheim goes so far as to say that the very idea of the covenant is "unintelligible" without the hope for a messianic outcome, and it must be the case that this outcome combines both a human contribution and a divine guarantee. Living towards redemption, the Jew is a covenantal partner with an unqualified confidence, even given his own limitations.

But Fackenheim explains that the very idea of a messianic future is complex and internally fraught. "The Jewish Messianic expectation is a dialectical togetherness of working and waiting, of action and prayer. The Midrash represents the Messiah as coming, on the one hand, when men are good enough to make his coming possible, and, on the other hand, when they are wicked enough to make it necessary."[31] Also, messianism does not allow that either the human or the divine contribution be absolute. Both are required, and each is qualified vis-à-vis the other. In Judaism today, the Jew's confidence in the coming of the messiah is no longer absolute.

The messianic idea in Judaism, then, is the appropriate complement to the centrality of covenantal existence in Judaism. Moreover, in the modern world, both must be true *within* history and not simply beyond it. For a Judaism threatened with utter destruction, there can be no authentic response that is not also a response in the world and in history, and that response must be one of resistance, of a refusal to abandon the Judaism that was so mercilessly assaulted. Fackenheim calls this an "uncompromising opposition," one that has become paradigmatic for the Jewish people as a whole. Furthermore, this opposition is normative: it is demanding, and the demands it makes are addressed to secular and religious Jews alike, which means that these terms, aligned as they are with the polarity of human freedom and divine power that remain now that Hegel's system has been left in fragments, must be redefined and understood in new ways.

This is the point at which we have been aiming. We have the idea of messianism as an appropriate complement to Jewish covenantal existence; we have a demand for an uncompromising opposition to the forces of Auschwitz; and we have the need to redefine, in order to understand that opposition, messianism's religious and secular dimensions. How does an opposition to Auschwitz that is both secular and religious contribute to the messianic anticipation that is central to a continuing Jewish existence? The answer, Fackenheim argues, comes to light when we recognize in the State of Israel and its citizens a paradigm of that opposition and also as a contribution to the realization of history's messianic future. That is, after Auschwitz, the Jew can remain loyal to Sinai and to the ideal of a messianic future only if he gives up dependency upon God in favour of a radical "secular" self-reliance. "And only by virtue of a radical 'religious' memory and hope can even the most 'secularist' survivor rally either the courage or the motivation to decide to remain a Jew, when every natural impulse tempts him to seek forgetfulness and even bare safety elsewhere."[32] This gives rise, Fackenheim says, to a new confidence. It is not the old confidence, timeless and absolute, but a *realistic* and historically contingent confidence that is based on a measure of hope and a measure of human initiative.

Finally, "this commingling of religiosity and secularity has found historical embodiment in the rebirth of a Jewish state." Jewish covenantal mutuality requires both human freedom and divine power, and so does the messianic promise. In our day, versions of the same polarity characterize an "uncompromising opposition" to the demons of Auschwitz and hence that paradigmatic opposition that is the Jewish state. For "after the Holocaust, the Israeli nation has become collectively what the survivor is individually."[33] Israel, to be what today it ought to be, Fackenheim says in the early 1970s, must be both religious and secular. It must take up arms in its own defence, but at the same time it must never give up the "religious" wish that the state be Jewish.

Temporary Result

Prior to the Holocaust, Fackenheim tells us, Jewish history was shaped by an absolute confidence that covenantal existence would ultimately be fulfilled. That was what the traditional notion of messianism represented: the guarantee that no matter how limited human beings are, the project of realizing God's purposes in the world – of creating a just and humane society – would be completed. That guarantee was absolute, and the messianic hope was for a divinely ordained agent to complete the task. After the Holocaust, Jewish history is fraught with the possibility of utter failure. At best, messianic agency will itself be historical and hence limited; no longer can Jews assume that human action will not be in vain. To create some degree of hope and of confidence in facing up to the challenges of evil and atrocity, what is needed is a historical exemplification of human self-reliant action dedicated to divinely inspired goals. This is what one finds, Fackenheim argues, in the State of Israel.[34]

By the early 1970s, then, Fackenheim's attitude towards the Jewish state and its importance for Judaism had changed dramatically, both psychologically and philosophically. From that time on, and until his death in 2003, the State of Israel – not the idea but more precisely the concrete reality – came to occupy a central place in his life and in his thought.[35] By the early 1980s, Rose – whose influence on Fackenheim's actions and on his thinking should not be underestimated – had convinced him that "intellectual probity" and existential honesty required that the Fackenheim family make a life-transforming decision: to make aliyah and to move to Jerusalem. The move was not an easy one, either for him or for Rose, and the next two decades were fraught with personal and professional challenges. Increasingly he felt emboldened to comment on the political life of his new homeland. Shadows from his past and memories of past failures led him, I think, to worry and even despair of Israel's future. But that is another story.

As I leave him in the early 1970s, however, it is obvious that the shift he had undergone had been nurtured by a sense of historical urgency and yet also by a high degree of romanticism and idealization. The spirit of the times, after the Six Day War, was elevating, and he shared in it. When he took Israel as the collective paradigm of a commitment to go on into a post-Holocaust future freely, by affirming human dignity while doing so as a religious response, both sides of his claim were subject to concrete evaluation, just as they are now. As Louis Greenspan, in an essay critical of Fackenheim's Zionism, puts it, "the status of this proposal is not clear. It raises the question of whether this proposal [concerning the secular and religious synthesis in Israel and in Zionism] belongs to the idea of Zionism or to the reality of present-day Israel. Are we supplying Zionism with norms it must meet, or are we describing what exists?"[36] Fackenheim never asked, though he could have, whether Israel's self-reliance was as uncompromising and as self-sufficient as he thought it was. Hannah Arendt, whom he never liked, had argued throughout the postwar years that Israel was too dependent upon the Great Powers and especially the United States. She argued that pandering to the Great Powers was a sign of subservience and of failed self-respect. Fackenheim simply assumed that in 1967 and thereafter, Israel was acting politically as a national "white knight" without any patronage or political dependencies. He never worried about how free Israel was, or, indeed, how free any of us are in political terms.

Furthermore, and perhaps even more importantly, Fackenheim never doubted Israel's religious purposes or her commitment to human dignity. He was certain in those early years that the state must be Jewish, and he has his own sophisticated understanding of what that meant, but he never adequately focused on what religious life in Israel meant for those not committed to the orthodoxy in power. Caught in a fog of idealization, he was insufficiently attentive to the intense and often embarrassing conflicts generated by religious pluralism. Moreover, while he was clear about Israel's need to be a liberal and democratic state, his single-mindedness about Israel's security and survival prevented him from responsibly considering and reflecting upon the problems of her democratic ideals, even when he acknowledged the problems and even though in his private life he was sensitive to others in a wholly open spirit.[37]

Fackenheim's fidelity to the State of Israel and his love for it remained firm for more than thirty years. But, one might argue, it was a fidelity grounded in intellectual honesty and in a sophisticated set of reflections about Judaism, messianism, modernity, and the Holocaust rather than in practical considerations. To be sure, his philosophical views were deeply historical and hence responsive to anti-Semitism and its role in modern Jewish life. But Israel was not for him a simple response to the Jewish plight; it was much more. It was a place to which he brought the painful recollections of his homeland and the opportunities and virtues of his Canadian sojourn. Family, memories, Judaism, and philosophy brought him to the Promised Land, where he lived and struggled for two decades and was finally laid to rest.

7
History and Thought: Meaning and Dialectic

From the 1950s through his initial reflections on the "epoch-making" character of the Nazi atrocities, Fackenheim thought deeply about the relationship between thought – especially philosophy and religious thought – and history or human experience and conduct. In his Aquinas Lecture at Marquette University, "Metaphysics and Historicity," he asked whether a conception of human selfhood as historically situated self-making and self-discovery could nonetheless still allow for philosophical transcendence. The lecture was surely a high point in his reflections on these issues. But this was by no means his only discussion of them. Indeed, the question of whether philosophical and religious thought must be thoroughly historical or whether there is a priori thought is one of the central problems on which all of his work pivots. In this chapter, we trace the most important developments in his thinking about these questions.

A provisional suggestion is that Fackenheim's conception of the relationship between thought and history or experience passes through two stages. In his early work, from the late 1940s through 1967–8, his approach is philosophical or analytical. During this period, he considers the nature of human selfhood, the character of philosophical thinking, especially metaphysical thinking, and the question of whether thought can attain what he calls "transcendence." Thomas Nagel in his widely read book *The View from Nowhere* argues that while human beings always aspire to an objective or detached point of view, there are features of one's subjective or personal point of view that are unavoidable and that limit the attainment of such objectivity.[1] Nonetheless, he adds, human beings aspire to objectivity and attain it to some degree. Fackenheim's question, in this early period, is whether a very radical conception of this subjective first-personal perspective, derived from Heidegger and Sartre, permits the attainment of this kind of objectivity. Another way of putting the issue is Hegelian: Is all subjectivity in the end assimilated to the perspective of philosophical consciousness, or is there a level of subjectivity or subjective particularity that is incomprehensible? And if so, is the thinking of that subjectivity ultimately always historical? However we formulate the issue, it is a matter of great importance for Fackenheim, for it has telling consequences for what philosophy and religious thought mean and for the historicity of language and thought.

The second stage of Fackenheim's consideration of this issue is concrete and substantive. From the late 1960s and his engagement with the Holocaust and the Nazi atrocities, Fackenheim's understanding of the historicity of thought is a feature of his reflection about the way that philosophy – and religious thought in particular – can or cannot comprehend, incorporate, and assimilate radical evil. An alternative way of putting this question is: Does the Holocaust show that there is no such thing as a priori thinking? Does it show that all thought is ultimately historical? Must Fackenheim accept an unconditional historicism?

Not only does Fackenheim's thinking about the historicity of thought – what I will call "historicism" – go through these two stages, from a purely philosophical analysis to a more concrete, substantive testing, so to speak; but it also shifts from the conviction that there is philosophical transcendence to the conviction that no concepts or principles or claims are unqualifiedly immune from historical modification and possibly even refutation. That is, in his early period, he thinks there is cognitive objectivity of an ultimate kind; in his later period, he denies there is. In this later period, he admits that all our thinking is historical, contingent, and pragmatic; in his early period, he does not. The point of this chapter is to explore these developments as well as changes in Fackenheim's treatment of this important set of issues.

Fackenheim was, in many ways, an original and perhaps even an isolated thinker and philosopher. He was familiar with the Western philosophical tradition, and he read widely in it. But he was not engaged in the ongoing philosophical communities, either continental or analytic. Both these communities, during the latter half of the twentieth century, were involved in questions regarding realism, foundationalism, objectivity, and relativism. Hermeneutics and interpretation and the historical and social contextuality of human existence and hence of language and thought, these were all central themes for Gadamer,

Ricoeur, Foucault, Derrida, and a host of others, from Richard Rorty to Stanley Fish.[2] Yet by and large, Fackenheim did not read this literature, nor did he study the ways in which contemporary analytic philosophers debated these issues. It is helpful, however, to use these discussions to clarify what Fackenheim claimed and his arguments and positions, for he was certainly engaged with these themes, albeit from his own distinctive point of view. In short, drawing on figures such as Richard Rorty, Charles Taylor, and Hilary Putnam can help us understand Fackenheim's views about historicism and the historicity of religious and philosophical thought.

One common strategy would be to begin with a discussion of the fact–value distinction. One might, for example, contrast moral claims and statements about secondary qualities with those that science makes about natural states of affairs. One approach would be to show what contextual features determine the meaning and truth of moral judgments, evaluative statements in general, and sensory claims and to show that they are not present in the case of claims in the natural sciences – that is, claims regarding scientific knowledge. In this regard, Bernard Williams comes to mind.[3] On the other hand, Putnam, in *Reason, Truth, and History*, argues that the same considerations that apply to moral judgments also apply to scientific ones; there is no sharp and clear distinction between factual and evaluative statements.[4] Even factual and scientific claims are qualified by evaluative considerations. All involve levels of evidence, degrees of justification, and so forth. Since we always argue and judge from within a framework of meaning and speaking, all our judgments are determined by the rules and practices within such frameworks. Still, there is objectivity, or standards of realism, within such frameworks; there is realism but it is an internal realism and not an external or detached realism. In a similar spirit, Rorty argues that all our talk and our thought is historically situated but nonetheless within our practices and that there are standards of what is acceptable and what is unconditionally condemned or rejected. In his collection *Contingency, Irony and Solidarity*, he puts this by saying that while we are all ironists, nonetheless there are some things – torture and cruelty – that we unconditionally oppose.[5] Although he does not put it this way, Fackenheim ultimately arrives at a position much like this, as we shall see.

But we are getting ahead of ourselves. To understand what Fackenheim, in his magnum opus *To Mend the World*, thinks about the historicity and hermeneutical character of human existence and hence about the historicity and hermeneutical character of human thought and speech, we need to begin at the beginning, and this means to return to his work of the immediate postwar period.

The Problem of History and Thought

What do I mean by the expression "the problem of history and thought?" If, by "history," I mean all that happens in the world, including natural occurrences and human actions, I could mean by this expression the problem of understanding how thought is *about* history – that is, how thought is about the natural events and human conduct that constitute what happens in the world. First of all, there is the problem of how thoughts – concepts, statements, and principles – can be about the world we experience at all. Second, there is the problem of how human beings, as thinking beings, can think about historical occurrences and worldly events. That is, the problem might be about the metaphysical question of how thought can be related to what is in the world, or it might be about the psychological question of how thinking can reach out and make contact with what happens in the world. Neither of these problems or issues is the one I have in mind, however. I am not interested in the representational aspect of thought or language, its capacity in some way or ways to signify or reach out to what it is about. I take it for granted that both thought and language do this.[6]

Let me put the problem as a question: Is all thought (and all language, all speech) historical? There are at least two ways in which this question can be understood. First, it could mean: Does all thinking and all speaking take place in history? Are all episodes of thinking and speaking historically situated in time and in space? Here I think the answer is obviously "yes," if by "episodes of thinking and speaking" we mean particular instances of a person's thinking something or saying something. In every particular case of a person's thinking or saying something, we can ask in what ways the person's attitudes, interests, recollections, goals, and understanding influenced the thought or the utterance; we can also ask how the person's situation – his cultural background, family upbringing, and so forth – affected what he was thinking or saying – that is, what he took it to mean, what he thought he was doing by saying it, and so forth. This set of issues could be what the question, whether all thought and language is historical, means. This is not the problem that Fackenheim has in mind.

But there is a second way of understanding the question. It could mean: Are all thoughts and all statements (or other linguistic tokens) in all cases determined by historical factors, and this means by factors that change from one time to another, one cultural and social setting to another, one overall historical context to another? That is, is it the case that while concepts and claims, words and statements, may look the same when introduced into different historical and cultural venues, their meaning, their point, and their truth are all essentially shaped or determined by these different venues? If the answer to this question is "yes," then no concepts, words, thoughts, or statements can be understood a priori or independently of an understanding of how and when they occur. When it comes to truth and knowledge, there is no truth and no knowledge that is independent of historically situated experience and understanding. All beliefs and all truths are historical. Or, put another way, all thinking and all speaking are hermeneutical, to apply a term that Gadamer appropriates from Heidegger, who uses it to characterize the situated and perspectival character of all human existence. For Gadamer and others like Ricoeur, human conversation and the understanding of texts are, like human existence itself, situated and perspectival in this way; they are hermeneutical. Human thought and speech are hermeneutical because human existence is. There are no timeless truths, ahistorical meanings, absolute principles, and so forth. Platonism is false.

It is this last problem that troubles Fackenheim.[7] It is a problem about whether certain truths are unconditionally true, that is, whether their meaning is fixed independently of historical contingencies and whether their truth is also determined independently of historical events of any kind. Most of the time, Fackenheim does not frame the problem as a problem about words or language or texts. Rather, he focuses on thought – on particular claims or principles and sometimes whole systems of thought or theories. Moreover, while the question of historicity concerns all of these, and since our commitment to the truth of a particular thought or claim is a claim to knowledge, Fackenheim often takes the issue to be one of whether our knowledge is wholly historical or not, and especially, when it comes to philosophy, whether the highest form of philosophical knowledge (i.e., metaphysics) is wholly historical or can achieve what he calls, "transcendence." Can knowledge, especially philosophy, transcend the limitations of worldly human experience and therefore transcend history?

If this is the problem that weighs upon Fackenheim throughout his career, it is one that engages him in different ways at different times. As I have said, basically he responds to it in two ways. Early in his career, especially with regard to philosophy and metaphysics, he is convinced that philosophy achieves its goal when it arrives at some truths that are timeless and general and unconditional. This at least is philosophy's goal – the goal of Plato, Aristotle, Aquinas, Maimonides, Descartes, Spinoza, Leibniz, Kant, Hegel, and a host of others. All Western philosophy seeks to understand the world and the human condition, but it seeks to arrive at an understanding that includes and is even founded on truths about the world and the human condition that are absolutely true, timeless, and completely general. As we have seen, around 1960, having been won over by the "existential" account of the human condition, an account derived from Heidegger, Sartre, Kierkegaard, and others, Fackenheim asks if his commitment to the transcendence of philosophy and metaphysics can survive exposure to that account. If human existence is historically situated self-constitution and self-discovery, can human thinking ever attain a wholly detached, impersonal point of view? Can it arrive at unconditionally objective truths? If the human condition is based on an existential account of human selfhood, and therefore if the first-person point of view of all human experience and agency is unavoidable, can thought still attain transcendence? As we shall see, his answer is "yes." And even when Leo Strauss pushes him to a deeper understanding of the implications of Heidegger's account of human *Dasein*, he still argues for the possibility and indeed actuality of timeless truth and metaphysical knowledge.[8]

In short, during the 1960s Fackenheim argues that no philosophical account of the human condition and no philosophical account of human understanding and knowledge, no matter how historically receptive and attentive, can threaten the highest accomplishments of reason, of thought at its most detached and transcendent. Thought cannot show that thought is limited historically.

But in 1966 or 1967, Fackenheim comes face to face with the question of whether philosophy and the commitments of religious thought or religious belief can confront an event of radical evil and still claim such transcendence. Here he confronts the problem not with a philosophical system or a philosophical analysis; rather he confronts it with an event, an utterly particular historical episode of a particular character, a character that may be too extreme, too idiosyncratic, and too anomalous to accommodate the transcendence of philosophical thought – indeed of any thought.

These two ways of confronting the question of the historicity or transcendence of thought and especially of philosophical and religious

thought mark the major steps in Fackenheim's examination of the issue. The outcome, however, is not a total victory for history over
thought, so to speak. Rather, as I suggested by introducing Putnam and
Rorty, if I am right about Fackenheim, in the end he believes that
thought and history are dialectically related. All thought is deeply and
essentially historical, but history is also deeply shaped and determined
by thought. They engage each other. We will, in the end, have to show
why and how this is so.

Philosophy and Religion in the Early Years: Schelling

As we have seen, Fackenheim's major project, from 1945 through the
late 1950s, concerned reason and revelation in German philosophy
from Kant to Kierkegaard. Reason, when employed in its most elevated
and purist fashion, attains to absolute truth; it arrives at timeless truths
about the world, God, and human nature. Revelation refers to the event
of a divine–human encounter and the linguistic, textual outcome of
such an encounter or event, but both – that is, the event and the text –
are utterly concrete and particular. Hence, the problem of understanding the relationship between reason and revelation is a problem of understanding one way in which thought and history are related, in the
sense that it is about how two ways of apprehending truths are related,
one being absolute and universal, the other being particular and concrete. But to take this problem seriously, at least to grasp it in the traditional way, Fackenheim had to assume that the two avenues of apprehending truths were distinguishable in the way I have described.
Reason would have to aim, ultimately, at absolute, universal truths,
while revelation would be restricted to contingent, particular, and historically determined truths. This was the way, for example, that Moses
Mendelssohn in *Jerusalem* distinguished the eternal verities and historical truths that, together with ceremonial laws, constituted the substance
of Jewish belief and practice.[9] But it was just this distinction that
Fackenheim came to doubt, for he came to wonder whether reason and
philosophy were, in the end, capable of arriving at absolute and universal truths.

I think that Fackenheim's doubts begin to emerge in the early 1950s,
when he turned to examine the philosophy of Schelling and especially
Schelling's later thought.[10] As Fackenheim understands the crucial shift
in Schelling's thought, it originates with a realization that there are
"facts which the system of reason cannot assimilate" and which require

a new foundation and a new way of thinking, in particular a new conception of philosophy and a new philosophy of religion.[11] These facts are "freedom and existence."[12] By "freedom" Schelling means first the free choice between good and evil and later the decision of faith, the decision to accept God; by "existence" he refers first of all to the existence of the Absolute, which reason by itself cannot understand even if experience grasps it, and then to the brute existence of the particular individual.[13] What Schelling comes to realize is that dialectical reason, as it gives shape to systematic comprehensiveness, cannot understand and justify these two brute facts. This is a crucial problem for the most successful of such systems, Idealism. In two important papers, Fackenheim seeks to reconstruct Schelling's critical response to the Idealism he had helped invent and thereby to expose the limitations of reason and the foundations of a new way of understanding the human condition. In the course of his reconstruction of Schelling's revolution against himself and those who followed him, Fackenheim also comes to see in Schelling an awareness of the problem of the historicity of reason itself.

The strength of Fackenheim's two papers on Schelling's later philosophy lies in his remarkable ability to mine Schelling's difficult texts for a clear account. With stunning precision, he is able to distil the path of Schelling's argument and hence to sketch the narrative of his thought. He makes what is often obscure appear utterly perspicuous, coherent, and precise. However, it is not necessary for us to review the technical details of the arguments of the two papers; what I want to focus on is the way in which Fackenheim shows that for the late Schelling, experience, in all its concreteness and temporality, comes to encompass rational thought, so that in the end his reading of Schelling raises the question of whether even rational thought itself is not essentially historical in the sense I have described.

Fackenheim shows this best at the end of the paper on Schelling's positive philosophy. After clarifying how the "positive philosophy" of Schelling's later period proceeds, he argues that Schelling himself saw that such a new philosophy ends in shipwreck. The problem it cannot solve is how to justify itself. That is, how is the positive philosophy in fact philosophy? How can rational thought explain its own possibility? Schelling has argued that rationality is grounded not in an idea or in reason but rather in an Absolute existent. But if so, it cannot be shown to be necessary. Hence, Schelling calls reason a "necessary accident" of the Absolute existent. To Fackenheim, however, this conclusion is an admission of failure. For if reason is an accident, it is not necessary, and indeed there is no ground for that necessity. The result is that reason or rationality is either "the mere play of the human mind" or "merely the dialectic … of man-in-his-environment." Fackenheim associates the leap that follows this outcome with "contemporary existentialism" and possibly with "certain types of pragmatism." That is, one can be confident about philosophy and dialectical reason and the results of positive philosophy only because one *chooses* to trust in them.

In his essay on Schelling's philosophy of religion in the later period, Fackenheim puts the same point a bit differently. The system of Idealism is possible, he says, only if "finite spirit can raise itself to identification with Absolute Spirit." Finite spirit is the experience of the historically situated agent, constrained by its first-person point of view. Idealism takes it that such experience can overcome its limitations and ultimately become objective: finite rationality can attain the "view from nowhere" or rather the "viewpoint of Absolute Spirit." But if Schelling has argued that human freedom cannot transcend itself, which is the point of his doctrine of the fall, then Schelling rejects the possibility of attaining such objectivity. No amount of redemption can be total; human finitude is irredeemably finite. As Fackenheim reads Schelling, after the fall, human beings are God-seeking and hence God-positing, but this is a form of idolatry, which "hangs over fallen man, like a heavy cloud." If so, then the history of religion is a history of mythology; "the philosophy of religious experience systematizes mere products of the human imagination." Reason cannot grasp God; human experience, when rationally transparent, can understand itself as a response to the call of the hidden Absolute; at its highest, it is an act of submission, of surrender to the divine revelation.

One might conclude that Schelling must abandon reason for revelation, philosophy for faith. But he does not do so. There is too much of the system builder still in him. Hence, as Fackenheim claims, Schelling shows how the surrender to revelation and the response to it can be articulated by reason in a philosophy of revelation. That is, "philosophy may achieve a meaningful concept of revelation, but … how can it hope to identify an actual revelation? … It might seem that a revelation can be asserted only on the basis of faith, and that Schelling therefore must choose between philosophy and revelation: a Philosophy of Revelation is impossible."[14] But, Fackenheim argues, Schelling shows that it *is* possible, as a philosophical and rational understanding of the world, starting with the revelation of the Absolute in an act of will and continuing to show how the metaphysical picture of nature can only be filled out by such acts of will. The story begins with the explanation of why there is anything at all alongside the Absolute. The only ground possible is an act of divine will, which is the meaning of the doctrine of Creation, and which explains existence only by turning to a brute, original act that is itself inexplicable. From this original fact emerges the world of nature and then, as a result of human freedom and the fall, the world as we know it, the stage for human history. It is a world of idolatry, of mythology, in which man suffers the anguish of his situation, seeking to redeem his world and to find the true God. In such a situation, Christianity arises as the vehicle for that redemption: it is the surrender of the human to a divine revelation. "Christianity claims to be an actual incursion of God into history, an incarnation whose purpose is the redemption of man from his fallen condition."[15] Indeed, with Christianity – not a doctrine or a belief but rather the fact of the divine incursion itself – the Philosophy of Revelation comes to an end: as Fackenheim points out, its content is revelation but its form is philosophical, for it is the rational understanding of "the need for revelation, and its meaning if and when it takes place."[16]

Schelling thus saves the philosophy of revelation by showing that the brute facts of freedom and existence can indeed be explained, but they can be explained only if reason ultimately shows that all is grounded on an unknowable Absolute. But that grounding can be understood only as acknowledging the necessity for revelation and then what rationally follows from it – that is, what it means for understanding existence, nature, history, and human selfhood. To return to the language of the subjective and objective points of view, Schelling realizes that all human experience is finite and situated; it begins with the subjective point of view. It strives to comprehend the totality of nature and history, and it succeeds up to a point. It manages some objectivity but only some, for it must admit that certain facts – freedom, existence, the hidden Absolute – are beyond its comprehension. They and what follows from them define a situation that no amount of objectivity can encompass. In the end, however, for Schelling, while human existence and human reason are finite and situated, they can nonetheless rise to a level of rational understanding that, while not complete and comprehensive, is nonetheless extensive and explanatory.

These conclusions are as far as Fackenheim reaches in his early examination of Schelling's late, positive philosophy and his philosophy of religion. His primary reason for turning to Schelling is to see how

Schelling deals with the problem of reason and revelation. As I pointed out, Fackenheim takes Schelling to have argued that a philosophy of revelation is still possible. Revelation, freedom, and existence are brute facts, beyond rational explanation. But given them, philosophy can articulate an empirically grounded but nonetheless coherent and systematic understanding of the world and history and hence of human existence. But that philosophy will not be unqualifiedly objective and comprehensive; it will be grounded in the philosopher's finite point of view, and it will be limited by the radical inexplicability of the facts of freedom, existence, and the revelation of the hidden Absolute, the *Urgrund*. In short, Fackenheim, by the mid-1950s, had yet to expose reason to the critique of its historicity that we associate with existentialism and in particular with the thought of Martin Heidegger. For that exposure, we need to turn to his Aquinas Lecture, published in 1961 as *Metaphysics and Historicity*.

Metaphysics and Historicity: Confronting Heidegger

The next stage of Fackenheim's thinking about the problem of historicity and the transcendence of thought begins with his Aquinas Lecture in 1960 and continues with his "The Historicity and Transcendence of Philosophic Truth," published in 1967 but delivered as a paper a year earlier.[17] The latter was a response to a letter from Leo Strauss that objected to Fackenheim's inadequate appreciation of Heidegger in the earlier lecture. In considering these pieces,[18] I want to clarify how in the two works Fackenheim advances his understanding of the historical character of philosophical rationality and the possibility of objectivity or timeless, unchanging philosophical understanding.

Fackenheim argues that there is no such thing as human nature; rather, human being or human existence is historically situated human agency. The central question of Fackenheim's lecture is this: "Does the doctrine of historicity [that human existence is a process of self-making in a historical situation] imply the surrender of the idea of timeless metaphysical truth?"[19] Or, as he later reformulates it: "If human being is an historically situated self-making, must all its activities be historically situated – metaphysics included?"[20] Fackenheim identifies four philosophers who historicize all human existence and hence philosophy itself – Dilthey, Croce, Heidegger, and Dewey. If they are right, then their conclusion applies to metaphysics as well, and accordingly, "all metaphysics … is reduced to a sequence of historically relative

Weltanschauungen."[21] How, at this point in his career, does Fackenheim himself respond to this historicist challenge to what we might call the objective claims of philosophy – as well as to certain sciences, religious belief, and more? In his mind, if the challenge is not met, there is a risk of scepticism, relativism, and historicism. Looking back from the early twenty-first century, this is the challenge of all anti-foundationalisms, of figures like Foucault and Derrida. It is also the challenge of the interpretation of science that one associates with Thomas Kuhn and later historians of science such as Steven Shapin.

The short answer is that Fackenheim's task in the lecture is to defend metaphysics against the historicist challenge, and it is a task that he takes himself to have accomplished. It is not his strategy to accept the doctrine of the historicism of human existence and to redefine philosophy or metaphysics to meet it. Rather, his strategy is to refute the historicist doctrine of human existence. How does he seek to accomplish that task? He takes the historicity of philosophy and metaphysics to be the reduction of metaphysical to historical questions and this to be what he calls "historicism." If the doctrine of the historicity of human existence implies historicism, and if historicism is false, then so is the doctrine of the historicity of human existence. And the historicity of human existence is false because it would have to "find room for transhistorical possibilities of self-making" – possibilities that include, he suggests, in addition to philosophy, religion and art.[22]

Let me translate Fackenheim's terminology in part, in order to make clear his argument. The hinge of his reasoning is the impossibility of historicism, and here he argues against historicism in a way that is familiar from traditional refutations of relativism. That is, if historicism or the doctrine that all truths are historical (and relative) is true, then either it too is only relatively true and hence there are times when it is false, which makes historicism internally inconsistent, or it is not a philosophical doctrine at all but simply the "facts on the ground." If so, however, then historicism is not historicism, Fackenheim says, but history itself. Alternatively, there is no possibility that the philosopher, reasoning from his subjective and finite point of view, can attain an objective and infinite point of view. But this means, in Fackenheim's terms, that the philosopher must give up metaphysics, since the latter cannot exist without "the notion of timeless metaphysical truth." In short, if human agency and experience are restricted to the subjective point of view with no hope of attaining any measure of objectivity, then metaphysics is impossible and with it religion and art as well.

In order to save metaphysics, philosophy, religion, art, and even science, then, a philosophical view of human agency and experience must "find room for transhistorical possibilities of self-making," as Fackenheim puts it. Here he turns to Hegel, but we can make his point by turning to someone like Nagel as well. The point is that "human self-making," or agency and experience, "must be composed of both finite or situated and infinite or non-situated aspects," one in tension with the other, or what Nagel would call both a subjective point of view and also a capacity to rise to objectivity. Can human agency be the struggle between these two poles – the constraint that makes first-person experience unavoidable and the aspiration that makes objectivity and a detached point of view desirable and attainable – and also achieve some measure of "philosophic self-understanding"? If so, then human agency as situated self-constitution does not rule out philosophical transcendence. Not all thought is historically determined if, at a minimum, individual self-understanding can have an a priori and universal character.

Here Fackenheim calls upon the existential tradition, so popular in the postwar period and to which he himself was committed. Today the vocabulary of existentialism is outdated, but we do have proponents of a similar view of agency or selfhood.[23] We might call it a hermeneutical account or an account of the self as historically situated agency. That is, Fackenheim argues that the heritage of Heidegger and Sartre, among others, provides us with an account of human existence and agency that exhibits the Hegelian tension as thoroughly historical and yet also as a timelessly true account of the human condition. The crucial feature of the historically situated self is that it cannot take up a wholly detached, objective point of view. It seeks to do so, but it cannot, for its situated and first-person perspective is unavoidable. No amount of detachment can enable disengagement with it. But – and this is the crucial point – while this self-understanding is always utterly particular or "radically individual," as Fackenheim puts it, still it is universal. Each particular I realizes this about itself, but in realizing it, the I also realizes that it is so for every I. The I realizes that "temporality and mortality are universally part of the human lot."[24] But there is one more step to Fackenheim's defence of the possibility of metaphysics. It is this. If the self is a process of self-making, of self-constitution in a natural and historical situation – that is, a cultural and social one – then it is possible that metaphysics is also the result of human constitution or construction. That is, there is nothing to prevent even metaphysics from succumbing to human autonomy. Both nature and culture could be human constructions;

subjective idealism might be true. But metaphysics is possible only if the universal truth about human selfhood identifies an unassimilable other- ness about every self. There must be a difference between the self that chooses and the self that is chosen and a dialectic that relates the one to the other. I want to ignore the technical details of his account here, ex- cept to note that Fackenheim's point is that "what emerges from this dialectic is the distinction ... between self and *authentic* self. The self is self whether or not it chooses itself. But only through self-choice does it become authentic self."[25]

This last step is the crucial one. Once the self as self-making or self- constitution is replaced with the self as self-choosing, metaphysics is redeemed, according to Fackenheim. Until this step is taken, even metaphysics, the most systematic and rational form of thought, could be a form of human artifice. "But once human being is understood as a humanly situated self-choosing, this possibility is at once wholly ex- cluded. For what situates man humanly is not produced by man but on the contrary the condition of all human producing. And in rising to metaphysics man recognizes this fact."[26] Put another way, if there is a distinction between self and authentic self – that is, if one must choose to be more or less true to oneself – then there is a sense in which there is something about ourselves that is given to us and not produced by us. And it is given to every self, just as the challenge of choosing for or against it is given to every self. All the content of particular selves might be a matter of context and history, but the form or structure of selfhood as a choosing for or against oneself is universal. It is a condition of pos- sibility of what it is to be a self. The doctrine of historicity, of the situ- ated character of selfhood, does not required abandoning metaphysics or the possibility of the transcendence of thought. Or, to put it in other terms, not all thought is historical. At least one thought – the transcen- dental account of the conditions of selfhood – is not historical but a priori and universal.[27]

In 1961, then, Fackenheim certainly appreciated the dialectical char- acter of the relation between thought and history, reason and human agency. At the same time, however, he had defended what he called the transcendence of philosophical thought and also of religion and art. He was still convinced that some thought was a priori and universal, that there were timeless truths and unqualified truths. But that was 1961, several years before he had completed his book on Hegel and before he dared face seriously the implications of Nazism and the horrors of the death camps for religious thought, philosophy, and much else.[28] We need to ask, was this a position that he continued to defend? Or did he abandon it and accept the historicity of all human conduct, thinking and reasoning included? And if he did accept the historical situated-ness of all thought, with what implications did he do so?

Hegel and the Holocaust: The Inexplicability of Radical Evil

As I showed in an earlier chapter, Fackenheim never abandons the no-tion of human agency and human selfhood as situated and historical. He always appreciates that ordinary agents are participants in the world and not simply spectators of it; they are situated within it and experience it in a first-person way. Even when they aspire to some de-gree of detachment, to a view from nowhere, thinkers – religious, philo-sophical, and more – can never escape this subjective point of view. But does this conception entail that all beliefs, world views, theories, and so forth are also essentially historical? Is there anything about the Nazi Holocaust and the serious, honest exposure to it that would require there be no a priori and universal truths?

In *To Mend the World*, which we shall discuss shortly, Fackenheim in-troduces the idea of the "epoch-making event." He suggests that there have been such events and that each constitutes an abyss, a break, be-tween past and present. But this graphic image, of a chasm separating one terrain from another, one plateau from another, needs to be trans-lated into another idiom before we can understand its meaning for the question of the historicity of thought.

To begin with, a chasm or abyss, between the past and present, repre-sents a challenge to anyone in the present who seeks to return to the past and to recover from it something to be used in the present. Let us suppose that what are to be recovered are concepts, terms, ideas, im-ages, metaphors, theories, principles, practices, and so forth. If so, then an abyss may make it difficult or even impossible to grasp them or to return with them to the present, or both. The progress or passage be-tween past and present is history or time; an epoch-making event or abyss (or caesura or rupture) marks off two time periods or historical periods as radically distinct; and in the terms I have suggested, what makes them distinct is that the concepts, terms, ideas, images, meta-phors, theories, and principles of the one do not automatically apply univocally to both periods. Their meaning or their truth does not carry over from one to the other. What they mean or what they claim in the one period is not automatically what they mean or what they claim in the other. The earlier or "past" repertoire is not automatically available in the later or "present" period or epoch. Even if the terms, claims, and theories occur in the later period using the same expressions, and even if they appear to carry the same meanings and the same truth values, they may not do so. Or, to be more precise, they do not carry over as a matter of assumed continuity. If an idea or term or principle does mean the same thing, it is because a later use has recovered that meaning from the earlier period and managed a way of employing it again, in the present, with that same or similar meaning. In short, any continuity must be earned; it will not be the default application of an assumed continuity but rather the earned continuity of an assumed discontinuity. The notion of an "epoch-making event" includes the idea that the periods or epochs prior to and subsequent to the event are radically different, like extremely different cultures or national civilizations. In such cases, translation is not easy; it is hard work. The assumption is opacity and not perspicuity.

Therefore, if there are "epoch-making events," then no two historical periods are in principle continuous. Most periods (days, months, years, decades) may be continuous, but that is because the continuity is easily earned, easily had. And that ease or facility occurs because no event intervenes that challenges the translation, the recovery. There is always recovery, but most often it is virtually automatic.[29] It is the presence of dramatic, extraordinary events that exaggerates the conceptual, linguistic, and cognitive differences between past and present. Such events, that is, make it clear that the default for communication – of ideas and discourse – is not continuity but rather discontinuity. Or, to put this is other terms, the presence of such events shows that all our ideas, terms, metaphors, and so forth are historically determined – their meaning, their application, and their truth. But this is to say that all thought, all *Weltanschauungen*, all culture, all discourse, is historical.

I want now to ask when Fackenheim comes to such a view and how, in his writings from the late 1960s through the publication of *To Mend the World*, he defends it and argues for it. I also want to say something about the most urgent and worrisome implication of such a view, which is the possibility that it might leave ungrounded a sense of unqualified opposition to evils such as those that contributed to the horrors, atrocities, and suffering of the Nazi Holocaust. For if it is true that all thought and all discourse are historical, then all opposition to evil is conditional.

Fackenheim's earlier commitment to the transcendence of philosophic and religious truth begins to show some erosion in 1968, which is the year he wrote the first chapter of *Quest for Past and Future*, in which he reflected on the development of his Jewish philosophy and Jewish thought and the recent changes they had undergone. In the course of this reappraisal of his thought, Fackenheim turns to the question of how to understand Judaism, and thus he takes up the existentialist critique of Buber and Rosenzweig to the "essence-approach to religion" and especially to Judaism. His conclusion is that the new approach to religion and to Judaism shows that "Judaism ... [is] a dynamic whole, which in its historical career is able simply to absorb some novel events and experiences, is forced to respond to others through an internal restructuring and – this must be considered at least possible – is vulnerable to experience so radical that the strain may be intolerable."[30] What this rules out is an "essence" – for example, an empty abstraction such as "ethical monotheism" – that is any more structured or fixed than this. Since Judaism is a historical tradition of responding to a God who speaks into the "historical here-and-now," it takes different shapes. As Fackenheim puts it, at any moment Judaism is grounded in the past but also open to novelty: "Jewish theological thought, however firmly rooted in past revelatory events, has always remained open to present and future, and this openness includes vulnerability to radical surprise." In short, no matter what Judaism has meant in the past, there is no guarantee that even its most central affirmations may not require reinterpretation and even rejection in the present and future.

In the light of this conclusion and as an application of it, Fackenheim turns to an understanding of traditional Jewish faith and his concept of what he calls the "Midrashic framework."[31] But before we follow him, let me ask what leads him to conclude that Jewish theological thought is "open to present and future" and is "vulnerable to radical surprise." This is how I understand Fackenheim's reasoning. First, he points out that the account of revelation that one finds in Buber and Rosenzweig and that Fackenheim takes to reflect accurately Jewish self-understanding involves a divine encounter with the human and a human response, appropriation, and interpretation in the world and in history. Moreover, he argues that the response is "by no means devoid of structure"; rather, insofar as it is called for by a divine speaking, this response must be a "hearing and a responding," for the revelation is "a Presence speaking to man which singles him out for response." That is, whoever receives a revelation does so at a particular historical moment and in a particular place; the believer who interprets and acts does so in his situation. But not any response will do; it must be a response to the call being made to

it. It is an interpretation that suits its response to a call. What this implies is, second, that "not all varieties of religious experience are assimi-
lable to Judaism." Those are excluded that take religious experience to
involve self-alienation or that identify revelation with some psychological attitude or state. That is, the first limit or constraint on a legitimate
religious experience is that it be a response to a call or claim.

Furthermore, Judaism or Jewish response is even more structured,
more limited than this. For it is not a single, isolated state at all, but
rather a historical process, a way of life rooted in the past and shaped
by it, but open to and responsive to new presents and novel futures.
Judaism is what Fackenheim calls a "dynamic whole," one that constantly responds to events and experiences as they occur. But if it is
dynamic and historical, it is also a whole. As time passes, Judaism's
essence may change, but there is some continuity and a good deal of
coherence. In short, Judaism does have an essence in a sense, which he
refers to as "at least the heuristic use of the concept of essence." As he
puts it, the existential account rejects only "caricatures" of what an essence is. That is, within the flow of Judaism as a tradition, there are elements and features that are more secure than others, and there are some
ways of framing the continuities that fail to do justice to the divine–
human encounter at its core and its historical character.[32]

At this point in his argument, Fackenheim has defended the idea that
Judaism is a historically situated, temporally ongoing tradition of responses to divine revelations, a sequence of events and experiences that
determine how Judaism occurs at any given time and at all given times.
In a passage I have already cited, he further clarifies this historical, continuous character of Jewish experience as "firmly rooted in past revelatory events" and yet "open to present and future," which "openness
includes vulnerability to radical surprise."[33]

The notion of "surprise" suggests reacting to something unexpected,
a response to a confrontation with the unknown, the unusual, and the
inexplicable. And "radical surprise" points beyond a state conditioned
by a temporary failure or lapse towards a deep and unbounded shock
or amazement that abides. In short, Fackenheim seems to be suggesting
that Jewish belief must not exclude as possible a sense of the unexpected, of utter disturbance or imbalance, of unconditional alteration or
rejection of what had been accepted and relied upon. What, however,
has led him to think so? Moreover, what has led him to think that traditional Jewish theology and its Midrashic framework have always been
open in this way, even if both are dialectical and whole?

"Openness" should be associated with receptivity to change, to alteration or modification, to rejection, or to something like being nullified or erased. Fackenheim uses the term "vulnerability," and this clearly suggests susceptibility to being overcome. The idea is one of not being fixed or firm, secure or permanent. When he says that Jewish belief òr Jewish theology is open, what he says bears these suggestions; and when he applies openness to the theology articulated in midrashic literature, he means that the midrashic system of belief, dialectically structured and a coherent whole, is nonetheless insecure and impermanent. I will say something in a subsequent chapter about what makes midrash a whole and also what makes it dialectical. Here, I want to focus on its receptivity to change and even to being refuted or overcome.

"The Torah was given at Sinai, yet it is given whenever a man receives it, and a man must often hear the old commandments in new ways ... Such openness is necessary if history is to be serious."[34] This vulnerability is a theoretical claim, about Jewish belief, Jewish faith and theology. Fackenheim follows that claim by proposing that until the twentieth century, such vulnerability was only a theoretical possibility, but now, after Auschwitz, the possibility is an actuality. That is, after the Nazi horrors, the threat to a post-Holocaust recovery of pre-Holocaust Jewish beliefs – punishment for sin, redemption, covenantal responsibility, and more – is real.

What led Fackenheim to such a conclusion, and what does it mean? First, we should realize that it is in fact only one aspect of a much larger, much more extreme view. It is a conclusion explicitly about Jewish belief, but by implication that conclusion applies as well to *all* religious belief, and more, to philosophy, art, science – to all thought. It is the claim that "if history is to be serious," then all thought is vulnerable to "radical surprise" – that is, if historical events are to carry some epistemic or cognitive weight, then thought must be vulnerable to finding historical events and experience recalcitrant, to being unable to comprehend, incorporate, or assimilate the surprises of history, to utter particularities of a cognitively resistant kind. And this means that for any domain of thought, history would make a difference. As we have explained, an event could occur that would make it impossible to recover in the present the meanings and truths of the past. That is, if history is always to matter, then there are no a priori concepts or principles.

In part, let me suggest, what led Fackenheim to this realization was his study of Hegel and something he came to see about Hegel's system and its relation to history. Furthermore, what led him to this conclusion was the special relationship between Hegel's thought and radical evil, an evil that cannot be explained or understood within even the most embracing, most comprehensive of philosophical systems. What did Fackenheim mean when he said that if Hegel were alive today, he would no longer be a Hegelian?[35]

Fackenheim's reflections on this question began at least with the last chapter of *The Religious Dimension in Hegel's Thought* of 1968. What he had in mind were the twin features of the Hegelian system that would today put it into question. The one is its claim to comprehensiveness; Hegel had argued that if Reason is divine and the essence of Spirit, then everything is included within it. Ultimately, all that is actual is rational. Every event, every experience, and every fact is meaningful; nothing is without a purpose, a role within a perfectly coherent whole. The second feature is that while the system is a whole of Reason, that Reason is realized in history. Hence, as Hegel famously put it in the Preface to the *Philosophy of Right*, philosophy comes on the scene with dusk, after the day, to paint its grey on grey. Philosophy does not change history; it *comprehends* history. Hegel's assumption is that the true philosophy, the Hegelian system, only comes on the scene when history has reached its ultimate rationality, and this means when all central differences and polarities have been overcome in higher syntheses or unities and when everything has found its place in a perfect social and political whole. But the combination of these two features of the Hegelian system leads to a kind of cosmic *modus tolens*: if history includes dichotomies that resist overcoming and unity, or if history registers facts that are wholly beyond rational meaningfulness and that resist explanation and understanding, then the system has been falsified.[36] What remains is a fragmented world, a world of differences and tensions that belie the completeness and the viability of philosophical system itself, to the degree that Hegel's system is the most successful version that has yet been produced. As Fackenheim puts it,

Hegel's "science" can appear on the scene only when the time is ripe for it. Reason is divine only because it has been revealed to be so by history … But what if Hegel's appraisal of his own age, and hence of all history, was radically mistaken? Or what if epoch-making events were to occur which destroyed all grounds of the Hegelian estimate, either of modern secular freedom, or of modern Protestant faith, or of the inner bond between them?[37]

In Fackenheim's eyes, in the end, I think that it is the twin realities of Judaism and the radical evil of the Nazi death camps that would be the levers of such a *modus tolens*.[38] In the background lies the fragmentation of the Western world, but against this background, for Fackenheim, the chief recalcitrant phenomena are the separation of the divine and the human and that of any good and an evil that is unredeemable, what he calls "radical anti-Spirit." The very existence of Judaism in the contemporary world and its vitality confirm the reality of a divine–human covenant that is grounded in the relationship between God and the Jewish people. The reality and the truth of Judaism, then, tell against the claim of the Hegelian system to unite the divine with the human and to find the divine in history and not beyond it.

In Nazi Germany "at work was an all-too-spiritual anti-Spirit that affirmed the modern identity of the divine nature and the human in an unprecedented, enthusiastic, self-sacrificing celebration of hatred, degradation, and murder."[39] Here all of our technological knowledge was subordinated to the most heinous purposes. In 1973 Fackenheim can say that "no philosophy has yet dared to face the scandal of the Nazi murder camp" and that Hegel's claim to a wholly comprehensive mediation of all differences, all tensions, leaves him with no excuses and no devices to avoid the task. Hence, "after Auschwitz, the principle of the universal mediation of all things" has been shattered in life and in thought.[40] As a result the Hegelian system, the philosophical thought with the most comprehensive goals, is shown to lie in pieces.

In short, the fact that Nazi evil is incommensurable with reason and hence with thought in its most compelling form, the philosophical system, shows that there are events that thought cannot comprehend. But this fact implies, as I have argued, that no two periods of history are continuous without that continuity having been earned. Or, in other words, the meaning and truth of the concepts, discourse, theories, and metaphors that we use must always be recovered in every period, by distinct audiences, in differing contexts. Meaning is constituted by the interaction between texts and readers, speakers and listeners, pasts and presents. History is a concatenation of events and experiences, in complex arrays and networks, and all our ideas and our thinking go on within it and are determined by those responding within it. And after meaning, then truth, for what constitutes accuracy, correctness, justification, understanding, and knowledge arise too within that flux, that array. The point – or at least one point – of Fackenheim's attention to the unprecedented character of the Holocaust as a historical rupture or break is the appreciation of the historicity of all thought and all discourse. This point is much of what it means to say that as an event it is epoch making.[41] In principle, every age or period could be radically separated from what precedes it, but in fact only some ages or periods are so severed. But the implication of the very concept of an epoch-making event is the historicity of thought, culture, and language, of what Hegel would have called objective spirit.

Epoch-making Events in *To Mend the World*

Earlier I suggested that if Fackenheim did indeed come to think that all thought is historical, then the risk is that with this claim we have lost all sense of objectivity, or of what we might call "absolute principle." In recent decades, this has been one kind of criticism levelled at the post-modernism associated with thinkers as diverse as Foucault, Derrida, Rorty, and Fish.[42] Old doubts arise at this point – doubts that circulate around the notions of scepticism, relativism, and historicism. Indeed, one wonders, if all meanings are historical and all truths are conditional, is there no such thing as an unconditional opposition to the extraordinary explosions of inhumanity and atrocity that we call the Nazi death camps and that mark the decades since those horrific events? Have we lost all groundedness? Are human dignity and worth negotiable commodities? To clarify Fackenheim's most mature views on these matters, we need to turn to *To Mend the World* and to his concept of "epoch-making events," his account of human existence as hermeneutical, and his conception of duty or obligation in a post-Holocaust world.

There is no more complex and subtle argument in all of Fackenheim's writings than the one we find in Chapter IV of *To Mend the World*. The chapter is titled "Historicity, Rupture, and *Tikkun Olam* ('Mending the World'): From Rosenzweig beyond Heidegger." In a sense, the title tells it all. Here Fackenheim formulates the historical situatedness of thought and life. He then shows that a commitment to such historicity leaves open the possibility of an event that would "rupture" the seeming continuities of the flow of history and pose a challenge to any recovery of the past in the present. But if one lives after such a rupture, such a break or caesura, one must go on. The question is how, and Fackenheim argues that in order to go on authentically, thinking and thought after the event must take the shape of repair, of mending if only partially the shattered whole of the past, of seeing the past through a glass darkly.

Hence, if traditional philosophy had already been surpassed by Rosenzweig's formulation of a new way of thinking – existential or hermeneutical, historically situated thinking – then the response to its openness to unconditional rupture, if it is seriously and responsibly historical and open to historical rupture, is to go beyond Heidegger's inadequate if resolute human existence and to take on some form of opposition and repair or another. This sketch tells us what this momentous chapter is about, but it is not sufficient. Although we cannot here explore all of its nuances, in order to grasp what Fackenheim means, we must clarify further some steps along the way.

In a footnote, Fackenheim recalls that as a young student he was told that the "great philosophical task was to 'overcome historicism.'"[43] What he means is that philosophy's goal is to identify and articulate a priori, absolute truths about the most fundamental things. It cannot survive the thought that all truths are historically relative. How can it "overcome" this obstacle? The greatest challenge to this ideal of philosophy is Heidegger's philosophy, for Heidegger provided in *Being and Time* a "thoroughgoing attempt to explicate radically the historicity of human *Dasein* as such and as a whole … [Human] thinking as well as his *Dasein* [existence] is toward death."[44] But, Fackenheim notes, the aspiration to transcendence, to objective truth, is embedded in ordinary life; it is a yearning still present even in the light of Heidegger's analysis. Thus, we are faced with the problem of historicism as Fackenheim formulated it in his earlier writings: If all human existence and human thinking is historically situated, how is it possible for thought to achieve genuine transcendence? In *To Mend the World* Fackenheim claims that the problem arises with Kant and the German Idealists. The Kantian–Fichtean formulation is: "To philosophize is to think neither about objects nor about subjects but rather about the subject–object relation; to do so is to transcend that relation: but how is such a transcendence possible for a subject that is a subject only by virtue of standing in that relationship?" The more Schellingian or Hegelian formulation replaces the framework of judgment, cognitive and logical, with the notion of experience: "Philosophy is an inescapable thought-activity about experience; as such it transcends all experience: but how is this inescapable activity possible for a self existing in the midst of experience?"[45] If philosophy is to be philosophy – so Fackenheim argues – and by implication if science is to be science and religious thought is to be truth about God and revelation, then somehow it must be possible for the thinking of historically, socially, and culturally embedded agents to rise in thought beyond the limitations and conditions of their situation. Here again we have the problem formulated by Fackenheim earlier and as central to Foucault, Derrida, Rorty, Taylor, MacIntyre, Putnam, and Nagel as it is to him and to the Idealist tradition. What makes the Heideggerian formulation so radical, Fackenheim then argues, is that unlike the Idealists, he refuses to allow as "an experiential matrix for transcending thought" anything beyond the finite and the historical; for him "*Dasein* is and remains bound to finitude, and is nowhere able to transcend it."[46] There is no room for the Absolute or the Infinite. Hence, with Heidegger, we get the most radical and most challenging posing of the question, and this is what Fackenheim means when he says of Heidegger that for him "historicity is itself inseparable from transcendence."[47]

But, Fackenheim now clarifies, the notion of historicity is not just tied to the question of finitude and also to contextual and situational limitations; it is also tied to a notion of temporality, of past and present and future, of being situated in a "river of time." In concrete temporality, then, the self is situated with others, in a community, and it is always provided with an inherited tradition whose resources it engages as it chooses and acts. For Heidegger, the self is engaged in a quest for Being in relation to the tradition of Western philosophy. Fackenheim is not concerned with such a quest; rather, he is interested in the historical situatedness of human existence and the self's aspiration to engage with the Absolute. For him, however the self seeks to act, it does so in terms of the resources of the past, and it does so in a way that must stay with history and that cannot flee it, if it is to be authentic. That is, the side of Heidegger that interests Fackenheim most here is the role of decision and decisiveness and hence of agency and action.

In Heidegger there are no independent standards for such decisions and such actions.[48] However, such decisions and actions, without any independent standards, are very much historical and concrete. They occur in time and in history, that is, in situations marked by cultural, political, economic, and other conditions. "But what, other than having the characteristic of authentic decisiveness, these actions ought to be or will be, the work [*Being and Time*] cannot say. This was the condition of Heidegger's thought when his own *Volk* [people, community] made a fateful decision, and when the ontological thinker Heidegger made an ontic [concrete, actual] decision of great consequence – the only such decision he was to make during his whole life."[49] Fackenheim is referring here, of course, to Heidegger's infamous decision to become a

Nazi and, as Rector of Freiburg University, to advocate the goals of Nazism and the rule of the Führer.[50] Whence have we come? And to what point have we arrived? In these early sections of Chapter IV, Fackenheim has reformulated his account of the challenge that an account of historically situated selfhood poses for the tradition of Western philosophy and also for science, religious thought, and other claims to cognitive transcendence, to the attainment of a priori and unconditional knowledge. He has also shown how Heidegger's analysis of human existence in *Being and Time* deepens that challenge. At this juncture, having emphasized the concrete historical nature of human existence and agency, he introduces an event that he takes to be "epoch making" and "disruptive." That is, in the next three subsections of the chapter he turns to the Holocaust and to Heidegger and others who, in life and in thought, acted towards Nazism and its atrocities in inauthentic ways. His purpose is to show that the events we associate with Nazism and the death camps posed "temporal and historical" challenges that immobilized such thinking. These events did – or at least seemed to do – what Theodor Adorno said they did: Auschwitz paralysed our metaphysical capacities.[51] In this way, in part, Fackenheim approaches his goal, which is to use the encounter with the atrocities of Nazism to characterize an "epoch-making event" and the role it plays in belief and conduct. His account ultimately will define an "epoch-making event" as an event with the special feature that a dialectical inquiry into its agency and its victims produces a picture of response to it that shows how that response involves (1) an awareness of the event as an absolute rupture, (2) a realization of its disruptive character, and (3) an action that resists or opposes it in virtue of its negative or disruptive character. In the course of this argument, moreover, Fackenheim shows how situated human agency and understanding can nonetheless be guided by independent, objective standards. I will explain how Fackenheim does this shortly.

For our purposes, Fackenheim's discussion of Heidegger's Nazism and its philosophical implications is not the main issue.[52] But it is interesting to note that Fackenheim himself took these pages and his treatment of Heidegger to supersede the brief analysis he provided in the final chapter of *Encounters between Judaism and Modern Philosophy* ten years earlier. In the earlier work, Fackenheim charged Heidegger's account of the human condition with Christian bias. He also argued that Heidegger's lapse, his affiliation with and endorsement of Nazism, was a grave one. Fackenheim called it a "philosophical failure" and not just a personal one, although he did not take it to indict what was, for him, "one of the profoundest philosophies of this century."[53] But all Fackenheim provided, as a justification for his indictment, was the fact that the idea of a *Volk*, because of its association with land and a common language, ruled out any authentic Jewish community, that it lacked variety and flexibility, and that it was conducive to a community of obedience and total surrender.[54] The argument in *To Mend the World* goes much further than this.

First, Fackenheim reiterates that the "scandal" is not personal but philosophical. Second, he notes that "the final judgment will probably be that whereas the thought of *Being and Time* and of the years immediately following did not 'compel' surrender to Nazism it was 'unable to prevent it.'" Thus, his basic position has not changed since the earlier work, but his reasons have. The crucial features of his thought that produce these results are two. One is that Heidegger's thinking "hovers between an 'ontological' historicity and an 'ontic' history," which grounds that thinking in history and yet prevents it from taking fully seriously any particular history. The other feature is that "*Being and Time* has exalted an ontological 'decisiveness' that is prescriptive of no particular ontic decision and hence ominously hospitable to all decisions."[55] That is, as we have seen, Heidegger's account of the historical situatedness of human agency can provide no standards outside of historically relative ones. There are within his thinking no safeguards against the most horrific perversions, as long as they are grounded in the teachings of a real leader and in the life of a community bound to that leader's direction.

There is more to Fackenheim's indictment of Heidegger – he goes on to discuss Heidegger's later thought and the notion of Being as *Ereignis* – but for our purposes we can move ahead; in the end, Heidegger should have taken the Holocaust to mark a radical break with the past, but he did not. Even by the standards of his own philosophy, "his thought lapses into inauthenticity,"[56] but so did that of many others – Fackenheim calls attention particularly to Gabriel Marcel, Martin Buber, Isaac Deutscher, Ernst Bloch, and Abraham Joshua Heschel, among others.

This conclusion regarding Heidegger brings him to a crucial question: "whether … it can be otherwise and whether, for an historically-situated thinker, other or deeper standards are available." That is, are there standards, transcendent or otherwise, that are more precise and more binding than the standard of authentic self-affirmation and self-consistency? Simply put, Fackenheim has exposed Heidegger's understanding of human existence and its historical character to the evils of Nazism and the horrors of Auschwitz, and Heidegger has been found wanting. Here we have an "epoch-making event," but how can one take it seriously and not cut oneself off completely from the past? Is it impossible for thought in all its abstractness and transcendence to face Auschwitz and survive? Fackenheim describes in this way the point to which his exploration has come:

> In an earlier exploration we concluded that thought cannot overcome the Holocaust, that where the Holocaust is overcoming thought is not, and that where overcoming thought is the Holocaust cannot be – a conclusion forcing us to assent to a way of philosophical thought that, immersed in history, is fully exposed to it. Now that our thought is exposed, and exposed to that history, must we not conclude that where the Holocaust is, no thought can be, and that where there is thought it is in flight from the event? Is, for thought vis à vis Auschwitz – philosophical, theological, other – unauthenticity the price of survival? Or, as Theodor Adorno put it, in a remark less famous than that about poetry but more ominous still, must it be and remain the case that, when confronted with the "real hell" of Auschwitz, "the metaphysical capacity is paralyzed"?[57]

Let me rephrase Fackenheim's conclusions and questions this way: suppose we start with a view of human agency, experience, and thinking as historically situated and hence as conditional through and through. Such a view, as we have seen, might seem to rule out any possibility that philosophy, religious thought, and such can be what they traditionally have been taken to be – objective, impersonal, detached, and unconditional. But even if all thinking is situated and conditional, why can it not be that the same words mean the same things in all periods and that the same principles or claims are true at all times? That is, even if all words, claims, and so forth are thoroughly historical, this does not rule out generality, continuity, and permanence. But this proposal assumes that continuity between any two periods is taken for granted. What might occur, however, if two periods or epochs were ruptured or radically separated? And what if the event that did so were of such a character that the recovery of past meanings and past truths was put in jeopardy and perhaps even prohibited? This is the proposal that Fackenheim makes with regard to the Holocaust and the events surrounding Auschwitz. And what makes such an event discontinuous with the past is the fact that no concepts or principles available to comprehend or overcome it can do so. By itself, this event is an abyss, a caesura or chasm. If it is unavoidable that one must go on after such an event, the question is how? If there is to be thought, can it be philosophical or theological thought? Can thought attain transcendence, or can it recover without distortion or revision from the past?

Against the background of this picture, and keeping these questions in mind, we can reformulate the issue in Heideggerian terms: Can there be authentic philosophical or religious thought after the death camps and the Nazi atrocities? Can thought survive?

This is precisely the way Fackenheim describes the task of the next two sections of Chapter IV, Sections 8 and 9, which are, without a doubt, the central passages in the book and the central steps in Fackenheim's argument. In these sections, he argues that thought can survive after the Holocaust only because thought survived during the events themselves; that is, subsequent thought is justified because there was already thought during the events. Moreover, thought survived only because life did. That is, as Fackenheim is fond of saying, in the spirit of Hegel, thought went to school with life.[58] Moreover, the thought and the life had content; both were aware of the assault on the humanity of the victims and were consciously resistant to that assault, all at once. It was a thought that opposed evil and that called for the good. Furthermore, it was a thought that could not remain thought but had to become action, to become ecstatic. As I have put it elsewhere, the ontological had to become deontological – normative and embedded in action. Thinking that human dignity ought to be defended demanded that the thinker indeed carry out that defence, oppose further assaults on human dignity, and support the cause of human worth and well-being wherever it called for such support.

I want to pass over the technical details of Fackenheim's argument, about which I and others have written elsewhere.[59] Suffice it to say that it is a remarkable, subtle, and dialectical thinking through of the levels of agency and the levels of resistance that occurred during the Holocaust, organized to show the depth of the evil and the nature of the horrors that the thought had to face and to show too the ways in which different forms of victimization and then resistance came to understand and to cope with that evil and those horrors. The outcome is a grasp of the "whole-of-horror" that issues in a shudder, and "the truth disclosed in that shudder … that to grasp the Holocaust whole-of-horror is not to comprehend or transcend it, but rather to say no to it, or resist it. The Holocaust whole-of-horror is (for it has been); but it ought not to be (and not to have been). It ought not to be (and have been), but it is (for it has been) … Only by holding fast at once to the 'is' and 'ought not' can thought achieve an authentic survival. Thought, that is, must take the form of resistance." It is, as Fackenheim puts it shortly, "a surprised acceptance and a horrified resistance … a horrified surprise and, since the thought that is in this surprise is forced to accept what is yet in all eternity unacceptable, thought is required to become 'ecstatic,' such as to point beyond resistance within its own native sphere, to a resistance that is beyond the sphere of thought altogether, and in the sphere of life."[60]

The point of this analysis – what Fackenheim calls a digression on resistance as an ontological category – is to acknowledge the ultimacy of the chasm that is Auschwitz, the way it severs past from present radically, and then to show how going on after that event can involve thought that recovers the past in the light of an opposition to the content of that chasm, that rupture, its evil, which is – roughly speaking – its investment in annihilating the very idea of the human and destroying any sense of human dignity and worth. As he puts it, "the excursus was necessary because only the astounding fact that existence was not wholly paralyzed during the Holocaust itself could give our thought any hope of breaking the impasse."[61]

Resisting thought and life, then, are possible, but are they morally (or practically) necessary? Are they obligatory? Fackenheim's answer is yes. He tells us that we can now see a way to "break the impasse" and return to the question of going on in thought after the Holocaust, and seeing a way, we also are aware of "an imperative that brooks no compromise." "Authentic thought was actual among resisting victims; therefore, such thought must be possible for us after the event: and, being possible, it is mandatory."[62] But whence comes that imperative? Earlier, in *God's Presence in History* and the writings of the late 1960s, Fackenheim had taken the imperative to be a divine command, at least for the believing Jew. Here he says nothing like that. He notes that at least one resisting victim, Pelagia Lewinska, had felt "under orders to live." She had experienced the horrors as an assault on her dignity and on her life and had felt a sense of duty to go on, to struggle to maintain her self-dignity and to survive. Her thought was an imperative; so is ours as well. To be aware of what threatens our humanity and our lives, we think that we must resist and go on. Her thought was normative and obligatory; so is ours. In lieu of deference to a divine commanding presence, Fackenheim gives us a minimum – a sense of duty or obligation without any effort to locate its source.

Although Fackenheim's next step is to introduce the concept that enables him to recover the past and continue with future thought – the concept of *tikkun* – I want to rush ahead and notice how he summarizes all of what we have discussed with the new notion of mending or repair. He does this by sketching a hermeneutical conception of the self, historical and temporal, by placing within it the challenge of the Holocaust, and then by indicating how, in view of the rupture, some measure of continuity is reclaimed. The role of the concept of *tikkun olam* (mending the world) is to provide a concept that unites absolute rupture with fragmentary recovery and thus that makes it possible to obey "the imperative that brooks no compromise."[63] It is this concept, Fackenheim claims, that makes possible thought – and life – after a radical rupture of evil that threatens any possibility of continuity with the past.

Section 11 of Chapter IV, "Historicity, Hermeneutics, and *Tikkun Olam* after the Holocaust," takes all of these conclusions and combines them into an account of historically situated human agency. I have already discussed this hermeneutical teaching in our discussion of selfhood and freedom; all that remains here is to call attention to those features that reflect his endorsement of the historicist account of the self together with his understanding of how post-Holocaust thought is possible.[64] He formulates this hermeneutic in six steps. First, the present agent is situated in history, and his interpretation of the past is grounded in a prearticulate grasp of that past. After Gadamer, Fackenheim calls this always-already-present, prearticulate grasp a "pre-understanding" or a "pre-judice."[65] Second, this link, this pre-understanding, makes a conscious, intentional interpretive recovery of the past possible. That is, continuity forward makes possible a new continuity backward. Third, the recovery in thought, the conscious interpretive return to the past, is grounded in a link to the past that is already present in life – that is, human existence is already hermeneutical even before hermeneutical thought arises.[66] Fourth, the past – text or otherwise – is not simply passive or inert, waiting to be interpreted. At one level, there is discontinuity or a gap between past and present, but there is also continuity. The past, texts and especially great texts, speak to the present even before the present agent listens to them. Fackenheim here claims that the present agent is "ministerial to the text" as well as an active reshaper of it. The point here is that the past and past texts are not simply unshaped or unformed material; there is something there. There is a meaning or a truth that speaks to the present.[67] Fifth, this kind of agency is neither Platonic, in which one simply submits to the past, nor Hegelian, in which everything is absorbed into the present but "dialogical" and always incomplete, Fackenheim says.[68] Finally, "what speaks through past texts may be the word of man. But it may also be a reality-higher-than-human."[69] That is, the texts and the past may have a divine or transcendent dimension; they may be a vehicle for revelation.

There are three crucial features of this hermeneutical account. The first is that Fackenheim takes it as demonstrated that all human agency, including that of the thinker or philosopher, is situated, which means that it is shaped and determined in various ways by context, and that context includes influences from the past, via the traditions, customs, practices, discourse, and beliefs of the communities of which he or she is a part. This is the inescapability of the first-person point of view that Nagel emphasizes; it is the notion of situated agency that Taylor articulates and defends, along with others in the Hegelian tradition, like Michael Sandel, and that is discussed in chapter 2. The second is that now, after Auschwitz, we realize that the continuity – which in feature number two is associated with the presence of a pre-understanding link with the past – can be ruptured. As Fackenheim puts it, there is no "unbroken historical continuity from past to present."[70] This was the point of the account of the Holocaust as an "epoch-making event" that we have already discussed. It was to show that while continuity is often, certainly in normal times, presupposed, it cannot be assumed to hold in times like our own. At such times, returning to the past will require a special perspective, and that perspective will approach the past – as David Tracy, following Paul Ricoeur, has put it – with a "hermeneutics of suspicion," that is, with a sceptical, questioning spirit, with doubts, reservations, and concerns that the intervening event may have opened an abyss between us and the past that cannot be bridged. Finally, the self's relation to itself and its past is "dialogical" and incomplete; even given the rupture, the return to the past will involve both listening and speaking, receiving and directing. Moreover, the purpose of such conduct is to determine what is meaningful and what is true in the present. Objectivity is not a matter of escaping from history to a detached, impersonal point of view; it is a matter of arriving at results in the course of a conversation or dialogue between the present and the past. But it is still objectivity – or it can be, if it meets standards that arise within that process and that are acceptable and compelling.[71]

The remainder of *To Mend the World* and much of Fackenheim's subsequent work takes this framework for granted and seeks to concretize it.

The shape of post-Holocaust human existence and thought he calls *tik-kun olam*, mending the world – the world of philosophy, of Christianity, of Judaism, and much else. That thought is, he says, cognizant of the radical rupture that threatens to sever every present from the pre-Holocaust past, and yet it is also responsive and active. It seeks to mend but realizes that, faced with such an immense, extreme rupture, all mending will be fragmentary and partial. But it realizes too that only by returning to the past and engaging in this conflicted and complex dialogue with it can the present self find standards or guides for making decisions about what ought to be done and what ought to be thought. Indeed, on this picture, then, even if all human agency and thought is historically situated, and even if we all see the past through the dark shadow of Auschwitz, still there can be philosophy, theology, and science; thought can achieve some measure of firmness and generality. Indeed, it is all the firmness and generality that we can hope to achieve.

Conclusions

The themes of this chapter – which centre on the dialectical relationship between thought and history (experience, concrete events) – were central to Fackenheim throughout his career. In chapter 8, for example, we will see how these themes are essential for understanding what Fackenheim calls the "Midrashic Framework." I have shown how those themes first appeared to him in the context of his early philosophical writings and how they developed and changed over the years. To be sure, there were times – certainly while he was working on his Hegel book – when the issues were of primary concern to him. Once he turned his attention to the Holocaust and its salience for philosophy and theology, those issues became intertwined with the concrete question of the impact of that momentous event and what post-Holocaust Jewish life and philosophy should look like, what shapes they should take. But even as a background consideration, it was ever present. And in *To Mend the World*, as I have shown, it is of fundamental importance.

Throughout this chapter, I have tried to clarify how the question of historicism, the historicity of human agency and selfhood, and transcendence, the aspiration to objective truth and unconditional knowledge, is couched in two different ways by Fackenheim. One concerns the relation at any given moment between the self's experiences, thinking, and actions and the historical and natural context in which they occur. The other concerns the relation between the self in the present and its past – that is, the texts, discourses, and traditions that shape that self and that that self often seeks to recover explicitly for itself and for the present. That is, the issues we have been addressing are at times configured temporally, and at times they are not. But I have tried to show that the two perspectives or the two configurations are intimately connected; they are part of one problematic and share features with each other and with general questions about interpretation and understanding. In view of these links, the questions that Fackenheim addressed throughout his career can be associated with larger movements in Western intellectual culture, from the debates about the methodology of the natural and human sciences of the late nineteenth century, to the influential challenges of Thomas Kuhn to our understanding of science, to the challenges to foundationalism that we associate with MacIntyre and Rorty, to the rise of structuralism, post-structuralism, and postmodernism in the writings of Foucault, Lyotard, Derrida, and others, to the debates within Anglo-American philosophy about realism and anti-realism. In short, Fackenheim's work shares the stage with a large drama. What he brings to that drama is of special interest. One issue is a primary concern with its implications for Jewish belief and Jewish life, another is an attention to the Holocaust as an event of radical evil that is as deep, if not a deeper, reason to engage this dialectic of thought and history than any found even in the work of those other philosophers who do pay the event some attention.

8
The Midrash and Its Framework: Before and After Auschwitz

In *An Epitaph for German Judaism: From Halle to Jerusalem*, his memoir, published in 2007, Fackenheim introduces the first teacher at the *Hochschule* whom he met in Berlin in 1935, Leo Baeck. He praises Baeck's character and recalls the awe he felt upon first meeting him. He also acknowledges him as his "main inspiration." Baeck taught both midrash and homiletics, and, Fackenheim recalls, his "favorite theological expression was *das Zwiefache* [the twofold]," the "main manifestation [of which] in Judaism was *Geheimnis und Gebot* (mystery and commandment) … He did not make 'moral autonomy' absolute, alone, by itself … For Baeck, beyond 'commandment' there is 'mystery,' a term that – with deliberate obscurity – refers to God. But why 'das Zwiefache'? There must be a reason, or even an overarching system. Perhaps I was already looking beyond Baeck for Hegel and, after Hegel, for Rosenzweig."[1]

Midrash was always extremely important to Fackenheim.[2] From his earliest theological writings of the late 1940s through his latest writings, Judaism was for him "midrashic Judaism." He cites midrashic texts in his earliest theological writings, and he is still citing them in *To Mend the World* and again in *What Is Judaism?*[3] Midrash was, as he liked to call it, the most ancient and foundational Jewish theology. His early essays call upon and use midrash extensively and centrally, and in *God's Presence in History* he articulates a virtual theory of how midrash serves that theological function by formulating what he calls the "Midrashic framework." I am not sufficiently expert to provide an exhaustive and technical account of how Fackenheim uses midrash, but I do want to discuss in this chapter what midrash meant to him and to his thinking, and I want also to explore how we can understand his use of midrashic texts and to ask whether the encounter with Auschwitz altered in any significant ways either specific readings or his overall approach to midrash.[4]

To begin, I want to extract a few important points from Fackenheim's reminiscences about his teacher and "his inspiration," Leo Baeck. First, Fackenheim learned midrash originally from Baeck, and there is good reason to think that his earliest readings of midrashic texts, from the late 1940s through the 1960s at least, were influenced by Baeck's approach to midrash, if not also by specific readings of Baeck's. Second, he was quite taken with Baeck's use of the expression "the twofold." The example he gives – that for Baeck, Judaism incorporated both mystery and commandment – is taken from an essay of that name by Baeck in his collection *Judaism and Christianity*.[5] His point is that for Baeck, Judaism is not exclusively one thing, a religion of law or ethics or a religion of faith or revelation. Rather, Judaism is both, and this requires that the apparent dichotomy be in fact a systematic or coherent whole. Third, what applies to Judaism may very well apply to many other phenomena. They too may not be a single uniform thing; they may instead be a polarity, and yet one that unites two features that are in tension with each other into a greater whole; in this respect, Fackenheim speculates, he may have found in Baeck, in a simple form, what he would later find in the most sophisticated way in Hegel and then in Rosenzweig. Finally, Baeck's fondness for the twofold, with its respect for polarities and wholes, if it applies to Judaism, also applies to midrash, which contains classic Jewish theological thought in the shape of comments on the biblical text.

These reflections on Fackenheim's recollections of Baeck provide us with some hints about his own love of midrash and his respect for its role in Jewish theology and self-understanding. But they are only hints. In order to capitalize on them, we need to look at Fackenheim's lifelong use of midrash and his more thematic claims about it. First, I want to look at midrash in his early theological essays, through the publication of *Quest for Past and Future* in 1968. Then I will turn to his rich remarks about midrash in the introduction to that collection and in Chapter One of *God's Presence in History* and his use of the notion of a "Midrashic framework." This brings us to the brink of his exposure to the Nazi atrocities and the Holocaust. Our third step will be to look at midrash in his essays of the 1970s, especially in the collection *The Jewish Return into History*, and then at his concept of "mad midrash" in the essay on Elie Wiesel, "Midrashic Existence after the Holocaust." Finally, I will look at his midrashic readings in *To Mend the World*, *What Is Judaism?*, and other late writings. Here he does not rethink how he understands midrash; he does continue to read midrashic texts, often ones he has cited many times, but at times he reads them in different ways. It will be important to understand those readings and to ask why they differ from earlier ones.

Midrash in the Early Theological Essays

Baeck was Fackenheim's first teacher of midrash. However, his reading of midrash was indebted not only to Baeck but also, I believe, to Kierkegaard and especially to Kierkegaard's reading of the Akedah in *Fear and Trembling*.[6] Fackenheim says as much in his first theological essay, "In Praise of Abraham, Our Father," published in *Commentary* in 1948.[7] How does he use midrash in this essay? And how is his reading indebted to Kierkegaard?

Human existence and hence a religious, and Jewish, reflection on it and response to it must recognize its tragic character. "There are conflicts in existence which can never be solved by a little more effort. Modern men have become aware of the tragic element in life."[8] In this early essay, this conviction, which Fackenheim finds in Kierkegaard, guides his reading of midrashic texts. Midrash as he reads it expresses this tragic element in human existence, and this means midrash reflects the contradictions and tensions of that existence without seeking to resolve them.

The only text we have in which Fackenheim discusses Kierkegaard is a short communication to the editor of the British journal *Philosophy*, published in 1941 and dated August 1939 from Aberdeen. In that short piece Fackenheim focuses on the existential crisis that Kierkegaard faced: How is one to deal with growing rationalism and yet find a way to "jump" into faith with reflection? So Fackenheim puts it. Kierkegaard's real problem is: "How can the finite subject (the individual, soul) find a way to the 'totally different,' the infinite, God? How can the individual, who is 'not in the truth' ... 'acquire the truth,' i.e., find existential belief?"[9] Fackenheim then asks what belief is, what faith is, and his answer is that for Kierkegaard "living in belief means a permanent struggle 'in the Paradox'" that does not seek to go further – as in Hegel – by mediating the divine–human encounter in something higher and in a system. That is, as Fackenheim reads Kierkegaard, faith and reflection on it "belong directly to this struggle." Such reflection is, he says, "existential thinking; it is dialectical thinking." The human condition exhibits paradoxes and contradictions; the reflection that precedes faith lives in the struggle and does not seek to ignore or dissipate these paradoxes and contradictions. Until one has the courage to leap into faith, that situation is tragic; only the leap and the relation with the infinite, with God, can enable one to give one's situation, one's life, meaning. Hence, for Kierkegaard, faith is immediacy after reflection or what he calls a "second immediacy."[10]

In the spirit of these Kierkegaardian reflections, Fackenheim reads midrash. As I have suggested, midrash shows Judaism as confronting contradictions or paradoxes and seeking to live with them and resolve them. This requires that these contradictions or tensions be articulated clearly and not ignored.[11] In order to see this early, let us turn to the Abraham essay and also to another early essay, of 1952, "Self-Realization and the Search for God."

In the Abraham essay Fackenheim contends that "Judaism is not identifiable with the bourgeois 'religion of reason,'" which took Judaism to claim that "man is free, though morally obligated; that God represents moral law; that the messianic age is to be brought about by human effort."[12] This picture of Judaism is too one-sided and is the result of emphasizing certain midrashim and ignoring others. For example, Fackenheim says, Jewish rationalists "stressed the midrashim asserting Israel's election as the result of its free choice, but ignored those that saw it as a supernaturally imposed fate."[13] Later, in *God's Presence in History*, Fackenheim will cite a famous text from *Midrash Rabbah* on the Song of Songs which reports the interpretation of R. Yochanan on Deuteronomy 5:22, that when the Israelites heard the first word of the commandments at Sinai, the word "I," their souls left them. The word *anochi* (I) flew up to God and complained that the God of life had sent it to speak to the living, but they were dead. God responded by "sweetening" or softening the word so that it could be received without overwhelming the Israelites. I take it that it is this kind of midrash that he had in mind even in 1948, when he claims that midrashic statements are not "scientific or systematic but ... dialectical." That is, "they express profound and irreducible tensions, struggles, conflicts – and resolutions – arising in and from the basic relationship of finite and infinite."[14] In this case, the tension is between divine power and human freedom. In the Abraham essay, in particular, Fackenheim alludes to several midrashim that have this character: they express contradictions that arise within the divine–human relationship in a dialectical way.

In this early essay, Fackenheim refers to midrashim that singly incorporate a polarity or tension, and he restricts the tensions to ones that

arise precisely because the religious situation involves an encounter between the human and the divine. For example, in this essay and then
again in "Self-Realization and the Search for God," he cites a passage
from the Talmud Yerushalmi, Tractate Berachoth (13a, line 17), a comment on Psalm 113:5–6, regarding the immediacy of the divine–human
encounter: God is farther than the "heaven of heavens" and yet so near
He can hear the whisper of one praying in a synagogue.[15] That is, in the
very same midrashic text, God is portrayed as far and near, transcendent and immanent. He also cites well-known midrashim regarding
God's justice and mercifulness.

But, in my estimation, the most important midrash that he paraphrases in these early essays comes from *Midrash Tehilim* on Psalm
123:1: "'Ye are My witnesses,' saith the Lord, 'and I am God.' (Is.43;12)
That is, when ye are My witnesses, I am God, and when ye are not My
witnesses, I am, *as it were*, not God."[16] Fackenheim takes this midrash
to express the mutuality of the divine–human relation and in particular
to emphasize the paradox of the dependence of the divine upon the human. As he puts it in the Abraham essay, "statements such as this reflect
fully and consciously the two-way, mutually-dependent, dialectical
character of the God-man relationship."[17]

Four years later, in "Self-Realization and the Search for God," when
he cites this midrash again, he is even more explicit about its special
virtues. The midrash illustrates the paradoxical character of the relationship between the human, which is finite and impotent yet free and
responsible, and the divine, which is infinite and omnipotent. This motif – the conjunction of divine power and human freedom – is a pervasive feature of the religious situation for Fackenheim throughout his
early career and indeed through *God's Presence in History*.[18] Fackenheim
claims that it is expressed in the Bible and in rabbinic literature "in a
well-nigh infinite variety of metaphors … [which should be understood
not] as 'impure' philosophical notions [but rather as] symbolic terms
designed to describe a relation which cannot be grasped in any terms
other than symbolic." Moreover, he says, it is the expression *kevayakhol*
("as it were"), a virtually technical term in rabbinic theology as he sees
it, that "indicates the symbolic character of the statement it qualifies."[19]
The statement, that is, is not to be taken literally; it signifies in concrete
terms a more abstract feature or relationship, in this case that of the divine dependence upon the human and more broadly the fact that the
divine–human relationship is mutually interdependent or dialectical.[20]

I will return to this midrash. For the moment, a few comments will
suffice. It is so important to Fackenheim that he not only cites it several

times in this early period but also quotes from it as the very last words of *To Mend the World*, noting there its early presence in "Self-Realization and the Search for God" and also remarking on how its meaning has changed for him since the early 1950s. The mere fact that this favourite midrash of Fackenheim's is cited early, late, and also frequently in the course of his career is proof by itself that midrash played a central role for him throughout his lifetime. The primary issue for us is not whether exposure to Auschwitz prohibited the recovery of past midrashic texts or the creation of new midrashim; it is, rather, what role or roles midrash can and should continue to play and what meaning old texts can have in a new era.

Fackenheim's treatment of this midrash is characteristic of his appropriation of midrashic texts. He cites it selectively and focuses exclusively on its paradoxical and dialectical meaning. A more robust reading might make note of other features of the text. Although it is a comment on Psalm 123 overall, the text itself presents a passage from Isaiah 43:12, "And you are my witnesses, says the Lord, and I am God," followed by an interpretation of that verse by R. Shimon bar Yochai. It is the latter comment that makes explicit the interdependency between human conduct and God's status. Fackenheim does not ask how Shimon bar Yochai's interpretation works, or how it illuminates Psalm 123:1, nor does he say anything about its author or the context of his interpretation. Nor is he interested in how and where Shimon bar Yochai's interpretation of Isaiah 43:12 is cited in the rabbinic tradition. For example, the occurrence he cites, which he finds in *A Rabbinic Anthology*, is from *Midrash Tehilim*, but the interpretation is also found in the *Pesikta d'Rav Kahana* (12:6; 102b) and *Sifre Deuteronomy* (346). In fact, the passage in *Sifre* is a virtual catalogue of midrashim concerning God's dependency upon human conduct.[21] To be sure, in a footnote, he cites another passage that uses the expression *kevayakhol*, but his purpose is largely to illuminate that expression. In short, Fackenheim does not seem interested in a literary or textual reading of the passage – that is, in exegesis of it; his sole interest is what he takes to be a particular theological point conveyed by a fairly straightforward reading of the text.

Fackenheim does not indicate what led him to this particular midrash as an especially salient expression of the divine–human interdependency. It is possible that he learned it from Baeck, of course, but more likely is that he learned it from Martin Buber or Franz Rosenzweig or both. Buber quotes the midrash from its occurrence in *Sifre* in "Jewish Religiosity," the second of Buber's second trio of lectures given to the Prague Bar Kochba society between 1912 and 1914. Those three lectures were published in 1916, and then again, with the first trio of lectures and other essays, in 1923, and again in a second edition in 1932.[22] Fackenheim had read those lectures and was, by the early 1950s, powerfully influenced by Buber. It is also possible that he learned the midrash from Franz Rosenzweig, who used it twice, first in "Atheistic Theology" and again in *The Star of Redemption*.[23]

In terms of how Fackenheim reads the midrash, the likeliest source is Rosenzweig's citation in the *Star*, for there it is used in the context of clarifying the subtle dialectic of lover and beloved that Rosenzweig employs to articulate the character of revelation. "The trusting faith of the beloved affirms the momentary love of the lover and consolidates it too into something enduring. This is requited love: the faith of the beloved in the lover. By its trust, the faith of the soul attests (to) [witnesses to] the love of God and endows it with enduring being. If you testify to me, then I am God, and not otherwise – thus the master of the Kabbala lets the God of love declare."[24] That is, for Rosenzweig, divine love is extended to the human beloved and within that very exchange, the beloved receives it with trust and confirms that love. In this way, as Rosenzweig says, God's love requires human testimony to "endow it with enduring being." While this is not exactly what Fackenheim takes the midrash to signify, it is close to it. In this regard, his use is more akin to this citation than to Rosenzweig's in "Atheistic Theology," the gist of which is that in nineteenth-century Jewish belief and even for some in the early twentieth century, God is a human construction, which is something that Rosenzweig rejects and that Fackenheim does as well.[25] To be sure, Rosenzweig's point is that in order to interpret Isaiah 43:12 in this way, the "master of Kabbala" had to use an "exegetical trick" – that is, reading the *vav* (and) as "if … then" – and hence even the interpretation in terms of divine dependency on human witness points beyond itself to a real word of God. But the sense of interdependency in the citation is at best muted. Nor is Fackenheim's reading like Buber's in "Jewish Religiosity," for Buber calls upon the passage to illustrate how "God's reality" is a function of human decision, which he associates with developments in the Kabbalah. That is, for Buber, the midrash expresses the idea that "God is man's goal; therefore, the force of all human decision flows into the sea of divine power."[26] A later development has human action aiding in the elevation of the *sheckinah*. Buber clearly takes seriously that the interpretation of the text from Isaiah is provided by Shimon bar Yochai, who by tradition is the author of the

Zohar. To be sure, Rosenzweig, in both places, does refer to him as the "kabbalistic master," but his use of the text in the *Star* is dialectical and not mystical.[27]

For the moment, we have said enough about this favourite midrash of Fackenheim's and its citation in these early works. But there is one final comment I would like to make before we turn to other midrashim. Fackenheim is not the only Jewish theologian who quotes this midrash frequently.[28] Another is Abraham Joshua Heschel. In *Heavenly Torah*, Heschel quotes it along with a number of other midrashim that all make the same point – that God's very being is dependent upon human action. In a talk given to Jewish educators, reprinted as "Jewish Theology" in *Moral Grandeur and Spiritual Audacity* (edited by Susannah Heschel), he reports that when he first cited it, people doubted that it even existed.[29] But for Heschel, as one might expect, this theme is very much cast in the shadow of the Kabbalah and Jewish mysticism, especially Hasidism. In later writings, of course, he translates it into an imperative to human responsibility and human action in behalf of social justice; but most importantly, it is indicative of his theme that God is in need of and hence is searching for human beings. It may be the ultimate source or at least a paradigmatic source for this idea. What one does not find in Heschel is what we find in Fackenheim in his early works – that is, its use as an illustration of how rabbinic literature and especially midrash express symbolically the tensions and paradoxes of the religious situation.[30]

I have been showing how Fackenheim uses midrash as the rabbinic resource for expressing the paradoxical or contradictory character of the religious situation. "The task," he says, "is to describe the living relation between this infinite God and finite man, and to do so as an inevitable participant."[31] This latter point is crucial: the polarities and tensions are found within the experience of the religious believer and from her own point of view. Moreover, when he can, he cites one midrash that portrays both poles of the tension and the dialectical relation between them. When he cannot, he draws on more than one midrash to express those poles. The midrashim he cites in order to demonstrate how divine justice and divine mercy coexist in the divine nature are like this. In some cases, one midrash expresses both; in other cases, one midrash expresses the necessity of divine justice, while another expresses divine mercy or compassion.[32] Furthermore, as he argues, in each case the virtue is "absolute and unqualified." For example, quoting from *Tanhuma*, Mishpatim, 41b, Fackenheim calls to mind that God says, "All I do, I do in justice. If I sought to pass beyond justice but once, the world could not endure." At the same time, there are several midrashic comments that speak of mercy and grace in the same way: citing from *Bereshit Rabbah*, "All men need grace, including Abraham, for whose sake grace came plenteously into the world."[33]

Fackenheim, then, treats the midrashic literature as a single corpus, not a series of books, anthologies, discrete texts, or historically distinguishable remarks. Rather they are a whole, a unity.[34] This presupposition is common among traditional readings of the rabbinic corpus, halakhic and aggadic passages included. One text can be used to gloss another or can be read together with another, no matter what their origin. A similar presupposition is formulated by Martin Buber, concerning the Hebrew Bible, in his famous essay, "The Hebrew Bible and the Man of Today." There Buber begins by saying that the Bible is a book of many books and yet "is really one book, for one basic theme unites all the stories and songs, sayings and prophecies contained within it. The theme of the Bible is the encounter between a group of people and the Lord of the world in the course of history."[35] That is, modern intellectual culture encounters the Bible with the tools of scholarship. It separates strata, distinguishes authorship, and so forth. But the Bible, as a corpus, is one work, as redacted and edited, so to speak; it bears the stamp of one voice and teaches one theme. Both Buber and Rosenzweig refer to that voice or authorship as R, which means redactor, but more importantly as rabbenu (our teacher). Fackenheim is not so committed to simplifying the teaching of midrash; he is fully aware of the complexity of Jewish theological claims. But he does think that underlying all midrash is its constant effort to reveal what Buber calls "the saga of heaven and earth" or the historical career of a group of people and the Lord of the world. Thus, all of midrash is a whole; one piece can be juxtaposed with another; and those pieces can be combined in any ways the reader sees fit to illuminate the central teachings of midrash.

When confronted with the kinds of contradictions, paradoxes, and tensions that Fackenheim takes to be characteristic of the religious situation and also therefore of midrash, the scholar or historian might be inclined to resolve the apparent conflict by one or more strategies. One would be to date the polar accounts or views from different periods and then to plot them to show development of one kind or another. Another strategy would be to assign them different authors and to frame them as the positions in a debate between opposing views. A variation on the first strategy would be to assign them to a single author but at different times in his career and to characterize the shift from one view to another as an internal debate or as a conversionary experience. These and other intellectual strategies would be available to someone seeking to dissolve or rationalize the oppositions and tensions. Fackenheim takes all of these options to be characteristic of a scholarly or intellectualist dissipation of the Jewish insight into the intrinsically conflicted and paradoxical character of human existence and the religious situation. All presume that the point of view from which the polar opposites should be viewed is objective and depersonalized. By contrast, he takes human and religious experience to be first-personal and participatory; it follows that so ought the reflection on them to be, as well as the midrashic and literary expressions of them. Whether the texts singly express these contradictions or do so only when separate midrashim are juxtaposed makes no difference. The tensions that give rise to dialectical interdependence are present simultaneously and are pervasive and permanent features of religious life.

Midrash in *God's Presence in History*

In the introductory retrospective to *Quest for Past and Future* and most fully in *God's Presence in History*, Fackenheim introduces a new concept, "the Midrashic framework," which incorporates a reflective account of his understanding of midrash. He then, in the third chapter of *God's Presence in History*, uses this new concept to expose Judaism to the horrors of Auschwitz in order to understand what post-Holocaust Jewish thought ought to be. This is a rare moment in Fackenheim's appropriation of midrash: it is the first time that he steps back and seeks to theorize about midrash, and by and large it is the only such moment in his writings. Later, he does discuss the Bible and how it should be read by Jews and Christians, and there he does use midrash; but theoretically there is nothing to compare with the theoretical reflections at this moment in his career.[36] Furthermore, it is the moment when he first begins to think about midrash in terms of what we might call its historicity, and this historical embeddedness involves its vulnerability to historical disruption.[37] Specifically, these theoretical reflections on the nature of midrash go hand in hand with a consideration of what the Holocaust means for appropriating today the midrashic world. In *God's Presence in History* there is an emphasis on history and temporality and on the hermeneutical character of Jewish life and Jewish belief. The world of the midrash is articulated for a Judaism long past; between that world and ourselves there is a deep, dark abyss. We are shaped by that past in a host of ways, preconscious and implicit, but any explicit return to that world inevitably involves a struggle. This is an almost pictorial or graphic image of identity construction, a process of recovering anew resources from a distant past, as if going on a journey to a land beyond a virtually impassable chasm in order to recover hidden treasure. The question raised at this point is how to understand that treasure in a sense both prior to and subsequent to that journey.

In his retrospective that introduces *Quest for Past and Future*, Fackenheim provides us with his first attempt to articulate the features and framework of the midrash.[38] This account recapitulates and elaborates on what we have already seen. He says that "midrash is dialectical, and it is a whole, and it is an open whole."[39] First, "midrash is dialectical because it must hold fast to contradictory affirmations." These are the paradoxes and tensions that we have discussed and illustrated. Moreover, he argues, these can be "held together" only if the thinking that does so employs certain literary devices; here, the four terms he uses are "symbol and metaphor," "stories and parables." Fackenheim never explains explicitly what he means by "dialectical," nor does he clarify why dialectical midrash must use symbolic and imaginative literary devices. In lieu of such explanation and clarification, which we could try to provide, let me just suggest that what Fackenheim has in mind is that midrashic thought and representation is neither rational in a traditional sense, so that contradictions are avoided and paradoxes resolved, nor didactic and literal. Instead, midrash juxtaposes polar opposites or contradictories and displays their interdependence – which is what makes the relationship "dialectical" – and furthermore, it does so in a variety of imaginative ways, for example, by telling stories or using parables or metaphors, rather than by formulating arguments and chains of reasoning. Midrash invites the reader to decipher its symbolic meanings; it does not call for the clarification and evaluation of rational argumentation.

Second, he says, "midrash, lacking system, is yet a whole, with a logic of its own. There is what may be called a Midrashic framework, which systematically resists philosophical or religious dissipation of its central affirmations."[40] What does it mean to call the midrash a "whole"? Once again, Fackenheim does not tell us. But we can surmise that by a whole, he means in part that we should not treat the midrash as a vast collection of discrete units that are unrelated to one another in terms of their internal sense and truth. The units cohere in some fashion or other.[41] He does, however, say explicitly that the midrash is not a "systematic whole," and by system he means the kind of system one finds in German Idealist philosophy or in a philosopher like Spinoza. That is, midrash is not an axiomatic or deductive system; nor is it a coherent rational system, like the Hegelian one. It is not founded on first principles; its links are not deductive or logical. But it is nonetheless a whole and a complete one, and the pieces are related one to another. There is organization, order, and pattern.[42] That pattern is its "framework" or its "logic," which is that it is made up of opposites or contradictories that relate to each other dialectically, as we have seen. They pull apart and yet also attract each other. Each dominates the other and is subordinated to the other.[43] The midrash is a network of oppositions that interact with each other dialectically, within a pattern of mutual interdependence. Moreover, by and large these contradictions arise because the participants are divine and human, infinite and finite.

Finally, the third feature of midrash is that "the Midrashic framework is an open framework." Fackenheim uses an image: the Torah was given at Sinai, but it is received whenever one hears it, and often enough one hears "the old commandments in new ways." If the world of the midrash is a historical world, then what the midrash means must be open to revision and even rejection "if history is to be serious." Moreover, in this century, after Auschwitz, this means that the Midrashic framework must be vulnerable to modification and revision or even rejection when exposed to the events of the death camps. Fackenheim refers to this as an "internal challenge" to the Midrashic framework because it raises questions from history, and midrash is about the history and concrete experience of Jews.

This brief account of the nature of midrash and its framework constitutes a theoretical or philosophical reflection on the corpus of midrash, a corpus that had provided him with his understanding of classical Jewish belief. What is new here is the explicit claim that the Midrashic framework, the logic of midrash, is open to historical events, which may require revision, modification, or rejection of features of the midrashic world. In later writings, as we have seen, this claim will become part of the hermeneutics of Jewish selfhood, so to speak. The Judaism that shapes the identity of the contemporary Jew, when it becomes a resource for the explicit and conscious recovery of Judaism for that Jew, must journey into that past by crossing or bridging the abyss that is Auschwitz; what it recovers, then, will be altered by the content of Auschwitz and its evil. What was comfortable in a pre-Holocaust world may no longer be comfortable or even possible.

In *God's Presence in History*, in the remarkable first chapter, Fackenheim elaborates the midrashic world and its framework, prior to its exposure to the challenges of the modern, secular world and to the challenges of Auschwitz. The chapter is much too rich to occupy us here in all its details. What I want to do is identify ways in which Fackenheim's use of midrash and what he says about it develop the preceding account.

As we have seen, in his early writings, Fackenheim cites or quotes a midrash and then gives it a reading. Unremarkably, *God's Presence in History* does the same. The midrash is from the *Mekhilta*, a comment of R. Eliezer on Exodus 15:2.[44] The text points out that Ezekiel, like other prophets, saw not God but rather similes and visions of Him, whereas the Israelites saw him directly. It compares the situation of the Israelites to one of people who see an earthly king and his retinue of earthly servants but have to ask, "which one is the king?" In contrast, "the Israelites at the Red Sea had no need to ask which one was the King: As soon as they saw Him, they recognized Him, and they all opened their mouths and said, 'This is my God, and I will glorify Him.'" Fackenheim then reflects that while this midrash expresses the direct and immediate presence of God in history, it is aware that this fact is astonishing and even paradoxical, for it realizes both that God is so distant that for the prophets similes and visions are necessary to experience Him and that at the same time He is so near that even "the lowliest maidservant at the Sea" experiences Him directly. Up to this point, then, Fackenheim has shown how the midrash expresses a paradox regarding the divine presence.

Fackenheim does not stop here, however. He continues with a quite extraordinary and fascinating analysis of how Jews today, R. Eliezer, Ezekiel, and the maidservants at the Sea are all related not in terms of their status or some other objective feature but rather in terms of what they experienced and what they know. This calls for a philosophical analysis of how memory works from link to link in this chain. What follows, then, is Fackenheim's exploration of what he calls "root experiences" and "epoch-making events" in Judaism. The gist of the account, for our purposes, is that the experiences that gave rise to Jewish faith, the "root experiences," must be capable of making a claim on later experiences and providing a standard; but at the same time, the present experience cannot simply occur or the agent have that experience but she must also know that it was had before. Specifically, R. Eliezer did not have the experience the maidservants did, but he nonetheless must know that they had it. Furthermore, the maidservants must have experienced the threat of doom and the gift of salvation, and Ezekiel and R. Eliezer and we today must have access to that same experience. Fackenheim refers to this "accessibility of past to present" as the "crucial condition" of a root experience in Judaism.[45] Thus far, then, Fackenheim has asked a question inspired by the midrash and analysed what it implies for the idea of a "root experience" in Judaism. Now, however, he asks what this accessibility amounts to, and in order to answer that question, he uses a text from Martin Buber's *Moses* to clarify further what it is to experience a miracle – that is, to have a root experience. What he finds in that passage is that a root experience involves an "abiding astonishment" and the presence of a "sole power," and that in re-enacting the natural–historical event, the Jew of the present re-enacts that abiding astonishment as well and hence experiences the influence of the sole power.[46] There is much that is unclear and subtle about this account, but for us what is relevant is that all of this constitutes an elaborate interpretation of the meaning of the midrash.

We get a different kind of elaboration and interpretation almost immediately, when Fackenheim turns from the divine presence as saving and redemptive to the divine presence as commanding and normative. The distinction is important for Fackenheim. He wants to show that God can be present in either way. But I want to focus on the midrash he uses to explore the complexity of the experience of God's commanding presence, for his reading of it is, in my estimation, the most subtle and precise account we have from him of the dialectical character of midrash. It is also a paradigm of how his work on Hegel had come to shape his reading of midrash.

The text that Fackenheim cites is the midrash of R. Azaryiah and R. Aha in the name of R. Yohanan that I earlier discussed briefly. It comes from *Midrash Rabbah* on the Song of Songs and relates how the Israelites, upon hearing the first word of the Ten Commandments, *anochi* ("I"), die of terror and then are revived by God when he sweetens or softens the word.[47] Using the notions of "abiding astonishment" and "sole power" from Buber's account of the experience of the miracle at the Red Sea, Fackenheim says that this commanding Presence is "paradoxical. For, being commanding, it addresses human freedom. And being sole power, it destroys that freedom because it is only human. Yet the freedom destroyed is also required."

Here, Fackenheim is drawing on a motif that he appropriates from Rosenzweig. At the very moment of revelation, divine power commands the human; if that command is absolute, then it threatens to overwhelm the human; and yet, for it to be received as a command, the human must receive it freely. Somehow, in the same moment, there must be divine power and human freedom, and the only way in which this can be so is if the freedom is given in the command itself – that is, if the command is a gift and not wholly a burden.[48]

The dialectic enshrined in this midrash, then, is complex. I have cited Fackenheim's description of it earlier in this book, but it is worthy of being repeated:

> Hence the divine commanding Presence can be divine, commanding, and present only if it is doubly present; and the human astonishment must be a double astonishment. As sole Power, the divine commanding Presence destroys human freedom; as gracious Power, it restores that freedom, and indeed exalts it, for human freedom is made part of a covenant with Divinity itself. And the human astonishment, which is terror at a Presence at once divine and commanding, turns into a second astonishment, which is joy, at a Grace which restores and exalts human freedom by its commanding Presence.
>
> According to the Midrash all generations of Israel were present at Sinai, and the Torah is given whenever a man receives it.[49] A man can receive it only if he reenacts the double astonishment. If he remains frozen in stark terror, he cannot observe the commandments at all. And, if he evades that terror, he may observe the commandments, but he has lost the divine commanding Presence. Only by reenacting both the terror and the joy can he participate in a life of the commandments which lives before the sole Power and yet is human.[50]

This reading of the midrash exposes its polarities and its complexity; it also elaborates the dialectical relation between the human and the divine. And in so doing, the reading prepares for a philosophical enumeration of the contradictions or tensions inherent in the religious situation that the midrash expresses. Fackenheim identifies three: between divine transcendence and immanence, or distance and presence; between divine power and human freedom; and between "divine involvement with history and the evil which exists within it."[51] With regard to these contradictions, Fackenheim's point is that while philosophy would seek to remove them, the midrash or "Jewish theological thought" refuses to do so but instead takes on "logical and literary forms which preserve the root experiences of Judaism despite their contradictions."[52]

These forms are midrashic, and in order to clarify what midrash is, Fackenheim proceeds to elaborate the account of midrash that he had given in *Quest for Past and Future*. Here he lists five features that characterize the "Midrashic framework," and while they are indebted to the earlier account, they reflect Fackenheim's new interest in the temporal or historical dimension of tradition, which makes more precise his earlier claim about "openness." As I pointed out earlier in this book, Fackenheim's analysis of how a present historian or agent is related to the actions of the past is indebted to R.G. Collingwood and in particular to his notion of sympathetic "reenactment."[53] Fackenheim had argued that the present believer, in recovering the meaning of a root experience, re-enacts the astonishment of the original actors; and in the case of Sinai, as we saw, that means re-enacting both the terror and the joy that arise from confronting the sole power that the original actor encountered. In view of this analysis, the first feature of the Midrashic framework is that "Midrashic thinking reflects upon the root experiences of Judaism."[54] That is, midrash involves "thinking" and not merely experiencing, and this is so even in the case of an experience of re-enacting the original experience. Midrash is reflective. It does not just experience the contradictions of the root experience; it is aware of them, and this is the second feature of midrashic thinking.

Hence, "unlike philosophical reflection, however, it a priori refuses to destroy these experiences, even as it stands outside and reflects upon them." Philosophy as rational inquiry avoids contradiction at all costs. Midrash is thinking but not rational thinking, certainly not of the philosophical kind. It is both inside and outside the experiences; this is its third feature. And it leads directly to the fourth, which is, that it does not resolve or dissipate those contradictions; rather, it lives with them and expresses them. As Fackenheim puts it, "this expression (a) is fully conscious of the contradictions expressed; (b) is fully deliberate in leaving them unresolved; (c) for both reasons combined, is consciously fragmentary; and (d) is insistent that this fragmentariness is both ultimate for human thought and yet destined to an ultimate resolution. Midrashic thought, therefore, is both fragmentary and whole."[55] This is its fourth characteristic. Fifth, and finally, such thinking finds its "adequate literary form" in "story, parable, and metaphor."

Fackenheim does not leave this abstract account as it is. Rather, he proceeds to use an array of midrashim, with his readings, in order to illustrate this account of what midrash is, how it reflects on and expresses the contradictions of Jewish experience, and finally how the confrontation with external, historical crises challenges any easy re-enactment and appropriation of the earlier experience and its meaning. A fascinating feature of this illustration is that he uses several midrashim that he has employed before, some of which we have discussed, and weaves them together into a unified interpretation. He shows thereby how midrashim from various collections can be brought together and interpreted as responding to one another. This type of "intertexuality," as it is called, is simply part of how Fackenheim takes the midrashic framework to be organized, not in its own terms but by the reader or interpreter.[56]

Fackenheim begins with the redemption at the Red Sea and two midrashim from the *Mekhilta*: one comments on the phrase "Adonai is His name" that it tells us that the same God reveals himself to different nations and in different situations; the other notes that all the nations universally abandoned idolatry at the sight of God's saving power. But, he claims, the two midrashim should be taken together, and when they are, they present the contradiction that a manifestation of absolute divine power at the same time shows that God needs human glorification. Another midrash from the *Mekhilta* confronts "this tension" by commenting on Exodus 15:7: "I will glorify Him." R. Yishmael asks: "Is it possible for a man of flesh and blood to add to the glory of His Creator?" Put another way, is the "sole Power" sufficient in itself, and is the "abiding astonishment" irrelevant? To answer, Fackenheim begins by referring again to the midrash of R. Shimon bar Yohai that we have already discussed and that is one of his favourites. This time he calls upon *Sifre*: "When I praise God, He is lovely; and when I do not praise Him, He is, so to speak, lovely in Himself." But even this midrash is not as extreme as the version from *Midrash Rabbah* on Psalm 123:1 and its comment on Isaiah 43:12: "You are my witness, and I am God." That is, "when the Israelites do God's will, they add to the power of God on high. When the Israelites do not do God's will, they, as it were, weaken the great power of God." As Fackenheim then concludes:

> Taking all the Midrashim together, we find that the contradictions between divine transcendence and divine involvement and between divine Power and human freedom are not resolved but only expressed; and, indeed, that the expression could not be more frank, open, and conscious.[57]

Here, then, we have a more complete example than we have yet seen of how a "collection" of midrashic texts can be coordinated into an interpretation that shows the way in which midrash is the conscious literary expression of those deep contradictions or tensions that are characteristic of Jewish religious experience. Moreover, as Fackenheim then comments, midrash occurs from the human perspective and not from a divine or detached, objective point of view in which the partial perspective of human experience is resolved and explained. For this reason, as Rosenzweig consistently shows in the *Star of Redemption*, the point of view of finite human agency is always fragmentary and incomplete.

Fackenheim's next question, which he takes up in the final pages of Chapter One and then develops in Chapter Three of *God's Presence in History*, is the critical one for him: What happens when the Midrashic framework is exposed to crisis in general or to catastrophe, and to the Holocaust in particular? Or, to put it differently, in what way can the past midrashic thinking be recovered in a post-Holocaust present?[58] When it confronts a historical crisis, does the classic midrashic literature seek to expose contradictions and then cope with them, and can the approaches of the past be applied again to the great twentieth-century catastrophe, the Holocaust?

Concerning the crises of ancient Judaism, "the rabbis remained within the Midrashic framework, and indeed, responded to the radical crisis [of the destruction of the Temple by Titus and the subsequent transformation of Jerusalem into a pagan city by Hadrian] with the most profound thought ever produced within that framework. This was because they both faced the present with unyielding realism and held fast to the root experiences of Judaism with unyielding stubbornness."[59] As Fackenheim reads the midrash, the concept of sin was no longer useful to understand these catastrophes, nor was the concept of God's hiding his face. God Himself suffered and went into exile with His people; that is the clarion call of R. Akiba's midrash, contained in the *Mekhilta*, which speaks of the Shekhinah going into exile.[60] Moreover, as he turns to the Holocaust, Fackenheim points out that in this case too the doctrine of "for our sins are we punished" is no longer acceptable; "however we twist and turn this doctrine in response to Auschwitz, it becomes a religious absurdity and even a sacrilege."[61] Nor are midrashim of martyrdom or protest acceptable. And even midrashim of divine powerlessness – as in the case of Akiba's midrash about the Shekhinah going into exile with the people and returning with them from it – will not do, for in the case of the death camps and the ovens, there was and will be no return.[62] In short, no attempt to understand Auschwitz within the framework of traditional midrashic thinking is satisfactory; if there can be post-Holocaust midrashic thinking, a post-Holocaust Jewish theology, it must have to chart a new direction.[63] The main thrust of Fackenheim's readings is to show how midrashic thinking confronts and attempts to cope with catastrophe and yet how a series of traditional ways of doing this are unsatisfactory when confronted with the Holocaust. To be sure, as we know from ample testimony, there were during the Nazi period and subsequent to it many traditional rabbis who returned to the midrash, found such motifs, and appropriated them.[64] Some did so with a sense of pious, unquestioning acceptance; others, however, only appropriated these midrashim with severe doubts and at times with bitterness. But our concern here is not that Fackenheim accepts that no such appropriation is possible, for it would lead to "absurdity and even sacrilege." Rather, what is important is, first, that Fackenheim naturally turned to the Midrashic framework to understand how classical Judaism conceived of the relation between God and history; and second, that in his readings of the midrashim, he heeded how in different ways they sought to cope with historical dissonance. Here the contradictions of the religious situation were often between the midrashic thinking and history, and while the tensions were never denied, there were traditional ways of coping with them.

Midrash in the Essays of the 1970s

In 1978, Fackenheim collected his essays of the previous decade in *The Jewish Return into History*.[65] As we saw in an earlier chapter, one change in Fackenheim's views from this period and beyond is that he no longer treats the human condition as characterized by unresolvable contradictions and tensions. He continues to see the human condition as situated agency and the religious situation as hermeneutical; but the role of contradictions and paradoxes, which he inherited from Kierkegaard and Hegel, has been replaced by the pluralism and complexity of human existence. So we might expect this change and others, regarding the possibility of revelation and the divine–human relation in a post-Holocaust world, to lead to changes in the way he reads midrash and in the substance of some of his readings.

Midrash is present in several of Fackenheim's essays from this period. I want to focus on two: one that deals with Hegel and a Hegelian-inspired way of reading midrash,[66] and another that reflects on the possibility of "new" midrash in the course of considering Elie Wiesel's literary-theological writings.[67] Each of these essays expresses in its own way what midrash can mean in a post-Holocaust world but does so in a different way. One elaborates the Hegelian or dialectical character of midrash; the other explores how post-Holocaust literature might constitute a creative literary response to the Holocaust, a new kind of midrash. I think it is quite clear that there is a good deal of continuity in the status Fackenheim accords to midrash and also in his thinking about it; what changes most of all is the midrash's content and its substance.

As we have noted, Fackenheim was introduced to Hegel in 1936. He studied Hegel when he was in Aberdeen in 1940, and then around 1952 he began to teach Hegel. In the decade prior to 1968 he studied Hegel intensely. I have suggested that Fackenheim's way of reading midrash early in his career was influenced by Baeck and Kierkegaard, but certainly – especially from the mid-1960s – Hegel was an equally important influence, if not the most significant one of all. The essay on demythologizing and remythologizing is an explicit case of his reading midrash in a Hegelian spirit and doing so after the Holocaust. That essay's theme is that literary and symbolic expression is necessary to religious life and hence to Jewish life in the form of midrash – necessary, but also insufficient. More is needed – specifically, philosophical reflection. "All this becomes inescapable for a Jewish philosopher who lives in an age in which old Midrashim are coming to new life and, indeed, new ones are born."[68]

First, we need to see how Fackenheim understands Hegel's philosophy of religion. Let me summarize his sketch of Hegel's philosophy of religion by quoting several statements from his description:

(1) "Every genuine religion … is a totality of existence in which the inwardness of feeling is united with outward action and external occurrence, through a representational meaning that permeates both." Philosophy understands this as a divine–human relationship, which is the way the believer experiences it.

(2) This representational meaning constitutes a "doubly representational religious existence. Doubly representational feeling is a togetherness of being-gripped by the Divine and free commitment. Doubly representational representation is a complex of symbols in which the Divine, its infinity notwithstanding, is involved with the human, and the human, its finitude notwithstanding, is an active partner in a divine-human relationship." For Hegel, Christianity is doubly representational; for Fackenheim, Judaism and the Divine–Jewish covenant are as well.

(3) Hegel seeks to "transmythologize" this doubly representational character by seeking to show that the doubly representational religious existence is a "single self-activity of Thought which can be described, not as human, but rather as human-divine." But this does not extinguish the doubly representational religious existence. "Even if the philosopher qua philosopher can rise to the single thought-activity of a transmythologizing divine-human Thought, he continues to exist, qua man, on the human side of a doubly representational divine-human relationship." Absolute consciousness, the self-activity of Thought, does not annihilate individual experience and thought from finite points of view.

(4) "Hence the task of philosophy is not only to transmythologize but also – if it can muster the power – to remythologize as well." This is the Hegelian accomplishment – to rise to complete and absolute philosophical comprehension but not without reinstating the existence that it comprehends.

(5) But if Hegelian transmythologizing is today impossible, "what, according to Hegel, would result if philosophical thought were confined to human finitude? … [It] becomes merely 'reflective' and demythologizes. Since, however, it transcends reflective finitude sufficiently to recognize the reductionist falsehood of such mere demythologizing, it points beyond reflection back to a religious immediacy which now, however, becomes (to use Kierkegaard's term) immediacy after reflection." Hence, "whether or not Hegel's transmythologizing thought-activity is possible, a remythologizing is necessary by which doubly representational religious existence is reinstated."[69]

Fackenheim finds this "doubly representational religious existence" in Martin Buber's description of the religious antinomy in *I and Thou*; he also finds it in midrash.[70] We have seen an excellent example of this in Fackenheim's description in Chapter One of *God's Presence in History* of the divine commanding Presence and the famous midrash from *Midrash Rabbah* on Song of Songs. In this essay he illustrates such a structure more fully. Hegel's role for Jewish philosophy, then, is to help the philosopher understand how to interpret Jewish literary expressions of the character of Jewish religious experience as a divine–human covenant, but it does so without demythologizing that experience or dissolving it into some higher synthesis or whole. If so, how is the "doubly representational" structure of Jewish religious existence expressed in midrash? Moreover, does an acceptable interpretation require a post-Holocaust rereading, a remythologized reinterpretation?

It is hardly surprising that in this essay Fackenheim resorts to three of his favourite midrashim and interprets them as a single unit. The first is the midrash about the event at Sinai in which R. Azaryiah and R. Aha, in the name of R. Yohanan, commenting on Deut. 5:22, take God to have softened the word "I" so that the Israelites can remain alive and not die in the moment of divine revelation. This is the same midrash from *Midrash Rabbah* on the Song of Songs that had been read in *God's Presence in History*. The third midrash is the early favourite from *Midrash Rabbah* on Psalm 123:1, about the interdependency of God's existence and human witness. The second, which mediates the two, is Shimon bar Yochai's midrash from *Sifre* on the song at the sea, Exodus 15:2, "This is my Lord, and I will praise Him," in which he takes the verse to mean that God is glorified whether or not the Israelites glorify Him. Fackenheim reads the three against the background of his account of Hegel's philosophy of religion. The first indicates that the midrash already goes beyond Hegel's understanding of Judaism as a religion of law: "In Judaism, grace is manifest in the gift of the commandment itself which, bridging the gulf between two incommensurables [divine power and human freedom], makes a human community partner in a divine-human covenant."[71] Then, as Fackenheim puts it, the second and third midrashim show that "the paradox and the grace," which are present at Sinai, are still features of later re-enactments of that moment. But why does he then cite two midrashim and not simply one? His answer is that the first, from *Sifre*, underscores the divine–human mutuality and that it does so by using the technical term "as it were" (*kivyakhol*), which indicates that the story is a story and yet must be told. The second, however, he reads in a different way, one that allows him to acknowledge the significance of the Holocaust for recovering these midrashim.

Fackenheim points to a remarkable difference between the second and the third midrashim. Both point to divine dependence upon human praise and testimony. But the third is more radical. The second presumes that God has saved the Israelites at the Red Sea and that He expects praise for His acts. Yet even if there is no such praise and God may not be secure without it, He is still God. The third, however, is aware of a "grim possibility inherent in the Jewish religious experience, and possibly unique to it."[72] Fackenheim explains it this way: Both midrashim admit that Jews may lack fidelity. But the earlier one admits that even with such infidelity, God will still be God. What the later midrash adds is that "if the people Israel failed to witness, not because of infidelity, but because of nonexistence," there would be no covenant at all. Or, as Fackenheim puts it, "Is [God] glorified in himself if his people are dead? Such religious smugness, if not obscenity, is avoided in the third Midrash. Remaining, as it were, open-ended, it implicitly contains a whole host of religious possibilities, such as protest, defiance and even despair."[73] That is, for those who lived during the time when the people was being annihilated, these are all options, and indeed, too, they are options for those who live afterwards and who seek to recover the covenantal relationship in a post-Holocaust world.

Before we turn to this open-endedness and what is now possible for midrash after Auschwitz, we should turn to the very last words of *To Mend the World*. There Fackenheim quotes this very same midrash, one that he had discussed, as we have seen, already in 1952. In a note he mentions this: "I first cited this Midrash nearly thirty years ago ... The careful reader will notice that its significance has changed for me in these many years – with an immense burden now falling on the 'as it were.'"[74] First, how has the significance changed? In that early essay of 1952 and throughout his early period and even through 1970, the midrash was a primary testimony in behalf of the dialectical mutuality of the covenantal relationship; that was its main significance. But, as we have just seen, after Auschwitz, the midrash must be read more literally, in a sense. It poses as a possibility that the Jewish people may not continue to testify in behalf of God, and Fackenheim takes this to mean that it may not exist in order to do so. Could this be what Fackenheim is alluding to in this footnote? Could this be the midrash's new significance? Second, however, he calls attention to the burden placed on the expression "as it were" (*kivyakhol*), which means that the statement is true in a way but not fully or perfectly true and yet is as much as we can know. But what does it modify? The whole statement "I am not God," or the predicate "not God"? I take it the latter: even after God has failed to reach out to save the people, God still speaks, but it is His affirmation of who He is, His being God, that He denies or admits, as if He is being chastised or reprimanded or denounced – and God can only admit the truth of the denunciation, the despair, the sense of abandonment.

This shift of sense and significance is on display in the last chapter of *What Is Judaism?*, "God in the Age of Auschwitz and the Rebuilt Jerusalem."[75] The old meaning is the same: the midrash expresses the dialectical relationship between divine intimacy and divine infinity, proximity and distance, presence and transcendence.[76] But in our age there is something more. Citing the midrash on Song of Songs, Fackenheim says that it acknowledges the possibility that Jews will abandon their allegiance to the covenant, through neglect perhaps but also through outright refusal to remain God's people. "Great, then, is the threat to divine revelation in history."[77] But refusal is one thing; the failure at Auschwitz is another. In the Nazi world there were, to be sure, those who rejected God and those who clung to faith. But most ominously there were those who could not testify because they were dead, and had Hitler won his battles and achieved his goals, that would be true of all Jews. "At Auschwitz Jews were not His witnesses – not because of infidelity but because they were murdered."[78] Fackenheim calls those who survived a "holy remnant," but he warns against exploiting their memory, the memory of the few: that "few could be witnesses" should not lead us to forget that "most were not witnesses but victims."[79] For them, Fackenheim here returns to the second midrash he had discussed in the essay on Hegel and midrash: "When I praise God He is lovely; when I do not praise God He is, as it were, lovely in Himself."[80] But now he asks: In view of those victims, those who died – the babies thrown into the burning pits at Auschwitz and the *Muselmänner* already dead in life – "did God remain 'lovely in Himself' at Auschwitz?" In short, we have here an elaboration of the reading introduced in the earlier essay and alluded to at the conclusion of *To Mend the World.* It is a brutally literal reading. Using the polarity of divine intimacy and divine infinity, he reframes the question: "Has [the Holocaust] fragmented the God of Israel, into an intimacy of absolute impotence, and an infinity of absolute indifference?"[81] That is, if the God of Israel has always been characterized in terms of the dialectical relation between absolute rule and parental concern, has the Holocaust destroyed that unity, that whole, and left God Himself in fragments?

It is at this point that one must turn, if one can turn at all, not to old midrashim, which still affirm what is no longer, but rather to new ones that express the new Jewish religious situation. Fackenheim broaches such a possibility, of new midrashic responses, in the essay on Hegel and midrash; he then explores it more fully in his essay on Elie Wiesel; and he returns to it here, in *What Is Judaism?*

New Midrashic Thinking after
Auschwitz: Mad Midrash and More

In our age, "not only old Midrashim have assumed new life," as we have just discussed. "New Midrashim have been born. They are still being born. They will continue to be born."[82] These new midrashim come in the form of testimony and stories, imaginative and realistic, and like their older forbearers, they harbour the tensions and dialectic of the religious situation. In the Hegel essay, Fackenheim simply reports three such stories. The first, from Wiesel's *Night*, is the famous scene with the young boy hanging on the gallows; the second is from a visit to Bergen-Belsen that records an interpretation of the rain as God weeping; the final one is from the Wall, in Jerusalem, from a survivor who calls for God's blessing daily on a people still alive in a Jewish state. Fackenheim makes no comment, offers no interpretation. He simply records the stories but in an order whose point is transparent. Overall, the three speak of divine impotence and divine renewal, of the death of faith and its revival, of despair and joy.

In "Midrashic Existence after Auschwitz," Fackenheim describes "midrashic existence" as a life that testifies to the experience expressed in midrash, and midrash as the authentic way of expressing the experience of holding fast to God, holding fast to the world, and "affirm[ing] a bond between them."[83] As we have seen, this bond is problematic and the experience of holding fast to it is conflicted and dialectical.[84] This is familiar; indeed, Fackenheim's description of midrash and midrashic existence calls to mind in detail the descriptions we have already discussed, especially the two from *Quest for Past and Future* and *God's Presence in History*.[85] But if classical midrash has endured the tensions and paradoxes precisely because it refuses to ignore or dissipate what is essential to the human and religious situations, one must now wonder if new midrash can endure the same tensions.

Fackenheim equivocates. On the one hand, he says: "Midrash is meant for every kind of imperfect world. It was not meant for Planet Auschwitz, the anti-world."[86] Here he surely means "classical midrash," that is, the midrash that he has continually read and interpreted, the midrash that articulates the polarities of human existence and divine–human relationship and expresses their dialectical relation. But on the other hand, when referring to Wiesel's writing, he writes that "no matter what its form – eyewitness reports, essays, a cantata, a play, to say nothing of the novels – it always has recognizable midrashic elements."[87] It is not clear what the difference is between a new midrash and a story or text that has midrashic elements, which he takes to mean that it confronts Auschwitz and yet affirms Judaism, past and future. Moreover, this togetherness, impossible as it is, "produces the unprecedented phenomenon of mad Midrash."[88] I do not recall Fackenheim ever using this expression again; nonetheless, it is a helpful one and appropriate. As he points out, the madness is not insanity, and neither is it irrationality.[89] Rather, it is a passionate clinging to a mad reality – to the realization, for example, that the time for the messiah is past – and yet to cling to hope all the same. This is to outdo Kierkegaard's conception of faith precisely by locating the paradox or tension of religious existence in a very dark place indeed.

It is to outdo Kierkegaard in another respect as well. It is not merely to be aware of the conflicts and the tensions of living in a post-Holocaust world; it is to *oppose* that world. Fackenheim's proposal takes this shape: If the world of the Nazis is an anti-world, then how can one hold fast to it and to God and Judaism at the same time? Only if a text can do this can it be midrash, and if it does so it is mad. But it is more than mad cognition if it registers an "absolute protest against the anti-world and its god." And "this protest is serious only if it turns into a determination to *restore* the world," and that is *our* world, the everyday world. But to restore it is not to restore it whole; that is impossible. It is to recover it as imperfect, or as fragmentary. This line of thinking clarifies that mad midrash is more than a story; it is also an act itself and in particular an act of resistance and opposition that calls for and seeks to implement a repair of a fractured world for the future. In *To Mend the World* this same line of thinking, which Fackenheim here uses to characterize a new form of midrash, leads to a notion of "mending the world." Here, however, he does not elaborate what content it might have. What he does is acknowledge its greatest risk and how it must confront it. The risk is that of aestheticizing itself, of shrinking inward and creating a world out of itself and thus of "descend[ing] from literature into aestheticizing."[90] To avoid this temptation, an author like Wiesel in his fiction charts a path from a near failure of faith to his support for Jewish affirmation in Soviet Russia and from death at the hands of the Nazis to sacrifice in behalf of the Jewish state. That is, Fackenheim finds indications in Wiesel's writings of "pointing beyond the theological Word to a praxis whose politics forever questions all theology even as it remains itself theologically questioned."[91]

Fackenheim concludes by describing midrashic existence as the only responsible way of going on as a Jew in a post-Holocaust world. This is doubtless an exaggeration. But this is how he uses the idea of midrash to frame the specifically Jewish mandate to "mending the world." He says that

midrashic madness points to *an existence in which the madness is transfigured*. Midrashic madness is the Word spoken in the anti-world which ought not to be but is. The existence it points to acts to restore a world which ought to be but is not, committed to the faith that what ought to be must and will be, and this is *its* madness. After Planet Auschwitz, there can be no health without *this* madness, no joy, no life. Without this madness a Jew cannot do – with God or without him – what a Voice from Sinai bids him do: choose life.[92]

The language in this passage points ahead, in detail, to Fackenheim's description of the ontological category of resistance in *To Mend the World*. His language of madness, more Nietzschean in spirit than Platonic, affirms a kind of eccentricity, a non-conformism that understands the horrors for what they are and their legacy and that at the same time affirms the future and what can be done to make it better. There is in this joint affirmation a kind of madness, to be sure. I am not sure that Fackenheim is right to dismiss the synonyms – insanity, irrationality. This is surely not mysticism, but it is, by everyday standards, disturbed and oblique. Moreover, it is an attitude of protest that expresses itself in conduct in behalf of a margin of restoration, even if no complete restoration seems possible. In this sense, the madness is "transfigured." It is not rejected or nullified, though it does take on a somewhat different look or shape. Rather than a "surprised horror" by itself, it becomes a transforming act of repair. What is transfigured is its passivity and its detachment; what midrashic existence becomes is active and engaged and adversarial, oppositional. In his reflections on the nature of midrash, now a midrash situated in a post-Holocaust world, Fackenheim goes no further than this.

Conclusions

In the course of his career Fackenheim gravitated to midrash consistently as the most characteristic expression of Jewish theology, especially in its traditional form. I have said this repeatedly, and it is true. It is a point that he never denied or abandoned. Throughout his writings, he cited and interpreted midrashic texts. In his earliest writings the context was his infatuation with the possibility of revelation, the nature of the divine–human encounter, and the life of faith. As he studies Hegel and in particular his philosophy of religion and its representational character, he explicitly analyses the nature of midrash and how it functions. Then, in the late 1960s, with his turn to the horrors of the Nazi era, his interests broaden and change; he takes rupture and fracture seriously and wonders whether midrash can be retained and even created in new ways. His answer is that a new form of midrash is possible, one that expresses these very deep breaks and sharp dissonances; then, rather than simply articulate the dialectic of the polarities that are present, he comes to see midrash as finally "transfigured" into opposition, protest, and fragmentary restoration.

Fackenheim is not a literary or historical reader of midrash. His engagement with this literature is theological and theoretical. It also has something in common with recent trends in the hermeneutics of midrash, especially regarding the ways in which midrashic texts refer intertextually and can be read in terms of one another. The common ancestry of recent theory and of Fackenheim's thinking in Hegel and German Idealism helps make this point less surprising than one might think. Still, his appropriation of midrash is never ungrounded and without conceptual structure, and his readings are not playful as much as dialectically serious and capable of philosophical articulation. He is not a traditional reader, but he is a rich and fascinating one.

9
Finding a Philosophical Voice

Some readers have noticed that with his engagement with the horrors of Nazi Germany and the death camps and his emerging commitment to the State of Israel, Fackenheim's prose became intense, passionate, and highly rhetorical. Some have even claimed that at this point – in the late 1960s – he abandoned philosophy for something else, literature or rhetoric.[1] I have argued in earlier chapters that central concepts in Fackenheim's philosophical repertoire remained stable throughout his career, while others underwent interesting developments. One concept that exhibited both features – continuity and modification – was his very conception of philosophical thinking. Moreover, he remained committed to that concept until his death in 2003. He always thought of himself as a deeply engaged philosopher and as a Jewish philosopher. If I am right that Fackenheim was an engaged philosophical thinker throughout his career and that the years between the publication of *To Mend the World* in 1982 and his death in 2003 saw that engagement take on a particularly ethical character, then the features and development of his philosophical voice ought to confirm these conclusions and express his special identity as a Jewish philosopher.

Voice is not the same as style but is certainly connected with it. Although Fackenheim was always a philosopher, a careful reader of his work will notice changes in his literary style, the tone of his writing, and various characteristic literary features. The early essays, both theological and philosophical, exhibit a clear and precise use of argumentation. The prose is accessible, direct, transparent, and generally detached. His essays of the 1970s are more artful and eclectic in the sources they use and in how they are interpreted, and with *To Mend the World* his writing becomes more technical, dense, and complex. His last writings are almost hermetic at times. Moreover, from the 1970s to the end of his career, his writings become more and more autobiographical, culminating in the intimacy of his memoirs.

This cluster of considerations – Fackenheim's philosophical voice, his changing literary style, and his increasingly autobiographical writings – coalesce in questions that come to me from the work of Stanley Cavell: How did Fackenheim find his philosophical voice? Did that voice undergo change during his career? And what are its distinctive features? These are not merely psychological matters; they are also philosophical ones, but in order to see why, we need to say something about this very elusive notion, "voice," and especially the idea of a "philosophical voice." Voice is not exactly or exclusively style or tone or dialect or inflection or method, but it is associated with all of these and more. It is a rich and elusive notion but one that can be helpful as I try to address the question of Fackenheim's authorial identity.

Stanley Cavell and the Search for a Philosophical Voice

No philosopher has taken up this notion of voice more directly and more deeply than Stanley Cavell. In his revealing study of voice in Cavell's work, *Hearing Things: Voice and Method in the Writings of Stanley Cavell*, Timothy Gould shows that the notion of voice is already exemplified in Cavell's earliest writings, even if it is introduced explicitly only later, in *The Claim of Reason* and thereafter, during the late 1970s and early 1980s.[2] As Gould shows, voice is a useful concept in understanding Cavell's philosophical work, but it is also more than that – it is a concept that Cavell himself makes the thematic core of his work, from his early infatuation with ordinary language philosophy, scepticism, Wittgenstein, and Austin to his involvement with Thoreau and Emerson and his elaboration of what he calls "moral perfectionism." That is, Cavell identifies a central lesson or moral of the philosophical inquiry into scepticism as a lesson about voice, and he takes his own philosophical endeavour as an attempt to find his own philosophical voice, to recover in his own way the human voice that he takes scepticism and philosophy – and especially metaphysics – to have occluded. This explicit attention to the discovery of voice and to its relationship to autobiography comes to a head in Cavell's Jerusalem-Harvard lectures, delivered in November 1992 at the Hebrew University and published two years later as *A Pitch of Philosophy*.[3] Throughout his career, then, Cavell uses the notion of voice to characterize the subject of his philosophical thinking and his own philosophical writing; it is a central theme in all of his work. Fackenheim does not thematize voice the way that Cavell does, but Cavell's conception of voice, and some of its most telling complexities, are exemplified in Fackenheim's writings in very intriguing ways. That conception can, therefore, provide an especially revealing lens through which to explore Fackenheim's persona as a philosopher and as a Jewish philosopher.

Voice is a function of communication, of speech and writing, of teaching. As one might expect, Cavell never gives a definition of voice, nor does he set out explicit criteria for its use. But he does help us gather a sense. What does it mean to "speak in a certain voice"? It has something to do with tone, as he puts it in one place, and the right to take up that tone. It also has to do with representativeness; one's voice may be idiosyncratic in some ways, but it regularly stands for or exemplifies an approach or stance or attitude that is shared by others, and indeed it may be what the speaker seeks to evoke in his audience. But that stance or attitude or tone is not accidental or eliminable for the speaker; it is constitutive of who that speaker is, of her or his identity. One's voice evokes or expresses much about who one is, and it is one vehicle for calling upon others to follow in one's footsteps, to take up that voice as well.

All of this is well and good, but for our purposes we need more help, and it may be that it comes best when Cavell begins to reformulate his interest in ordinary language philosophy, scepticism, and metaphysics in terms of the notion of voice. There is a statement of these matters – exemplified in some of the essays in *Must We Mean What We Say?* and *The Claim of Reason* – in an essay published in 1982 and reprinted in *Themes Out of School* in 1984:

> For me it is evident that the reign of repressive philosophical systematizing – sometimes called metaphysics, sometimes called logical analysis – has depended upon the suppression of the human voice. It is as the recovery of this voice (as from an illness) that ordinary language philosophy is, as I have understood and written about it, before all to be understood. I am prepared, or prepared to get prepared, to regard this sorting out of the issue of the voice as a further stage of intellectual adventure, for certainly I do not claim that it is amply clear *why* the procedures of ordinary language philosophy strike me (not me alone, I believe) as functions of voice, nor clear what voice is felt in contrast with; nor do I claim that this function cannot be interpreted as an effect of what might be seen as writing.

What I claim is that no such interpretation will be of the right thing from my point of view unless it accounts for the *fact* that the appeal to the ordinary, as an indictment of metaphysics, strikes one, and should strike one, as an appeal to the voice.[4]

In this passage Cavell is distinguishing between two perspectives: that of metaphysics or philosophical systematizing, and that of the human voice. Elsewhere he refers to both of these as voices: the voice of philosophy (i.e., traditional Western philosophy) and the voice of ordinary, everyday speech.[5]

The former is the voice of detached, objective, and impersonal philosophical thinking – what Thomas Nagel famously called the "view from nowhere" and what Charles Taylor calls the perspective of the atomistic self.[6] The latter is the voice of the engaged agent, embedded in forms of life, who engages with others in the world in complex, nuanced ways. Cavell takes it that in different ways, both Austin and Wittgenstein seek to expose how the subtlety and complexity of everyday speech, the "human voice," is obscured – "suppressed" or "repressed," to use the Freudian term – by the "voice" of traditional Western philosophy. Moreover, for Cavell there is a central epistemological problem – scepticism about the existence of the external world and about other minds – that when properly understood exposes this suppression or repression. The real "moral" of scepticism is precisely this exposure of the false "philosophical" or "metaphysical" presuppositions about independently existing subjects and objects – with essential and accidental properties and relations – and thereby the disclosure of the complex and nuanced relationships that characterize the lives of persons with other persons in the world and the speech used by persons in such relationships – ordinary, everyday language. As Gould puts it, for Cavell, scepticism is a condition that supports the quest for knowledge and the conditions that underlie it; it is "a contemporary version of the ancient human effort to escape the limitations of the human ... [and] a wish to repudiate the world."[7]

The tone of one's writing and one's speech, the character of one's approach or approaches, one's rhetorical or literary style, and one's perspective, which includes one's right in taking it up – all of this (and doubtless more) is what Cavell calls "voice." Voice attaches to a multitude of ways of speaking and writing – indeed, perhaps to all ways. For Cavell, the difference between these two voices – the metaphysical and the human – is especially telling and important. In addition to much else, his philosophical thinking is about the richness of the human voice and the ways in which philosophy has obscured it. In his terms, the quest for knowledge often leads to avoidance – the avoidance of love, intimacy, and concern and of the various modes of acknowledgment associated with them, the stuff of tragedy.[8] Furthermore, his project is about his search for his own philosophical voice and the relation between that search, that philosophical voice, and his own autobiography. As I have said, one culminating stage of this project comes in *A Pitch of Philosophy*, but the project surely continues, even in his most recent autobiographical work, *Little Did I Know: Excerpts from Memory*.[9]

The engaged voice of ordinary life has idiosyncratic features, but at the same time, it must have features that can be shared. In particular, a voice in philosophy must call to one's audience to share in what is said or what is written; there must be something to communicate, and an audience is called upon to respond, to understand, and more. Gould, discussing Cavell, refers to this as the representativeness of voice. But Gould notes that Cavell's prose is distinctive, demanding, frustrating, and disturbing and that indeed Cavell wants it that way – for his writing to produce discomfort, restlessness, and frustration.[10] But one risk of such an idiosyncratic and demanding style is that it will be dismissed as unintelligible or self-indulgent. It has been said that Cavell allows a personal element to intrude so thoroughly into his writing that it is no longer philosophy but rather the product of intuition, spontaneity, mannered and inflated, without order, plan, or rigour.[11] Gould's book is a careful defence of Cavell against such charges, but those charges surely have some basis, and similar ones can be made against any philosopher whose writing is highly literary or rhetorical and who speaks often and regularly in the first person, filling his works with memoir and recollection. Especially in the autobiographical recollections that permeate a work like *A Pitch of Philosophy* – recollections about his mother and father, his involvement in music, his experiences as a teenager, his classes with Ernst Bloch and others, and the Jewish side of his youth and his life – one might wonder what place such narratives and reflections have in philosophical work and how they link up with Cavell's more philosophical themes, such as scepticism, ordinary language philosophy, and moral perfectionism. Gould's answer concerns method. There are times when Gould distinguishes between voice and method, "between the need to find the words that will let you articulate the depth of your position and the need to find words that will let others acknowledge your position as one that they can share."[12] But it may be more helpful to approach voice and method as two dimensions of one thing, the collection of features that makes Cavell's writing sensitive to ordinary, everyday life but nonetheless philosophically informative, communicable.

Voice can expose and express; it can also occlude and suppress, or, as Cavell often puts it, repress. I hesitate to enter Freudian territory, except to note that to repress is to hide from oneself as well as, most likely, from others. The important point, for our purposes, is that voice can be suppressed or obscured; thus, there can be a compelling need to expose it and indeed to take it up oneself. Cavell in his writings first turned to ordinary language philosophy in order to show how traditional philosophical formulations, distinctions, and such obscured how expressions were used and what they meant in ordinary, everyday settings. For Cavell, Austin and Wittgenstein and then Thoreau and Emerson were exemplary archaeologists of the human voice. Cavell next turned to external-world scepticism and its legacy to show how the assumptions that underlie the sceptical question and attempts to dispose of it are indicative of traditional philosophy – epistemology and metaphysics – and distort how persons live and talk with others in the world in everyday life. Cavell came to see Shakespearean tragedy as an exemplary way of expressing this situation, in which these same conditions for scepticism and the aspiration for certainty and knowledge lead to an "avoidance of love" and thus provide the terms of tragedy, the tension between knowledge and acknowledgment, distance and engagement, detachment and intimacy. This is Lear's tragedy and that of Othello as well.[13] Scepticism, as Gould puts it, is our response to our anxieties about how we are related to others; it abolishes the intimacies we have for one another.[14] It is the tragic dimension that Kierkegaard despairs of and that Levinas calls the "temptation of theodicy" – that is, the situation of being tempted to theoretical reflection about suffering in the face of what makes a claim upon us for care and loving kindness. In short, voice can suppress or obscure, and it can be obscured and in need of exposure. It can refer to the tonality and expressive character of a discourse that hides another or that is hidden by another.

Fackenheim's Early Writings and the Emergence of a New Tone

We have said enough about how the notion of voice functions for Cavell. We can now use the idea to ask how we might understand features of Fackenheim's writing as a philosopher and a Jewish philosopher as part of his project of discovering and developing his philosophical voice. To begin, let me propose that during his career Fackenheim sought to expose and articulate three modes of voice that had been suppressed or obscured. In each case, he not only made an effort to identify the voice but also sought to appropriate it himself, so that its exposure was carried out by him from the perspective of that voice. The first of these suppressed voices is the voice of revelation as an event of divine–human encounter. This is the voice of faith, a voice obscured by the speech of secular humanism and by the naturalistic discourse so often used to express it. I have discussed this theme in chapter 1 and elsewhere, especially the way in which Fackenheim appropriated the teachings of Buber and Rosenzweig and their voice of revelation. The second of these suppressed voices is the voice of Judaism and Jewish faith, a voice suppressed by Christianity in general and particularly, for Fackenheim's purposes, by a Western philosophy that is explicitly and implicitly permeated by Christian terms, themes, and commitments. Perhaps his most explicit and effective effort at disclosing the distinctive voice of Judaism and Jewish thought comes in his *Encounters between Judaism and Modern Philosophy*, but it is a theme also found prominently in *To Mend the World* and later in *The Jewish Bible after the Holocaust: A Re-reading.*[15] Finally, Fackenheim sought to expose the ways in which the voice of Auschwitz, the voice that described and grasped the radical evil of the Nazi death camps and the Nazi universe, had been and continued to be occluded by a discourse that evaded this historically unprecedented evil by treating it only within existing categories and by explaining it as part of theories of human conduct and political programs. Fackenheim would have called this the "voice of the victims" of the Nazi horror. It was a singular responsibility of his to oppose any attempts to hide or distort or dismiss that voice.

In Fackenheim's effort, then, to discover his "voice in philosophy" (as Cavell would have put it), he sought to identify and then expose the voices of revelation and faith, Judaism and Jewish philosophy, and Auschwitz as radical evil and opposition to it. Moreover, in so doing, he identified and exposed the distortions and falsifications of the voices that carried out such acts of suppression and occlusion. These are the voices of secularist humanist thinking, Western philosophy, and Christian theology insofar as they ignore or distort Judaism and Jewish experience, as well as those of "liberal" strategies of avoiding the radical evil of Auschwitz and all it stands for. Since I have dealt with various aspects of these voices or modes of discourse, I will not review them here.

What I do want to explore, however, is a feature of the voice of philosophy that Gould has emphasized is central to Cavell and that I will argue is also central to Fackenheim. It concerns the way in which the voice of philosophy is idiosyncratic and personal but also shareable and representative and the way in which it is connected with autobiography yet is still a communicable voice. How, that is, does the increasingly personal and rhetorical character of Fackenheim's writing contribute to the development of his philosophical voice? And how does his changing literary style express his changing views about what it is to take up that philosophical voice, to speak as a post-Holocaust philosopher and Jewish philosopher?

At one point in *Hearing Things*, Gould tries to locate the aspect of Cavell's philosophical writing that is available to others in voice, and he distinguishes this from what is personal and idiosyncratic, which he calls "style" and which is "the development of that singular, seductive sound to his prose." He refers to voice as "something that needs to be communicated and, in that sense, shared," and he associates it with the "representativeness" of Cavell's writing, with what the listener or reader can take away as something to be shared.[16] This is Gould's way of calling attention to what we might call the particularity and generality in Cavell's philosophical writing.

In Fackenheim, who uses a more traditional vocabulary, the issues raised by this distinction concern how philosophy can at the same time be the thinking and writing of a particular, engaged individual, and also convey meanings and truths, teachings, that transcend that personal, historically located point of view. We saw this problem emerge in earlier chapters. We noted that Fackenheim wondered how Jewish philosophy is even possible, and we also appreciated how this problem was a salient one not just for Jewish philosophy but indeed for all philosophy, once philosophy was taken to be engaged and historically embedded, the thinking of a particular individual at a particular time. Another way of putting it would be to ask how existential philosophy is possible. Or, in Rosenzweig's terms, can the new thinking be philosophy? For Cavell, as for Fackenheim, the individual agent is embedded in everyday life, and the philosopher – Cavell himself, as well as Fackenheim – is such an agent, such a philosopher.

One side of Gould's point about Cavell, then, is that all philosophy is unavoidably personal. The other side is that, if it is philosophy, it is unavoidably philosophical. Gould notes that Cavell was fond of saying that there is no such thing as metaphilosophy. There is no place outside philosophical activity that allows one to take a perspective on it that is not already an occurrence of it; there is no place outside philosophy from which one can describe it that is not itself already philosophical.[17] That is, there is no model of a philosophical procedure or method that is not already itself part of some further philosophical practice. Fackenheim's lifelong articulation and rethinking of what philosophy is inevitably occurs as itself a part of a philosophical practice or inquiry. But since philosophy is historically embedded, transcendence is avoidance; there is no unconditional universality. What there is instead is communicability or representativeness, philosophy's availability to be shared, appropriated, taken up.

Style, then, is not voice, and as Gould also points out, philosophy for Cavell is not the same as autobiography: even if Cavell has taught us "to trace the autobiographical edge of philosophical writing, autobiography is not, in itself, philosophy."[18] The mere recalling of past experiences and events is story-telling; it is not philosophy. Philosophy makes a point; it informs, articulates, exposes, and teaches. It is not mere description or recollection. Yet the voice of philosophy is personal and autobiographical in a sense. Cavell warns that philosophy is ambivalent about autobiography. Philosophy is not the same as personal recollections; nonetheless, in order to discover one's voice, as a philosopher, one can and perhaps must engage in autobiographical reflections about one's experiences, one's conversions and education, and one's readings of texts, films, and more and what they mean.

Do we find in Fackenheim such a project of discovering his philosophical voice, one that involves changes in literary style and autobiographical reflections and readings, conducted so as to provide something that is communicable and representative for his readers, his audience? Do we find him willing and even eager to take with increasing seriousness his own engaged agency as a concrete, particular philosophical thinker and author? And, at the same time, do we find him seeking a voice that is exemplary and that can be appropriated? And does his own writing express the moral edge to that philosophical voice that we have argued is characteristic of what a genuine post-Holocaust philosophy ought to be?

Fackenheim's early theological essays, his philosophical essays on Kant and Schelling, the Aquinas Lecture *Metaphysics and Historicity*, and his book on Hegel are all somewhat different from one another in writing style, but all are written in straightforward, reasoned, philosophical prose. There are moments of self-conscious reflection, as well as very occasional first-person passages, but by and large Fackenheim's early philosophical voice presents arguments and engages in analysis and explication that is dialectical but quite traditional.[19] Fackenheim's early writings, both his exclusively philosophical works and his essays in Jewish theology, are scrupulously philosophical and carefully reasoned. There is little doubt that the voice he was cultivating aimed at clarity and rational precision; it also sought to involve his readers and listeners in that reasoning process, to engage them in thinking through what to believe and how to understand themselves and their situation. But he leaves no doubts about the deep forces that moved him and the challenges that pressed upon him most profoundly. The stakes of philosophical and theological thinking were very high. Existentially, as he put it, the meaning of Jewish existence and Jewish history was at the centre of his thinking: Why be and remain a Jew? In the years of the greatest catastrophe for the Jewish people and thereafter, this was the central problem he addressed.[20]

Only in the late 1960s, especially with his turn to the Holocaust and his early attempts to engage it, did his prose and his voice begin to change.[21] His writing continued to be precise, but it also became increasingly personal and rhetorical. Especially after 1967, his writings became more personal; the words on the page voiced his state of mind, his sense of urgency, his emotion, and the depth of his concern. What had been sober and detached was becoming, in these years, richer and more compelling; even the rhythm and tempo of his sentences was changing, which added to the emotion of the prose. The personal point of view was not intended to limit the scope of the discussion; rather, it was a means to express that the issues needed to be engaged from the point of view of the subject or agent and not objectively or in a detached way. Moreover, his prose became more literary, employing a variety of devices to move the reader and to add drama and concreteness to his writings. At crucial moments he turned to literature and to testimony and witnesses' reports and reflections. Compared to his earlier writings, many essays and books from the crucial decade – roughly 1967 to 1977 – seem more dramatic and rhetorically crafted. Fackenheim's style was changing and so was his philosophical voice.

Some of this sense of drama and urgency begins to emerge, I think, in the last major essay in *Quest for Past and Future*, "On the Self-Exposure of Faith to the Modern Secular World: Philosophical Reflections in the Light of Jewish Experience."[22] This essay, which first appeared in the winter of 1967 in *Daedalus*, is an early expression of his then recent commitment to take seriously the Nazi atrocities and the horrors of the death camps.

I have long believed that Fackenheim had decided to confront explicitly and seriously the Nazi Holocaust some time prior to the Six Day War of June 1967. Dating his turn to the Holocaust prior to June 1967 is a fairly straightforward matter. The *Judaism* symposium "Jewish Values in the Post-Holocaust Future," where he first articulated the 614th commandment, was held in New York on 26 March of that year. In conversation, Fackenheim regularly contended to me that his first essay on these matters was his contribution to a conference on hope, at the University of California, Santa Barbara, convened in 1968, but I believe that a draft of the material at the *Judaism* symposium and the somewhat later "Jewish Faith and the Holocaust: A Fragment," published in *Commentary* in August 1968, had already been presented to colleagues at a Segal Conference in Quebec in the summer of 1966.[23] Eugene Borowitz reported to me that in August 1965, after hearing Irving Greenberg present a paper on the Holocaust at the Segal Conference in the summer of 1965, Fackenheim admitted that he could no longer avoid the issue. The last two sections of the paper on faith and modern secularism show him taking a first step in this direction, marked by a crisis of faith that deepened with a self-exposure to Auschwitz.

Early in "On the Self-Exposure of Faith to the Modern Secular World," Fackenheim locates the problematic situation of the contemporary Jew as he or she faces secular humanism from outside Judaism and a secular–religious split even within it. But then he acknowledges an experience that "overshadows and dwarfs" any other in our generation, he says. It is an experience that is

> wholly unassimilable. The events that are associated with the dread name of Auschwitz still pass human comprehension. But they have shaken Jewish existence to the core, even when they are uncomprehended. They call everything into question: for the believing Jew, for the unbelieving Jew, for the Jew who is neither believer nor unbeliever but merely asks unanswered or unanswerable questions. Only one thing is as yet clear. The Jew may not authentically think about religion, or its modern crisis, or the goods and ills of the modern-secular world as though Auschwitz had not happened.[24]

What a remarkable, surprising, and dramatic statement this is. Auschwitz is introduced into Fackenheim's writing with a singular claim and a singular, if as yet unclear, imperative. The claim is that the Holocaust is beyond comprehension: it has not been and cannot be assimilated by and into our ways of thinking, our theories and systems, and that is true for all of us, no matter what our beliefs and convictions. Honesty requires that we acknowledge as much. But even if there can be no comprehension, there is nonetheless an implication, which takes the form of this imperative: not to go on thinking about religion, life, our situation, as if Auschwitz had not occurred. That is, the imperative is not to forget and not to allow ourselves to ignore or reject or hide the dark window that will always separate us from our past and even from our present. This claim and this imperative would shortly be elaborated into what he would come to call the 614th commandment, and the structure of that elaboration would form the core of Fackenheim's thinking about Auschwitz and life thereafter. Here we have what appears to be a simple, forthright statement, but it begins to release a pent-up sorrow and guilt – and more, a precise philosophical reflection on the dark events of the recent past.

The essay becomes, in effect, a book review of four works on the recent crisis of religion, in particular Christianity, in the modern secular world. Those four works are Dietrich Bonhoeffer's *Letters and Papers from Prison*; Harvey Cox's *The Secular City*; Paul Van Buren's *The Secular Meaning of the Gospel*; and Thomas Altizer's *The Gospel of Christian Atheism*. By and large, the four reviews are organized to dig more and more deeply into contemporary critiques of the secular world (i.e., the secularization of Christianity) and then to expose the theologians' failure to articulate faith in a sufficiently compelling way to meet the challenges. He then offers a summary of Buberian themes and of the challenges that a Buberian view of faith and revelation faces.[25]

All of which brings us to the critical moment in Fackenheim's essay. If the contemporary religious situation and human situation requires a self-exposure not only to secularity and secularism but also to that "unassimilable event, all that is associated with the dread name of Auschwitz," where does that leave Buber's account of the "Biblical openness to the divine-presence" when, to all appearances, there *was* no such presence? Fackenheim poses a striking problem for Buber and the Buberians: "committed to the thesis that God speaks constantly, *I and Thou* stakes all responsibility for 'hearing' on a human 'turning.' But the weight of such responsibility was too great even in Biblical times. In the modern-secular world it is intolerable."[26] How, that is, can even a compelling account of the divine–human relation and covenantal existence survive the Holocaust? How does one deal with divine absence?

At this point, Fackenheim turns to Buber, but his account of Buber's own response in *Eclipse of God* does not sound convincing. That account as he frames it is, that if there is a time of divine concealment or an "eclipse" that blocks one's view of God, one "accepts a divine eclipse" and "listens even in a time of silence, in the trust that the divine word will again be heard." Here is faith as trust, as confidence even in the face of absence. Fackenheim asks what characterizes the situation facing the modern Jew in such a world, and he finds – as he often does – a world of contradictions that are not faced with sufficient candour and appreciation. Among those contradictions is the appreciation that although the world contains an Auschwitz, one must "refuse a despair of this world which, wholly contrary to Judaism, would hand still another victory to the forces of radical evil."[27] Moreover, while there has been a commitment on the part of many to Jewish survival and "insofar as the Jew [thereby] has already taken a stand against these forces," Fackenheim refuses here to believe that "survival-for-survival's sake" is an "adequate stand." As we shall see shortly, this is a denial that Fackenheim would come to rescind. Here, however, his tone is cautious yet confident and encouraging: "the Jew can go beyond [the stand of survival-for-survival's sake] only if he can reopen the quest of Jeremiah and Job, who for all their agony refused to despair either of God or of the world." In short, Fackenheim finds something appealing in Buber's optimism, that even in the face of divine absence, there should be trust in the future and confidence that even after Auschwitz, Jewish existence can retain a sense of meaning and purpose.

Yet at the same time that Fackenheim seems hopeful, he admits that his own voice is inadequate to say anything about "an authentic Jewish enduring of the contradictions of present Jewish existence."[28] For guidance and for some assistance, he invites the reader to listen not to a philosopher or a theologian but to a novelist. This is a distinctive and crucial move in Fackenheim's development; it marks the turn to confession, literary testimony, and autobiography. The essay's final section is a relatively short collection of five quotations from four books by Elie Wiesel, woven together with Fackenheim's own very brief comments. In a note, he cites Steve Schwarzschild, who had, in the spring of 1966, referred to Wiesel as "the one man who spoke and protested and stormed the heavens and implicated Israel most tellingly for our generation and for our hearts, and for our hopes, and for our tragedy ... The *de facto* High Priest of our generation."[29] The first quotation is the famous passage from *Night* that depicts the hanging scene; Fackenheim calls it "an eye-witness account of the most terrible actual darkness ...

the document of our time of the impact of radical evil on Jewish faith."
Subsequent quotations – from *The Accident*, *The Town Beyond the Wall*,
and *The Gates of the Messiah* – express the loss of faith, protest, and a
margin of recovery. And with these quotations the essay ends, with
Wiesel's words, with no further comment.

What has happened to Fackenheim's authorial style, his voice, in
these final pages of this essay? In many ways, his writing remains as it
was: clear and precise, albeit a little more moving than before. What we
find in this final section, however, is something different. Here he has
abdicated his voice altogether, or, perhaps better, he is asking to speak
through another's words, and this time the other is a novelist, whose
words are the words of a witness, albeit in a fictionalized testimony.
Furthermore, while the words are Wiesel's, the organization is Fackenheim's. His point is that to be exposed to Auschwitz is to surrender everything and to grope towards recovery without ever failing to give
Auschwitz its due; it is to see the past through its dark glass. Indeed, it
is to abandon and then recover faith only by means of reflection on the
experience of the death camps. What begins here with these quotations
from Wiesel will continue in virtually every one of his essays of the
1970s and then in *To Mend the World* – reflection on the agency of the
perpetrators and then on the responses and experiences of the victims,
through reports and testimony, reflection that is interpretation that
bears philosophical results. In this way, Fackenheim's writing continues
to be philosophical only to the degree that it becomes concrete, and that
concreteness brings with it greater literary artistry and rhetorical force.
Fackenheim is on the way to a more lofty, sermonic tone, one that never
ceases to be rigorous but dresses that rigour in dramatic and moving
prose. Here this voice is expressed in literary quotation; as time goes on,
such quotation or paraphrase will become one component in a set of
dialectical reflections on the meaning of such testimony, reflections that
encompass both narratives of episodes and personal recollections.

Confession and Autobiography
in the Writings of the Late 1960s

Around this same time, in writings that mark his explicit engagement
with Auschwitz, Fackenheim's style becomes strikingly personal and,
as he himself calls it, confessional. Cavell's confessional and autobiographical writing is modelled after Augustine, Rousseau, and Thoreau.
Fackenheim's models are not as obvious, but the change is important

and will be encountered in all his writings thereafter. To understand this turn to confessional and personal recollections, let me examine passages in two papers that Fackenheim wrote that initiated his post-Holocaust Jewish thinking. The first, which still sounds like his older papers in many respects, is his contribution to the *Judaism* symposium on 26 March 1967; it includes his earliest formulation of the 614th commandment. The second is his *Commentary* essay, "Jewish Faith and the Holocaust: A Fragment."[30]

The short statement from the symposium begins in a familiar way. The word "crisis," which Fackenheim has used earlier to refer to the contemporary "crisis of faith" in the modern secular world, occurs throughout the paper's early paragraphs. He asks that his audience accept two presuppositions: that there is a crisis that all Jews need to face, and that whatever the response, it must involve a "stubborn persistence in our Jewishness." So his first task is to understand the crisis, a task that he confronts, as he often does, by articulating contradictions that permeate the contemporary situation. But what makes the essay sound familiar – this appeal to contradictions – is something that Fackenheim will soon come to abandon. To be sure, he will continue to reason by means of contrariety and oppositions, but he will abandon quite soon the almost formulaic strategy of characterizing the human condition, the religious situation, and the contemporary situation in terms of paradoxes or contradictions.[31]

Having described these contradictions and the crisis they frame, Fackenheim turns to responses, and here he makes a move that will become characteristic of his thinking for some time; it is what he will call "thought going to school with life."[32] In order to determine what an authentic response to this crisis would be, he turns to past responses to see what we can learn from them. Here he identifies two types of response: a commitment to Jewish survival, and a commitment to Jewish unity.[33] Our first reaction might be surprise; after all, not long ago we saw that he had rejected any appeal to survival for survival's sake. Has he called attention to such a response here only to reject it?

As Fackenheim considers Jewish survival, his tone becomes deeply personal and, in his own words, "confessional." He admits to his past views and to a change of thinking, and he does so in a thoroughly autobiographical way.

I confess I used to be highly critical of Jewish philosophies which seemed to advocate no more than survival for survival's sake. I have changed my mind. I now believe that, in this present, unbelievable age, even a mere collective commitment to Jewish group-survival for its own sake is a momentous response, with the greatest implications. I am convinced that future historians will understand it, not, as our present detractors would have it, as the tribal response-mechanism of a fossil, but rather as a profound, albeit as yet fragmentary, act of faith, in an age of crisis to which the response might well have been either flight in total disarray or complete despair.[34]

If earlier, in "Judaism and the Idea of Progress," Fackenheim used an autobiographical style in order to bring the reader into the perspective of his argument and invite her to join in his reasoning, here his confession is more provocative still. He admits that his old "liberal" scruples have failed him, and for a very particular reason. Arguments are not abstract; they are concrete. What makes them compelling or not is contextual and historical. What may have been worthy of rejection at other times is now, in a post-Holocaust world, urgent and compelling. A commitment to Jewish survival, after Auschwitz, may not be everything, but it is *something*. At a time when Jews might well have abandoned Judaism or clung to it but without any hope, to remain Jewish with some sense of pride, any at all, is a "fragmentary act of faith." This is a dramatic and serious confession, and it is also a powerful recommendation and appeal. As always, his eye is on the argument and the issue. It may be Fackenheim who places his integrity on the line, but it is more than a personal matter.

That this deeply personal admission and appeal is intended to involve the reader is made utterly clear by the fact that Fackenheim almost immediately shifts from the first-person singular to the first-person plural. In fact, this stage is the third in a dialectical movement: the two responses are those that Jews have already made; endorsing them is something that Fackenheim admits for himself; now we return to the meaning and implications of those two responses. "Whether aware of what we have decided or not, we have made the collective decision to endure the contradictions of present Jewish existence. We have collectively rejected the option, either of 'checking out' of Jewish existence altogether or of so avoiding the present contradictions as to shatter Jewish existence into fragments."[35] That is, Jews have faced Auschwitz, not "checked out" – an ordinary idiom if ever there was one – and have taken the contradictions of Jewish life seriously. Fackenheim asks: Can we go beyond these fragmentary commitments? Can we do more than face Auschwitz and survive? There is an argument here, to be sure, but it is also an exhortation, a highly rhetorical appeal to step beyond survival to some kind of duty, obligation, and orientation and not to settle for a "fragmentary act of faith."

Fackenheim's voice rings with passion, encouragement, and hope. As I read him, I also hear a kind of liberation, or release, as if he had lived too long with the weight of guilt and shame but now feels able to speak his mind, for he has now finally *found* his mind: "Not accidentally has it taken twenty years for us to face this question, and it is not certain that we can face it yet." And then, a few sentences later: "We have lived in this contradiction for twenty years without being able to face it."[36] Who is this "we," and what is it that cannot be faced? *We* are all those who have continued to live as Jews but have struggled with the tension between going on as a Jew and living with despair, without confidence or hope. *We* are all the theologians who have ignored or avoided Auschwitz. And *we* includes Fackenheim himself, who has repressed the memories and avoided confronting explicitly the momentousness of the event at the risk of having also to face his guilt as a person and his inadequacies as a philosopher.

I have always been struck by the way in which Fackenheim, at this juncture, introduces the 614th commandment: "Unless I am mistaken" and of course he could be, "we are now beginning to face [the contradiction of affirming death and affirming life in the present and future in the shadow of the catastrophe], however fragmentarily and inconclusively." Is Fackenheim here at last speaking for himself and his newfound courage to return to the memories and to face the trauma of having survived and the guilt of having left family behind? "And from this beginning confrontation there emerges what I will boldly term a 614th commandment: *the authentic Jew of today is forbidden to hand Hitler yet another, posthumous victory.*"[37] One can only be baffled – I certainly am – about where such a commandment and indeed where any commandment comes from. He says it "emerges from" what has begun to be done. Does this mean that it has emerged "after" such a beginning or that it has emerged "out of" the very confrontation? And is it the commandment or imperative or obligation that "emerges" or the *awareness* of such a commandment or imperative? And who is it that grasps this fact, this commandment? The ordinary Jew or the Jewish philosopher or, hopefully, both?

Immediately Fackenheim opens a parenthesis and justifies his formulation, in particular three features of it, and the momentary aside shows his self-consciousness, the mixture of boldness and reticence that marks this important step. First, he explains why he has chosen to call the imperative a 614th commandment: it is to acknowledge that while nothing supersedes the original 613 commandments, "something radically new has happened." Second, the Nazi atrocities did have content – the extermination of six million – so the formulation of an imperative must be negative; it must be an imperative to resist and oppose. Third and finally, the utter particularity of this event requires that it be denominated in some way; reluctant as one might be, using the name of Hitler is unavoidable to respect what he here calls the event's "uniqueness," and this means in order to avoid simply assimilating it into broad, general categories. Whether these are the only questions that immediately come to mind or whether they are the ones that seem most worrisome is not the issue. What forces a reflection and a defence are Fackenheim's doubts, his self-doubts, and his self-consciousness about the step he is here taking. In the text, as he turns to consider who hears the commandment, he shows that he has Rosenzweig in mind at this moment. What this means is that he has come to think that to face Auschwitz seriously, one must treat it as momentous and determinative, as orienting. And if so, then it either is or is akin to a divine–human encounter, a revelatory event. Moreover, the best account of what impact such an event has and how we should understand the human response to it comes, for him, from Rosenzweig and Buber; and on their view the commandment, with its precise content and its formulation, lies in human hands; it is a matter of human interpretation. Fackenheim does not here come right out and say this, nor does he make explicit the link to the Buber–Rosenzweig account of revelation. But to the reader attuned to Fackenheim's vocabulary and writings, the connection is unavoidable. In other words, to call the imperative that "emerges" from the encounter with Auschwitz a "commandment" and to identify it as the "614th," as well as to give it the content he does, "not to hand Hitler yet another, posthumous victory," all of this is a human interpretation of what facing up to Auschwitz means. "But for whom?," we might ask. And the answer here is certainly, "For Emil Fackenheim, Jew and Jewish philosopher." Hence, all that he has said and all that follows as he articulates the four fragments that give this imperative its content count as proposals to his readers. They are Fackenheim's account of what opposing the forces of Nazi evil means – what we ought to stand for in order to stand against that evil.

Fackenheim brings these brief reflections to a close with the following question: It is one thing to be bound by a necessity and to understand what that necessity – moral and religious – requires of us; it is another to be confident that we can abide by it, that we can fulfil it. But "how can we possibly obey these imperatives?" That is, how can we survive as Jews, remember the victims of Auschwitz, not deny or despair of God, and, finally, remain committed to the world and to human existence as meaningful and worthwhile?[38] To do all of this will require the ability to endure the contradictions that mark this event; it will take a kind of will, of courage, that cannot but remain uncertain. Still, this uncertainty and doubt is no reason not to act and to do what we can. This at least is the climax of his plea, of his exhortation.

Fackenheim often said that his contribution to the *Judaism* symposium was his first public statement about the Holocaust and its significance for Judaism and that it caused him tremendous anxiety.[39] For this reason alone, it is of special importance. But it is a brief statement, and he would eventually dismiss some of its features, most notably the emphasis on contradictions. Moreover, its argument for the 614th commandment is severely truncated, which heightens the statement's homiletical qualities. As it proceeds, it acquires the tone of a pronouncement and an appeal, not a philosophical reflection. The essay "Jewish Faith and the Holocaust: A Fragment," published in *Commentary* in August 1968, maintains that tone, but at the same time it is a much richer and fuller account. Along with *God's Presence in History*, it is the major work of this period.

In this 1968 essay Fackenheim brings together three things, two of which have long been important to him and one that will come to be his central preoccupation. The first is the line of thinking that leads to the 614th commandment; the account in this essay is more precise and more detailed than the one we have just surveyed, and together with the account in Chapter Three of *God's Presence in History*, it would become normative for him. Second, he discusses the response of the Christian churches to the Holocaust and to the contemporary Jewish situation. The relationship between Judaism and Christianity had been an important one for him for years and would be represented in several essays in *Quest for Past and Future*. Finally, Fackenheim turns to the events of June 1967 and comments on the role of Israel for Judaism in a post-Holocaust world. From this moment until his death in 2003, his writings would regularly – virtually always – speak of the State of Israel and its centrality for Judaism and Jewish life.[40]

Near the paper's beginning, Fackenheim turns to the Holocaust, and his tone is not academic or detached but charged and urgent:

To avoid Auschwitz, or to act as if it had never occurred, would be blasphemous. Yet how face it and be faithful to its victims? No precedent exists either within Jewish history or outside it. Even when a Jewish religious thinker barely begins to face Auschwitz, he perceives the possibility of a desperate choice between the faith of a millennial Jewish past, which has so far persisted through every trial, and faithfulness to the victims of the present. But at the edge of this abyss, there must be a great pause, a lengthy silence, and an endurance.[41]

The sense of drama and urgency in this introductory statement is hard to miss. Avoiding Auschwitz is more than a mistake or an error; it is blasphemous, yet there is no precedent available to us that would help us confront that blasphemy. These are extreme terms. The choice between faith in Judaism and taking Auschwitz seriously is a desperate one, and then finally, the Jewish religious thinker – one can no longer assume he is a theologian – stands on the "edge of an abyss" and pauses in silence, yet endures. Fackenheim's vocabulary has become more exaggerated and dramatic, and the pitch of his prose elevated, almost tragic.

Section II of the essay follows this introduction and explores, in more precise terms, the line of thinking that Fackenheim had initiated at the *Judaism* symposium. Its first paragraph sets the stage for this argument:

Men shun the scandal of the particularity of Auschwitz. Germans link it with Dresden; American liberals, with Hiroshima. Christians deplore antisemitism-in-general, while Communists erect monuments to victims-of-Fascism-in-general, depriving the dead of Auschwitz of their Jewish identity even in death. Rather than face Auschwitz, men everywhere seek refuge in generalities, comfortable precisely because they are generalities. And such is the extent to which reality is shunned that no cries of protest are heard even when in the world community's own forum obscene comparisons are made between Israeli soldiers and Nazi murderers.[42]

There is a rhythm and a pulse to this paragraph that never ceases to inspire as well as to communicate in stark terms Fackenheim's criticism of all those who suppress or repress the "voice" that honestly speaks of Auschwitz, a voice that he now seeks to appropriate. He twice uses the term "shun": first, when he decries all of those who do not face up to the very particular features of the Nazi atrocities and the horrors of the death camps; and second, when he remarks on the "obscenity" that is permitted to occur without "protest" in the United Nations. To avoid or ignore the horrific events is reprehensible or negligent; to "shun" them is even more so, for the failure is deeper, the repression more disturbing. It is to be aware yet to still refuse to pay attention; it is to express a kind of disdain or at least a self-satisfying avoidance. The tempo of the sentences to follow elaborates the culprits – Germans and American liberals, Christians and Communists alike – and their ultimate failure, which takes the form of hiding behind generalities simply *because* they are generalities.

Now, to these failures, Fackenheim adds the Jewish one. In the paragraphs that follow, he charts the hestitant but emerging Jewish responses; often using a rhetoric of question and answer, he plots the requirements that Jewish responses must satisfy. Jews too cannot lapse into generalities, but at the same time they cannot diminish the significance of other catastrophes and other atrocities. Every horror is distinctive, and this means that so is Auschwitz. He argues that the evil was unprecedented and that the victims were particular. Fackenheim introduces features of the event, as well as vocabulary that he will continue to employ for some time: both Auschwitz and Hiroshima are horrific, but "Eichmann was moved by no such 'rational' objective as victory when he diverted trains needed for military purposes in order to dispatch Jews to their death." Also, "Torquemada burned bodies in order to save souls. Eichmann sought to destroy both bodies and souls." And "where else and at what other time have executioners ever separated those to be murdered now from those to be murdered later to the strain of Viennese waltzes?"[43] He calls upon evidence like this – as awful and disturbing as it is vivid and moving – to show that there is sufficient evil in these events to warrant a response that it distinctive and not universal. From this point on, especially in his essays and then in *To Mend the World*, his writing uses historical evidence of this kind, as well as reports and testimony, extensively and as part of his argument. That argument reaches a crucial stage when Fackenheim contends that

there is not, and never will be, an adequate explanation. Auschwitz is evil for evil's sake, an eruption of demonism without analogy; and the singling-out of Jews, ultimately, is an unparalleled expression of what the rabbis call groundless hate. This is the rock on which throughout eternity all rational explanations will crash and break apart … No purpose, religious or non-religious, will ever be found in Auschwitz. The very attempt to find one is blasphemous.

Yet it is of the utmost importance to recognize that seeking a purpose is one thing, but seeking a response quite another. The first is wholly out of the question. The second is inescapable. Even after two decades any sort of adequate response may as yet transcend the power of any Jew. But his faith, his destiny, his very survival will depend on whether, in the end, he will be able to respond.[44]

Explanation, and with it meaning and purpose, all are impossible; once again, he uses the term "blasphemous" to underline the almost sacred affront that is involved in seeking respite by domesticating the horror and making sense of it. Yet response is necessary. Fackenheim's word is "inescapable," as if the issue is not an abstract decision but rather a personal, concrete choice that faces each Jew – and others too – and that cannot be evaded or escaped, however much one might be moved to do so.

Fackenheim asks how Jews have tried to confront evil in the past, and he emphatically refuses to allow such explanations to be applied in this case:

The one million Jewish children murdered in the Nazi Holocaust died neither because of their faith, nor in spite of their faith, nor for reasons unrelated to faith. They were murdered because of the faith of their greatgrandparents ... Like Abraham of old, European Jews some time in the mid-nineteenth century offered a human sacrifice, by the mere minimal commitment to the Jewish faith of bringing up Jewish children. But unlike Abraham they did not know what they were doing, and there was no reprieve. This is the brute fact which makes all comparisons odious or irrelevant. This is what makes Jewish religious existence today unique, without support from analogies anywhere in the past. This is the scandal of the particularity of Auschwitz which, once confronted by Jewish faith, threatens total despair.[45]

With this repeated reference to the "scandal of the particularity of Auschwitz," Fackenheim has closed the circle on these early paragraphs, the aim of which is to defend and then measure this "particularity," this "brute fact" that makes the dread name of Auschwitz stand for an event that ruptures our ways of thinking and leaves us without familiar moorings. It "threatens total despair" because it leaves us without any resources for coping, for going on. This is what the talk of a lack of explanation, meaning, and purpose is about. It marks the location of a historical event whose evil and whose particular subject – the Jewish people – make it something different, radically so. Moreover, this crucial stage in his argument has been carried out in highly rhetorical, compelling terms. For a large part of the case is to take seriously what Auschwitz stands for, and in order to do so one must grasp and indeed "feel" its horror, its extremity.

As in the *Judaism* symposium, Fackenheim here makes a confession, but whereas there it was about changing his mind about survivalist arguments, here it is broader and deeper. The passage makes it clear how personal and transformative these thoughts are for Fackenheim; his words express his deepest convictions and at the same time draw us into his reasoning. They are the words of "passionate reason" at its most compelling:

> I confess that it took me twenty years until I was able to look at this scandal, but when at length I did, I made what to me was, and still is, a momentous discovery: that while religious thinkers were vainly struggling for a response to Auschwitz, Jews throughout the world – rich and poor, learned and ignorant, religious and nonreligious – had to some degree been responding all along. For twelve long years Jews had been exposed to a murderous hate which was as groundless as it was implacable. For twelve long years the world had been lukewarm or indifferent, unconcerned over the prospect of a world without Jews. For twelve long years the whole world had conspired to make Jews wish to cease to be Jews wherever, whenever, and in whatever way they could. Yet to this unprecedented invitation to group suicide, Jews responded with an unexpected will to live – with, under the circumstances, an incredible commitment to Jewish group survival.[46]

Scandalon is the Greek word for "stumbling-block." We have seen Fackenheim use "scandal" in this essay before, where he refers to Auschwitz and especially to its particularity, its utterly brute historical character and what makes it a radical rupture. In Christianity, the scandal is Jesus as the Christ and the incarnation, the presence of the divine in the human.[47] Fackenheim is resorting to this notion of a "momentous" obstacle not simply to faith but to going on at all. And once again, he is making a very personal admission – that he had neglected or repressed the event, and yet once he had faced up to it, he noted that for all the theological inadequacies, there *had* been responses – by ordinary, everyday Jews, of all kinds – and that their doctrinal commitments aside, they shared something "momentous," a will to survive. Fackenheim underscores the importance of this commitment by repeating, rhythmically, the phrase "for twelve long years" to show how long and how deep was the hatred, the assault, and the indifference with which Jews had had to live. This use of repetition has the effect of making the conclusion all the more striking and compelling. Indeed, he then turns to that commitment's very remarkable meaning in a confessional passage that condenses, in highly rhetorical terms, a very precise argument:

> In ordinary times, a commitment of this kind may be a mere mixture of nostalgia and vague loyalties not far removed from tribalism; and, unable to face Auschwitz, I had myself long viewed it as such, placing little value on a Jewish survival which was, or seemed to be, only survival for survival's sake. I was wrong, and even the shallowest Jewish survivalist philosophy of the postwar period was right by comparison. For in the age of Auschwitz a Jewish commitment to Jewish survival is in itself a monumental act of faithfulness, as well as a monumental, albeit as yet fragmentary, act of faith. Even to do no more than remain a Jew after Auschwitz is to confront the demons of Auschwitz in all their guises, and to bear witness against them. It is to believe that these demons cannot, will not, and must not prevail, and to stake on that belief one's own life and the lives of one's children, and of one's children's children. To be a Jew after Auschwitz is to have wrested hope – for the Jew and the world – from the abyss of total despair.[48]

To my ear, the cadence and terms of this further admission and its revision are perfect. We are told that a commitment to Jewish survival could be mere atavism, but it all depends on the times, the context. Now it is more, so much more – it is an act of faithfulness of enormous depth and power, to the Jewish people; and possibly, for some, it is an act of faith in its God. Moreover, even if one simply opposes the assault on humanity and on the Jewish people, that is itself a "monumental" act, and the way we can weigh its significance is by realizing that the price for that act is paid with the lives of one's children and grandchildren. Fackenheim chooses vivid images to portray his reasoning, and he leaves just enough to the reader to fill in. For example, instead of speaking, didactically, of the contempt that Nazism had for human dignity and worth and of its unqualified hatred of Jews, he refers to the "demons of Auschwitz" and personifies the horrors and opposition to them.

Let me deal with the other two themes of the essay more hastily. On the question of Jewish–Christian relations, on how "the Nazi Holocaust has brought Jews and Christians closer together – and set them further apart," Fackenheim continues to take the deeply personal, confessional stance that he had earlier employed. He recalls how he had previously been convinced that the separation between Jews and Christians had been superseded by a common opposition to Nazism, and in a moving paragraph he indicates why the confessional Church and figures like Barth and Tillich had meant so much to him. "To this day," he says, "I am supported in my Judaism by the faithfulness of Christians to their Christianity," and he feels abandoned when Christian theologians speak of the death of God. But at the same time, he admits, he has come to realize that Christians have not always spearheaded efforts at Jewish emancipation; he has become increasingly realistic about dialogue between Jews and Christians, and he reports two examples of German Christians who opposed Nazism and yet whose attitudes towards Judaism were seriously qualified. Those two were Cardinal Faulhaber and Dietrich Bonhoeffer, the latter of whom remained committed to the tradition of the curse and seemed never to have repudiated it. In these pages Fackenheim's style becomes almost conversational and virtually colloquial, a clear shift in tone from his more philosophical writings. And his conclusion is similarly concrete and direct: "And the truth, as I am now forced to see it, is that the organized Christian forces will find it easiest to drop the ancient charge of deicide, harder to recognize roots of antisemitism in the New Testament, and hardest of all to face up to the fact that Jews and Judaism are both still alive."[49]

The litmus test of such convictions and such realism came, for Fackenheim, during the Six Day War and the events of May and June 1967. These provide him with a vehicle for clarifying vividly the issues for Jewish–Christian dialogue after the Holocaust and also for beginning to consider the role of Israel in that context. Fackenheim has a cascade of questions for Christianity and Christian leaders about Israel, her Arab neighbours, and such, and his rhetoric belies his doubts that most would have much to say. Furthermore, he uses that trope of repetition once again – this time "For two long weeks in May" – in order to underscore the indifference, the silence of so many of churches at a moment of extreme risk. "For two weeks [the worldwide Jewish community] longed for Christian words of apprehension and concern. But whereas some such words came from secular sources, from the churches there was little but silence. Once again, Jews were alone."[50] Fackenheim's point, as he puts it, is that "Hitler tried to create an abyss between Jews and Christians; he succeeded; and – this is the horror – he continues to enjoy posthumous successes." He goes on to explain that the churches failed to appreciate the risk of a second Holocaust in 1967, because they failed to acknowledge the responsibility for the abandonment that contributed to the former one.

Fackenheim's final comments in the paper turn to Israel's significance for Jews in a post-Holocaust world. At this stage, he is still groping to understand what is possible in such a world. What can Israel – and a kind of salvation – mean? Or a margin of hope and joy? He is puzzled, and his halting final questions and reflections indicate as much. He affirms that the events of May and June 1967 are somehow connected to Auschwitz and that this "military victory [did] acquire an inescapable religious dimension." But he chooses, at the essay's end, not to try to say what that religious dimension was. Instead, just as he had chosen to end his essay on faith and the modern secular world by calling upon Elie Wiesel, here he calls upon a letter from Harold Fisch of Bar-Ilan University, who recounts a conversation with a colleague, a psychologist, who reported to him the way in which Israeli soldiers saw a connection between the Holocaust and the challenges they had faced during the June war. In short, Fackenheim once again turns to a more concrete, almost testimonial text that expresses, from the participant's point of view, the sense of command from Auschwitz that was heard during those weeks in June 1967. This approach to grounding the connection between Israel and the Holocaust and the command or obligation for which he has argued is one that will recur in his writings, most vividly and importantly in *To Mend the World*.

Cavell sought his voice in philosophy by finding resources (in ordinary language philosophy, scepticism, the writings of Thoreau and Emerson, Shakespeare, and film) for exposing the suppression of the human voice and then by drawing on autobiography and recollections to link his own identity to the exposure of the rich diversity of that voice. Fackenheim's route to the discovery of his philosophical voice differs. For him, the route carried him through a familiarity with traditional Western philosophy and metaphysics; and then through a commitment to what he called existential philosophy and the hovering between engaged, historically embedded experience (in particular religious experience) and detached, philosophical reflection; and then through a felt duty – religious and moral – to expose the repressed voice of Auschwitz, the human voices of victims and survivors, of perpetrators and collaborators, whose speech reveals the horrific events in all their particularity and concreteness. As we have seen, it is a route that carries Fackenheim into the realm of personal, confessional writing and into the domain of the reflective interpretation of testimony, fictional texts, and narratives. The new use of autobiographical reflection and the introduction of these kinds of texts, together with the increased intensity and lyricism in his prose – these are practices that would become regular features of his writing from late 1960s through the late 1970s. The chief works of that period – *God's Presence in History*, *Encounters between Judaism and Modern Philosophy*, and the essays collected in *The Jewish Return into History* – provide many examples of these practices and the skill with which Fackenheim masters them.[51]

Only rarely will Fackenheim's prose reach again the peak of lyricism that one finds in these works of the 1970s. That prose, when it does so, will continue often to be confessional and personal, and it will regularly use testimony, narrative reports or paraphrases, and readings of texts. And it will have moments when it flows with an ease reminiscent of the early essays and is as accessible, especially in the book written for a wide popular audience, *What Is Judaism?* Moreover, there will be times when it is as sophisticated and philosophically deep as it has ever been, perhaps more so. But from this moment in the late 1970s through to his death in 2003, Fackenheim's writing by and large shifts into a different register, more difficult, arcane, complex, and at times almost hermetic. This begins with *To Mend the World*.

Voice out of the Depths: From *To Mend the World* to *An Epitaph for German Judaism*

In a review of Fackenheim's *The Religious Dimension in Hegel's Thought*, W.H. Walsh describes the book as "packed with argument and composed with great care and skill." It is, he says, "a powerful and persuasive ... piece of exegesis" and "in its own terms strikingly lucid, though it may not seem so to those used to a different style of philosophy."[52] This is a fair description of all of Fackenheim's philosophical and theological writings of the early period, through the late 1960s. His approach is rational and filled with arguments, although his style of argumentation is not that of Anglo-American analytic philosophy.

For Fackenheim in those years, his focus on the relation between faith and reason and his defence of the Buber–Rosenzweig conception of revelation and religious experience were the context in which the problem of the method of philosophical inquiry arose. The issues raised by the particular, historically embedded character of human experience as the subject matter of philosophy, and by the concrete, personal experience of the philosopher and of philosophical thought, were really problems about perspective. In those days, he was seeking a method that would not avoid or distort the concrete, personal point of view of engaged experience and yet would be reflective and detached enough to draw general or universal conclusions. He spoke about moments of re-enactment and reflection and of a thought that "hovered" between the subjective and objective points of view. Even when he took seriously his own engaged point of view as a Jewish philosopher, he still spoke in these terms and sought to confront the problems that faced such philosophy in this way. But as we have seen, once he turned to the encounter with the dark times of the Nazi era, the problem of finding for himself a philosophical voice – an identity and perspective – that had been suppressed or repressed seemed to require more. He began to employ confession and autobiography and reflective interpretation of testimony, narrative reports of witnesses, and more. Yet these activities, which had a personal dimension, had to be presented as bearing a representative weight. Autobiography could not be exclusive and private, and personal interpretations and readings could not be strictly his own. They had to have a shareable content, the stuff of teaching and communication, to use Cavell's terms.

This communicable content was available because these writings of the late 1960s and beyond still were "packed with argument," to use Walsh's expression, although the argument was of a different sort. Of course, even though the terms and vocabulary that Fackenheim used were sometimes drawn from ordinary, everyday use and sometimes were technical and were appropriated from Heidegger, Schelling, Hegel, and others, what really made the writing shareable and available to an audience was how it employed argument. I have argued, for example, that there is a very precise argument in "Jewish Faith and the Holocaust" and the third chapter of *God's Presence in History* of a transcendental sort, one that begins with the attempt to explain and understand the Holocaust and results in an imperative of opposition to the Nazi assault on Judaism, human dignity, and more and then issues in various hermeneutical, interpretive readings of what content such an imperative (duty or obligation) might been given. But Fackenheim's very notion of what counts as an argument is not narrow, and hence what is required to make his very personal confessions and interpretive readings communicable is not just one thing. What is important is that there be some kind of reasoning going on and that the audience or reader be able, be encouraged, be motivated to follow it and appropriate it. Even at times when there may seem not to be argumentation, there may be.

In commenting on the sense in which Emerson and Thoreau should be treated as philosophical professionals and not merely as amateurs, Cavell notices that "they propose, and embody, a mode of thinking, a mode of conceptual accuracy, as thorough as anything imagined within established philosophy, but invisible to that philosophy because based on an idea of rigor foreign to its establishment."[53] He goes on to point out that what leads to such a dismissal of Thoreau and Emerson is the identification of rigour with argumentation; the corresponding charge against Fackenheim in his later writings might call attention to his lack of arguments of a familiar kind and his indulgence in highly rhetorical descriptions and speculations. But Cavell offers a helpful corrective: "But suppose that what is meant by argumentation in philosophy is one way of accepting full responsibility for one's own discourse. Then the hearing I require [in order to appreciate the philosophy in Thoreau and Emerson] depends upon the thought that there is another way, another philosophical way ... of accepting that responsibility. This other philosophical way I am going to call reading; others may call it philosophical interpretation."[54] In Fackenheim's later work, then, what we may find, amidst the autobiographical passages and the extensive use of testimony and narrative reports, is a form of argumentation that takes up the task of "accepting full responsibility" for what he claims by a process of "philosophical interpretation." As we turn to selections from these later writings, I suggest that this is precisely what we do find, so that in this way his philosophical voice retains its personal character while at the same time reaching out to an audience whom it seeks to motivate and persuade.

To Mend the World is Fackenheim's magnum opus, the culmination of all that preceded it and the foundation for all his later work. In it we hear the sounds of a different voice emerging. It is a composition that is, as I have said, far more complex and demanding than earlier work, constructed out of a highly technical philosophical vocabulary together with historical reports and testimony, at times evocative and compelling and at times dialectic and almost hermetic. The book contains lengthy encounters with Rosenzweig, Spinoza, Hegel, Heidegger, and many others, and it incorporates discussions, some new and some old, of a host of people, events, debates, issues, and challenges. Most of all, the book shows Fackenheim taking problems and issues that he has already considered in earlier writings and pushing his thinking about them beyond anything we have yet seen. It breaks new ground again and again, but its novelty and its advances require him to search for and to construct a vocabulary and a way of speaking that can help him succeed. The result is a different philosophical prose, a distinct new tone, and a voice that combines the technical, the everyday, and the esoteric.

What can we say about Fackenheim's style and his voice in *To Mend the World*? Let me put it in a word: his prose has become *dense*, where that term points to a combination of features. To be sure, the length of his analyses and arguments, and their complexities, make the prose denser, thicker, more packed. But there are also added complexities – longer and more convoluted sentences, a use of Heideggerian terminology and other terms from German philosophy, and a use of parentheses and other ways of breaking up sentences and introducing digressions or interruptions. The book demands to be read slowly and carefully. In short, the writing is heavier, weightier, and more ponderous – and it is also more cryptic or internalized than in the past. The book is written with Fackenheim giving his memory of favourite terms, expressions, tropes, and themes full play. And the result is that like many great works, it creates its own discourse, its own terms for treating its themes. To be sure, Fackenheim draws on others – Rosenzweig, Spinoza, Heidegger, Hegel, Schelling, Buber, Strauss – but the result is a new creation: a new world that has to be entered, or a symphony with a new sound that one has to be educated to appreciate.

Furthermore, if Fackenheim's voice has become dense – weighty and intricate – it also has taken on a certain height or loftiness. But this loftiness is not the lyrical hortatory style of the essays of the 1970s; it is by and large lofty and pronounced but without the rich tapestry of figures and metaphors. In a sense, Fackenheim has returned to the podium of the German university; he gives free rein to all his erudition, all the expressions and motifs and snatches of vocabulary that have filled his mind through his labours as a historian of philosophy and his readings of poetry, history, and more, and he uses all of this to frame his new type of analysis and his new argument.

Let me give an example of the result. At the end of the important and complex digression in Chapter IV, Sections 8 and 9, in which Fackenheim gives an account of "resistance as an ontological category," he summarizes the outcome of this analysis:

With this monumental conclusion [i.e., that our ecstatic thought must point to their resistance – the resistance in thought and the resistance in life – as ontologically ultimate. Resistance in that extremity was a way of being. For our thought now, it is an ontological category] what may be called a necessary excursus, extending over the last two sections of the present exploration, has come to a climax and an end. Prior to these sections we reached an impasse with the question whether perhaps no thought can be where the Holocaust is; whether perhaps all thought is "paralyzed" vis-à-vis that event; and whether perhaps paralysis at this catastrophic point calls into question significant post-Holocaust thought everywhere. The two sections that followed were an excursus in that that question was suspended; and the excursus was necessary because only the astounding fact that existence was not wholly paralyzed during the Holocaust itself could give our thought any hope of breaking the impasse. Now that the astounding fact has been confronted, contemplated, explored, the suspended question returns; and there arises for future thought – the focus of our concern is Jewish thought, but also involved are philosophical and, to a lesser extent, Christian thought – an imperative that brooks no compromise. Authentic thought was actual during the Holocaust among resisting victims; therefore such thought must be possible for us after the event: and, being possible, it is mandatory. Moreover, their resisting thought pointed to and helped make possible a resisting life; our post-Holocaust thought, however authentic in other respects, would still lapse into inauthenticity if it remained in an academically-self enclosed circle – if it failed to point to, and help make possible, a post-Holocaust life.[55]

How ought we, Fackenheim's audience, to read this passage?[56] First, it almost immediately refers back to what preceded it. By itself, this backward demonstrative does not add to the burden of reading the passage. What does, however, add to that burden is that "this monumental conclusion" refers to a conclusion that needs to be recovered from several sentences and not from a simple statement. Moreover, that conclusion is itself not transparent. It uses the idea of an ontological category, but the term "ontological" is being used here in a very precisely Heideggerian sense, and while Fackenheim has used the term before and its contrast with "ontic," he does not really stop to explain it – rather, he is utilizing it here in order to clarify the Heideggerian notion of an ontic–ontological circle.[57] All of this would by itself make the reference to his "conclusion" a demanding one, but there is more. He also uses the term "ecstatic," which he has introduced in a technical way in the argument, as well as the distinctions between thought and life and between resistance in life and resistance in thought. In short, the reader's first steps into this summary paragraph make very substantial demands, and this is before the first sentence is barely underway.

The second sentence refers even further back, to the question that had been set aside when the digression began. Here Fackenheim gives three formulations or three dimensions of the question. And as the reader wrestles to identify each formulation or dimension precisely, he or she also must ask how the three are related to one another. Furthermore, Fackenheim uses a strange locution that he has used before – or rather two such locutions: the first, the idea of thought being where some event occurs, and second, the idea of thought being paralysed.[58] He has used them earlier, of course, but since he never defines or clarifies such notions but rather uses them in differing contexts, their use here asks the reader once again to seek to grasp them and their interrelation.

The next sentence calls on the reader to think back and recall what went on in the previous two sections, 8 and 9, and to ask *why* the question as just formulated has to be suspended and *how* it is suspended. The sentence ends by suggesting that the question marks an impasse and that unless that impasse is broken or somehow destroyed, the inquiry cannot go on. This implies that the excursus or digression in effect has destroyed this impasse, and Fackenheim says how, by showing that "existence was not wholly paralyzed during the Holocaust itself." To understand this, the reader must recall how this claim was shown in the previous sections. Moreover, the reader may wonder whether that is the point of the digression or only part of the point, since there is more than description going on – there is also reflection and analysis.

Fackenheim does say that this "astounding fact" was "confronted, contemplated, explored," but he also says that the "question returns." One must ask, of course, what the question was or which formulation Fackenheim has in mind. In fact, what Fackenheim then says is striking but also perplexing. He says that "there arises for future thought ... an imperative that brooks no compromise."[59] Why is this proposal perplexing? Because it refers to an "imperative." Here the reader familiar with Fackenheim's work might think back to earlier writings such as "Jewish Faith and the Holocaust" and *God's Presence in History* and the 614th commandment. But this idea has not played any role in *To Mend the World*. What Fackenheim has shown is that during the Holocaust there was resistance and even knowing resistance. Hence, thought after the Holocaust – say, philosophical reflection on action and evil or Jewish theological thought – is possible because during the event it had occurred, and what was real then is possible thereafter. But Fackenheim goes a step further in the very next sentence. He writes that "authentic thought was actual during the Holocaust among resisting victims; therefore such thought must be possible for us after the event: and, being possible, it is mandatory." It is the last step of the argument that seems, on the face of it, an utter non sequitur. Even if the reader can understand the next sentence, in which Fackenheim says that resisting thought during the Holocaust led to resisting life, and hence that it ought to do that for us too, the idea of an imperative somehow arising out of a possibility seems almost incomprehensible. Or, at least, it requires some very serious additional thinking before the reader can make sufficient sense of it to go on to the last sentence, and beyond that, to the next paragraph.

Let me stop here. In these initial steps at a reading of this passage I have been concerned most of all to show how demanding this paragraph is for the reader. Fackenheim is being very precise about its content, about what he wants the paragraph to do and how it functions as a transition between the analysis and argument of Sections 8 and 9 and what is to follow, which is the introduction of a new category that is required in order for the imperative to be obeyed, as he puts it. Indeed, this manner of talking to the reader – didactically explaining what has been accomplished and where he is going – is new in Fackenheim's prose. But while he may be very careful about the paragraph's role and its content, he does not make it easy on the reader. The terminology, the allusions and references, and the ideas themselves are not easy to grasp; they require either a good deal of independent understanding or a very comprehensive recollection of earlier passages or very intricate thinking. Without these, the reader will find the paragraph opaque.

This authorial and philosophical voice is quite different from what we have seen in Fackenheim's early essays and then in his books and essays of the 1970s. *To Mend the World* is, as I have described it, dense and weighty, carefully modulated; its arguments use an eclectic and often novel terminology that Fackenheim has created in order to carry out his project. He continues to call upon figures, particular expressions or quotations, and much else that have become his intellectual and philosophical repertoire. But the whole is cast in a way that weaves everything together in very challenging units. Even when he tells the reader where he is, where he has gone, and where he is going, he does so in a way that takes a great deal of effort to fathom. Most of the time there is little lyricism or literary elegance, and if the reader has the sense of an authorial presence, it is very much an intellectually serious and weighty presence. Fackenheim is not so much concerned to provoke or move the reader or to elevate her; his sole concern is the complex analysis and reasoning of the work itself and all the details that constitute these. Moreover, the text's complexity is underscored by its heavy use of parentheticals within sentences (parentheses, dashes, and so on); it is also revealed in the fact that the text uses both endnotes and footnotes, although there is no obvious system at work for dividing up the documentation in this manner.

Another way of describing Fackenheim's voice in *To Mend the World* is to say that it has taken on a very "internal" character; he seems to be talking to himself much of the time or to very familiar conversation partners. His entire effort is absorbed by the work's argument, each and every stage of it, as he works out its details with the greatest care and precision. To be sure, the reasoning is designed so that he can take "responsibility" for its outcomes and so that others, we readers, can share in so doing. But for the most part, the passion and emotion of the essays of the 1970s have been subdued for the sake of this greater purpose. The explicit, rhetorical concern with speaking to or writing for others is subordinated to the demands of the project, to the working out of the argument on which future thinking – Jewish, philosophical, Christian, and much else – is to be built and then future life.

Another word that comes to mind to describe the writing and the tone of *To Mend the World* is "fragmented." To be sure, as I have emphasized, the work is organized around a very complex argument, with themes that Fackenheim has constantly in mind. Yet he brings so much to bear on the argument, so many phrases and motifs, and so many allusions and references that the overall impression is that of a chopped-up and constantly interrupted conversation rather than a smooth whole. It definitely is a whole, and it does have a very precise organization. But simultaneously the book seems quite fragmented, strikingly so. This is not surprising, given that one of its central themes is the fragmentary character of all post-Holocaust responses, of all life and all thought.

Finally, much of the book's philosophical reasoning is conducted by means of readings of historical events or selected quotations, what Cavell called "philosophical interpretation." This affords the book a feeling of concreteness and an impression of transparency; yet the result is that the precise steps of Fackenheim's reasoning are not always easy to identify and that his argument's flow is not easy to discern. The reader may wonder how a line of reasoning can possibly move along on the back of particular examples or cases, and Fackenheim's reading of incidents or reports or testimony can at times seem highly idiosyncratic and arbitrary, even when it is imaginative. At other times it may seem simply enigmatic.

In several ways, the writing of *To Mend the World* marked a watershed for Fackenheim. At the very moment he completed the book, he moved to Jerusalem. His life changed; his primary audience was now thousands of miles away and spread over the entire globe. In Israel he was not as singular a voice as he had been in North America. Eventually he would come to think that he had an important audience in Europe and in particular in Germany, and some of his last writings were aimed at communicating the importance of the Holocaust for German self-understanding. But the change for him was not solely about audience and venue. He had also in the book developed a vocabulary and a style that would dominate his later writings and whose features would become exaggerated as time went on. One might say that except for his popular book, *What Is Judaism?*, most of his writing (and speaking) thereafter would be conducted in the shadow of *To Mend the World*. It would be marked by thinking *through* and *with* concrete, historical events and particular quotations, in often cryptic terms, in sometimes dense and demanding prose, yet with a rhetorical edge.[60] Many of his essays would draw on themes, arguments, and images from *To Mend the World* and extend them in a similar style.

During his last years, from the late 1990s until his death in 2003, Fackenheim's writings exhibited an increasingly cryptic and fragmented style. More and more, he couched his thoughts in the context of recollection and memory. Remembering was a difficult and demanding task for him. Moreover, his decision to engage in such remembering was itself a difficult and conflicted one. For a long time, he refused to commit himself to such recollections or to writing his memoirs. When he did decide to engage in this process, moreover, it was with the proviso that memories always involve philosophical reflection and that it was these reflections and not the memories themselves that would be of paramount importance. Put another way, personal recollections were for him a way of making vivid and concrete more abstract and general philosophical points; they were a form of shareable teaching. We can see these matters develop if we pass over his writings from 1983 into the mid-1990s and focus instead on his last writings.[61] In them we hear the voice of memory in its most developed form.

What I have called the "voice of memory" in Fackenheim's late writings can best be assessed by examining the two essays he contributed to *The Philosopher as Witness*, the talks and essay included as appendices in *An Epitaph for German Judaism*, and, finally, that book, his memoirs.[62] Increasingly in these writings, he weaves together his recollections and his intellectual, philosophical reflections. The opening lecture at the conference held in his honour on his eighty-fifth birthday is a good example. Its title, "In Memory of Leo Baeck and Other Jewish Thinkers in 'Dark Times': Once More, 'After Auschwitz, Jerusalem,'" already hints that the lecture will be a collection of more or less episodic memories and thoughts about a variety of thinkers – Baeck, Hans Jonas, Mordecai Kaplan and Moshe Davis, Martin Buber, Leo Strauss, Franz Rosenzweig, and Primo Levi. The essay is marked by its lack of fluidity as well as by its abruptness. It presents snapshots of figures, memories, and ideas, almost like a collage, and it calls upon the reader and the listener to receive (to determine) its message in new ways. He begins with Leo Baeck:

> The last time I spoke in public was at Hebrew Union College, Jerusalem, on November 7, 2000, just two days before the anniversary of *Kristallnacht*, the event I would understand – in retrospect, many years later – as the beginning of the Holocaust. Two days later, someone in Berlin would mention Rabbi Leo Baeck, no more than his name, for who would still know him? But I had been a student of his, in the period 1935–1938, at the Berlin *Hochschule für die Wissenschaft des Judentums*.[63] *another ideology of which Christianity is not.*

These opening words and the entire essay that follows them sound like the verbal traces of memory working by association. The almost clumsy first sentence is condensed to the point that the reader has to parse the temporal relations. Once one works out what Fackenheim is trying to say, they are clear, but the text compresses the temporal locations, the date of the lecture he had given, the date of *Kristallnacht*, and the moment when he would come to treat that event as the initial act of the Holocaust. The second sentence begins "two days later," and while it is easily seen that Fackenheim means two days after the lecture at the Hebrew Union College, the word "later" is unclear as it stands. Moreover, one wonders how Fackenheim then found himself in Berlin, and here also a sentence compresses a great deal, patching together three thoughts in three clauses separated only by commas. The final sentence begins with "But" and leaves it at that, even though a fuller phrase is required to clarify that what Fackenheim means is "But I did know him, since I had been a student of his ..." In short, this very first paragraph warns us that Fackenheim's "memorial voice" will speak in highly compressed ways: it will juxtapose or list thoughts one after another, strung together with commas, and leave a great deal to the reader, including working out the temporal relationships involved. The second section of the essay begins this way:

> The aforementioned is in summary of an address I gave more than half a year ago. Then I also reported how Baeck taught Midrash. The biblical *Song of Songs* is understood by the rabbis, not as love between the sexes but between God and Israel. *Song of Songs*, 2:7, "adjures the maidens of Jerusalem to awaken not, nor stir up love until it pleases."
>
> I recall Baeck teach[ing] a Midrash on this verse in Berlin, but did he teach it also in Theresienstadt? Half a year ago I was sure; now I am no longer.
>
> When, after the war, I visited him in London I did not dare to ask about Nazi crimes, and all he would tell me was that, when he and another had to pull a heavy wagon in Theresienstadt, they were discussing Plato and Isaiah.[64]

In these pages on Baeck, a person for whom Fackenheim had the greatest respect, Fackenheim seems to be struggling to deal with the complexity of Baeck's conduct during the Nazi period. How much did Baeck understand? What did he allow himself to see and to believe? Was the real horror lost on him or did he confront it courageously and with dignity? But Fackenheim wants to condense his thoughts into the least number of sentences, so he sets aside any idea of telling a story in fluid and narratively coherent terms. Instead he places bits and pieces alongside one another and leaves out all the connectives and transitions that would make it easy for the reader. The result is like a modernist painting or a surreal dream image. He ignores normal protocol. For example, in the second sentence of this section he comments that in the previous lecture he had mentioned that Baeck taught midrash. In fact, he had already mentioned it in the first section of this talk, just two paragraphs before. Then he introduces a verse from Song of Songs. It is one that Baeck had taught and a verse on which Baeck had introduced a midrash and examined it in class. The verse is about the love between God and Israel. Fackenheim says nothing about what the verse means or what the midrash was. But he asks if Baeck also taught it at Theresienstadt and says that a year ago he was sure but no longer. He does not say, however, whether he had been sure that Baeck did teach it or not, nor does he say whether he is no longer sure Baeck had taught it or whether he is no longer sure he had not. He concludes these reflections by recalling his meeting with Baeck in London after the war and after the Holocaust, a story he often repeated. But what is its point? Does he admire Baeck for dealing with the horrors by teaching Plato and Isaiah or does he take this to mean that Baeck was somehow avoiding those horrors? In the next paragraph Fackenheim does say something that suggests – but not clearly – that the story about Baeck teaching Plato and Isaiah is evidence that he did not know the horror or failed to see it for what it was or was avoiding it. But it is hard to tell. Or did he know but maintain silence about it? This is something that Fackenheim in the next few paragraphs introduces as a possibility. But not until then. Here, in the paragraphs I have cited, he does not tell us.

The text goes on to say that Fackenheim's point in introducing the Holocaust is to underscore the need for honest and serious openness to the horrors of Auschwitz. He takes this to be the task of philosophy, for, he asks, "must not philosophy, the more self-critical it is, be the more *ruthless* in facing the Holocaust as being both 'real-and-impossible'?"[65] But while he makes this challenge obvious and emphasizes it, he leaves the connections between the anecdotes and the reflection about Baeck and this task of philosophy quite unclear.

It is not necessary to continue examining this essay in detail; the stylistic features we have identified are present throughout: the abrupt shifting of focus and topic; the cascading series of comments, summoned by memory and separated only by commas or dashes; the economy or condensation; the lack of transitions or fluid narrative; the prominence of fragmented and almost fractured sentences. The essay moves from figure to figure, and in each case Fackenheim's patchwork of thoughts expresses juxtapositions, questions, affirmations that have become his philosophical repertoire. One reads the essay and hears a voice that cannot say enough at one time, that abbreviates thoughts and strings them together, as if time is running out and there will not be sufficient opportunity again to say what needs to be said, to say *everything* that needs to be said. The prose is rushed, compressed – as I have suggested, a "collage." It bursts on the page, one thought after another.

And the personal and the reflective are inseparable in the essay. It is a bundle of memories, and since Fackenheim's memories are often of Germany, his reflections are studded with German expressions. These features are present everywhere but most of all in a short section near the end called "Hallel and Handel."[66] Fackenheim came from Halle, and in this section he notes that Halle was also home to Reinhard Heydrich, whom he recalls – as he often did – was a neighbour to Curt Lewin, who was a friend of Fackenheim's father Julius.[67] It was also the birthplace of Georg Friedrich Handel. In trying to show how German culture and Judaism were interwoven and how the Holocaust had torn that fabric beyond repair, he uses Handel:

The world-famous person, born in Halle, was Georg Friedrich Händel, of great composers surely alone in his love not only of biblical but also post-biblical Judaism: he composed *Israel in Egypt*, *Jephtah*, and many other Old Testament works, but also the postbiblical *Judas Maccabaeus*. Despite his words in his *Matthaeus-Passion*, which disturbed my mother, who loved Bach's music, even though Rosenzweig recommended Bach, Händel is better in that even his *Messiah* contains no anti-Jewish words. More, love of Händel was with us not only personally, for we often heard *Hallel* (Psalms 113–118) in synagogue, on *Pesach*, *Shavuot*, and *Sukkot*, to the great hymn from *Judas Maccabaeus*; this also was sung in Berlin synagogues, but in Halle it was special.

In 1998, on a visit to Halle, I went to the *Marketplatz*, not for other *Sehenswurdigkeiten*, "things to see" – such as the *Rote Turm* or the *Marienkirche*, in which one of Bach's sons, Wilhelm Friedemann, had once been organist – but just for one purpose: to see whether Händel's statue is still there. They had smashed Mendelssohn's in Dresden and changed the text of Händel's *Israel in Egypt* to "*Opferseieg von Walstatt.*"

Twelve years of Nazism had been enough to make Germany *judenrein*, but too short to "cleanse" her of "Aryan Jew lovers": Händel's statue is still there.

Even so, my attitude to Germany remains ambivalent, for in *Kristallnacht* they destroyed the Halle synagogue and, soon after, through expulsion or murder, "cleansed"' her of Jews. True, there are Jews again in my *Heimatstadt*, even a *Bethaus* in the cemetery, but "*Hallel and Händel*"? Once a possibility, even an actuality, but *nimmermehr*, "never again."[68]

If we read this passage carefully, we can see a clear image and grasp Fackenheim's very precise point. But in order to do so, we have to fill in gaps, accept the abruptness and the sharp juxtaposition of thoughts and observations, and more. It is almost as if Fackenheim is giving us a pile of fragments and a hint about what one can find in them; our job is to construct an image and an account out of that pile. Look, for example, at the second sentence, in which Fackenheim piles together a point about Bach's negative comments about Jews with a recollection about his mother, who loved Bach and yet was disturbed by the comments, and a comment about Rosenzweig, all to make the point that Handel, in the end, did think well of Jews.[69] Rather than construct a few sentences and a narrative to explain how all of this is connected in his mind, Fackenheim bundles the points together and leaves it to us to construct or reconstruct that narrative, and then to go on.[70]

The essay ends, leaping into the present, with this sentence: "'After Auschwitz, Jerusalem': the 'comma' means no cause-effect relation obtains between these two, only links: one hope, the other resolve."[71] Fackenheim had already called attention to the fact that he was speaking in Jerusalem and that for his audience there, the point of all his reminiscences was especially salient – not to forget the rupture that the Holocaust has caused in Jewish memory and the demands that are placed on all Jews to go on as Jews. In this sentence he refers to the subtitle of his talk and to the role of the "comma." His point, so condensed and so cryptic, is the same one that he had made in the 1970s, especially in "The Holocaust and the State of Israel: Their Relation." There he had juxtaposed hope with catastrophe and response: in the face of Auschwitz, one seeks to recover hope through the response that is the State of Israel. Here he replaces "response" with "resolve," for there is no response without resolute action, commitment, an act of will. But what had been accomplished years ago in a long and rhetorically powerful essay is here presented in a single, highly condensed sentence.

The "voice of memory," with all the characteristic features I have identified, is present everywhere in Fackenheim's late writings. We find it too, for example, in the talk with which he ended the conference in 2001, "Hegel and 'The Jewish Problem,'" which is structured as a series of reminiscences of his own encounters with Hegel and hence is personal, engaged, but also just as fragmentary, abrupt, and cryptic as the earlier essay on Baeck and "Jewish philosophers." We also find it in the various lectures, given in Germany, that are collected as appendices in *An Epitaph for German Judaism* and indeed throughout that memoir as well. Consider, as one example, a passage from a lecture given at the *Martin Luther-Universitat* in Halle on 22 October 1998, "On the SS

Murder of My Uncle Adolf Goldberg, and in Memory of Leo Baeck," in which Fackenheim reflects on Baeck in a slighter fuller account than we saw in the 2001 talk:

> Baeck taught midrash and homiletics. One midrash he taught was on Song of Songs 2:7: "O daughters of Jerusalem, I adjure you / Do not awaken Love until it is ready."
>
> This may be a secular love song, but for the midrash, the Love is between God and Israel. Baeck taught this midrash in Berlin, perhaps also in Theresienstadt. By a Gestapo error he survived, but the pious had waited for divine love too long, and then came Auschwitz and Treblinka.
>
> I visited Baeck in London, after all was over, and he told me how he and another had discussed Plato and Isaiah while pulling a heavy wagon in Theresienstadt. He did not speak of Nazis, and I did not dare to ask him. But he did make a few comments in Hans Adler's *Theresienstadt 1941– 1945*, just in the one page preface, for him that was enough. Theresienstadt was a place for Jewish dying, not for Jewish living, and it was designed to force or manipulate Jews into crime, in order then to "punish" them.[72]

These are the same memories that Fackenheim recalls in the other essay, and similarly they are delivered in a fairly cryptic and condensed fashion. We are never told exactly which midrash on the verse Baeck had taught, although it is suggested that it was about waiting for God to initiate revelation and not calling for it before the time is right. Here too Fackenheim adds a comment about Baeck's preface to a volume on the concentration camp, but without discussion, clarification, or elaboration. Once again, the memories are personal; they are delivered in a condensed form, abruptly, briefly, without excessive comment or indeed comment at all.

As I have indicated, one finds all of these features of Fackenheim's late authorial voice, what I have called the "voice of memory," in his memoirs, *An Epitaph for German Judaism*. It is a work that Fackenheim left nearly finished but incomplete at his death at eighty-seven in September 2003; he had been at work on it for about a dozen years. Given this lengthy period of composition, the text is marked by an unevenness of style and tone and also by the changes in Fackenheim's life during this period. Overall, however, it exemplifies the tone and style we have found in his late writings. This late philosophical voice was his last.

I have been showing how Fackenheim's later writings, after *To Mend the World*, exhibit an escalating employment of confessional and autobiographical reflections. At the same time, however, he utilizes methods of argumentation and presentation, of philosophical interpretation, that make his writings available to his audience and indeed make great demands on that audience to receive his writing and his thinking. This is what Cavell had called a "way of accepting responsibility for one's discourse" and is what accounts for its "representativeness." It is what replaces, in Fackenheim's later writings, the method of the re-enactment of personal experience and the hovering between the subjective and objective points of view. Does it also, however, illustrate the moral character that, as I argued in chapter 3, Fackenheim claims is characteristic of a genuine post-Holocaust philosophy? It does.

Gould points out that Cavell wants his writing, his voice, to agitate and to produce discomfort, restlessness, and frustration.[73] Certainly, at least since the late 1960s, Fackenheim could agree. He saw in his audience so much avoidance and neglect that he wanted the same – to agitate in behalf of the "victims of Auschwitz" and their memory, to produce discomfort, restlessness, a frustration with the status quo and a change of heart – and of life. In his writings after *To Mend the World*, one can add to these a sense of fragmentariness – of hope interlaced with realism about what can be accomplished as much as what ought to be sought. Who then is the ideal audience for such a message? Who needs such a teaching and who could respond to it?

In *Sense of Walden*, comparing Wittgenstein to Thoreau, Cavell says a valuable word about their audience, and what he says, I think, applies to Fackenheim as well:

> The writer has secrets to tell which can only be told to strangers. The secrets are not his, and they are not the confidences of others. They are secrets because few are anxious to know them; all but one or two wish to remain foreign. Only those who recognize themselves as strangers can be told them, because those who think themselves familiars will think they have already heard what the writer is saying. They will not understand his speaking in confidence.[74]

If a secret is something that "few are anxious to know," then Fackenheim's philosophical understanding of Judaism, revelation, and the Holocaust is a secret. Those who think they are Fackenheim's familiars – his friends and associates, as it were – will not listen carefully; they will think they have already heard what he has to say and so will not understand him as "confiding" in them something unheard, a secret. A few of these associates will not need to hear what he is saying, but many will, and their understanding will be blocked by a kind of self-deception. Hence, Fackenheim's true audience must be strangers, some sympathetic and some not – or at least they must be an audience willing to approach his writings and listen to him with a sense of unfamiliarity. To use language he might use, they should read him with a sense of surprise or astonishment. And if they do, they may come to hear what he has to say and be disturbed by it, discomforted, and changed. In this sense, Fackenheim's writings would be genuinely philosophical. If successful, they would open something to view, agitate, and motivate.

In *To Mend the World*, in the Introduction, in the section where he discusses language and its use to describe the horrors of the Holocaust, Fackenheim makes the following argument. First, if one wants to use language today in order to help others grasp and then articulate, how to respond in life to the Holocaust and to live in its shadow, one cannot go beyond the witnesses themselves, such as Jean Améry or Chaim Kaplan, Primo Levi or Elie Wiesel. Second, for them, language could be neither "objective" nor "self-indulgent" but rather "subject to disciplined restraint." Third, this means that "the language necessary … is one of sober, restrained, but at the same time unyielding outrage."[75] Finally, the language necessary for writing today about what it is to live in a post-Holocaust world must also have these features. For the writer today must still "go to school with life," and "the going-to-school of thought with this life is not a temporary necessity but permanent."[76]

In his own way, in *An Epitaph for German Judaism*, Fackenheim does indeed follow his own strictures. His writing is sober, but it is the sobriety of memory. It is also restrained, especially if restraint is expressed in economy and compression. Finally, it does express a kind of "unyielding outrage," for it is driven to express something about the German Judaism that Nazism destroyed and that will, as he sees it, never again exist. Hence, it is about trying to recover the fragments of a world that is lost, both in general for all to see and for him personally in terms of a recovery of memories and his reflections on them and their meaning.

In the early chapters of his memoirs, Fackenheim takes time with his stories and his reflections on them. The narrative is as full as his memory allows, and the comments are developed and clear. But as the book goes on, especially in Part 3, "Israel," the style and tone become more condensed and fragmented, more like that of the essays we have just examined. Throughout, Fackenheim begins with a memory but then, in commenting on its significance, allows himself to move forward to more recent events and even to the situation when he was writing. The book has, therefore, a dynamic character; his thoughts seem to hover back to Germany, then Aberdeen, and Toronto, and then forward to Israel and to the years of the book's writing, from 1993 to the early years of the new century. And the hovering in time is also a hovering in space, from one locale to another, often from Germany and Toronto to Israel and back. The composition thus draws together past, present, and a kind of timelessness, all into moments, images, and insights. The effect is to allow the book to be both about Fackenheim, his life and career, and about German Judaism, Judaism in Canada, and then the role of the Holocaust and Israel for Jewish thought and Jewish life. The book is also about the tradition of Western philosophy as Fackenheim read, analysed, and engaged with it, and finally about how, in his thought and work, the two – Judaism and Western philosophy – at times interacted and at times were kept separate. This theme – of "wearing two hats," as he puts it – is central to the book throughout.

Several drafts of the "Epilogue" for these memoirs exist, but the essay finally chosen for this purpose begins with an admission that part of Fackenheim's motive for writing his memoirs was his personal sense of guilt:

> When I started *An Epitaph for German Judaism* I did not plan to write about myself at all. But one of my personal catastrophes was shared by all survivors, even those of Auschwitz and, so one hopes, much of the world. That no human being is innocent is a belief shared by Jews and Christians, which is why Jews have Yom Kippur, Christians the Crucifixion.
>
> But guilt after the Holocaust is *particular*: did I, personally, do enough for my brother [Alexander] left behind, think enough of my murdered uncle [Adolf]? Did *the world* do enough for the six million, countless Russians, Czechs, Poles?
>
> The real guilt, of course, belongs to Germans, yet others, too, have no mere *feelings* of guilt, for psychologists to deal with: *the guilt is real.*[77]

Fackenheim goes on to discuss briefly Karl Jaspers, who wrote a book on guilt – individual, collective, and then "German guilt about Hitler Germany as 'metaphysical' and this, he asserted, consisted of being alive."[78] He then calls upon the evidence of his high school classics teacher, Adolph Lörcher, to refute Jasper's claim and to show that staying alive could be an act of rejection and not one of guilt.

Why write about guilt – personal and shared? Why write about German Judaism, about the Nazi assault on human dignity, on Judaism, and more? Why write about Judaism and philosophy and a sense of life's meaning and purpose? Fackenheim's admission is that he only wrote about himself insofar as his experience was not utterly distinctive but rather shared, so that both the experiences recalled in his memoir and his reflections on their significance could have a general and independent value. The same is true of all his later writings, at least from the early 1970s. To him, the memoirs were not merely personal recollections. They were more than that. They were personal entranceways to common experience and to matters of the gravest concern and urgency for all of those who would listen and who needed to listen. Fackenheim always saw himself as a philosopher, and although his understanding of human selfhood and agency was what he called "existentialist" and engaged, so that philosophers as well as everyone else had to be understood as historically situated and as participants, not as spectators or detached observers, he still took philosophical results to be communicable and shareable. The last thing he would have agreed to do was write about himself for the primary purpose of putting himself on exhibit. His experiences and his memories were windows to a broad and common horizon.

As I have tried to show in my "Foreword" to *An Epitaph for German Judaism*, the fragmentary and compressed style of the work, and its interruptive and digressive character, with its unflagging effort to recall the significant and memorialize all of those in his past who meant something to him, all of this exemplifies Fackenheim's own conclusions about how an authentic *tikkun* (mending) of one's life ought to be conducted.[79] No mending today is or can be perfect or complete; no life is coherent, smooth, and comprehensive. All one can hope to accomplish is to recover to some degree and to mend in whatever ways one can. Let me quote a passage here that I quoted there, one in which Fackenheim called upon Hegel at the end of the second edition of *To Mend the World*, published in 1989:

> Hegel once said that the wounds of Spirit heal without leaving scars. He could no longer say this today. To speak of a healing has become inappropriate. Scars of the wounds of Spirit remain and will continue to remain. But a mending is possible, and therefore necessary.[80]

As in mending, so in writing – the scars remain. They are present in the philosophical voice that Fackenheim discovers and in the discourse we have described. Furthermore, in writing his memoirs and in the long process of remembering and returning to the past, Fackenheim was in fact writing his life and mending it, without hiding the complexity, the pain and the guilt, and the commitments that marked his persona in his last years. As he closed in on death, as time was running out, he found the will to assemble his thoughts and his memories as best he could, delivering a eulogy to one Judaism that had been destroyed and expressing his hopes for another Judaism yet to be, both with a "restrained but unyielding outrage." In so doing, he took upon himself the responsibility of genuine post-Holocaust philosophical thought and found the voice to do so.

10
Fackenheim's Legacy:
Resources for Mending the World

It is about a decade since Fackenheim passed away in Jerusalem. Is it too early to attempt to assess his significance and to consider his legacy? And if we do want to ask what his legacy is, what he has passed on that is valuable and important, ought we not first to ask what kind of legacy we have in mind and whom its recipients might be? If we want to ask what is living and what is dead in his writings and in his thought, for whom is this question being asked?

Some years ago, on a visit to Australia, I was invited to speak at the Holocaust museum in Sydney. Before the talk I was introduced to a white-haired man, a retiree. He was a Holocaust survivor – Sydney has a very large population of Holocaust survivors, as does Melbourne – and, if I recall correctly, he had once owned a grocery store. I had been asked to speak on Fackenheim's work, and this man had come to the lecture. He explained that he had heard Fackenheim years before in Sydney and had been so moved, so engaged by him and his thinking, that he had begun to read his works. In fact, as we talked, I realized that he had not merely read Fackenheim's books; he had pored over them, studied them, lived with them. He knew the central themes; he knew words and phrases; he knew footnotes. Fackenheim had become for him a voice that spoke to his life in profound ways; he had become his "teacher" and his guide. This man was not alone. I have met many people like him; they are everywhere.

For the last forty years of his life, Fackenheim was a Jewish intellectual and especially a Jewish theologian and philosopher of international reputation. His writings were read in North America but also in Europe, South America, South Africa, and Australia. Moreover, he spoke and lectured widely not only at universities but also in numerous public venues and often in interfaith contexts; thousands heard him, met him, and were affected by his thinking and by him personally. No final chapter of a book dedicated to understanding his thought and in particular the sense in which he was a philosopher and a Jewish philosopher can deal with this broad impact. Nor should it; his psychological and social significance for the lives of many is for historians to gauge; it is not the business of a philosopher. Rather, what we can do is ask about various themes and views he addressed and positions he held, whether they can be and perhaps should be of special importance for those who seek to continue the project or projects of Jewish philosophy. And a bit more broadly, what features of his writings and his thinking can and should be important for anyone interested in understanding Jewish existence, the situation of Judaism and Christianity in a post-Holocaust world, and in general religion and contemporary life? In *To Mend the World* he sought to establish "foundations for future Jewish thought," and in the book's last pages he sketched what "mending the world" for Judaism, Christianity, and Western philosophy might look like. In this spirit, we can ask, at the end of our study: What does his thinking contribute to Jewish philosophy today and in the future?

I have no doubt that if he were asked, at the end of his life, what his central contribution had been, he would have answered: he had explained and defended the duty of a joint commitment to take seriously the Holocaust and to take God seriously. Perhaps this is a good place to begin. What does such a two-part commitment mean? What does it mean "to take something seriously," and what does Fackenheim mean by the "Holocaust" and by "God?"

The phrase "to take something seriously" can of course be used in an ordinary, idiomatic way, to mean "to pay some attention to something rather than to ignore it or to be indifferent to it," and perhaps "to pay some significant amount of attention to something, that is, to commit some time and effort to something or to considering it." But Fackenheim uses the expression to mean something philosophically deeper than this – for someone to consider something's claims and implications as demanding or binding, as unavoidable and inescapable, and to reject any account of it that would reduce it to something else. These terms – "unavoidable and inescapable" – are ones that Fackenheim uses frequently. They suggest that we are not talking about a narrowly philosophical matter. The expression "to take something seriously" is not for him an exclusively logical or epistemological expression; rather, it is "existential." It connotes that one should be willing to give up a good deal to face up to something, to pay a steep cost, a high price, and to do so because the weight of the issue or the thing is so great that avoiding or escaping it is not possible; and that when one faces up to it, this will not be easy.

When the phrase is understood in this way, we can see why Fackenheim would say that the Holocaust is this sort of event. He wants us to realize that facing up to it is a weighty business; it is inescapable and will cost us a good deal. Much is at stake. No account that assimilates it to other bad or horrible events treats it this way; no account that homogenizes it, or that underestimates the importance of its distinctiveness and avoids its "particularity" and generalizes its negative features, is acceptable. To whom? To anyone with human sensitivity, human concern, honesty. Moreover, this taking-seriously in all its particularity and distinctiveness applies to all suffering, all horrors, all atrocities, and all evil. In each case, each of us has a responsibility to the victims that must be respected.

But let me treat these two deep concerns of Fackenheim's – the Holocaust and God – as the poles of our discussion. The Holocaust as a concern first arose for him explicitly and thematically in 1966–7; but God and revelation were interests of his from his earliest days, and arguably they remained important to him throughout his life. So let us begin with revelation and the divine–human encounter; then, after introducing a number of other matters, at the end of our consideration of his legacy for contemporary Jewish philosophy, we will return to the Holocaust.

Revelation as Orientation: Judaism as Covenantal Mutuality

Since I want to speculate on what Jewish philosophers might find valuable in Fackenheim's work, let me be unabashedly autobiographical, at least to begin with. I have found his thinking about revelation and the divine–human relationship very provocative and compelling, in part because of what he clearly believes about these matters and in part because his appropriation of Buber and Rosenzweig on them raises just the right questions about the meaning and role of revelation in Jewish existence. Let me explain.

What does Fackenheim mean when he says that the contemporary Jew ought to take God seriously? The word "God" here stands for the religious significance of Judaism, that is, its character as a way of grasping and understanding the divine–human relationship, the relationship between the absolute and the conditioned or the finite, the human. Therefore, it stands for all the problems relating to revelation and faith that Fackenheim had taken to be the core issues for his earliest work. Fackenheim's point, that the Jew today must take God seriously, means that even in the light of modern science, scepticism about transcendence, and much else, and in the shadow of the horrors of the death camps, the Jew today should not glibly and easily abandon God, faith, the idea of revelation, and the centrality of the covenant to Judaism. To abandon them would be to give up on Judaism. Certainly, the relations today between the individual Jew and God and between God and the Jewish people may not be simple and unproblematic, and there will be many ways of understanding what content such a relationship should have. But still, if Fackenheim is right, no recovery of Judaism today will do that does not incorporate some understanding of and commitment to these ideas and their reality in Jewish life.

Moreover, facing up to this question is "inescapable and unavoidable" in our day. To take God seriously may not lead everyone to commit him or herself to God, to the covenant, and to transcendence, but there are no facile answers. Even a renewed commitment to such features of Judaism should, in our day, not come easily. It should be a conflicted and troubled return.

If I am right, revelation and the divine–human relationship, according to Fackenheim, are core features of any attempt to understand Jewish existence. What revelation is, its role, and its implications – these ought to be central preoccupations of any genuine Jewish philosophy. He argued that Judaism without revelation is seriously deficient. What, however, does this mean? And what would Fackenheim contribute to contemporary treatment of these issues?

To begin, we ought think for a moment about *why* revelation was such a central preoccupation of Fackenheim's and why he thought it was central to understanding Judaism – why, in fact, at least in his early writings, until the late 1960s, he took it to be among Jewish ideas the most central one. It is clear that Fackenheim took the modern crisis of religion and religious faith to be about the challenges posed by modern thought and modern life to the possibility of a divine–human relationship and of religious experience. He did not seem to think that it was simply a matter of doubting the existence of God, in view, let us say, of developments in the sciences and the pre-eminence of naturalism. What concerned him was not knowledge of God and God's existence; rather, it was the possibility – and the necessity – of living with God.

When he discusses his crisis of faith, he has in mind figures like Feuerbach, Marx, and Nietzsche – he does not mention Freud as well, but he might have – and an overall cultural attitude that seemed to treat religious experience as an aberration or as somehow anomalous.

In addition, what he thinks endangers Judaism is not Christianity or opposing religious impulses or movements. It is secularism, where he takes that to mean a world view that is by and large naturalist and scientistic, enamoured with the natural and social sciences, with technological advances, and with organizational and bureaucratic models grounded in the sciences. In Judaism, a serious and responsible view of Judaism as a covenantal faith is not threatened as much by parochialism as it is by Jewish forms of secularism and naturalism. For much of his career, he saw this as one kind of threat and one kind of concern.[1]

This way of looking at the chief opponent of religion and of Judaism led him to treat revelation as the central issue in understanding Judaism. To be sure, it is not the only important Jewish concept – Fackenheim gives creation and redemption their due – but it is the central one. He clearly felt the need to show how revelation is possible and why it is necessary for Judaism; he also considers what its role is, that is, how it ought to be understood as a feature of human existence when that existence is understood from a Jewish point of view.

Why did Fackenheim feel that without revelation, Judaism was somehow inadequate and inauthentic? The answer to this question is neither surprising nor obscure. If being and remaining Jewish, in the face of anti-Semitism and worse, the Nazi persecutions and atrocities, were to be worthy tasks, compelling and binding, then there must be some reason for being Jewish that is unconditional or absolute. Judaism cannot just be an ethnic or cultural affiliation; it cannot be a matter of inertia or whim or unquestioned acceptance. The reason for remaining a Jew cannot be to cultivate an identity or to make one's family happy or to prevent various colourful and interesting rituals and texts from falling into disuse; and it cannot be for no reason at all. Fackenheim found that philosophers who were unsettled by conditional and qualified answers to questions about Judaism's significance for Jews or who were generally unsatisfied with the possibility of religious or cultural relativism or similar views believed that one had to link human existence somehow to an absolute, to something unconditioned. Philosophers as diverse as Plato and Descartes, Kant and Hegel, thought this. One might or might not be able to say much, if anything, about that absolute by itself, but one could say *some*thing about its relationship with finite, limited creatures like ourselves. One could say how human life, what we call "religious" life, was somehow grounded in that relationship: it made sense of our lives or gave them meaning that was unconditionally secure in its ground; and it did not permit such meaning to be rooted only in temporary, changing things. The anchor had to be more than what nature provides, for what nature provides is subject to change, partiality, and limits.

In part, I think, Fackenheim felt this about Judaism because he was a Jew, growing up in Weimar Germany, seeing around him the persecutions that targeted his father, his uncle, and others in his family and eventually him, and realizing that if he were to remain firm in his commitment to Judaism, that commitment would have to be matched by some reason why Judaism was worthy of it. It had to be worth it to continue being a Jew – especially when it made one a target of genocidal hatred and more.

One thing that Fackenheim teaches us, then, is that there are intellectual, historical, moral, and human reasons for finding at the core of Judaism a relationship between an utterly finite and vulnerable people and an absolute, transcendent God. Revelation, from one angle, then is about this fact, this relationship, which provides an unconditional framework in which Jewish life and Jewish history gets worked out. It is the heart of the covenant.

I have always thought, having read Fackenheim and those who influenced him in this regard – Kierkegaard, Buber, and Rosenzweig most of all – that in order to place revelation at the heart of Judaism, one must have a *concept* of revelation. Some have thought that revelation is a text and thus that it is linguistic; others have thought that it is rational and that the content of revelation is what our reason, operating at its highest levels, produces and discovers – for example, science and metaphysics. There are other views about the concept of revelation. Fackenheim's great contribution, I think, is to synthesize from Buber and from Rosenzweig a plausible and compelling account of revelation as a dialogical – as a first-person–second-person–event, an encounter between the finite and the infinite, the human and the divine. In an earlier chapter, I set out the features of this account; there is no need to review it here. It is a philosopher's attempt to appropriate features of two earlier views and to construct out of them a coherent account that he then articulates in terms of its internal dialectical character. This latter, of course, is helped once he takes his understanding of Kierkegaard, Buber, and Rosenzweig and enriches it with a Hegelian understanding of the historical and dialectical interdependence between Divine power and human freedom and other relevant polarities within that relationship. One does not find such a sophisticated and subtle account in any other postwar Jewish theologian or philosopher, not in Heschel or Soloveitchik or indeed in any other figure working in the latter half of the twentieth century.[2]

At one point, we should remember, Fackenheim refers to revelation as the Jewish theological category of existence; it deals with human existence of the individual. More precisely, it is the category of selfhood or what I would call *meaningful selfhood*. If creation is the way in which the divine is related to all nature and hence is the category of the natural, and if redemption is the category of history and community, insofar as it joins individuals into a community with a historical purpose, then revelation is what mediates the two. It gives meaning to the individual person's natural life and provides the sense of purpose that is common to all individuals, as a community, and that becomes their historical task.

This framework or network of concepts is one that Fackenheim himself develops in some of his early essays. Although he does not put it this way, such a framing places the concept of revelation at the centre of Judaism's normative project. What I mean is this. Broadly speaking, Judaism as a way of life is about how Jews ought to live – what they ought to believe and how they ought to act. It is about the meaning of life from a Jewish point of view. But "oughts" must be grounded in something in order to carry normative weight or to have normative force. There must be some authority behind them; they must be grounded in some reasons. And ultimately, those reasons must be unconditional if the normative project is to be secure. The concept of creation responds to the experience of our sheer existence and the existence of the world in which we live by articulating the dependence of our existence, its contingency, and at the same time the sense that it is ordered. The concept of redemption responds to the sense we have that the historical process is not pointless and without purpose and that while the responsibility for taking that purpose seriously rests on humankind and human communities, it is also somehow guaranteed and ensured. Finally, then, the concept of revelation responds to the sense that we are more than merely natural beings and that what meaning and purpose there is to human life is confirmed for each of us as individuals. Our lives are not without a point and purpose, and we are, each of us, engaged with the project of recognizing this and taking this on as members of one or more communities that hope to realize it.

The Divine–Human Relation and the Ground
of Normativity in Judaism

Ever since Kant raised doubts, epistemological and ethical, about the possibility of taking moral normativity to rest upon Divine will and to be grounded on Divine command, the pressure to locate the ground of moral force or moral weight or authority has increased. To be sure, philosophers like Hobbes and Spinoza, and many others, felt that pressure, but it comes to a head after Kant, in the thought of figures like Hegel, Kierkegaard, Nietzsche, Sidgwick, and Moore, and more recently throughout the twentieth century. The two main options to this question of the ground of moral normativity have been nature and rationality, and twentieth-century meta-ethical inquiries on this matter have taken on the look of a return to Hume or to Kant, in one way or another. Fackenheim's formulation of a concept of a determinative divine–human relation, engaged and dialectical, provides Judaism with a way to think about moral force and normative authority without an explicit return to the idea of divine command. To be sure, he cites and interprets midrashim that refer to God as delivering commands, and he at times uses this language of divine command. But in fact, the role of revelation for him, along with the way he articulates it – in the tradition of Kierkegaard, Buber, and Rosenzweig – uses the idea of command as a metaphor and transfigures moral normativity from law and statute to the claims and responsibilities that arise in a determinative relationship. In other words, revelation becomes the vocabulary for the way that moral and religious responsibilities arise in interpersonal relationships insofar as they express the responsibilities and expectations of the divine–human relationship, that is, the covenantal relationship.

To the degree that Jewish philosophy today and in the future ought to reflect on the normative character of Jewish life and its foundations, I take Fackenheim to have provided a valuable resource for so doing. To be sure, not everyone will agree with this as an important issue. There will be those, for example, who may want to treat this normative dimension of Jewish life as legal and as worthy of exploration and analysis only internally, in terms of how it functions and how it is configured as a legal system. There are those, in other words, who may want to leave the theological question wholly aside, as beyond or at least outside the realm of worthwhile exploration and examination. What is, for some, interesting and worth exploring are the methods, values, complexity, multivalence, and such of the Halakhah as a legal system.

Indeed, there are those who will doubt that such a system has any transcendent or external ground. It is simply a system, anchored in a consti-
tutional text and then interpreted within a complex and rich textual
tradition. And even if others would affirm that the Halakhah is grounded in its relationship with God, they might take it to be the perfect expression of Divine will and Divine intellect. Human responsibility is to
elaborate and articulate that perfect expression in all its details, to incorporate more and more of what may appear to be excluded into what
is in its ideal form a complete divine representation of the world and all
that orders it. And since it is normative, human responsibility is also to
adhere to the norms, to obey the law, thereby fitting one's actions and
one's life into this ideal divine map of all reality.

This is not the place to debate these options and others regarding the
status and role of law in Judaism and the nature of commandment. My
point is that if the contemporary Jewish philosopher takes the divine–
human relationship to be formative for Judaism and takes responsibility for understanding that relationship, then there is no escaping the
reflections on it that we find in the nineteenth and especially the twentieth centuries. Among those reflections, Fackenheim's is especially interesting, as a clear and deep late-twentieth-century consideration and
recovery of a tradition of thinking about such matters that includes
Hegel, Kierkegaard, Buber, Rosenzweig, and many others.[3]

Of special interest, I believe, is a comparison between Fackenheim
and Emmanuel Levinas, and while there are many reasons to consider
them together and to evaluate their work in terms of each other, I think
that on this issue of the ground of normativity in Judaism, the comparison is especially salient.[4] What I have in mind is this. For Levinas, there
is a dimension of every interpersonal encounter we have that contains
a claim that the other person makes upon the self, an appeal the other
makes to the self for acceptance, aid, and support, and the responsibility of the self to the other for that acceptance and aid. In short, if we
were to ask where the sense of obligation we have towards others
comes from, the answer is that it is a structural feature of every relationship a self has with each and every other person. Moreover, unlike other relations we have and other features of them, this one never arises at
a given moment; it is always already there, in the relationship. And the
aspect of it that carries a kind of command or ought, its moral weight or
authority, is manifest in it. It lies deep within it and does not derive
from anything else. In his later writings, from about 1963, Levinas refers to this intrinsic moral force or weight with the expression *Illeity*,

and he associates the term with the everyday term "God" in the sense that this term is used in contexts where one wants to bring to mind the special force carried by moral duty or obligation to others.[5]

In a sense, Fackenheim might find much of this congenial, especially insofar as it is presented as an alternative to Heidegger's account of *Dasein*, of human existence. Whereas Heidegger takes human existence to be a particular kind of manifestation of Being, and hence an ontological matter, Levinas wants us to see that ethics is more fundamental than ontology. Put another way, *ought* is more fundamental than *is*. Fackenheim does not have a systematic account of human existence or a philosophical anthropology. However, he does think that human existence in its everyday or ordinary setting does have a dimension that conveys normative force to it. Ordinary life – in particular, interpersonal relationships – can be interrupted by episodes of intense, meaning-conferring relation, where the encounter between a particular self and a particular other person either establishes or confirms or redirects a way of acting and living that is oriented around that relationship. Unlike in Levinas, this encounter is an episode; it is something that happens between the self and the other. And the burden of it falls on the "betweenness" or the relation, which is mutual, giving, open, and all-inclusive. It is a matter of two individuals being wholly involved with each other, as if there were nothing going on anywhere that was somehow not incorporated into that moment and that "meeting." For Levinas, as we have said, the face-to-face relation is not a separate event or episode; it is a dimension of every social interaction, sometimes more dominant and explicit, sometimes less so.

Furthermore, if we were to call this moment for Fackenheim (after Buber, he calls it an "I–Thou" encounter) ethical, what we might mean is that it gives life the meaning it has or confirms some meaning that one already had in sight. But in order to carry that weight, to be normative in this absolute sense, it must be grounded in a relation with God. Revelation is not a separate event; it is a supervenient one. It occurs at the same moment when an intimate interpersonal event is occurring. It is distinguishable but not separable. For Levinas, as we saw, the relation of the self to the other, at its fundamental level – its ethical level – is a dimension of all interpersonal relations, and the presence of *Illeity*, while like the divine presence, is not really that, in any factual sense. In other words, Levinas is even less attracted to talking about God ontologically than Buber is. Buber is willing to talk about Divine presence but not Divine existence; Levinas is only willing to talk about Divine *absence*, in the sense that "God always has already passed by," so to speak.

Why do these matters worry Fackenheim? And why should they worry Jewish philosophers today? I believe – and I am not alone; I would contend that philosophers as diverse as Hilary Putnam, Donald Davidson, Bernard Williams, Thomas Nagel, Charles Taylor, and Richard Rorty would agree – that a central, if not *the* central philosophical problem of the twentieth century is whether we can meet the challenges of scepticism, relativism, and nihilism with regard to our understanding of our everyday lives, of science, and of morality. In the area of morality, for example, can we have a secure understanding of what justice requires of us and what we ought to do to make life better for ourselves and others? In science, can we have a secure and productive understanding of the world around us? Can we have knowledge confidently and securely? Can we rebut the challenges of cultural and historical relativism? Can we say that torture and cruelty are wrong, period and without qualifications? Can we condemn Hitler and Nazism as horrific and abominable, without placing any conditions on our judgment?

In his early years, Fackenheim saw what a challenge this kind of question is. He was convinced that one had to understand human existence and human agency as situated and perspectival. We are never simply observers or examiners of the world and our experience. Rather, we are participants, involved agents. Yet even given this necessarily subjective point of view, so to speak, we could rise to a point of view that is detached, impersonal, and unconditional or absolute. Thomas Nagel argues for this in his widely read *The View from Nowhere*, and he is not alone.[6] This is not the place to discuss this issue in detail. My point is that although Fackenheim held a view like this in his early period, the more he studied Hegel and the more he focused on the Holocaust and its horrors, the more convinced he became that no such absolute and wholly objective point of view is possible for us, as finite and limited human beings. He framed this point by talking about how history and thought are related.[7] As he came to realize, all thought – philosophical and metaphysical, religious, and moral – is historical. That is, its terms and claims can always be modified and refuted by new historical realities. There is no such thing as a claim that is wholly immune to historical modification and even refutation.

The Dialectic of Thought and History: Historicism and Relativism

The Holocaust and the various threats to the comprehensiveness and completeness of the Hegelian system exposed this claim to him and also raised the spectre of disaster. That is, at first Fackenheim believes that there is such a thing as absolute truth, at least philosophical and probably also religious. But then intellectual honesty leads him to admit that no such transcendence, as it were, is possible. All thought is historical and historically vulnerable. But if so, then nothing counts unconditionally against Nazism and radical evil. This conclusion, however, is intolerable. How does one respond to it? Not by revisiting the issue about the totally historical character of human existence – including human thought – but rather by arguing that the only authentic way to confront the horrific – such as the Nazi atrocities – in our daily lives is by setting aside intellectual and explanatory endeavours and by confronting atrocities and evil in the only way appropriate for us, who adhere to humane values, to human dignity and worth. That way is, by opposing the evil and by doing what we can to support the cause of human dignity wherever and however we can.[8]

Fackenheim – following, I believe, in the footsteps of a host of others, including Hegel, Rosenzweig, Barth, and Marcel – takes the dialectic between thought and history to be central to understanding religion and much else about ourselves and our lives. I think he is right and that many debates in history and historiography, in science and the history of science, in literary criticism and interpretation, and in the study of religion and religious belief make this completely clear. The debate in the wake of Thomas Kuhn's *The Structure of Scientific Revolutions*, for example, shows precisely this, as do the controversies over structuralism and deconstruction, and postmodernism and traditional thought. Arguably, these twentieth-century debates go back to the discussion about the *Naturwissenschaften* and the *Geisteswissenschaften* in the late nineteenth century. The postwar controversy over Wittgenstein's later philosophy has raised similar issues, as has the impact and influence of Heidegger's early philosophy in *Sein und Zeit* and the slow but highly influential transmission of French and European thought to America – from Foucault and Lyotard and Derrida to later figures, many of whom react against those three on political grounds.[9]

We discussed this dialectic in an earlier chapter. It is one of the most vital issues in twentieth-century intellectual circles. Thought, of course, comes in a various forms: religious, scientific, ethical, philosophical, and political, to mention only a few. The problem of the historicity of thought can be formulated this way: In what ways are the meaning and truth of statements in a particular domain of thought – say geometry or socialist thought or epistemology – qualified by the historical situation in which they are produced (uttered or published)? Or, alternatively, are there any such statements – or any ideas or concepts that such statements employ – whose meaning and/or truth are not qualified by their historical situation? Fackenheim is especially interested in philosophical claims and also religious ones, but others – Kuhn and MacIntyre and a host of philosophers – are interested in science, in logical principles, and in general principles of rationality.

Fackenheim, that is, wonders whether any philosophical claims can be essentially transcendent – that is, whether they can be unqualifiedly general and universal. As I have tried to show, he becomes convinced that after Auschwitz, no religious claim is in principle immune from historical modification or refutation. But this belief is tantamount to saying that all religious claims are historically qualified and hence relative. Facing up to this possibility, appreciating how deeply historical situations influence the ways we think and speak, all of this is critical to any understanding of ourselves and our world. But such a view may appear to risk lapsing into relativism, and it ought to make someone like Fackenheim worry about how any standards for authentic or responsible opposition to Nazism, genocidal hatred, and acts of inhumanity are possible. And even if, as with someone like Michael André Bernstein, one doubts that there are such standards, surely one might take opposition to evil and inhumanity and barbarism as in some sense absolute and unconditional.[10] But if what Fackenheim fears is true – that in philosophy, ethics, and religion, no truths are a priori in a strong sense – how is absolute opposition grounded? What explains its absoluteness? Even if one disagrees with Fackenheim about what role the Holocaust plays in this matter, he is surely a guiding light in pointing out how serious the issue is for Judaism and Jewish philosophy.

My own view is that the issue is central and that nonetheless, within the ways we view and understand the world, we do articulate rules of thought and practise habits of deliberation and decision and thereby arrive at what we consider degrees of confidence about what we believe and what we take to be true and binding.[11] This is as much certitude and as much objectivity as we can hope for and all that we regularly operate with. Any claim that we can detach ourselves from all finite or personal points of view and arrive at an absolute or impersonal perspective is a fiction, at best an ideal that we imagine for ourselves from within the finite points of view that we occupy as participants and agents and that are ineliminable for us.[12] Fackenheim knew this; he found it in Kant and also took it to be one of the outcomes of the "breakdown of the Hegelian middle," as he referred to it. So, in fact, I think that the position I would hold is also one for which Fackenheim had a good deal of sympathy. It is not something about which he is very explicit, although it is implied, I think, in the Gadamer-style hermeneutical account of human existence that he formulates in *To Mend the World*.

The Holocaust as Epoch-Making Event

One thing shared by Fackenheim and many of these continental figures – as in the case of Levinas, whom I already mentioned – is an apprecia-tion of the monumental impact of the Nazi atrocities and the horrors of the death camps on our thinking and on our lives. Terms like difference, rupture, transcendence, and the like came naturally to these postmod-ernist thinkers and also, given his Hegelian background, to Fackenheim, for whom the expression "epoch-making event" was so central in his later period.[13] To many of them, the issue was about the conditions that, though constitutive of our lives, nonetheless are beyond expressing. Fackenheim too is interested in what everyday language and rationality cannot possibly grasp and in what cannot be captured even in the rich-est and most comprehensive philosophical thought – God, the concrete, utterly particular individual, and even the thing-in-itself. When he ar-gues that the radical evil of Auschwitz and all that is associated with the dreaded event also lie somehow outside our explanatory systems and our ordinary conceptual apparatus, he is thinking in the same terms. In the waning years of his life, Fackenheim surely felt that his greatest con-tribution and yet the one most in jeopardy was his claim that the Holo-caust deserved our greatest attention and that responding to it seriously and honestly was one of our most important responsibilities.

This is one area where Levinas and Fackenheim do differ, I think. Richard Bernstein has argued that the Holocaust is at the root of all of Levinas's thinking, and there is certainly an element of truth in think-ing that the Holocaust played an important role for him.[14] But Levinas does not think about the Holocaust as a uniquely momentous event, or even an evil one, in Western history. Rather, he is inclined to think of the entire twentieth century, with all of its genocidal acts – the Holocaust of course, but also Cambodia, Serbia, and others – as one of horror, atroc-ity, and suffering. To him, these events represent a vast failure of hu-manity and justice, of human kindness and concern and generosity of spirit. So to begin with, Fackenheim is more inclined than Levinas to focus on the very particular event of the Nazi Holocaust and the death camps and its unprecedented character, its capacity to mark off all the past from a new epoch, a post-Holocaust epoch.

Levinas and Fackenheim do agree that the Holocaust cannot be explained or understood using conventional categories and theories about human behaviour, politics, social psychology, and such. No explanations, social scientific, historical, or religious, are capable of answering the questions one is inclined to ask; no explanations provide intellectual satisfaction. In fact, in a very important essay, "Useless Suffering," in which Levinas does discuss the Holocaust and refers explicitly to what Fackenheim says in Chapter III of *God's Presence in History*, Levinas remarks on just this claim of Fackenheim's that we can find no meaning, no purpose, and no explanation for the Holocaust.[15] Levinas reads this as an endorsement of a view that he calls the "end of theodicy," arguing that we should never be tempted to respond to events like the Holocaust with theodicies. His use of this expression is very broad. For Levinas, all explanatory schemes or theories – religious, ethical, metaphysical, social scientific – are theodicies. They all attempt to explain why evil and suffering take place and to make their existence reasonable, understandable. Of course, what counts as understandable varies greatly depending upon what kind of scheme or theory one is talking about, but Levinas's point is that the Holocaust marks a historical moment when we ought to realize that the primary way to respond to suffering and atrocity is not with explanations and intellectual accounts. Rather the right or appropriate response to such events is one of opposition or resistance – to use Fackenheim's word – or, in Levinasian language, it is to take one's responsibility to the victims, to those who suffer, seriously, to reach out to them and to do what one can to reduce that suffering. In this respect, then, there is a strong similarity between Levinas and Fackenheim. Both claim that overintellectualizing one's response to evil and suffering is unacceptable and flawed; one should never abandon the suffering, no matter what the cost.

However, this is also a moment when Levinas and Fackenheim differ, for to Fackenheim the responses are always particularized and hence can be articulated in terms of duties falling upon Jews, Christians, and so forth. For Levinas, the responses are particularized to the situation, but they are always responses to the needs of the other, whether this involves acceptance, or assistance, or respect, or something else. In other words, on the face of it, at any rate, Levinas's focus is on the ethical and hence the universal dimension of response to suffering, whereas

Fackenheim's focus is hermeneutically determined by the point of view from which one engages the situation and the victims. I am tempted to think that in reality, there is not as much of a difference here as Levinas himself would think. But even if we were to accept this as a difference between them, what it points to is a deeper difference: the way in which Fackenheim's account is without the metaphysical foundation (if I may call it that) that we find in Levinas's account. In other words, the two differ with regard to their philosophical anthropologies. What do I mean by this?

Both Fackenheim and Levinas are philosophers. Both articulated accounts of human existence or the human condition. Levinas's philosophical writings constituted a lifelong engagement with this task. Fackenheim's attention to it was more diffuse; he confronted it in "Metaphysics and Historicity" in the course of asking whether philosophy – metaphysics in particular – is still possible if we affirm a view of human agency and selfhood as historically situated and engaged. Where they differ, to put it briefly, is that Fackenheim adheres to an existential or hermeneutic conception of the self as freedom in a situation (his debt here is to Heidegger, Kierkegaard, Sartre, and Buber), whereas Levinas breaks sharply with this tradition. Famously, he takes the primary relationship for human existence to be interpersonal and ethical. One implication of this difference is that for Levinas there are ethical and moral considerations – responsibilities – that arise almost directly from the claims others make on us for acceptance, concern, and aid and that apply to us always in every situation. It may be true that for Levinas we are, in our everyday lives, always particularizing, prioritizing, and orchestrating such claims, but they are always there. For Fackenheim, the demands of social existence are always mediated and identified contextually and always with an overriding regard for the divine–human relationship, which operates as a kind of overarching orientation for all our moral decisions and their content. There is, for this reason, more indeterminacy about Fackenheim's conception of our moral obligations and responsibilities. To be sure, at any given moment, we articulate what we are responsible for doing and why we operate within a tradition of past determinations and decisions, by others and by us, so our decisions are not wholly indeterminate or without guidance or direction. Clearly there *is* direction. But for Levinas, every situation comes already prepared, so to speak, with claims to justice and generosity, to kindness and goodness, prior to any articulations or decisions.

Thus, for Levinas, the Holocaust cannot be an absolute rupture; it cannot cut us off totally from the past and leave us with the imperative and also the problem of recovery of a radical kind. For Fackenheim, this is precisely what the Holocaust does. Just as the law is both a bar and a bridge between God and the human, so the Holocaust is a bar and a bridge to the past and to recovery. It is a bar in that it puts everything into question and requires a leap into the past to retrieve anything; it is a dark chasm between us and all we had taken for granted. It is also a bar to complete recovery; its "scars" are permanent and cannot be covered over completely. Only fragmentary recovery is possible, Fackenheim argues. But in addition to that, the Holocaust originates an imperative of opposition and hence of recovery, and in this regard it is a bridge, albeit a difficult one to traverse. This is how Fackenheim depicts the role that the Holocaust plays in Jewish life and indeed in all life and for all thought.

Levinas takes the Holocaust very seriously for the failure and abandonment it involved and that it expresses, as a paradigm of the horrors and suffering of the entire century. But the Holocaust was not a caesura or a rupture so much as a failure. The ethical as the character of all human relationships was present before the Holocaust; it was present during the Holocaust; and it is present today. In Levinas's thinking, the ethical is a corrective to all totalities; it underlies them and is a standard by which they are all to be judged. But we – humankind – have not always been attuned to the ethical and responsive to it. During the Nazi era and especially within the Nazi regime, there was a wholesale abandonment of the ethical, and the result was horror, atrocity, and the death and suffering of millions. There is no other way to recover from this failure than to extend care and concern for others, personally, socially, nationally, and globally.

Hegel and Beyond

I mentioned in an earlier chapter Fackenheim's recollection of the night in Berlin when Arnold Metzger first introduced him – and a select group of other students – to Hegel's *Phenomenology of Spirit* and what an impression that night made on him.[16] All that mattered that night was the "presence" or "absence" of Hegel's "Absolute" in Nazi Berlin. What was it that struck Fackenheim as so momentous about that night's discussion? One possibility was its relevance: it taught him that real philosophy was not an ivory tower reflection on abstract and dead texts. It was about making old texts and problems come alive in the present. But another possibility is that what excited him about Metzger's teaching that night and about the *Phenomenology* was that in it one could find a monumental exploration of the question of the presence or absence of the Absolute in life. That is, for Fackenheim one of the things that made Hegel so important to him and one of the things that he took to be fundamental to the *Phenomenology* was the central theme of that text and of human selfhood as Hegel saw it – that the self is the arena for the divine–human encounter. It is in this spirit, I think, that he chose the following passage from Hegel's *Lectures on the Philosophy of Religion* as a prologue to the chapter on the *Phenomenology* in his Hegel book:

> I raise myself in thought to the Absolute ... thus being infinite conscious-ness; yet at the same time I am finite consciousness ... Both aspects seek each other and flee each other ... I am the struggle between them.[17]

Why, then, was Hegel of so much importance to Fackenheim? And should the contemporary Jewish philosopher follow in Fackenheim's footsteps?

Let me put the point in my own words. There are two opposing ten-dencies in Western philosophy and Western culture with regard to tran-scendence and divinity and concreteness and worldliness. One is Pla-tonism, which in its most extreme forms – its Gnostic and Manichean forms – exalts the transcendent and ideal and at the same time deni-grates the earthly, the natural. The other is materialism or naturalism, which, once again, in its extreme forms either forecloses and rejects the transcendent and ideal altogether or reduces it to something material or natural. Fackenheim always was committed to the falsity of these extremes, although he was convinced in the partial truth of both. Any responsible understanding of human existence must appreciate fully our embodied and concrete physicality; yet at the same time, it must ap-preciate our ability to stretch beyond the limits of our physical abilities and character so that we find ourselves in touch with something that is wholly beyond the physical and the concrete, something unconditional, utterly particular, and determinative. Aristotelianism and Christianity of certain kinds affirmed such a mediation but did so with an inclination towards the natural; Judaism, on the other hand, affirmed such a media-tion but with a firm commitment that if the human and the transcendent were to come into relation, it could only be with the understanding that the two are nonetheless separate and distinct. But the point I am trying to make is that what attracted Fackenheim to Hegel, at least in part, was that he could fathom all of this and take it seriously. Unlike other philosophers – Spinoza or Hobbes or Leibniz or Berkeley – Hegel could take cognizance of this dialectical character of human existence and appreciate how it permeates all of human experience, at every level and in every way. Thus Fackenheim's thinking, like that of Buber, Rosenzweig, Heidegger, and others, can find a place for naturalism and other forms of thinking that are, by Fackenheim's lights, one-sided and even reductionist or exclusionary, whereas the only way materialists can accommodate Fackenheim's acknowledgment of the Absolute or the Infinite – to use these terms of art – is to reduce it to a distortion, phantasm, or error.

In short, what appealed to Fackenheim on that night in 1937 or 1938 in Berlin was the openness to transcendence that he found in Metzger and Hegel. It was the willingness to take seriously the "absence or presence" of the Absolute and what that might mean for human existence, for a way of life, and for a *Zeitgeist*. All culture, art, religion, and society live in the engagement of transcendence and the world. What distinguishes us as selves is how we negotiate that enterprise, that encounter. As Hegel says, "we are the struggle between them."

Jewish philosophers today may look in different directions for their philosophical guidance. If they look to German philosophy, they may turn to Kant or Heidegger rather than to Hegel. If they direct their attention to French philosophy, they may turn to later figures such as Foucault or Derrida or Levinas. And they might even turn their gaze towards Anglo-American philosophy and find interlocutors in philosophers such as John Dewey or Ludwig Wittgenstein or Bernard Williams or Hilary Putnam or Charles Taylor or Alasdair MacIntyre or Stanley Cavell. But if contemporary Jewish philosophers learn any lesson from Emil Fackenheim, it will be this one, I think: that a serious interlocutor from the tradition of Western philosophy will be one who takes seriously and is open to two dimensions of the human experience, the transcendent (or divine or ideal) and the historical (or concrete or worldly). Only by considering both and by negotiating the tensions and interplay between them will a responsible Jewish philosophy emerge – for our day and for the future.

Only in Christ is the real answer to unity and that means His Church will survive in these turbulent times Suffering for sure will follow Christ's believers but the Church of Christ will survive. He promises that life in Him will mean Eternity in His presence.

Notes

Introduction

1 That such an aspiration is natural and desirable is a central theme of Thomas Nagel's *The View from Nowhere* (Oxford: Oxford University Press, 1989).

2 See Martin D. Yaffe, "Historicism and Revelation in Emil Fackenheim's Self-Distancing from Leo Strauss," in *Emil L. Fackenheim: Philosopher, Theologian, Jew*, ed. Sharon Portnoff, James A. Diamond, and Martin D. Yaffe (Leiden and Boston: Brill, 2008), 107–24; Kenneth Hart Green, "Leo Strauss's Challenge to Emil Fackenheim: Heidegger, Radical Historicism, and Diabolical Evil," in *Emil L. Fackenheim*, 124–60; Sharon Portnoff, "Fackenheim's Hegelian Return to Contingency," in *Emil L. Fackenheim*, 161–78; Sol Goldberg, "The Holocaust and the Foundations of Future Philosophy: Fackenheim and Strauss," in *The Philosopher as Witness: Fackenheim and Responses to the Holocaust*, ed. Michael L. Morgan and Benjamin Pollock (Albany: SUNY Press, 2008), 75–86; and Catherine H. Zuckert, "Fackenheim and Strauss," in *The Philosopher as Witness*, 87–102. See also Martin Kavka, *Being and Non-Being* (PhD diss., Rice University, 2000), 49–79.

3 See Fackenheim, *An Epitaph for German Judaism: From Halle to Jerusalem* (Madison: University of Wisconsin Press, 2007), 46, 105. Fackenheim's essay "The Historicity and Transcendence of Philosophic Truth" (in *The God Within*, ed. John Burbidge [Toronto: University of Toronto Press, 1996], 148–63) was written in response to a letter from Strauss in which he criticized Fackenheim's facile dismissal of Heidegger's historicism in *Metaphysics and Historicity*, n43; see in *The God Within*, 227–8.

4 Especially in Michael L. Morgan, *Discovering Levinas* (Cambridge: Cambridge University Press, 2007) and *The Cambridge Introduction to Emmanuel Levinas* (Cambridge: Cambridge University Press, 2011).

5 See Morgan, *Discovering Levinas* and *The Cambridge Introduction to Emmanuel Levinas*.

6 See Morgan, *Discovering Levinas*, ch. 10, "Beyond Language and Expressibility."

7 The notions of transcendence and rupture are related. For now, I want to separate them. See Martin Jay's two papers on the "event": "Historical Explanation and the Event: Reflections on the Limits of Contextualization," *New Literary History* 42 (2011), 557–71; and his paper in a forthcoming festschrift for Steven Aschheim. See also Gary Gutting, *Thinking the Impossible: French Philosophy Since 1960* (Oxford: Oxford University Press, 2011).

8 John McCumber argues that Fackenheim shares this theme with postmodernist philosophers; see McCumber, "The Holocaust as Master Rupture: Foucault, Fackenheim, and 'Postmodernity,'" in *Postmodernism and the Holocaust*, ed. Alan Milchman and Alan Rosenberg (Amsterdam: Rodopi, 1998), 239–64. See also Susan Neiman, Claudia Card, and Richard Bernstein, all on evil, radical evil, and atrocity.

9 Others – such as Leo Strauss, Abraham Joshua Heschel, Mordecai Kaplan, and Gershom Scholem – are important, but their contributions to Jewish philosophical thought are limited in ways that are not true of the others I mentioned. Hannah Arendt and Hans Jonas are even more marginal to the enterprise of understanding Judaism in ways that engage philosophical issues. Even lower down on any list would be Leo Baeck, Isaac Breuer, Jacob Petuchowski, Norman Lamm, and Robert Gordis. I restrict myself to figures who are no longer living.

10 Early on, he discusses Aristotle, Plotinus and Proclus, Alfarabi and Maimonides; later Strauss, Arendt, and Sartre; but the extent of these encounters is nothing like that with those mentioned above.

Chapter 1

1 Fackenheim, "Can We Believe in Judaism Religiously?" *Commentary* 6 (1948), 521–7; reprinted in Fackenheim, *Quest for Past and Future* (Bloomington: Indiana University Press, 1968), ch. 3. All references to the latter.

2 Fackenheim's first essay, "Our Position toward Halacha," written in 1938, while he was still a student in the *Hochschule*, as part of a project with his fellow students, and unpublished until he translated it for inclusion in

Michael L. Morgan, *The Jewish Thought of Emil Fackenheim* (Detroit: Wayne
State University Press, 1987), 21–5, was on the theme of revelation,
covenant, and Jewish practice.

3 This is a central theme of Rosenzweig's *Star of Redemption* (New York:
Holt, Rhinehart and Winston, 1970, 1971). This is, one might argue,
precisely the challenge that Rosenzweig poses – of staying with the "old
thinking" or moving on to the "new" or of remaining within the confines
of Part One of the *Star of Redemption* or of pushing on to Part Two. In a
sense, it is the difference between clinging to Heidegger or turning to
Rosenzweig, Buber, and those associated with them.

4 Fackenheim uses this expression on several occasions. See, for example,
"Self-Realization and the Search for God," in *Quest for Past and Future*, 46.

5 Perhaps to Barth and Bultmann as well.

6 I discuss the emergence of this movement in Michael L. Morgan, *Beyond
Auschwitz: Post-Holocaust Jewish Thought in America* (Oxford: Oxford
University Press, 2001), ch. 1. See also Robert G. Goldy, *The Emergence
of Jewish Theology in America* (Indiana: Indiana University Press, 1990).

7 Buber makes this claim, a central one, in Part Three of *I and Thou*. Fackenheim explores the status of this Buberian claim in "Martin Buber's Concept
of Revelation," originally in Schilpp and Friedman, *The Philosophy of
Martin Buber* (Chicago: Open Court, 1965); reprinted in Michael Morgan,
ed., *The Jewish Thought of Emil Fackenheim*, and in *Emil L. Fackenheim: Jewish
Philosophers and Jewish Philosophy* (Bloomington: Indiana University Press,
1996). In other terms, all relations to God can only be first-person to
second-person.

8 See Fackenheim, "The Revealed Morality of Judaism and Modern
Thought," in *Quest for Past and Future*, 218–24. Originally this essay was
published in Arnold J. Wolf, ed., *Rediscovering Judaism* (Chicago: Quadrangle Press, 1965).

9 Franz Rosenzweig, *The Star of Redemption* (New York: Holt Rhinehart and
Winston, 1970, 1971), 156–204.

10 See Rosenzweig, *The Star of Redemption*, 167–168.

11 See Fackenheim, "Can There Be Judaism Without Revelation?" in *Quest
for Past and Future*, ch. 4.

12 The essay was originally published in *Commentary* in 1965; it is reprinted
in *Quest for Past and Future*, ch. 16.

13 See Martin Buber, *I and Thou* (New York: Scribner's, 1970), 157–60.

14 The review was originally published in *Judaism* 2 (1953), 367–72; it is
reprinted in Morgan, ed., *The Jewish Thought of Emil Fackenheim*. Cf. his
review of Will Herberg, *Judaism and Modern Man*, in *Judaism* 1 (1952): 172–6.

15 See "Self-Realization and the Search for God."
16 Morgan, *Quest for Past and Future*, 314–15.
17 Originally in *Commentary* (1964); reprinted in *Quest for Past and Future*, ch. 15.
18 I discuss this terminology and Fackenheim's use of midrash in chapter 8.
19 Morgan, *Quest for Past and Future*, 17.
20 Fackenheim, *To Mend the World* (New York: Schocken Books, 1982), 13; see also 6–9.
21 On the dialectic between thought and history, see chapter 7.
22 This was in part what Fackenheim as a young student learned from reading Strauss's *Philosophie und Gesetz*. It was one access for him to debates between the old humanism and the movement of dialectical or crisis theology and others – for example, Barth, Gogarten, Bultmann, and the young Tillich.
23 Emmanuel Levinas identifies this tendency toward intellectualizing the problem of evil and suffering and calls it the temptation of "theodicies." See Levinas, "Useless Suffering," in *The Provocation of Levinas*, trans. Richard A. Cohen, ed. Robert Bernasconi and D. Woods (London and New York: Routledge, 1988), 156–67.
24 Ideally, we should also look at *What Is Judaism?*, published in 1987, where he seeks to speak most clearly and candidly to *amcha*. For my purposes in this chapter, I omit this treatment, which follows the others and is carried out in a more homiletical fashion. On 24 April 1997, in his Inaugural Lecture included in the Franz Rosenzweig Memorial Lecture Series, Fackenheim could still say that "my main work has been – still is – the problem and fate of revelation in modernity, except that in more recent years the Holocaust has replaced modernity." The lecture is printed as Appendix B in Fackenheim, *An Epitaph for German Judaism* (Madison: University of Wisconsin Press, 2007), 240–6; the passage is on 243.
25 I am not concerned here with Munk's criticism of Fackenheim or the latter's reply. What I am interested in is what Fackenheim says about his views about revelation.
26 Louis Greenspan and Graeme Nicholson, eds., *Fackenheim: German Philosophy and Jewish Thought* (Toronto: University of Toronto Press, 1992), 268; see generally 268–72.
27 That is, he is more concerned with how one should respond to the imperatives or obligations that arise out of an encounter with the horrors of Nazism than with whether one takes such imperatives or obligations to be grounded in divine presence or in some rationally apprehended value or whether indeed they seem ungrounded in any determinate way.

28 Fackenheim's reading of Rosenzweig is the traditional or orthodox one. But I think it needs clarification. All people are responsible for humane and caring treatment of others – love of others – Jews included. But as members of the Jewish people, Jews do have a special commitment and a particular role or task to play in the course of history and with regard to the historical goal of realizing in the world social forms of life that exemplify such humanity and concern to the greatest possible degree, to the degree that they can be realized in history.

29 Greenspan and Nicholson, *Fackenheim*, 270; see also 272.

30 Martin Buber, *Moses* (New York: Harper Torchbooks, 1958), 75–7; quoted in *God's Presence in History* (New York: Harper, 1970/1972), 12–13.

31 Fackenheim's account here is more consciously phenomenological than ever before.

32 I discuss this midrash in ch. 8.

33 Fackenheim, *God's Presence in History*, 14–16. For the Hegelian background of the dialectic in this passage, see ch. 5.

34 See Fackenheim, "On the Eclipse of God," in *Quest for Past and Future*, ch. 15.

35 Fackenheim, *God's Presence in History*, 83.

36 This would involve arguments against naturalist and rationalist accounts; arguably Fackenheim should have provided more in this regard than he did. See Zachary Braiterman, *(God) After Auschwitz*, for discussion of such arguments.

37 See Fackenheim, *The Jewish Return into History* (New York: Schocken Books, 1978), 23. The comment occurs in "The 614th Commandment," which is a reprinting of Fackenheim's contribution to the symposium "Jewish Values in the Post-Holocaust Future," in *Judaism* (Summer 1967).

38 In *I and Thou* Buber cites the passage at 158; see Friedrich Nietzsche, *Ecce Homo*, trans. Walter Kaufmann (New York: Vintage, 1967), 300. The sceptic or secular Jew has a kind of moral intuition and a moral sense of a claim being made upon him or her – and he or she has intuitive understanding of what it requires to stand up to and oppose such horror and atrocity. But that is all.

39 Fackenheim, *An Epitaph for German Judaism* (Madison: University of Wisconsin Press, 2007), 243.

40 Fackenheim, *What Is Judaism?*, 81; see also 88–103.

41 For the present I set aside his general book *What Is Judaism?*

42 See chs. 2 and 5 especially.

43 Here Fackenheim focuses on Rosenzweig. Insofar as Fackenheim's account of revelation is indebted to Rosenzweig, this is the appropriate place to look for illumination about his own views. But his account is also indebted

to Kierkegaard, and so it is useful to look back at his discussion of Kierkegaard in section 9 of ch. 3, where he is considering the "dialectical results"
of the breakdown of the Hegelian mediation or synthesis; see Fackenheim,
To Mend the World, 121–3, and especially his analysis of what Kierkegaard
means by "immediacy after reflection."
44 Fackenheim, *To Mend the World*, 141; see 136–46.
45 See Fackenheim, *What Is Judaism?* (New York: Summit Books, 1987), the
last chapter.

Chapter 2

1 See Rosenzweig, *The Star of Redemption*, trans. William H. Hallo (New York:
Holt, Rinehart and Winston, 1970, 1971), 156–98.
2 For an account, from the analytic point of view, of the aspiration to
objectivity and the unavoidability of the first-person point of view, see
Thomas Nagel, *The View from Nowhere* (Oxford: Oxford University Press,
1989).
3 On situated and embedded agency, see Charles Taylor, "Engaged Agency
and Background in Heidegger," in *The Cambridge Companion to Heidegger*,
ed. Charles Guignon (Cambridge: Cambridge University Press, 1993),
317–36; also Taylor, "Self-Interpreting Animals," in *Human Agency and
Language: Philosophical Papers I* (Cambridge: Cambridge University Press,
1985), 45–76.
4 This was first published as the Aquinas Lecture by Marquette University
Press in 1961; reprinted as "Metaphysics and Historicity," in *The God Within*,
ed. John Burbidge (Toronto: University of Toronto Press, 1996), 122–47.
5 See Charles Taylor, *Sources of the Self* (Cambridge: Cambridge University
Press, 1989), 3–107; also "What is a Person?," in *Human Agency and
Language.*
6 See Fackenheim, "Self-Realization and the Search for God," in Fackenheim, *Quest for Past and Future* (Bloomington: Indiana University Press,
1968), 46–7.
7 In "Self-Realization and the Search for God," for example, Fackenheim
lists the alternatives that are possible for man when confronted by God;
in the end, in addition to all the ways of avoiding or rejecting God, man
can make "the decision of faith ... He can accept the 'yoke of the Kingdom
of Heaven.'" *Quest for Past and Future*, 45; see also 47.
8 Fackenheim, "An Outline of a Modern Jewish Theology," in *Quest for Past
and Future*, ch. 6.
9 Fackenheim, "An Outline of a Modern Jewish Theology," 110–11.

10 See Franz Rosenzweig, *On Jewish Learning* (New York: Schocken Books, 1955), 72–94.

11 Fackenheim is recalling Buber's use of a famous midrash from T. Berachoth 64a on Is.54:13: "Rabbi Elazar said in the name of R. Chanina: 'Talmidai Chachamim increase peace in the world,' as it says, 'And all your children will be taught of Adonai, and great will be the peace of your children' – do not read *banayikh* 'your children,' but rather *bonayikh* 'your builders.'"

12 See Fackenheim, "The Dilemma of Liberal Judaism" and "The Revealed Morality of Judaism and Modern Thought," in *Quest for Past and Future*, chs. 8 and 14.

13 Alasdair MacIntyre popularized a notion of the narrative self. See Marya Schechtman, *The Constitution of Selves* (Ithaca: Cornell University Press, 1996), esp. Pt 3; John Christman, "Narrative Unity as a Condition of Personhood," *Metaphilosophy* 35, no. 5 (2004): 696–713; and Kim Atkins, *Narrative Identity and Moral Identity* (New York and London: Routledge, 2008).

14 For a case of traditional Judaism being honest with itself in this way, see David Hartman, *A Living Covenant* (New York: Free Press, 1985); and Walter Wurzburger, *Ethics of Responsibility: Pluralistic Approaches to Covenantal Ethics* (Philadelphia: Jewish Publication Society, 1984).

15 This comment is from a famous letter of Rosenzweig to Buber, 16 July 1924; see "The Builders" in *On Jewish Learning*.

16 This account of freedom, commandment, and revelation is the crux of "The Dilemma of Liberal Judaism," 141–5.

17 See "The Revealed Morality of Judaism and Modern Thought," 222 and 221–7.

18 "The Revealed Morality of Judaism and Modern Thought," 227. One finds a similar view about human freedom as a divine gift in the thought of Eliezer Berkovits. For Berkovits, however, that freedom is the ground of human responsibility and therefore a feature of the rabbinic conception of divine providence; see Berkovits, *Faith after the Holocaust* (New York: Ktav, 1977). Berkovits bases his account of the relation between divine power and human freedom on an interpretation of the biblical motif of *hester panim* (God's hiding of His face), but as Paul Franks has pointed out to me, a more natural source is the kabbalistic notion of *tsimtsum* (divine contraction), which may very well play an important role in the German Idealist tradition that is so important to Fackenheim.

19 Fackenheim, "Metaphysics and Historicity," reprinted in *The God Within*, 122–47.

20 Fackenheim, "Metaphysics and Historicity," 126. All my citations come from this reprint of the original monograph.
21 Fackenheim, "Metaphysics and Historicity," 128.
22 See Taylor, "Engaged Agency and Background in Heidegger."
23 See "Metaphysics and Historicity," 143.
24 In an important note to this conclusion, Fackenheim quotes Kierkegaard's account of the self as self-choosing in *Either/Or* (Princeton: Princeton University Press, 1944), II, 179ff. He notes too that for Kierkegaard this choosing involves the "recognition and free acceptance of its own finitude, which, if authentically performed, is its 'absolute.'"
25 Sartre says that the anti-Semite chooses to be a stone, that is, to be passive with respect to how others view her.
26 See Jean Paul Sartre, *Anti-Semite and Jew* (New York: Schocken Books, 1948), 53–4, 59–60. Sartre portrays the human condition, human selfhood, as transcendence and facticity, that is, freedom as a process of interpretion and action in a situation. In *Anti-Semite and Jew* he uses different terms but the point is the same. This formulation, in ch. 2, captures what is central to Fackenheim's conception in *Metaphysics and Historicity*, where he characterizes human agency as self-making (and then self-choosing) in a situation.
27 For a nice treatment of the emergence of this account of selfhood, see Charles Taylor, *Sources of the Self* (Cambridge: Harvard University Press, 1989). See also Alain Renaut, *The Era of the Individual* (Princeton: Princeton University Press, 1997).
28 Reprinted as "The 614th Commandment," in *The Jewish Return into History* (New York: Schocken Books, 1978), 22.
29 See Rosenzweig, *On Jewish Learning*. See also Rosenzweig's famous remark on Exodus: "*vayered*, 'He came down,' *vayomer*, 'he said' is already human interpretation." See also *Star of Redemption*, 161.
30 The interpretive character may be implicit, given the role of text and midrash as expressed in *God's Presence in History* (New York: NYU Press, 1970), ch. 1, but Fackenheim does not distinguish between argument and interpretive reading when it comes to the 614th commandment.
31 Fackenheim, *To Mend the World*, 256–9.
32 Fackenheim, *To Mend the World*, 256–9 and 345n96. See also Hans-Georg Gadamer, *Truth and Method* (New York: Crossroad, 2004); Rudolf Bultmann, *The New Testament and Mythology and Other Basic Writings* (Philadelphia: Fortress, 1984); and Paul Ricoeur, *Hermeneutics and the Human Sciences* (Cambridge: Cambridge University Press, 1981) and *The Conflict of Interpretations* (Evanston: Northwestern University Press, trans. 1974).

33 Taylor uses the vocabulary of identity and the constitution of identity in *Sources of the Self.*

34 Fackenheim, *To Mend the World*, 260.

35 For the impact of the Holocaust on the idea of martyrdom, see Fackenheim, "On the Life, Death, and Transfiguration of Martyrdom: The Jewish Testimony to the Divine Image in Our Time," in *The Jewish Return into History* (New York: Schocken Books, 1978), ch. 15 (orig. in *Communio* 4, no. 1 [1977]). Hannah Arendt also notes that the death camps made martyrdom impossible; see "The Concentration Camps" and also "Total Domination" in *The Origins of Totalitarianism* (New York: Harcourt, Brace, Jovanovich, 1951), 451–2.

36 In ch. 1 in *Quest for Past and Future*, Fackenheim rejects the essentialist approach to Judaism (12–16), but the present point is more extreme and more serious.

37 We will discuss this idea of the Midrashic framework more fully in ch. 7.

38 Fackenheim, *To Mend the World*, 24, citing *God's Presence in History*, 92.

39 See Arendt, *The Origins of Totalitarianism*, 437–59. Arendt called the result "superfluous persons," that is, persons who had been stripped of their juridical status, their moral character, and their individuality – persons who were redundant and whose distinctiveness was irrelevant.

40 I will refer to three primary texts: the essay "On the Life, Death, and Transfiguration of Martyrdom" (originally delivered in the spring of 1976); *To Mend the World*; and "The Holocaust and Philosophy" (see next note).

41 Fackenheim, "The Holocaust and Philosophy," in *Jewish Philosophers and Jewish Philosophy*, ed. Michael L. Morgan (Indiana: Indiana University Press, 1996), 133, see also 129–36; reprinted from *Journal of Philosophy* 82, no. 10 (1985): 505–14.

42 Fackenheim, *To Mend the World*, 215.

43 Fackenheim, "The Holocaust and Philosophy," 133.

44 See Martin Heidegger, *Being and Time* (New York: Harper, 1962). For commentary, see Richard Polt, *Heidegger: An Introduction* (Ithaca: Cornell University Press, 1999), 85–100; and Stephen Mulhall, *Heidegger and Being and Time*, 2nd ed. (New York: Routledge, 2005), 120–52.

45 See Giorgio Agamben, *Remnants of Auschwitz: The Witness and the Archive* (Brooklyn: Zone Books, 2002), 41–86.

46 Fackenheim, "On the Life, Death, and Transfiguration of Martyrdom," 241.

47 Fackenheim, "On the Life, Death, and Transfiguration of Martyrdom," 244.

48 Arendt, "Total Domination," in *The Origins of Totalitarianism*; see also Jean Améry, *At the Mind's Limits* (Indiana: Indiana University Press, 1980), 1–40.

49 Arendt, "Total Domination," 251.

50 Arendt makes this observation in *The Origins of Totalitarianism*, 459.
51 Fackenheim, "The Holocaust and Philosophy," 135.
52 Fackenheim, "The Holocaust and Philosophy," 136.
53 Arendt recognizes that her account of the "new criminal of the twentieth century" and of the "banality of evil" does not apply to Goebbels, Heydrich, Streicher, Hitler, et al. both in *The Origins of Totalitarianism* and then in Hannah Arendt, *Eichmann in Jerusalem* (New York: The Viking Press, 1963).
54 See Fackenheim, "Holocaust and *Weltanschauung*: Philosophical Reflections on Why They Did It," in both *The God Within* and *Jewish Philosophers and Jewish Philosophy*; originally published in *Holocaust and Genocide Studies* 3, no. 2 (1988): 197–208.
55 I have discussed these matters in *Discovering Levinas* (Cambridge: Cambridge University Press, 2007), and in *The Cambridge Companion to Emmanuel Levinas* (Cambridge: Cambridge University Press, 2011).
56 In his famous paper, "Freedom and Resentment," P.F. Strawson calls special attention to various forms of punishment and moral condemnation and to attitudes such as gratitude, resentment, forgiveness, love, and hurt feelings. See Strawson, "Freedom and Resentment," originally published in the *Proceedings of the British Academy* in 1960 and reprinted in many places, including *Freedom and Resentment and Other Essays* (New York: Methuen, 1970).
57 Susan Shapiro, "'For Thy Breach Is Great Like the Sea; Who Can Heal Thee?,'" *Religious Studies Review* 13, no. 3 (1987): 211.
58 See Fackenheim, *To Mend the World*, 336; cf. 217. And for discussion, see Benjamin Pollock, "Thought Going to School with Life? Fackenheim's Last Philosophical Testament," in *Emil L. Fackenheim: Philosopher, Theologian, Jew*, ed. Sharon Portnoff, James A. Diamond, and Martin D. Yaffe (New York: Brill, 2008), 79.

Chapter 3

1 For a wonderful and rich account of ancient philosophy as a way of life, see John M. Cooper, *Pursuits of Wisdom* (Princeton: Princeton University Press, 2012).
2 To others, of course, what replaces philosophy or thought is life, ordinary experience.
3 Fackenheim, "Human Freedom and Divine Power," *Quest for Past and Future* (Bloomington: Indiana University Press, 1968), 195–203, esp. 200.
4 Fackenheim, "Human Freedom and Divine Power," 196–9.

5 Fackenheim, "Human Freedom and Divine Power," 200.
6 Thomas Nagel, *The View from Nowhere* (Oxford: Oxford University Press, 1989).
7 Fackenheim, "Human Freedom and Divine Power," 201.
8 Since, for Fackenheim, after Buber, the divine–human encounter cannot involve taking up an objective or detached point of view, he might well not agree that the special case is typical of all philosophy.
9 Fackenheim, "Human Freedom and Divine Power," 201.
10 For some comments on Fackenheim's early reading of Kierkegaard, see ch. 7; for his reading of Hegel, see ch. 5.
11 Fackenheim, "Human Freedom and Divine Power," 203.
12 For evidence that he was influenced by his reading of Hegel, see Fackenheim, *The Religious Dimension in Hegel's Thought* (Bloomington: Indiana University Press, 1967), ch. 3. The essay I am discussing was published in 1963. Fackenheim had been teaching Hegel since 1952, and he was at work on the Hegel book from 1957 to its publication a decade later. See below, ch. 5.
13 Fackenheim, "The Revealed Morality of Judaism and Kantian Thought," in *Quest for Past and Future*, 204–28, esp. 204.
14 Fackenheim, "The Revealed Morality," 204.
15 Fackenheim, "The Revealed Morality," 205.
16 That is, it is the particularity of experience that needs to be accommodated into an inquiry that seeks universal and general results. In the case of Jewish experience, that particularity concerns commitments that are made by a Jew and that would not be made by others. This may seem to be a different type of particularity, and it is. But it has the same effect.
17 The proposal is reminiscent of the position taken by Peter Winch in his Wittgensteinian work *The Idea of a Social Science*. Alasdair MacIntyre delivered a famous critique. The debate is reprinted in Bryan R. Wilson, ed., *Rationality* (Oxford: Blackwell, 1970).
18 Fackenheim himself, in a later essay, points out that the problem of other minds is similar to the problem of relating to God and that in order to understand the confusions of the both problems, it is important to realize that human experience, like the divine–human encounter, is a matter of participating in a lived nexus. The ideas relevant to this discussion are relevant to understanding how interpersonal communication goes on and hence how philosophical reflection on human experience works. See Fackenheim, "On the Eclipse of God," in *Quest for Past and Future*, 240.
19 Fackenheim, "Metaphysics and Historicity," in *The God Within*, ed. John Burbidge (Toronto: University of Toronto Press, 1996), 136: "Does the

doctrine of historicity imply the surrender of the idea of timeless metaphysical truth? … If human being is an historically situated self-making, must all its activities be historically situated – metaphysics included?"

20 Fackenheim, "Metaphysics and Historicity," 137.

21 Fackenheim, "Metaphysics and Historicity," 141.

22 Fackenheim, "Metaphysics and Historicity," 146. The conclusion that Fackenheim arrives at concerning philosophical self-understanding is one instance of a larger claim concerning the historicity of philosophy that is the central issue in a later paper, "The Historicity and Transcendence of Philosophic Truth," reprinted, with a new introduction, in *The God Within*, 141–63. See esp. 154: "How can philosophic thought be rooted in history, and emerge from history, and yet reach a truth which is transcendent?" This is the central problem of the paper.

23 The passage is from Martin Buber, *Moses* (New York: Harper, 1958), 75–7.

24 Fackenheim, *God's Presence in History* (New York: NYU Press, 1970), 9.

25 Fackenheim, *The Religious Dimension in Hegel's Thought*, and also ch. 5.

26 It is no mere coincidence that in the years that Fackenheim was working on Hegel and framing his understanding of philosophical method, his colleague Bill Dray was deeply engaged with Collingwood's contribution to our understanding of historical inquiry and explanation. See William H. Dray, *Perspectives on History* (London: Routledge and Kegan Paul, 1980) and *History as Re-enactment: R.G. Collingwood's Philosophy of History* (Oxford: Oxford University Press, 1995).

27 In his *Journals*, for 11 May 1848, Kierkegaard states: "This means that most ppl. never attain faith at all. For a long time they live in immediacy, finally move on to a bit of reflection, and then die. The exceptional ones begin from just the opposite end, dialectically, from childhood onward, i.e., without immediacy; they begin with the dialectical, with reflection; [they] live like this year after year (about as long as others live in pure immediacy), and then, at a more mature time, the possibility of faith appears for them. Faith is an immediacy that follows reflection." On a number of occasions, he describes a second immediacy or direct divine–human condition as having passed through the stage of reflection or doubt after an initial stage of immediacy; see *Stages on Life's Way* 63f., 123, 157f., 162f., and especially 412 and 414. There are many passages in the *Concluding Scientific Postscript* about second immediacy. For discussion about Kierkegaard on this notion of faith as immediacy after reflection, I want to thank Noreen Nhawaji.

28 Fackenheim, *God's Presence in History*, 16.

29 Fackenheim, *God's Presence in History*, 20.

30 This is at least true of the first three chapters and perhaps the fourth. The fifth is less successful and provides a weak conclusion to an otherwise strong work. The first chapter deals with an encounter between Judaism and modern analytic philosophy, the second with an encounter between Judaism and Kantian moral philosophy (and Kierkegaard as a Kantian philosopher), and the third with Judaism and Hegel. The fifth chapter, in much less elaborate form, presents confrontations between Judaism and modern existentialism in the form of Sartre and Heidegger.

31 Fackenheim, *Encounters between Judaism and Modern Philosophy* (New York: Basic Books, 1973), 153. It is a question Fackenheim had asked at the end of his Hegel book in 1968 and again in an essay of the same title in 1970: "Would Hegel Today Be a Hegelian?," *Dialogue* 9 (1970): 222–6. The question generated an interesting debate with Fackenheim's student, who was teaching at Dalhousie University, James Doull. For a discussion of the debate, see David Bronstein, "Hegel and the Holocaust," *Animus* 10 (2005), www2.swgc.mun.ca/animus.

32 The implication is: only a genuinely post-Hegelian philosophy of some kind could.

33 Fackenheim, *Encounters*, 154. He is referring to Hegel's *Introduction to the Philosophy of History*.

34 Fackenheim, *Encounters*, 154.

35 Fackenheim, *Encounters*, 157.

36 Fackenheim, *Encounters*, 157–8.

37 Fackenheim, *Encounters*, 158.

38 Fackenheim, *Encounters*, 158.

39 Fackenheim, *Encounters*, 165–6.

40 Fackenheim, *Encounters*, 166.

41 Fackenheim, *Encounters*, 167.

42 Fackenheim, *Encounters*, 167.

43 It is hardly necessary to itemize what might very well strike the reader as extremely controversial about Fackenheim's claims. Why not respond by jettisoning the entire Hegelian framework and simply opt for an other-worldly escape or a this-worldly secular response? And even if one continues to accept the Hegelian framework, why take Judaism to be the only or the best response to this historical situation? And even if one does accept the primacy of Judaism, why think that Israel is the best exemplification of an authentic response?

44 Fackenheim, *To Mend the World* (New York: Schocken Books, 1982), 247.

45 What begins as a Hegelian–Rosenzweigian exposition culminates in a Schellingian outcome.

46 Fackenheim, *To Mend the World*, 249.
47 Fackenheim, *To Mend the World*, 267–77. For accounts of the White Rose, see Inge Scholl, *The White Rose: Munich, 1942–1943* (Middletown: Wesleyan University Press, 1983); Jud Newborn and Annette Dumbach, *Sophie Scholl and the White Rose* (London: Oneworld, 2007). Huber was trained as a philosopher but was teaching musicology in Munich; while incarcerated he completed a book on Leibniz, which was published posthumously after the war. For further discussion of Huber, Kant, and Fichte, see ch. 4 below.
48 Huber's last words, which Fackenheim says are a quotation from Fichte, in fact come from the poem "Fichte an jeden Deutschen," the second and last stanza, by Albert Matthai (1853[1855?]–1924), a German writer and editor. The poem was inspired by Fichte's *Reden an die deutsche Nation* and was written during the New Year's holiday in 1922. Huber's wife, Clara, found it on the reverse side of a calendar for a Tuesday, 12 May, which must have been 1925, 1931, 1936, or 1942. The heading was missing. The calendar was the source for Huber's citation. He probably thought it came from Fichte. (These details come from an article by Wolfgang Huber, "Die Bedeutung der Literatur für den Widerstand der Wiessen Rose," *Einsichten und Perspektiven* 4 [2010].)
49 Fackenheim, *To Mend the World*, 275. "Given strength" here means that the idea somehow motivated Huber and compelled him. It had the normative force of a moral ideal. An anonymous reader suggested to me that one might associate this force of the idea with "the orders to live under which Pelagia Lewinska felt bound," and I would agree.
50 Fackenheim, *To Mend the World*, 276.
51 Later, in *An Epitaph for German Judaism* (Madison: University of Wisconsin Press, 2007), Fackenheim reaffirms his praise for Huber and his conception of a post-Holocaust philosophy: "Philosophers similarly troubled need not despair of philosophy. Professor Kurt Huber's intended address at Roland Freisler's *Volksgericht*, though he was prevented from giving it, was resistance as well. But in philosophy, too, there were only few, mostly Huber's students of the Munich 'White Rose.' If Christians think of Lichtenberg, philosophers should think of Huber, as they already do of Socrates" (219). The text dates from 2002–3.
52 See Emmanuel Levinas, "Useless Suffering" (1982), in *Entre Nous* (New York: Columbia University Press, 1998).
53 For discussion of Fackenheim's late thoughts on these matters, see Benjamin Pollock, "Thought Going to School with Life? Fackenheim's Last Philosophical Testament," in Sharon Portnoff, James A. Diamond,

and Martin Yaffe (eds.), *Emil L. Fackenheim: Philosopher, Theologian, Jew* (Leiden: Brill, 2008), 55–87; reprinted from *AJS Review* 31 (2007): 133–59.

Chapter 4

1 Fackenheim completed and defended his dissertation in 1945. The title is "Substance and Perseity in Medieval Arabic Philosophy, with Introductory Chapters on Aristotle, Plotinus, and Proclus." He published four early articles on medieval philosophy, the most important of which is on creation: "The Possibility of the Universe in al-Farabi, Ibn Sina, and Maimonides," *Proceedings of the American Academy for Jewish Research* 16 (1947): 39–70. In 1950 he contributed an essay, "Medieval Jewish Philosophy," to *A History of Philosophical Systems*, edited by Vergilius Ferm (New York: Philosophical Library, 1950), 178–84.
2 See Fackenheim, *An Epitaph for German Judaism* (Madison: University of Wisconsin Press, 2003), 149: "After some years of teaching I started on a project for which I received a Guggenheim fellowship. 'From Kant to Kierkegaard' would trace the challenge to the 'otherness' of the scriptural God, from Kantian 'autonomous' Reason to Hegel's Absolute Spirit, the overcoming, finally, of Divine 'otherness,' or total internalization. But after Hegel's death the whole enterprise was called into question, first, by none other than Schelling, himself the first to reach the Absolute, and, following him and his 'positive' philosophy, by Soren Kierkegaard." See also Fackenheim's comment on the project in *The God Within: Kant, Schelling, and Historicity* (Toronto: University of Toronto Press, 1996), xvii.
3 See ch. 5.
4 The most important piece is "The Revealed Morality of Judaism and Modern Thought: A Confrontation with Kant," in *Rediscovering Judaism*, ed. Arnold Wolf (Chicago: Quadrangle Books, 1965), 51–75. The essay was reprinted in Fackenheim, *Quest for Past and Future* (Bloomington: Indiana University Press, 1968), 204–28; also in *Contemporary Jewish Ethics*, ed. Menachem Kellner; and in *The Jewish Thought of Emil Fackenheim*, ed. Michael L. Morgan (Detroit: Wayne State University Press, 1987). A slightly modified, more popular version appeared earlier as "Kant and Judaism," *Commentary* 34 (1963): 460–7.
5 This chapter is an expanded version of the paper on Kant and the revealed morality of Judaism; in it he contrasts Kant with Kierkegaard and then places both treatments of religion and morality in a post-Holocaust context.

6 See his "Kant and Radical Evil," *University of Toronto Quarterly* 23 (1953): 339–53; "Kant's Concept of History," *Kantstudien* 58, no. 3 (1956–7): 381–97; and "Immanuel Kant," in *Nineteenth Century Religious Thought in the West*, ed. Ninian Smart, John Clayton, Stephen Katz, and Patrick Sherry (Cambridge: Cambridge University Press, 1985), I:17–40. The last of these papers was the bulk of the first part of Fackenheim's project on reason and revelation from Kant to Kierkegaard, which he had planned during the postwar years and which became the theme of the project proposal for the Guggenheim Foundation fellowship that he held in 1957–8. In *The Religious Dimension in Hegel's Thought* (Bloomington: Indiana University Press, 1968), he refers to this book by the title *The God Within*. It never appeared. In 1996, John Burbidge edited Fackenheim's essays on German philosophy together with several other important essays in *The God Within: Kant, Schelling, and Historicity*, published by the University of Toronto Press. The Kant essay was published in that same volume under the title "Kant's Philosophy of Religion" together with the other two Kant essays, on radical evil and history. All references to these three essays are to the chapters reprinted in *The God Within* (1996). Fackenheim also translated Kant's "Conjectural Beginning of Human History," which appeared in a volume of translations of Kant's short works in Immanuel Kant, *On History*, ed. Lewis White Beck (Indianapolis: Bobbs-Merrill, Library of Liberal Arts, 1963), 53–68.

7 Fred Beiser takes this to be a central goal of Kant's moral faith, to deal with such dualism; see Beiser, "Moral Faith and the Highest Good," in *The Cambridge Companion to Kant and Modern Philosophy*, ed. Paul Guyer (Cambridge: Cambridge University Press, 2006), 590.

8 Allen Wood argues for a naturalistic interpretation of Kant's account of radical evil, but he makes the excellent point that it is a naturalistic, rational interpretation of the Christian doctrine of original sin; that is Kant's purpose, to give an account of original sin in rationalist terms and then to reinterpret salvation in a similar way. See Wood, "The Evil in Human Nature" (unpublished), 1–2, 17–18. See also David Sussman, "Perversity of the Heart," *The Philosophical Review* 114, no. 2 (2005): 153–77.

9 Gordon Michalson, *Fallen Freedom* (Cambridge: Cambridge University Press, 2008) and *Kant and the Problem of God* (Oxford: Wiley-Blackwell, 1999); Henry Allison, *Kant's Theory of Freedom* (Cambridge: Cambridge University Press, 1990); and Philip J. Rossi, *The Social Authority of Reason: Kant's Critique, Radical Evil, and the Destiny of Humankind* (Albany: SUNY Press, 2006).

10 There have been a number of excellent recent accounts of Kant's views
    about God and religion, by Beiser, Wood, Michalson, and others. We have
    no interest in reviewing Fackenheim's general account, which is like many
    of these; what we want to do is identify what is distinctive about his
    approach, and that involves his conviction that Kant's account harbours
    contradictions, which Kant attempts to reconcile rather than avoid or
    dissolve.
11 Fackenheim, "Kant's Philosophy of Religion," 5–6.
12 It is also indebted to his reading of Kierkegaard, most likely *Fear and
    Trembling*, *Philosophical Fragments*, and *Concluding Unscientific Postscript*.
13 Fackenheim, "Kant's Philosophy of Religion," 9.
14 Fackenheim, "Kant's Philosophy of Religion," 9.
15 Fackenheim's essays are regularly cited in the recent work on Kant on
    religion, evil, and history, but such citation is for his references to Goethe
    and others and rarely for any features of his own account. Kant scholars
    typically examine Kant's *Religion* and the second *Critique* for expository
    purposes; they want to understand Kant as best they can. But there are
    some who investigate Kant as part of a larger project of understanding
    his role in nineteenth- and twentieth-century theology, especially Christian
    theology. Probably the best of these and the one whose thinking comes
    closest to Fackenheim's overall is Gordon E. Michalson, Jr. I am thinking
    especially of two of his books: *Fallen Freedom: Kant on Radical Evil and Moral
    Regeneration* (Cambridge: Cambridge University Press, 2008) and *Kant
    and the Problem of God* (Oxford: Wiley-Blackwell, 1999). Michalson's deep
    interest is in the role that Kant plays in a development that later includes
    Kierkegaard, Marx, Nietzsche, and twentieth-century Christian theology,
    and there is, in his work, a systematic interest that guides it all. By
    contrast, the sympathy with the importance of the religious dimension
    in Kant's work that one finds in the work of Allen Wood and Fred Beiser
    is by and large historical; to them, it is historically inaccurate and irre-
    sponsible to treat Kant as a thoroughly secular and naturalistic philoso-
    pher. For them, that is to miss something essential in what Kant took
    himself to be doing.
16 Martin Buber, *I and Thou* (New York: Scribner's, 1970), 143–4.
17 Fackenheim takes the metaphysical goal of Kant's account very seriously.
    Beiser does so as well; his reading is aimed at showing the systematic role
    of Kant's account of moral faith and especially its metaphysical commit-
    ments. In this regard, as he points out, his account takes issue with those
    recent interpreters who sanitize and secularize Kant's treatment of the
    Highest Good and what results from it. See Beiser, "Moral Faith and the

Highest Good," 589; and the references to articles by Thomas Pogge, Onora O'Neill, and Andrew Heath in 624n5; see also 599–604.

18 Fackenheim, "Kant's Philosophy of Religion," in *The God Within*, 10.

19 For an analytic approach along similar lines, see Thomas Nagel, *The View from Nowhere* (Oxford: Oxford University Press, 1986), ch. 7.

20 Ibid.

21 Beiser points out that this is traditional Christian doctrine; redemption is required only because human beings have natural desires and feelings that "cannot be eradicated." What Beiser does not note is that the Christian commitment to the duality of body and soul is already present in its Jewish heritage. See Beiser, "Moral Faith and the Highest Good," 596.

22 Fackenheim, "Kant's Philosophy of Religion," 10.

23 Fackenheim, "Kant's Philosophy of Religion," 11.

24 Fackenheim, "Kant's Philosophy of Religion," 11.

25 Fackenheim, "Kant's Philosophy of Religion," 12.

26 Fackenheim, "Kant's Philosophy of Religion," 12.

27 Fackenheim, "Kant's Philosophy of Religion," 13.

28 Fackenheim, "Kant's Philosophy of Religion," 13.

29 Fackenheim, "Kant's Philosophy of Religion," 14.

30 Fackenheim, "Kant's Philosophy of Religion," 14.

31 Fackenheim, "Kant's Philosophy of Religion," 15.

32 Fackenheim, "Kant's Philosophy of Religion," 15.

33 One commentator who sees things this way and who appreciates that this point is central to Fackenheim's reading of Kant is Gordon E. Michalson, Jr. See his *Fallen Freedom*, 6–7 and especially 144n8.

34 Beiser shows in a brief but excellent portrait of the religious context of Kant's work what makes this position historically distinctive; see Beiser, "Moral Faith and the Highest Good," 590–3. He also examines precisely what Kant means by the "primacy of practical reason" (610–13). Fackenheim's argument for the ultimacy of the standpoint of the engaged moral agent is intended to serve the same purpose, but Beiser's account stays much closer to Kant's terms and to his understanding of reason.

35 Fackenheim, "Kant's Philosophy of Religion," 15.

36 This is a slightly modified paraphrase of what Fackenheim himself says in comparing the "postulating" of God and the immortal soul to the argument for freedom in the Kant's *Foundation for a Metaphysics of Morals*.

37 The most recent discussion I have is Allen Wood, "The Evil in Human Nature" (unpublished); in his notes, Wood cites much of the recent literature.

38 Fackenheim repeats Goethe's reprimand that Kant had introduced the idea of radical evil in order to pander to Christians looking for a surrogate in his thinking for the doctrine of original sin; see "Kant and Radical Evil," 21; Fackenheim is often cited for having called attention to Goethe's slur, in a letter to Herder.

39 Fackenheim, "Kant and Radical Evil," 24.

40 Fackenheim, "Kant and Radical Evil," 24–6. Michalson claims that Fackenheim's account is mistaken precisely because it fails to understand the distinction between *Wille* and *Willkür* and, if I understand him correctly, because he fails to take seriously the distinction between the form and the content of a maxim. See Michalson, *Fallen Freedom*, 34–7 and 148n2. On the distinction, see also Richard J. Bernstein, *Radical Evil* (Cambridge: Polity, 2002), 13–19.

41 I take it that Michalson and others would argue that even without the terminology, Kant does take freedom to be a broader notion than autonomy; in Michalson's terms, Kant argues that what determines the kind of will is the form and not the content of the maxim.

42 Bernstein, *Radical Evil*, 28. This well-known point – that moral evil and radical evil are not a matter of man's becoming diabolical or devilish – is widely discussed. See Michalson, *Fallen Freedom*, 73–6, 81–2; Sharon Anderson-Gold, "Kant's Rejection of Devilishness: The Limits of Human Volition," *Idealistic Studies* 14 (1984): 35–48; and Bernstein, *Radical Evil*, 36–42.

43 Fackenheim, "Kant and Radical Evil," 28–9.

44 Fackenheim, "Kant and Radical Evil," 29.

45 Michalson has an extensive discussion of Kant's terminology (*Fallen Freedom*, 34–47); there is also a very helpful account in Bernstein, *Radical Evil*, 14–35. A "maxim" for Kant is a subjectively held principle or program or policy; there are short-term maxims and long-term or overarching ones. The latter he calls "propensities" or "dispositions" when they are incorporated into us as determining features of our character or personality.

46 Fackenheim, "Kant and Radical Evil."

47 Fackenheim, "Kant and Radical Evil," 31.

48 Fackenheim, "Kant and Radical Evil."

49 Fackenheim, "Kant and Radical Evil," 32.

50 Fackenheim, "Kant and Radical Evil." Michalson discusses this process of "moral regeneration" and the biblical language that Kant uses to describe it in *Fallen Freedom*.

51 Fackenheim, "Kant and Radical Evil."

52 That is, in *Fallen Freedom*. Later, in *Kant and the Problem of God* (Oxford: Blackwell, 1999), Michalson argues that in fact Kant himself is a reductionist. While Kant's sensibility inspires various mediating theological strategies, he himself reduces religion to morality and hence is the proper godparent of the atheistic developments we associate with Hegel, Feuerbach, and ultimately someone like Marx.

53 For similar comparisons, see Henry Allison, "Reflections on the Banality of (Radical) Evil: A Kantian Analysis," in his *Idealism and Freedom: Essays on Kant's Theoretical and Practical Philosophy* (Cambridge: Cambridge University Press, 1996), 169–82 (orig. 1995); and Bernstein, *Radical Evil*, 11–45.

54 Allison emphasizes this a priori feature of Kant's account – that Kant wants to show how consistent his thinking is by grounding moral evil in a free choice between good and evil – in "Reflections on the Banality of (Radical) Evil." See also Robert Louden, "Evil Everywhere," in Sharon Anderson-Gold and Pablo Muchnik, eds., *Kant's Anatomy of Evil* (Cambridge: Cambridge University Press, 2010), 93–115.

55 Fackenheim, "The Revealed Morality of Judaism and Modern Thought: A Confrontation with Kant." This essay first appeared in Wolf, *Rediscovering Judaism*, 51–75. It has been reprinted in *Quest for Past and Future*, 204–28; also in Kellner, ed., *Contemporary Jewish Ethics*, and in Morgan, ed., *The Jewish Thought of Emil Fackenheim*. All references here are to the version printed in *Quest for Past and Future*. In a sense, in the early essays Fackenheim takes Kant to be opening up the possibility of a mediating strategy between an openness to transcendence and a reduction to the human; in the later essay, he focuses on autonomy as the centrepiece of Kant's reductionist approach to religion. It is the latter with which Judaism as a revealed religion must cope.

56 Fackenheim uses the expression "liberal" here to refer to the view that acknowledges the epistemological and practical, moral primacy of the free, rational person. Hence, a liberal Judaism is one that at least wrestles with this primacy of the individual vis-à-vis the roles of community, tradition, and God in Judaism.

57 Fackenheim, "The Revealed Morality of Judaism and Modern Thought," 211–15.

58 Fackenheim, "The Revealed Morality," 214. In a note, Fackenheim mentions Samuel Hirsch as an excellent example of a nineteenth-century Jewish philosopher who faced and failed to cope with just this dilemma; see 328.

59 Fackenheim states the need to find an account of Jewish morality that combines divine givenness with human receptivity very clearly; see his "The Revealed Morality," 216–17.

60 See Fackenheim, "The Revealed Morality," 218–20 and 221ff.

61 This is how Fackenheim describes the philosophical problem; see "The Revealed Morality," 220.
62 See Fackenheim, *The Religious Dimension in Hegel's Thought*, ch. 3.
63 Fackenheim, "The Revealed Morality," 221–2.
64 Fackenheim, "The Revealed Morality," 222.
65 Fackenheim, "The Revealed Morality," 222–3. Fackenheim cites Micah 6:8 and in the footnote a midrash from the *Pesikta d'Rav Kahana* XV that makes the same point about the interdependence of interpersonal justice and divine–human intimacy. For Fackenheim's way of reading midrash, see ch. 8.
66 Fackenheim, "The Revealed Morality," 224.
67 Here I am thinking of Stephen Darwall, R. Jay Wallace, and Michael Thompson. See Darwall, *The Second-Person Standpoint: Morality, Respect, and Accountability* (Cambridge, MA: Harvard University Press, 2006); Wallace, "The Deontic Structure of Morality" (unpublished ms); and Michael Thompson, "What is it to Wrong Someone? A Puzzle about Justice," in *Reason and Value: Themes from the Moral Philosophy of Joseph Raz*, ed. R. Jay Wallace, Philip Pettit, Samuel Scheffler, and Michael Smith (Oxford: Oxford University Press, 2004), 333–84.
68 See Michael Morgan, *Discovering Levinas* (Cambridge: Cambridge University Press, 2007); and *The Cambridge Introduction to Emmanuel Levinas* (Cambridge: Cambridge University Press, 2011).
69 This statement needs to be qualified in the light of Levinas's notion of *Illeity* and of the trace of the Other. But suffice it to say that this notion must be distinguished from the role of God for Fackenheim and of the Divine Presence or Eternal Thou for Buber.
70 Fackenheim, "The Revealed Morality," 225–7. Fackenheim gives a more precise formulation of this dialectic between divine power and human freedom in *God's Presence in History* (New York: NYU Press, 1970), 15–16: "If the astonishment abides [when the divine Presence commands], it is because Divinity is present in the commandment. Because it is a commanding rather than a saving Presence, however, the abiding astonishment turns into deadly terror. Indeed, such a Presence is, in the first instance, nothing short of paradoxical. For, being commanding, it addresses human freedom. And being sole Power, it destroys that freedom because it is only human. Yet the freedom destroyed is also required … As sole Power, the divine commanding Presence destroys human freedom; as gracious Power, it restores that freedom, and indeed exalts it, for human freedom is made part of a covenant with Divinity itself. And the human astonishment, which is terror at a Presence at once divine and commanding, turns into a second astonishment, which is joy, at a Grace which restores and exalts human freedom by its commanding Presence."

71 Fackenheim, *To Mend the World* (New York: Schocken Books, 1982), 24. In this later work, he rejects it as an inadequate account, for reasons we will mention later.

72 See Franz Rosenzweig, *The Star of Redemption* (New York: Holt, Rhinehart and Winston, 1970), 156–85.

73 See Rosenzweig, "The Builders," in *On Jewish Learning: Franz Rosenzweig*, ed. N.N. Glatzer (New York: Schocken Books, 1955), 85.

74 Immanuel Kant, *The Conflict of the Faculties*, trans. Mary J. Gregor (Lincoln: University of Nebraska Press, 1992), 115.

75 Fackenheim, "Abraham and the Kantians," in *Encounters between Judaism and Modern Philosophy* (New York: Basic Books, 1973), 33–4.

76 Fackenheim, "Abraham and the Kantians," 34–5. See Søren Kierkegaard, *Fear and Trembling* (Princeton: Princeton University Press, 1974), passim.

77 See Martin Buber, "The Question to the Single One," in *Between Man and Man* (New York: Macmillan, 1978), 40ff. (orig. 1936).

78 Fackenheim, "Abraham and the Kantians," 53.

79 Fackenheim, "Abraham and the Kantians," 54–5. The question is telling, for it poses the challenge of being faithful both to God and to humankind.

80 Fackenheim, "Abraham and the Kantians," 57.

81 Fackenheim, "Abraham and the Kantians."

82 See Fackenheim, "Abraham and the Kantians," 63. Moshe Halbertal, *On Sacrifice* (Princeton: Princeton University Press, 2012).

83 Fackenheim, "Abraham and the Kantians," 66, where Fackenheim cites *Midrash Genesis Rabbah 55.5.*

84 Fackenheim, "Abraham and the Kantians," 66. Throughout the essay, Fackenheim is perhaps insufficiently attentive to the social dimension of the recovery; he certainly neglects to introduce the social dimension of Kant's understanding of history and its goal, an ethical commonwealth. Recent discussion of Kant on radical evil and history takes this social dimension very seriously. See Wood, "The Evil in Human Nature"; Rossi, *The Social Authority of Reason*; Sharon Anderson-Gold, *Unnecessary Evil: History and Moral Progress in the Philosophy of Immanuel Kant* (Albany: SUNY Press, 2001); and Michalson, *Fallen Freedom*.

85 Fackenheim, "Abraham and the Kantians," 68.

86 Fackenheim, "Abraham and the Kantians," 69.

87 Fackenheim, "Abraham and the Kantians," 70. Compare the language of re-enactment from *God's Presence in History*, ch. 1. As I have indicated, Fackenheim's debt is to Hegel and to Collingwood.

88 Ibid.

89 Fackenheim interpolates between the midrashic past and the post-Holocaust present a medieval episode from 1096 in order to show how

child sacrifice was transmuted, in the Jewish historical imagination, into martyrdom; see Fackenheim, "Abraham and the Kantians," 72–3.

90 Fackenheim, "Abraham and the Kantians," 75.

91 Fackenheim, "Abraham and the Kantians," 77. For an elaboration of this same theme, see Fackenheim, "On the Life, Death, and Transfiguration of Martyrdom: The Jewish Testimony to the Divine Image in Our Time," in *The Jewish Return into History* (New York: Schocken Books, 1978), ch. 15, 234–51 [orig. in *Communio* IV, no. 1 (1977)].

92 Various Kant scholars, from Henry Allison to John Silber, and others – for example, Richard Bernstein – ask whether Kant's doctrine of radical evil and his rejection of "devilishness" can apply to Auschwitz and the Holocaust. See note 94 below. Fackenheim does not appear to be familiar with this literature. Some of it is early enough for it to have been available to him; some was published quite late in his life. It would be a valuable project to consider how he might respond to this body of work.

93 I have begun such an account in Morgan, "The Central Problem of Emil Fackenheim's *To Mend the World*," *Journal of Jewish Thought and Philosophy* 5, no. 2 (1996): 297–312; and in *Beyond Auschwitz* (Oxford: Oxford University Press, 2001), ch. 10.

94 Since our primary interest here is Kant and Fackenheim, it is not necessary to consider the Arendt literature. There are, however, three accounts that deal with Kant and Arendt, and they will be especially helpful: Allison, "Reflections on the Banality of (Radical) Evil"; Richard J. Bernstein, "Arendt: Radical Evil and the Banality of Evil," in *Radical Evil*, 205–24; and John R. Silber, "Kant at Auschwitz," in *Proceedings of the Sixth International Kant Congress*, vol. 1: *Invited Papers*, ed. Gerhard Funke and Thomas M. Seebohm (Center for Advanced Research in Phenomenology and University Press of America, 1991), 177–211.

95 Allison, "Reflections on the Banality of (Radical) Evil," 175.

96 This is what Richard Bernstein calls "the intentional adoption of evil maxims," Bernstein, *Radical Evil*, 214.

97 Allison, "Reflections on the Banality of (Radical) Evil," 176–7, citing Allen Wood, *Kant's Moral Religion* (Ithaca: Cornell University Press, 1970), 210–15.

98 Allison, "Reflections on the Banality of (Radical) Evil," 177.

99 One can also find an account along these lines in Allen Wood, *Kant's Ethical Thought* (Cambridge: Cambridge University Press, 1999); and in David Sussman, "Perversity of the Heart," *Philosophical Review* 114, no. 2 (2005): 1–24. Wood defends his account against criticisms in "Kant and the Intelligibility of Evil," in Anderson-Gold and Muchnik, eds., *Kant's Anatomy of Evil*, 165–70. See also Wood, "The Evil in Human Nature" (unpublished).

100 Allison, "Reflections on the Banality of (Radical) Evil," 178.
101 Jaspers uses this expression in a letter to Arendt in 1946; see Lotte Kohler and Hans Saner, eds., *Hannah Arendt/Karl Jaspers: Correspondence 1926–1969* (New York: Harcourt, Brace Jovanovich, 1992), 62; cited by Bernstein in *Radical Evil*, 214–15. The letter concerns how to characterize Nazism. Arendt agrees with Jaspers that one must "combat all impulses to mythologize the horrible" (*Correspondence*, 69).
102 See Louden, "Evil Everywhere," 105–8.
103 Allison, "Reflections on the Banality of (Radical) Evil," 178–9.
104 Bernstein emphasizes the contrast in Arendt's account between doing evil thoughtlessly and doing it for evil motives – for greed, lust for power, sadistic purposes, or even for anti-Semitic reasons; see *Radical Evil*, 215–16. Clearly, part of Arendt's reasons for calling the extreme evil of the Nazis extreme and not radical is that it does not have depth or go to the roots. She also thinks it is ordinary or commonplace and not extraordinary or remarkable.
105 Bernstein, *Radical Evil*, 218–24.
106 I am not convinced that either Allison or Bernstein has understood Arendt correctly or at least not fully, although both accounts are helpful. Neither understands the kind of detachment that Arendt intends when she uses the term "thoughtlessness." Eichmann and those like him were motivated by reasons that were not connected in thought to the outcomes or ends of their actions. Their reasons pointed to one set of ends, while their actions brought about horrific ends that they did not have in mind. For the confusions in various accounts of what Kant means by rejecting the idea of a "diabolical being," see Louden, "Evil Everywhere," 103–8.
107 Richard J. Bernstein, "Arendt: Radical Evil and the Banality of Evil," 205–24. Arendt, of course, in *The Origins of Totalitarianism*, considers both the Nazi concentration and death camps and the Stalinist labour camps. For convenience, I will treat her account as if it was solely about the Nazi horrors – indeed about all the horrific acts and policies of the Nazi state – and not solely about its conduct in the camps. I will assume this scope throughout.
108 Bernstein, "Arendt: Radical Evil and the Banality of Evil," 209.
109 Bernstein, "Arendt: Radical Evil and the Banality of Evil," 209–12.
110 Bernstein, "Arendt: Radical Evil and the Banality of Evil," 208.
111 Silber, in "Kant at Auschwitz," esp. 194–201, distinguishes between Hitler and Speer and those like them, on the one hand, and the lesser functionaries, on the other. Kant might help us to understand the latter, but nothing he says touches the former. "Kant's theory can comprehend

the motivation of an Eichmann, a functionary whose efficiency and zeal were motivated almost entirely by careerist concerns; but it cannot illuminate the conduct of a Hitler" (194). As we have seen, others such as Wood, Louden, and Allison defend Kant's account against the charge. It is possible that Fackenheim, in 1982, knew about Silber's earlier account (which took the same position), but he showed no indication of it. And Silber indicated no familiarity with Fackenheim's work.

112 Wood points out that Kant's account focuses on evil decisions and actions, on what we do; see Wood, "Kant and the Intelligibility of Evil," 145.

113 Silber, "Kant at Auschwitz," 200.

114 See Wood, "The Evil in Human Nature," 5 and 5n5. See also his "Kant and the Intelligibility of Evil," 152–7.

115 Fackenheim, *To Mend the World*, 206. The crucial pages are 182–90, 206–15, and especially 230–48.

116 This theme, that the Holocaust cannot be explained and has no meaning or purpose, goes back to Fackenheim's earliest writings about these matters and reaches its peak in these pages of *To Mend the World*. See his "Jewish Faith and the Holocaust: A Fragment," in *The Jewish Return into History*, reprinted from *Commentary* 46, no. 2 (August 1968): 30–6; and reprinted in Morgan, ed., *The Jewish Thought of Emil Fackenheim*; and Morgan, ed., *A Holocaust Reader* (Oxford: Oxford University Press, 2001).

117 Fackenheim, *To Mend the World*, 183; in a note Fackenheim remarks that this description of the agents or perpetrators is indebted to the work of historians such as Yehuda Bauer and Raul Hilberg. A few pages later, commenting on a famous speech by Himmler, Fackenheim says: "The leading Nazi spirits were not perverts or opportunists or even ordinary jobholders but rather extraordinary idealists, i.e., criminals with a good conscience and a pure heart" (186).

118 Fackenheim, *To Mend the World*, 187.

119 Fackenheim, *To Mend the World*, 208–9.

120 Fackenheim, *To Mend the World*, 210. Fackenheim admits that not all shared this view, but it was sufficient to set the "tone" for the "world of Auschwitz."

121 Fackenheim, *To Mend the World*, 231.

122 The same would go for the motive or program of redemptive anti-Semitism, employed as an explanatory device by Saul Friedlander and appropriated from Uriel Tal, *Christians and Jews in Germany* (Ithaca: Cornell University Press, 1975).

123 Fackenheim mentions both, although he focuses on Schelling. The implication of his acknowledgment, I think, is that Schelling, unlike Kant,

does recognize the notion of demonic evil and also that he takes it to be grounded in what lies outside conceptual systems. See *To Mend the World*, 234, 240.

124 Fackenheim, *To Mend the World*, 235–8.

125 Fackenheim, *To Mend the World*, 237.

126 In fact, as already mentioned, Arendt excludes Goebbels, Streicher, Hitler, and others from her account of the "new criminal" of the twentieth century, which occurs in *The Origins of Totalitarianism*. It is this account that anticipates the later account of Eichmann and which she calls then "banal."

127 Fackenheim, *To Mend the World*, 236–7; cf. 247.

128 Fackenheim takes the "thought" to be philosophical thought trying to grasp the evil, I think, while it is clear to me that for Arendt the relevant thought is the deliberative reason of the agents. The gap between the agents' intentions about what to do and the action itself insofar as it contributed to the horrific outcomes is what makes the evil "thoughtless."

129 At this point, Fackenheim asks how philosophical thought responds to this realization. He says it is haunted by it and is forced to move from the evil system to the banal doers, back and forth. Hence, philosophical thought moves in a circle. Following Hegel and then Schelling, this moving in a circle that grasps a whole, when the whole is a whole of horror, leads to resistance, and from resistance in thought, it moves to resistance in life. But this is Fackenheim's argument and beyond our interest here. See *To Mend the World*, 238–40.

130 Fackenheim analyses Hoess's comments in his autobiography about his choice to join the SS and his later split-vision about watching the suffering and the torture. He resists letting Hoess avoid responsibility; he made choices, and Fackenheim focuses on revealing them. See *To Mend the World*, 241–3. The same holds for Eichmann and Himmler.

131 Fackenheim, *To Mend the World*, 241.

132 On the issue of intentionality, Arendt's account is more complex than Fackenheim perhaps appreciates or at least acknowledges. Even bureaucrats have motives and reasons for what they do, but the relationship between these reasons and motives and the descriptions of what they do in acting is complicated.

133 Fackenheim, *To Mend the World*, 263.

134 Fackenheim, *To Mend the World*, 266.

135 Kurt Huber (1893–1943) was professor of philosophy at the Ludwig Maximilian University of Munich from 1920. Later, when unable to find a position in philosophy, he taught musicology.

136 This is my point, not Fackenheim's. For a recent, important discussion of that encounter, see Peter Eli Gordon, *Continental Divide: Heidegger, Cassirer, Davos* (Cambridge, MA: Harvard University Press, 2010).

137 See Tom Rockmore, *On Heidegger's Nazism and Philosophy* (Berkeley: University of California Press, 1997), 56, who associates the text with Platonism (at 313nn121, 122, Rockmore cites Fackenheim's comments in *To Mend the World*). Also, for background about the poem and its author, Albert Matthai, see my comments on Huber and this poem in ch. 3.

138 I say that Fichte singles out Germans alone, but since the poem is by Matthai, he is the real speaker. As I've noted, however, Huber thought Fichte was the author, and Fackenheim follows him. So I treat Fichte as the subject.

139 Fackenheim, *To Mend the World*, 267–70.

140 Fackenheim, *To Mend the World*, 270; then 270–3 and 273–7.

141 Fackenheim, *To Mend the World*, 270.

142 Fackenheim, *To Mend the World*, 272.

143 Fackenheim, *To Mend the World*, 273.

144 Fackenheim, *To Mend the World*, 275–6.

145 Fackenheim, *To Mend the World*, 276.

146 Fackenheim, *To Mend the World*, 277.

Chapter 5

1 Arnold Metzger (1892–1974) was Edmund Husserl's assistant from 1920 to 1924. He taught at the *Hochschule* from 1934 to 1937. His *Phenomenology and Metaphysics*, on the problem of relativism and an argument that it cannot be solved by phenomenology, was published in 1933. *Freedom and Death* was published in 1955. Fackenheim never acknowledges any influence, but, as we shall see in chapter 7, the problem of thought and history or historicism and relativism was a lifelong issue for him.

2 Fackenheim, "Hegel and 'The Jewish Problem,'" in *The Philosopher as Witness*, ed. Michael L. Morgan and Benjamin Pollock (Albany: SUNY Press, 2008), 16.

3 See Fackenheim, "Hegel and 'The Jewish Problem,'" 17; Fackenheim, *An Epitaph for German Judaism* (Madison: University of Wisconsin Press, 2007), 147–9.

4 Fackenheim, "Would Hegel Today Be a Hegelian?," *Dialogue* 9 (1970): 222–6; "On the Actuality of the Rational and the Rationality of the Actual," *Review of Metaphysics* 23 (1970): 690–8 (reprinted in *The God Within*, ed. John Burbidge [Toronto: University of Toronto Press, 1996],

164–71). See also his "Hegel and Judaism: A Flaw in the Hegelian Mediation," in *The Legacy of Hegel*, ed. J.J. O'Malley, K.W. Algozin, H.P. Kainz,
and L.C. Rice (The Hague: Nijhoff, 1973), 161–85.

5 Fackenheim, "Demythologizing and Remythologizing in Jewish Experience: Reflections Inspired by Hegel's Philosophy," in *The Jewish Return
into History*, 112–26 (originally in *Myth and Philosophy: Proceedings of the
American Catholic Philosophical Association* 45 [1971]: 16–27); "On the Life,
Death, and Transfiguration of Martyrdom: Divine Image in Our Time,"
in *The Jewish Return into History*, 234–51 (originally in *Communio* 4 [1977]:
19–35).

6 Fackenheim, *The Religious Dimension in Hegel's Thought* (Bloomington:
Indiana University Press, 1967), 9. Cf. 22–3. The centrality of religion for
Hegel is controversial and has been since his death. For an excellent
discussion, see Frederich Beiser, *Hegel* (New York and London: Routledge,
2005), ch. 6. The issue is closely connected with the role of metaphysics
for Hegel; for this too, see Beiser, *Hegel*, ch. 3. Virtually every review of
Fackenheim's book noted that his strong argument for the central role that
religion plays in Hegel's system is the book's most important feature, as
well as its most controversial one. See James Doull, review of RDHT,
Dialogue 7, no. 3 (1968): 483–91; David Burrell, "Religious Life and Understanding," *Review of Metaphysics* 22, no. 4 (1969): 676–99; Frederick G.
Weiss and Howard P. Kainz, "Recent Work on Hegel," *American Philosophi-
cal Quarterly* 8, no. 3 (1971): 203–22, esp. 210–12; Quentin Lauer, "Emil L.
Fackenheim's RDHT," *International Philosophical Quarterly* 8, no. 4 (1968):
630–5 (reprinted in *Essays in Hegelian Dialectic* [New York: Fordham
University Press, 1977], 107–12); and W.H. Walsh, review of RDHT,
Philosophical Quarterly 23, no. 90 (1973): 77–9. See also Robert L. Perkins,
"Hegel and the Secularisation of Religion," *International Journal for
Philosophy of Religion* 1, no. 3 (1970): 130–46.

7 Fackenheim, *The Religious Dimension*, 10.

8 This is precisely what Kant, in the Transcendental Dialectic in his *Critique
of Pure Reason*, claims is the central and dominant aspiration of Reason,
as distinct from sensory perception and understanding. For discussion,
see Henry Allison, *Kant's Transcendental Idealism*, 2nd ed. (New Haven: Yale
University Press, 2004); and Michelle Grier, *Kant's Doctrine of Transcendental
Illusion* (Cambridge: Cambridge University Press, 2007).

9 Fackenheim, *The Religious Dimension*, 11. We touched upon one implication
of this claim in ch. 3.

10 Fackenheim, *The Religious Dimension*, 12.

11 Fackenheim, *The Religious Dimension*.

12 See Fackenheim, *The Religious Dimension*, 32, 33–7.
13 See, for example, A.W. Moore, *Points of View* (Oxford: Oxford University Press, 2000).
14 See Fackenheim, *The Religious Dimension*, 23–5, esp. 23.
15 See Fackenheim, *The Religious Dimension*, 26–7; see also 72.
16 See Fackenheim, *The Religious Dimension*, 51–8.
17 Fackenheim, *The Religious Dimension*, 51.
18 That is, as a challenge to the conception of the self as self-constituting.
19 Fackenheim's account is on page 52 of *The Religious Dimension*.
20 Fackenheim, *The Religious Dimension*, 54.
21 See Fackenheim, *The Religious Dimension*, 56–7.
22 Fackenheim, *The Religious Dimension*, 57.
23 This is the central theme of Friedrich Meinecke's *Cosmopolitanism and the Nation State* (1906). Meinecke was Rosenzweig's doctoral supervisor at Freiburg, the person under whom Rosenzweig wrote *Hegel and the State*.
24 Fackenheim, *The Religious Dimension*, 65.
25 Fackenheim, *The Religious Dimension*, 66.
26 Fackenheim, *The Religious Dimension*, 68–9.
27 Fackenheim, *The Religious Dimension*, 72.
28 Fackenheim, *The Religious Dimension*, 76–7.
29 He refers to these as right-wing and left-wing interpretations. One wonders whether Fackenheim would reject similar excesses when it comes to Spinoza and the crucial IIP7 of the *Ethics*. Is Spinoza a materialist as Stuart Hampshire argues? Or is he an Idealist? Or is his a double-aspect theory?
30 In religious terms, the system must integrate Sunday with the workaday week. One without the other is unacceptable. But Sunday is the true meaning of the week. See Fackenheim, *The Religious Dimension*, 106: "The philosophical Sunday is no other-worldly joy, indifferent to the grief of this world, against which indifference the unredeemed world would rise as an unconquered witness and accuser. It is a this-worldly joy, which can *be* joy only because its very life is the conquest of the world's grief."
31 Fackenheim, *The Religious Dimension*, 106.
32 Fackenheim, *The Religious Dimension*, 108. Idea is the "logical Idea" or what Hegel examines in the Logic, that is, what might be called metaphysical form or structure. Spirit is manifest in consciousness, thought, feelings, culture, art, and so forth. Nature is the world of natural beings. With a little licence, one can, I think, translate Fackenheim's account into ordinary terms. The basic conception is of mind, world, and the structure that is grasped by mind and informs the world.

33 Fackenheim, *The Religious Dimension*, 109.
34 See Fackenheim, *The Religious Dimension*, 109.
35 Fackenheim, *The Religious Dimension*, 110–11.
36 Fackenheim, *The Religious Dimension*, 111.
37 Fackenheim, *The Religious Dimension*.
38 See Fackenheim, *The Religious Dimension*, 112.
39 Hegel, *Encyclopedia of the Philosophical Sciences*, Preface (*Werke*, VI:xxi ff.); see also his *Lectures on the Philosophy of Religion*, I:19; cited by Fackenheim in *The Religious Dimension*, 116.
40 Fackenheim, *The Religious Dimension*, 117.
41 His account is at *The Religious Dimension*, 119–27. I think this exploration influenced Fackenheim's own understanding of midrash and traditional Jewish faith, especially in *God's Presence in History*, ch. 1.
42 Fackenheim, *The Religious Dimension*, 123.
43 Fackenheim, *The Religious Dimension*.
44 This kind of understanding of faith is a Hegelian-inspired articulation of what Fackenheim had appropriated from figures such as Buber and Rosenzweig on the Jewish side and Barth and others on the Christian side.
45 Fackenheim, *The Religious Dimension*, 124.
46 The five points are made in Appendix I to ch. 5 of Fackenheim, *The Religious Dimension*,155.
47 See Fackenheim, *The Religious Dimension*,195: "All genuine religions are totalities of feeling, representation, and cult geared to the Divine, and the totalities differ as does the Divine to which they are geared." See below, ch. 8.
48 Fackenheim, *The Religious Dimension*, 124–6.
49 Fackenheim, *The Religious Dimension*,138; cf. 139–43. This redemptive event, which is grounded in the incarnation, is the death of Jesus as the Christ (see 141–2).
50 Fackenheim, *The Religious Dimension*, 140.
51 Fackenheim, *The Religious Dimension*, 142.
52 Fackenheim, *The Religious Dimension*, 143–9.
53 Fackenheim, *The Religious Dimension*, 161.
54 Fackenheim, *The Religious Dimension*, 164.
55 Fackenheim takes up this challenge at *The Religious Dimension*, 184–92. The crucial point is that the religious content is the divine–human relation, which involves divine activity and human receptivity, that is, the human heart. Philosophical thought must grasp the relation from the point of view of the divine without destroying the human heart that receives it. Fackenheim sees this dialectic in Martin Buber in *I and Thou* (see *The*

Religious Dimension, 143–4), but without the philosophical transcendence. That is, he takes Hegel's account of the one double-activity in Christianity, divine Grace and human freedom, with the latter a divine gift, to be characteristic of Judaism as Buber describes it. The Hegelian picture of Judaism as a divine master and human slaves or subjects is false to Judaism as it is. See Fackenheim, *The Religious Dimension*, 188–9.

56 Fackenheim, *The Religious Dimension*, 165. These are the right- and left-wing critiques that Hegel wants to deflect, although, as Fackenheim notes, it is not clear that he is able to do so.

57 Fackenheim, *The Religious Dimension*, 206.

58 Fackenheim, *The Religious Dimension*, 206–7.

59 Fackenheim, *The Religious Dimension*, 207.

60 Fackenheim, *The Religious Dimension*, 211.

61 Fackenheim, *The Religious Dimension*.

62 Fackenheim, *The Religious Dimension*, 212.

63 Fackenheim, *The Religious Dimension*, 213.

64 Fackenheim, *The Religious Dimension*, 224: "Hegel's 'science' can appear on the scene only when the time is ripe for it. Reason is divine only because it has been revealed to be so by history, divine as well as human, philosophical as well as nonphilosophical."

65 Fackenheim, *The Religious Dimension*.

66 Fackenheim, *The Religious Dimension*; see also 235: "For our contemporary Christian West, unlike Hegel's own, is characterized by a fragmentation which is all-pervasive and inescapable."

67 Fackenheim, *The Religious Dimension*, 230.

68 Fackenheim, *The Religious Dimension*, 232–3.

69 See Fackenheim, *The Religious Dimension*, 233.

70 Fackenheim, *The Religious Dimension*, 236.

71 See Fackenheim, *The Religious Dimension*, 237.

72 Fackenheim, *The Religious Dimension*, 241–2.

73 This ideal, actual in Judaism, Fackenheim clearly states as early as the final paragraphs of his paper on the Jewish Hegelian Samuel Hirsch. See "Samuel Hirsch and Hegel," in *Studies in Nineteenth Century Jewish Intellectual History*, vol. II, ed. A. Altmannn (Cambridge: Harvard University Press, 1964); reprinted as ch. 2 in *Jewish Philosophers and Jewish Philosophy*, ed. Michael L. Morgan (Bloomington: Indiana University Press, 1996), 39–40.

74 Fackenheim, "Hegel on the Actuality of the Rational and the Rationality of the Actual," reprinted in *The God Within*, 171.

75 Fackenheim, "Hegel on the Actuality."

76 Although the long chapter (90 pages) is heavily indebted to Fackenheim's Hegel book, it is material that was not previously published and is by and large new. The first, second, and fourth sections of the book, on the other hand, derive from previously published material.

77 See Fackenheim, *Encounters*, 118–20. That the messianic redemption lies in the future is one of two central teachings that Judaism provides for Christianity, according to Rosenzweig. The other is the claim that the God of creation and the God of Redemption are one and the same God.

78 Fackenheim, *Encounters*, 84–5.

79 Fackenheim, *Encounters*, 88.

80 Fackenheim, *Encounters*, 88.

81 Fackenheim, *Encounters*, 91.

82 See Fackenheim, *Encounters*, 93–4.

83 Fackenheim, *Encounters*, 94.

84 Fackenheim, *Encounters*, 95.

85 See Fackenheim, *Encounters*, 97–9.

86 As Fackenheim points out, this is all the more surprising, since in his *Early Theological Writings*, the young Hegel viewed messianism as central to Judaism. See Fackenheim, *Encounters*, 99.

87 Fackenheim, *Encounters*, 101–2.

88 See Fackenheim, *Encounters*, 118–20.

89 Fackenheim, *Encounters*, 119.

90 Fackenheim, *Encounters*, 120.

91 Fackenheim, *Encounters*, 120; see also 125: "For at long last we have discovered the ultimate reason why the concept of covenant does not appear in Hegel's account of Judaism and why Jewish Messianism is not even mentioned: by the standards of a divine-human freedom, which is a divine self-othering in the human, any freedom remains 'unfree' which remains human in its relation to the Divine; and any God is Lord only who remains other-than-human in His relation to the human."

92 Fackenheim, *Encounters*, 126.

93 See Fackenheim, *Encounters*, 129–30.

94 Fackenheim, *Encounters*, 131.

95 For Fackenheim's most sustained examination of Cohen, see his *Hermann Cohen – After Fifty Years*, The Leo Baeck Memorial Lecture (New York: Leo Baeck Institute, 1969), reprinted in Fackenheim, *Jewish Philosophers and Jewish Philosophy*. For Rosenzweig's ahistoricism, see *To Mend the World*.

96 Fackenheim, *Encounters*, 135.

97 Fackenheim, *Encounters*.

98 Fackenheim, *Encounters*, 153.

99 Fackenheim, *Encounters*, 153; see also "Would Hegel Today Be a Hegelian?" See also ch. 3.

100 Fackenheim, *Encounters*, 154.

101 Fackenheim, *Encounters*, ibid.

102 Fackenheim, *Encounters*, ibid., 155.

103 Fackenheim, *Encounters*, 157. This encapsulates what Fackenheim means when he says that the Holocaust is a manifestation of "evil for evil's sake." See ch. 4.

104 See Fackenheim, *Encounters*: "Claiming to mediate all things, divine as well as human, [Hegel's thought] requires a world in which, except for the sphere of philosophic thought, so total a mediation is already actual. Yet in our time an absolute anti-Spirit has exploded precisely that mediation, in the heart of what once was Hegel's Europe. Had Hegel lived through this hell in his native land his thought would have been forced into paradox."

105 Fackenheim, *Encounters*, 158.

106 As we have indicated before, Fackenheim is drawing upon Buber, *I and Thou* (New York: Scribner's, 1970), 143–4.

107 Fackenheim, *Encounters*, 161.

108 As Fackenheim puts it, "with the Notion vanished, a Hegelian way of philosophical thought supplies the means – we are bold enough to assert, for the first time in the history of philosophy – of doing conceptual justice to the inner logic of Judaism." Fackenheim, *Encounters*, 162. The next two pages of *Encounters* are taken from Fackenheim's "Demythologizing and Remythologizing in Jewish Experience: Reflections Inspired by Hegel's Philosophy," reprinted in *The Jewish Return into History*, 120–3. See ch. 8 for discussion of the essay and the role of midrash in it.

109 Fackenheim, *Encounters*, 165. The account of messianism in this chapter (164–8) and of the role of the Holocaust and the State of Israel in a contemporary recovery of it is indebted to Fackenheim's "The Holocaust and the State of Israel: Their Relation," in *The Jewish Return into History*, 273–86.

110 Fackenheim, *Encounters*, 166.

111 Fackenheim, *Encounters*, 166. Fackenheim's most sophisticated account of how the encounter with Nazi evil becomes radical opposition to it occurs in *To Mend the World*, Chapter IV, 8–9, 201–50.

112 Fackenheim, *Encounters*, 167.

113 See Fackenheim, "The Holocaust and the State of Israel: Their Relation," in *The Jewish Return into History*, 273–86. Also in *The Jewish Return into History*, see "Israel and the Diaspora: Political Contingencies and Moral

Necessities; or, the Shofar of Rabbi Yitzhak Finkler of Piotrkov," 188–209; and "Post-Holocaust Anti-Jewishness, Jewish Identity and the Centrality of Israel: An Essay in the Philosophy of History," 210–33. For additional essays on Israel, see "Diaspora and Nation: The Contemporary Situation," *Forum: On the Jewish People, Zionism and Israel* 50 (Winter 1983–4), reprinted in *The Jewish Thought of Emil Fackenheim*, ed. Michael L. Morgan (Detroit: Wayne State University Press, 1987), 295–305; "A Political Philosophy for the State of Israel: Fragments," *Jerusalem Center for Public Affairs* (1988), 1–18, reprinted in *Jewish Philosophers and Jewish Philosophy*, 195–208; and "Pillars of Zionism," *Midstream* (December 1992): 13–15, reprinted in *Jewish Philosophers and Jewish Philosophy*, 209–14. See also ch. 6.

114 Fackenheim, *Encounters*, 167.

115 The book was completed prior to the Yom Kippur War and is still a product of the line of thinking initiated in the period before and after the Six Day War. For his thinking in the period after the war in 1972, one should turn to the essays collected in *The Jewish Return into History*. See ch. 6.

116 Fackenheim, *To Mend the World* (New York: Schocken Books, 1982), 105.

117 Fackenheim, *To Mend the World*, 106; see especially footnote *.

118 That is, how is revelation in Jewish modernity the determinative feature of Jewish distinctiveness?

119 Fackenheim, *To Mend the World*, 108–10.

120 Franz Rosenzweig, *The Star of Redemption*, 7; cited in Fackenheim, *To Mend the World*, 115; see also 105 and 105n.

121 Fackenheim, *To Mend the World*, 115.

122 Fackenheim, *To Mend the World*, 116–17.

123 Fackenheim, *To Mend the World*, 117.

124 See Fackenheim, *To Mend the World*, 118–19.

125 See Fackenheim, *To Mend the World*, 119–20 and then 120–30.

126 We can see evidence of both extremes, both failures, even today. One can be found in the movements toward spiritual renewal and meditation; the other occurs in naturalist critiques of religion such as those found in semipopular books such as Richard Dawkins, *The God Delusion* (New York: Houghton Mifflin, 2006); Daniel Dennett, *Breaking the Spell* (London: Allen Lane, 2006); Christopher Hitchens, *God Is Not Great* (New York: Random House, 2007); and Sam Harris, *The End of Faith* (New York: W.W. Norton, 2005). In Judaism, we have both tendencies: pseudo-Kabbalistic psychological spirituality and secular affirmations of Jewish peoplehood and nationality.

127 Fackenheim, *To Mend the World*, 127.

128 Levinas, among others, also recognizes the failure; it is a central theme
     of *Totality and Infinity* and other of his early writings. And one finds it in
     his essay "Useless Suffering" as the warning against being tempted by
     theodicies. We should recall that in the latter essay, Levinas refers to
     Fackenheim and *God's Presence in History*. There is no evidence that he
     knew *To Mend the World*, but it is tempting to imagine how he might have
     responded to that book.
129 Fackenheim, *To Mend the World*, 129.
130 See Fackenheim, *To Mend the World*, 130–6.
131 Fackenheim, *To Mend the World*, 135.
132 See Michael L. Morgan, *Beyond Auschwitz* (Oxford: Oxford University
     Press, 2001); and "The Central Argument of Emil Fackenheim's *To Mend
     the World*," *Journal of Jewish Thought and Philosophy* 5, no. 2 (1996): 297–312.
133 See ch. 1.
134 See ch. 2.
135 Cf. Yitzhak Y. Melamed, "Acosmism or Weak Individuals? Hegel,
     Spinoza, and the Reality of the Finite," *Journal of the History of Philosophy*
     48, no. 1 (2010): 77–92.
136 Fackenheim, *To Mend the World*, 138.
137 Fackenheim, *To Mend the World*, 139.
138 Fackenheim, *To Mend the World*, 141.
139 Rosenzweig always struggled with the problem of worldliness. See
     Benjamin Pollock's new book on the 1913 conversation between Rosen-
     zweig and Rosenstock that focuses on the problem of Marcionism and
     Gnosticism in Rosenzweig's thinking from the period prior to 1913
     through to the writing of the *Star of Redemption*. Benjamin Pollock,
     Overcoming Marcionism: Rethinking Franz Rosenzweig's Conversions
     (Bloomington, IN: Indiana University Press, forthcoming).
140 Fackenheim, *To Mend the World*, 142.
141 Fackenheim, *To Mend the World*. There is valuable recent work on the
     question of Israel's character as a Jewish and democratic state. See, for
     example, Chaim Gans, *A Just Zionism: On the Morality of the Jewish State*
     (Oxford: Oxford University Press, 2011). There is an important debate over
     Samuel Smooha's account of Israel as an ethnic democracy; see Smooha,
     "Ethnic Democracy: Israel as an Archetype," *Israel Studies* 2, no. 2 (1997):
     198–241. See also Ruth Gavison, "Jewish or Democratic? A Rejoinder to
     the 'Ethnic Democracy' Debate," *Israel Studies* 4, no. 1 (1999): 44–72; and
     "The Jews' Right to Statehood: A Defense," *Azure* 15 (Summer 2003).
142 Fackenheim, *To Mend the World*, 143. As Fackenheim goes on to argue that
     Zionist thought has had to work hard to find the religious dimension of

Zionism compelling and to take it seriously, he uses an expression that he had appropriated in *God's Presence in History* from Martin Buber's account of the experience of a miracle, the expression "abiding astonishment": "[Zionist thought] can hope to do better justice only if, before all else, it allows itself to be filled … with abiding astonishment." That is, it cannot treat the Zionist enterprise, the establishment of the state, its successful defence, and so forth, as a purely natural consequence of human action, without any sense for its extraordinary success.

143 See Fackenheim, *To Mend the World*, 144.
144 Fackenheim, *To Mend the World*, 145.
145 See Emil Fackenheim, *An Epitaph for German Judaism*, passim. See also note 2 above.
146 See Fackenheim, "Hegel and 'The Jewish Problem,'" in *The Philosopher as Witness*, 20.
147 Fackenheim, "Hegel and 'The Jewish Problem,'" 20–1. All of this is familiar from Fackenheim's earlier writings on Hegel. As I discuss in a later chapter, his style here however is condensed and cryptic, leaving the reader to fill in the details.
148 Fackenheim, "Hegel and 'The Jewish Problem,'" 21. Fackenheim cites two essays by Shlomo Avineri on this theme: "Hegel's Views on Jewish Emancipation" and "Hegel Revisited," both from the 1960s.
149 Fackenheim, "Hegel and 'The Jewish Problem,'" 21.
150 Fackenheim, "Hegel and 'The Jewish Problem,'" 22.
151 Fackenheim, "Hegel and 'The Jewish Problem.'" Fackenheim first discusses the *Verein*, to the best of my knowledge, in "Moses and the Hegelians," in *Encounters*, 126–8. There he treats its central impulses as Hegelian in spirit, the opposition to conversion to Christianity and the affirmation of a sense of Jewish fidelity – the "inner necessity of our continued existence [as Jews]." But the project failed, with Gans and Heine converting. Fackenheim notes that Graetz ascribed the failure to Hegelian ideas.
152 Fackenheim, "Hegel and 'The Jewish Problem,'" 23. This is in fact the final stanza of a poem found in Heine's literary papers remains. The poem is the second of two called "The Rabbi of Bacharach," sometimes titled "The Stars in Heaven Are Weeping" or "Old and Young Are Weeping." Heine also left behind an unfinished novel titled *The Rabbi of Bacharach* (circa 1840). The German original is "Und alle die Tränen fleißen / Nach Süden, im stillen Verein, / Sie fleisßen und ergießen / Sich allen den Jodan herein." Does the word *Verein* in l.2 allude to the group of which Heine had been a member? Perhaps.

Chapter 6

1   In traditional Jewish thinking about ultimate redemption, the coming
    of the messiah is taken to preceed the final redemptive goal, which is the
    "world to come" (*olam ha-ba*). In Maimonides, the former is taken to be
    historical and political, the latter personal, intellectual, and other-worldly.

2   See above 5n113, for a number of his essays. Many more occasional pieces
    appeared in *Canadian Jewish News* and in other popular venues.

3   The review is reprinted in Michael L. Morgan, ed., *The Jewish Thought of
    Emil Fackenheim* (Detroit: Wayne State University Press, 1987), 65–8.
    Buber's book is currently available as *On Zion: The History of an Idea*
    (Syracuse: Syracuse University Press, 1997). The best collection of Buber's
    writings on Zionism is *A Land of Two Peoples*, ed. Paul Mendes-Flohr
    (Oxford: Oxford University Press, 1983).

4   See especially the writings collected in Buber, *A Land of Two Peoples*.

5   See 5n109.

6   These quotations are all from Fackenheim, "The People Israel Lives,"
    Christian Century, 6 May 1970, 563–8, and reprinted in *The Jewish Return
    into History* (New York: Schocken Books, 1978), 43–57, esp. 54.

7   Fackenheim, *God's Presence in History* (New York: NYU Press, 1970), 86.

8   Fackenheim, "Jewish Faith and the Holocaust: A Fragment," in *The Jewish
    Return into History*, 40–1. I believe that Fackenheim met Harold Fisch at a
    meeting of the I. Meier Segal Center for the Study and Advancement of
    Judaism in Quebec. In the summer of 1969, at a meeting of the group, Fisch
    was involved in an intense conflict with Steven and Henry Schwarzschild
    regarding Israel's military victories and Zionism in general. The argument
    led to a breach that seriously divided the group, which continued to meet,
    but with deep divisions. Henry Schwarzschild resigned from the advisory
    board of the journal *Shma* in 1982, after the Lebanon War and the atrocities
    at Sabra and Chatila, saying that he renounced the State of Israel as a
    chauvinist and repressive nationalist regime. Fisch's passionate defence
    of Zionism can be found in *The Zionist Revolution* (New York: St Martin's
    Press, 1978).

9   These quotations are from "From Bergen-Belsen to Jerusalem," in *The
    Jewish Return into History*, 142–3.

10 Fackenheim, "From Bergen-Belsen to Jerusalem," 139.

11 The central role that messianism plays in Fackenheim's understanding of
    the State of Israel and its place in post-Holocaust Jewish life is underlined
    by his use of that idea in the final pages of "A Political Philosophy for the

State of Israel," which was first published in 1988 by the Jerusalem Center for Public Affairs and is reprinted in *Jewish Philosophers and Jewish Philosophy*, ed. Michael L. Morgan (Bloomington: Indiana University Press, 1996), 207–8.

12 There is a vast literature on the idea of messianism in religious Zionism. See, for example, Aviezer Ravitzky, *Messianism, Zionism, and Jewish Religious Radicalism* (Chicago: University of Chicago Press, 1996); Jacob Katz, "Israel and the Messiah," in *Essential Papers on Messianic Movements and Personalities in Jewish History*, ed. Marc Saperstein (New York: New York University Press, 1992), 475–91; Menachem Kellner, "Messianic Postures in Israel Today," in *Essential Papers*, 504–18 (orig. *Modern Judaism* 6, no. 2 [1986]: 197–209); Menachem Friedman, "*Habad* as Messianic Fundamentalism: From Local Particularism to Universal Jewish Mission," in *Accounting for Fundamentalism: The Dynamic Character of Movements*, ed. M.E. Marty and R.S. Appleby (Chicago: University of Chicago Press, 1994), 328–60; Motti Inbari, *Jewish Fundamentalism and the Temple Mount: Who Will Build the Third Temple?* (Albany: SUNY Press, 2009); and *Messianic Religious Zionism Confronts Israeli Territorial Compromises* (Cambridge: Cambridge University Press, 2012).

13 See Fackenheim, "Judaism and the Meaning of Life," in *Quest for Past and Future* (Bloomington: Indiana University Press, 1968), ch. 16.

14 This is a central Rosenzweigian theme.

15 In these paragraphs I draw upon "Can There Be Judaism without Revelation?" 78–80 and "An Outline of a Modern Jewish Theology," 106–9, both in Fackenheim, *The Quest for Past and Future*. See also ch. 1, above.

16 Fackenheim, "Judaism and the Meaning of Life," 249–62 at 254.

17 Fackenheim, "Judaism and the Meaning of Life," 257.

18 Fackenheim, "Judaism and the Meaning of Life," 259. Of course, many Jews still take the messiah to be parochial and political in a narrow sense.

19 In line with traditional sources, Fackenheim does distinguish the wholly individual expectation for the "world to come" from the "days of the Messiah." See his "Judaism and the Meaning of Life," 261–2.

20 As I said above, the literature here is enormous. For a valuable collection of papers, see Saperstein, ed., *Essential Papers*. See also especially Katz, "Israel and the Messiah," 475–91; and Kellner, "Messianic Postures in Israel Today," 504–18. An outstanding book on messianism and religious Zionism is Ravitzky, *Messianism, Zionism, and Jewish Religious Radicalism*.

21 Louis Greenspan wonders whether in fact he remained firmly committed to rejecting such explanatory connections; see Greenspan, "Fackenheim as Zionist," in *Fackenheim: German Philosophy and Jewish Thought*, ed.

Greenspan and Graeme Nicholson (Toronto: University of Toronto Press, 1992), 206–16. I think that he did. What he came to reject was any sort of explanatory adequacy – in other words, historical accounts do provide some illumination but not enough.

22 At least, it should, but much depends on how the state conducts itself, on what kind of a state it is. During his lifetime, Fackenheim would admit to political failings, but he resisted serious criticisms of Israeli policies and practices of the sort that are so widespread today. But one can imagine how such criticisms regarding inhumane and repressive conduct might influence one's estimate of Israel's messianic accomplishments.

23 This statement may be shocking. There are ways to mitigate the shock and to make it sound less extreme. But it may never lose its sting, so to speak – and the risks it implies. In a sense, what Fackenheim is arguing is that at a time when trust in God's messianic role is lost, one needs to trust in something, and that something is, for many, the security and opportunities that come with political sovereignty in a Jewish state. There are many who would not share Fackenheim's optimism about such trust.

24 For an overview of the central Talmudic texts, especially those from Tractate Sanhedrin 98–99, see Jacob Neusner, *Messiah in Context* (Baltimore: University Press of America, 1988), 168–91.

25 Fackenheim, "The Holocaust and the State of Israel," in *The Jewish Return into* History (New York: Schocken Books, 1978), 277–8.

26 Fackenheim, "Moses and the Hegelians," in *Encounters between Judaism and Modern Philosophy* (New York: Basic Books, 1973), 165–8.

27 See chs. 3 and 5 above.

28 See Fackenheim, *Encounters*, 158ff.

29 Buber, *I and Thou* (New York: Scribner's, 1970), 143–4; we have already seen how important this passage is to Fackenheim.

30 Buber, *I and Thou*, 162.

31 Fackenheim, *Encounters*, 165.

32 Fackenheim, *Encounters*, 167.

33 Fackenheim, *Encounters*, 167.

34 At the end of his essay "Diaspora and Nation," written in the early 1980s, Fackenheim calls upon Nahmanides, who, commenting on the redemption and the coming of the messiah, said that a true sign would be when one sees trees growing in the land. Fackenheim comments that once, after a long, dusty ride from the Galilee to Jerusalem, he recalled Nahmanides's claim: "I saw the trees of Galilee, and was astonished" (*The Jewish Thought of Emil Fackenheim*, 305). It is not hard, especially in hindsight, to read such comments, written after the decade of the 1970s, as highly romantic; I am

sure that many would do so. But Fackenheim shows a willingness to be surprised by historical events that is at least understandable. Farms, irrigation, crops – he takes nothing for granted.

35 To him it exemplified how post-Holocaust Judaism ought to look, at least formally: realistic, hopeful, with serious moral goals yet offering no excuses for the need to act, often in difficult circumstances, out of a concern for survival and self-preservation.

36 See Greenspan, "Fackenheim as Zionist," 218.

37 As Greenspan puts it, in 1992, "a Jewish state that is democratic is possible only if the view that Jewish hegemony over all the land of Israel must take priority over its democratic character does not prevail. But it may not." Greenspan, "Fackenheim as Zionist," 219. See also Fackenheim, "Diaspora and Nation: The Contemporary Situation," *Forum* 50 (1983–4), reprinted in *The Jewish Thought of Emil Fackenheim*, ed. Michael L. Morgan (Detroit: Wayne State University Press, 1987), 298. In "A Political Philosophy for the State of Israel," published in 1988, he does acknowledge the internal problems; see the essay, reprinted in Morgan, ed., *Jewish Philosophers and Jewish Philosophy* (Bloomington: Indiana University Press, 1996), 198–208.

Chapter 7

1 Thomas Nagel, *The View from Nowhere* (Oxford: Oxford University Press, 1989).

2 There is evidence that later in his career, by the early 1980s, Fackenheim had read Gadamer and Ricoeur. But he never read Derrida or Foucault and was certainly not familiar with the work of E.D. Hirsch, Stanley Fish, and other literary critics, nor with the discussion generated by Thomas Kuhn's work in the history of science or by the work of Richard Rorty, Charles Taylor, and Alasdair MacIntyre concerning the historical character of philosophy. It may be that the person who influenced his interest in the problem of historicism was Leo Strauss. Arnold Metzger, with whom Fackenheim studied in Berlin, had published a work in 1933 that argued that phenomenology was unable to refute relativism, and Fackenheim may have been somewhat familiar with that work, although I know of no evidence to support this.

3 See, for example, Bernard Williams, *Ethics and the Limits of Philosophy* (Cambridge, MA: Harvard University Press, 1985).

4 See Hilary Putnam, *Reason, Truth, and History* (Cambridge: Cambridge University Press, 1981); see also Putnam's *The Collapse of the Fact/Value*

Dichotomy and Other Essays (Cambridge, MA: Harvard University Press, 2004).

5 See Richard Rorty, *Contingency, Irony, and Solidarity* (Cambridge: Cambridge University Press, 1989).

6 That is, the problems about intentionality and reference are ones that Fackenheim never explored; in discussing his thinking, there is no need to enter this thicket of issues.

7 Fackenheim calls attention to this problem in "The Historicity and Transcendence of Philosophic Truth," in *The God Within* (Toronto: University of Toronto Press, 1996), 151: "Historical circumstances may favour or hamper this attainment [i.e., the philosopher's ascent to an apprehension of the Forms and hence philosophic truth in Plato's *Republic* VII]. They are in either case accidental to the truth attained" (151).

8 In response to receiving a copy of Fackenheim's *Metaphysics and Historicity*, Strauss wrote to Fackenheim, criticizing the inadequacy of his dismissal of Heidegger. See n45 (in *The God Within*, 227–8). Fackenheim's attempt to deal with Strauss's criticism is his essay "The Historicity and Transcendence of Philosophic Truth" (1967), reprinted in *The God Within*.

9 The distinction stems from Mendelssohn's rationalism. See Moses Mendelssohn, *Jerusalem: Or on Religious Power and Judaism* (Hanover: University Press of New England, 1983), 127.

10 Kierkegaard, whom Fackenheim read in Aberdeen, may already have been an influence.

11 Fackenheim, "Schelling's Philosophy of Religion," *University of Toronto Quarterly* 22 (1952), 1–17; reprinted in *The God Within*, 92–108 (all references to the reprinted version), esp. 93.

12 See Fackenheim, "Schelling's Philosophy of Religion," 95ff.; and "Schelling's Conception of Positive Philosophy," *Review of Metaphysics* 7, no. 4 (1954): 763–82, reprinted in *The God Within*, 109–21, esp. 112.

13 Technically speaking, what the free choice or leap accepts is not yet God but rather an absolute existent individual prior to all thought, and hence prior to being God. It is this Absolute that explains the existence of the world and that is expressed through the idea of Creation. For clarification, see Fackenheim, "Schelling's Conception of Positive Philosophy," 116.

14 Fackenheim, "Schelling's Philosophy of Religion," 101–3.

15 Fackenheim, "Schelling's Philosophy of Religion," 105.

16 Fackenheim, "Schelling's Philosophy of Religion," 106.

17 Reprinted in Fackenheim, *The God Within*, 148–63.

18 Except for one footnote, I will not consider the second of these texts, which elaborates Fackenheim's refutation of Heidegger's historicism.

19 Fackenheim, *Metaphysics and Historicity* (Milwaukee: Marquette University Press, 1961); reprinted in Fackenheim, *The God Within*, 122–47, esp. 124–5, 136.
20 Fackenheim, *The God Within*.
21 Fackenheim, *The God Within*, 137.
22 Fackenheim, *The God Within*, 138–9.
23 That is, it is not the current vocabulary – replaced as it has been by tendencies such as postmodernism and beyond. But existentialism is still a subject of interest and does have a legacy. See Steven Crowell, ed., *The Cambridge Companion to Existentialism* (Cambridge: Cambridge University Press, 2012), esp. ch. 1.
24 Fackenheim, *The God Within*, 142. This is a point that Donald Davidson makes when he says, in his famous paper "On the Very Idea of a Conceptual Scheme," that one cannot take up a position outside of all conceptual schemes; there is no such position. Claiming that one can is a fiction of Western philosophy. Stanley Cavell makes the same point in his understanding of the "moral of skepticism."
25 Fackenheim, *The God Within*, 143.
26 Fackenheim, *The God Within*, 144.
27 Something along these lines is Strawson's reading of Kant's transcendental deduction in *The Bounds of Sense* (London: Methuen, 1966). Also relevant is Charles Taylor's notion of strong evaluation in *Sources of the Self* and in earlier essays. For the self to be a self, something must be given to it; not everything can be constructed by it.
28 Fackenheim still argues for the transcendence of philosophic truth in 1967, in the essay "The Historicity and Transcendence of Philosophic Truth," in *The God Within*. See, for example, 151: "Philosophic thought seeks radical universality, and the truths to which it lays claim transcend history even if they encompass not eternity but merely all time or all history." The essay goes on to defend this claim against the Heideggerian critique. Later in the essay, Fackenheim puts its central question this way: "How can philosophic thought be rooted in history, and emerge from history, and yet reach a truth which is transcendent? For, as will be seen, philosophic thought can reach nothing less and still be philosophical" (154).
29 From minute to minute, it certainly is – virtually automatic. The default condition is one of a taken-for-granted continuity. Only under certain conditions do we question the default view and wonder what old terms mean in new circumstances.
30 Fackenheim, *The Quest for Past and Future*, 14.

31 The crucial pages are Fackenheim, *The Quest for Past and Future* (Blooming-ton: Indiana University Press, 1968), 12–17.

32 When Fackenheim refers here to a kind of essence, he is suggesting that there is what I have called elsewhere a kind of internal objectivity; see Morgan, *Interim Judaism* (Bloomington: Indiana University Press, 2001), ch. 1, esp. 44–5. It is an analogue to what Putnam means by the realistic aspect of "internal realism."

33 Fackenheim, *The Quest for Past and Future*, 16.

34 Fackenheim, *The Quest for Past and Future*, 17.

35 I pointed to this question in my discussion of philosophy after the Holo-caust in ch. 3; see also ch. 5. See also Fackenheim, *Encounters between Judaism and Modern Philosophy* (New York: Basic Books, 1973), 153. It is a question that Fackenheim had asked at the end of his Hegel book in 1968 and again in an essay of the same title in 1970: "Would Hegel Today Be a Hegelian?," *Dialogue* 9 (1970): 222–6. The question generated an interesting debate with Fackenheim's former student, who was teaching at Dalhousie University, James Doull. See Doull's review of RDHT in *Dialogue* 7, no. 3 (1998); and also Fackenheim's response and Doull's reply in *Dialogue* 9, no. 2 (1970): 222–35. For a discussion of the debate, see David Bronstein, "Hegel and the Holocaust," *Animus* 10 (2005), www.swgc.mun.ca/animus.

36 Fackenheim calls these two features "realism" and the system's "all-encompassing demands" – that is, its "comprehensiveness" – in Facken-heim, *The Religious Dimension in Hegel's Thought* (Bloomington: Indiana University Press, 1968), 229.

37 Fackenheim, *The Religious Dimension*, 224. Fackenheim shows that Hegel's system must incorporate both life and thought, bringing them together just as it appreciates their separateness; see 229–30.

38 See Fackenheim, *The Religious Dimension*, 235: "For our contemporary Christian West, unlike Hegel's own, is characterized by a fragmentation which is all-pervasive and inescapable." He refers to the weakening of faith in the West and the global reality of a host of non-Western, non-Christian faiths. Furthermore, self-confidence is shaken by wars and dehumanizing forces and by technological advances that strike us with terror as much as hope and optimism. See 236.

39 Fackenheim, *Encounters*, 157.

40 Fackenheim, *Encounters*, 157–8.

41 In *To Mend the World*, as we shall see, "epoch-making event" comes to mean "an event that cannot be assimilated to existing categories and to which opposition, arising out of uncomprehending thought, is an auto-matic response."

42 Strauss also opposes historicism for similar reasons, but unlike Facken-heim, his favoured response is a return to pre-modern thinking, something that Fackenheim takes to be impossible.
43 Fackenheim, *To Mend the World*, 152.
44 Fackenheim, *To Mend the World*, 153.
45 Fackenheim, *To Mend the World*, 157.
46 Fackenheim, *To Mend the World*, 159.
47 Fackenheim, *To Mend the World*, 160.
48 See Fackenheim, *To Mend the World*, 166.
49 Fackenheim, *To Mend the World*, 166.
50 There is a large literature on Heidegger's politics and his relation to Nazism. Over the years Fackenheim read some of it, but by and large he does not engage with recent discussion. He definitely was more interested in the views of people like Karl Löwith, Hans Jonas, and Otto Pöggeler than he was in the more recent discussions of Richard Wolin, Berel Lang, and Thomas Sheehan. French discussion also seems to have been of little interest to him.
51 Fackenheim is here alluding to Theodor W. Adorno's famous statement in *Negative Dialectics* (New York: Continuum, 2003), 353. See *To Mend the World*, 132.
52 Fackenheim, *To Mend the World*, 166–81.
53 Fackenheim, *Encounters*, 217.
54 Fackenheim, *Encounters*, 217.
55 Fackenheim, *To Mend the World*, 170.
56 Fackenheim, *To Mend the World*, 190.
57 Fackenheim, *To Mend the World*, 200. Fackenheim is quoting from Adorno, *Negative Dialectics*. His reference to an "earlier exploration" is to page 135 and a discussion stimulated by an essay of Jean Améry but with distinctly Hegelian overtones. His use of the expression "overcoming" refers to Hegel's notion of the "negation of negation."
58 For discussion of this expression, see Benjamin Pollock, "Thought Going to School with Life? Fackenheim's Last Philosophical Testament," in *Emil L. Fackenheim: Philosopher, Theologian, Jew*, ed. Sharon Portnoff, James A. Diamond, and Martin D. Yaffe (Leiden: Brill, 2008), 55–87.
59 See Michael L. Morgan, "The Central Problem of Emil Fackenheim's *To Mend the World*," *Journal of Jewish Thought and Philosophy* 5, no. 2 (1996): 297–312.
60 Fackenheim, *To Mend the World*, 239, 247.
61 Fackenheim, *To Mend the World*, 249.
62 Fackenheim, *To Mend the World*, ibid.

63 See Fackenheim, *To Mend the World*, 250–5.

64 To be precise, Fackenheim uses the expression "the present interpreter of the past," but the context makes clear, I think, that he is referring to the historical agent who is situated in the present and who seeks to utilize concepts, motifs, and teachings from the past in the course of understanding his situation, planning for his future, and making decisions about what to do and what to believe. See Fackenheim, *To Mend the World*, 257.

65 The terminology is appropriated from Hans-Georg Gadamer's *Truth and Method*.

66 A similar conception can be found in the work of Charles Taylor, regarding identity as constituted in part by what is given to the self, its language, practices, and so forth, what Taylor calls "background," after Heidegger and Wittgenstein. See Taylor, *Sources of the Self* (Cambridge: Cambridge University Press, 1989); and also "Engaged Agency and Background in Heidegger," in *The Cambridge Companion to Heidegger*, ed. Charles B. Guignon (Cambridge: Cambridge University Press, 1993), 317–36.

67 There is a Kantian sensibility at work here: the forms of intuition, space and time, and the concepts of the understanding, are presented with something, which they organize and order. This is not a free play of the imagination; it is an interweaving of form and content. Empirical knowledge and experience require both intuitions and concepts, but also both spontaneity and givenness.

68 See Fackenheim, *To Mend the World*, 259.

69 Fackenheim, *To Mend the World*.

70 Fackenheim, *To Mend the World*, 260.

71 This is where practical considerations arise or "internal" notions of warrant, confirmation, and such. Although Fackenheim has his own way of understanding this alternative, it is similar in spirit to what Hilary Putnam calls "internal realism."

Chapter 8

1 Fackenheim, *An Epitaph for German Judaism: From Halle to Jerusalem* (Madison: University of Wisconsin Press, 2007), 44–5. On Baeck, see also *An Epitaph*, Appendix D, 253–4. At his death in 2003, Fackenheim left the memoirs in a very full but incomplete fashion. After some years, the memoirs were published in 2007. Fackenheim's reading of the terms mystery and commandment is interesting and distinctive. Often Baeck's distinction is taken to refer to faith and reason or emotion and reason. Fackenheim takes it mean something like revelation and law.

2 For interesting reflections on midrash, see Fackenheim, *An Epitaph for German Judaism*, 154–6.

3 Robert Eisen, in his paper on midrash in Fackenheim's post-Holocaust thought (see n4 below), claims that the central question is whether Fackenheim thinks there can be midrash after the Holocaust. But this is not the central question: it is obvious that there can be. The real issue is what citing midrash can mean and what form new, creative midrashic thinking and writing might and should take.

4 The only paper on the subject of which I am aware is Robert Eisen, "Midrash in Emil Fackenheim's Holocaust Theology," *Harvard Theological Review* 96, no. 3 (2003): 369–92. Eisen is an expert who understands midrash in ways I do not. In this chapter I try to place Fackenheim's attraction to midrash in a larger conception of his work than Eisen does. But what he says is helpful; I will return to it later.

5 "Mystery and Commandment" is translated by Walter Kaufmann in a collection of five of Baeck's essays titled *Judaism and Christianity* (Philadelphia: Jewish Publication Society, 1958). In his translator's introduction, Kaufmann notes Baeck's predilection for use of the expression "the twofold" and for compound titles of the form "A and B."

6 Later, it would be indebted to Hegel, I think, but Kierkegaard was an important early influence. Fackenheim had read Kierkegaard by 1939. In 1941 he published a one-page piece titled "A Communication on Kierkegaard" in the journal *Philosophy* (64): 334–5. It is a response to a review of English translations of Kierkegaard's *Journals* and *Fear and Trembling*. The comments are dated August 1939 from Aberdeen, where Fackenheim had fled after his release from Sachsenhausen. In them he refers to several of Kierkegaard's works, *Der Augenblick*, *Philosophical Fragments*, *Der Begriff der Angst*, and *Fear and Trembling*, and there are reasons to think that he had by that time also read *Concluding Unscientific Postscript*.

7 Fackenheim, "In Praise of Abraham, Our Father," *Commentary* (December 1948): 521–7; reprinted in *Quest for Past and Future* (Bloomington: Indiana University Press, 1968), ch. 3, 52–65. All references are to the reprinted version. See, for example, 52: "In taking Abraham with such seriousness, I readily admit that I was influenced by Kierkegaard's magnificent *Fear and Trembling*." Also, 64: "To return to Father Abraham – for at last I have regained him as father and guide. And I have regained him not without the help of Kierkegaard."

8 Fackenheim, "In Praise of Abraham, Our Father," 58.

9 Fackenheim, "Correspondence to the Editor," *Philosophy* 64 (1941): 334.

10 For discussion of this theme in Kierkegaard, see Heiko Schulz, "Second Immediacy: A Kierkegaardian Account of Faith," 71–86, and Merold Westphal, "Kierkegaard and the Role of Reflection in Second Immediacy," 159–79, both in *Immediacy and Reflection in Kierkegaard's Thought*, ed. Paul Cruysberghs, Johan Taels, and Karel Verstrynge (Leuven: Leuven University Press, 2003). See above 3n27.

11 A similar attentiveness to the tensions in central Jewish ideas and texts can be found in Gershom Scholem – for example, in his classic discussion of the tensions in the messianic idea in Judaism; see Scholem, "Toward an Understanding of the Messianic Idea in Judaism," in *The Messianic Idea in Judaism and Other Essays* (New York: Schocken Books, 1971), 1–36, esp. 2–4.

12 Fackenheim, "In Praise of Abraham, Our Father," 59.

13 Fackenheim, "In Praise of Abraham, Our Father," 59.

14 Fackenheim, "In Praise of Abraham, Our Father," 60; see also *God's Presence in History* (New York: NYU Press, 1970), 15. See below for discussion of his dialectical reading of this midrash.

15 See Fackenheim, "In Praise of Abraham, Our Father," 60; "Self-Realization and the Search for God," 38. At 320n10, Fackenheim points out that in the latter essay, he uses the translation from Montefiore and Loewe, eds., *A Rabbinic Anthology*, and that he does so throughout the essay. This practice continues throughout Fackenheim's early essays; it is not clear when he begins to use alternative translations, but I imagine it is not until the 1970s at the earliest.

16 Ps.123:1 says "I lift up my eyes to you, to you whose throne is in heaven." The commentator cites Is.43:12 and interprets the relation between God's being and human testimony, in order to clarify God's being enthroned and its relation to the psalmist's act of lifting his eyes. That is, the commentator implies that God would not be enthroned in the heavens if the psalmist did not look to the heavens for Him.

17 Fackenheim, "In Praise of Abraham, Our Father," 60.

18 It is central to his account in Chapter One of *God's Presence in History*; it is the topic of "Human Freedom and Divine Power," ch. 13 in *Quest for Past and Future*; and it is present in other essays in the collection.

19 For a comprehensive treatment of the expression *kivyakhol* in rabbinic literature, see Michael Fishbane, *Biblical Myth and Rabbinic Mythmaking* (Oxford: Oxford University Press, 2003), Appendix 2, "The Term *kivyakhol* and its Uses," 325–404. Fishbane comments on this midrash at 385, where he says, "Theologically speaking, this teaching marks a limit case for God's dependence upon humans." Fishbane's appendix provides sufficient evidence, if it were needed, that Fackenheim was right to take the

term *kivyakhol* to be a technical term, although its role may be far more complex than Fackenheim suggests when he points to the fact that it signals a statement's "symbolic character."

20 Fackenheim's use of this midrash extends the traditional attention to God's dependence upon the human by focusing on the dialectical interdependence of the divine and the human.

21 For discussion of the role this midrashic text played in Hebrew political thought, see Joseph Isaac Lifshitz, "The Political Theology of Maharam of Rothenburg," *Hebraic Political Studies* 1, no. 4 (2006): 383–412, esp. 405. The emphasis is on human cooperation and coordination and the way they serve divine purposes.

22 See Martin Buber, "Jewish Religiosity," in *On Judaism*, ed. Nahum N. Glatzer (New York: Schocken Books, 1967), 79–94, esp. 84–5.

23 See below, nn 24 and 25.

24 Franz Rosenzweig, *The Star of Redemption* (New York: Holt, Rinehart and Winston, 1970), 171.

25 See Franz Rosenzweig, "Atheistic Theology," in his *Philosophical and Theological Writings*, trans. and ed. Paul W. Franks and Michael L. Morgan (Indianapolis: Hackett, 2000), 23–4 and n24.

26 See Buber, "Jewish Religiosity," 84–5. In a famous passage in Part Three of *I and Thou*, 143–4, Buber does not use this midrash but nonetheless does illuminate the paradoxical character of the human religious situation by contrasting the tension between divine power and human freedom with Kant's famous third antinomy, of human freedom and causality. This theme is in Buber, but, I would venture to say, not as early as the Prague lectures.

27 For recent discussion of Rosenzweig's attitude towards the Kabbalah and some helpful comments on his use of the midrash I have been examining, see Moshe Idel, "Franz Rosenzweig and the Kabbala," in *The Philosophy of Franz Rosenzweig*, ed. Paul Mendes-Flohr (Hanover: University Press of New England, 1988), 163–71; and Rivka Horwitz, "From Hegelianism to a Revolutionary Understanding of Judaism: Franz Rosenzweig's Attitude toward the Kabbala and Myth," *Modern Judaism* 26, no. 1 (2006): 31–54, esp. 35–6.

28 For a comprehensive discussion of the use of this midrash in modern Jewish thought, see Michael Marmur, "Are You My Witnesses? The Use of Sources in Modern Jewish Thought," *Modern Judaism* 32, no. 2 (2012): 155–73. For comparison, I focus here on only one case, that of Abraham Joshua Heschel. I recently noticed that Jon Levenson quotes the same midrash as evidence for the human role in the covenant in *Creation and the Persistence of Evil* (Princeton: Princeton University Press, 1988), 139.

29 He cited it from the *Sifre*, which is the *locus classicus* and the earliest source. See Heschel, *Moral Grandeur and Spiritual Audacity* (New York: Farrar, Strauss & Giroux, 1997), 162–3. See also 125, 269, 163, and 204. See also Heschel, *The Insecurity of Freedom* (New York: Noonday, 1967), 250, 281. For all of these references and the content of this paragraph, I thank Shai Held.

30 See Abraham Joshua Heschel, *Heavenly Torah* (New York: Continuum, 2006), 109–10; and "No Time for Neutrality," in *Moral Grandeur and Spiritual Audacity* (New York: Farrar, Straus and Giroux, 1997). See also Edward K. Kaplan, *Holiness in Words: Abraham Joshua Heschel's Poetics of Piety* (Albany: SUNY Press, 1996), 105 and 186n23. It is clear that Heschel likes to quote this midrash and that his primary motive is to clarify the notion of God's pathos regarding or need for human action – that is, of God's searching for man, His interest in human beings, and also the role of divine–human cooperation for humane and just purposes.

31 Fackenheim, "Self-Realization," 38.

32 See Fackenheim, "Self-Realization," 39–41.

33 Fackenheim, "Self-Realization," 41; see *Bereshit Rabbah, Hayye Sarah*, LX, 2.

34 A hallmark of the Buber–Rosenzweig translation of the Bible and of their reading of the Bible is that they treat it as a unity. Fackenheim does the same with the midrashic corpus. For brief discussion of this feature of Rosenzweig's reading of the Bible, see Mara Benjamin, *Rosenzweig's Bible* (Cambridge: Cambridge University Press, 2009), 140–6.

35 See Martin Buber, *On the Bible* (New York: Schocken Books, 1987), 1–13.

36 See Fackenheim, *The Jewish Bible after the Holocaust: A Re-Reading* (Bloomington: Indiana University Press, 1991).

37 To a significant degree, this is a result of his study of Hegel and his increasing appreciation of what historically embedded agency means.

38 See Fackenheim, "These Twenty Years," in *Quest for Past and Future*, 16–17.

39 Fackenheim, "These Twenty Years," 16.

40 Fackenheim, "These Twenty Years," 16–17. As many contemporary students of midrash point out, midrashic discourse takes itself and the Bible it comments upon to be wholes; Fackenheim would argue, I think, that a responsible reading of midrash must take seriously its own perception of itself, from its own point of view. See Reuven Hammer, "Introduction," in *The Classic Midrash* (Mahwah: Paulist Press, 1995), 13–50, esp. 26–37.

41 One proposal he does not consider is that midrashic collections might form authorial wholes or wholes representative of a particular school or tradition. Much recent discussion of aggadic texts and Talmudic ones is along these lines, but Fackenheim's interest is not historical or literal in this sense.

42 What Fackenheim has in mind by the pattern that unites the midrashic corpus into a whole is not what someone like Max Kadushin took to be the coherent pattern of rabbinic midrash. See Kadushin, *The Rabbinic Mind* (New York: Basic Books, 1952); see also Simon Greenberg, "Coherence and Change in the Rabbinic Universe of Discourse," 19–43, and Richard S. Sarason, "Kadushin's Study of Midrash: Value Concepts and Their Literary Embodiment," 45–72, both in *Understanding the Rabbinic Mind: Essays on the Hermeneutic of Max Kadushin*, ed. Peter Ochs (Marietta: Scholar Press, 1990).

43 In order to appreciate how old and important this notion of the coordinated compresence of opposites is, one needs to return to pre-Socratic Greek philosophy, especially to Heraclitus and then later to Plato and Aristotle.

44 For discussion, see David Joel Halperin, *The Faces of the Chariot: Early Jewish Responses to Ezekiel's Vision* (Tübingen: J.C.B. Mohr, 1988), 211; and James Kugel, *How to Read the Bible* (New York: Free Press, 2007), 227ff. Cf. Rashi on Ex.15:2, who refers to the maidservants' seeing more than the prophets; he is probably relying on Mekhilta on Beshalach. See also Elliot Wolfson, *Through a Speculum that Shines* (Princeton: Princeton University Press, 1994), 40.

45 See Fackenheim, *God's Presence in History*, 9–11.

46 See Fackenheim, *God's Presence in History*, 13–14.

47 The midrashic interpretation, originally from R. Yochanan, is a comment on Song of Songs 5:16, "His mouth is most sweet" or "His mouth is sweetness itself." Drawing on 5:6, "My soul expired at His word," the midrash turns to Deuteronomy 5:22. When God spoke with a loud voice, the Israelites heard him and died. Hence, He sweetened his voice, so that they might hear Him and live.

48 I discussed this motif in chs. 1 and 2.

49 Fackenheim cites *Midrash Tanhuma*, Yitro, as one source for such a theme.

50 Fackenheim, *God's Presence in History*, 15–16.

51 Fackenheim, *God's Presence in History*, 17.

52 Fackenheim, *God's Presence in History*, 18.

53 See ch3n26 of this volume for William Dray's work on Collingwood. See also R.G. Collingwood, *The Idea of History*, rev. ed. (Oxford: Oxford University Press, 1994).

54 Fackenheim, *God's Presence in History*, 20.

55 Fackenheim, *God's Presence in History*, 20.

56 See Daniel Boyarin, *Intertextuality and the Reading of Midrash* (Bloomington: Indiana University Press, 1990), for a now classic discussion.

57 Fackenheim, *God's Presence in History*, 21–3.
58 The key passages are Fackenheim, *God's Presence in History*, 25–30 and 69–78.
59 Fackenheim, *God's Presence in History*, 25–26.
60 *Mekhilta* I, 114f.; see Fackenheim, *God's Presence in History*, 28.
61 Fackenheim, *God's Presence in History*, 73.
62 Fackenheim, *God's Presence in History*, 77.
63 See Fackenheim, *God's Presence in History*, 78: "Jewish faith thus seems to find no refuge in Midrashim of divine powerlessness, none in otherworldliness, none in the redeeming power of martyrdom, and most of all none in the view that Auschwitz is punishment for the sins of Israel. Unless the God of history is to be abandoned, only a prayer remains, addressed to divine Power, but spoken softly lest it be heard."
64 For some examples, see Steven T. Katz, Shlomo Biderman, and Gershon Greenberg, eds., *Wrestling with God: Jewish Theological Responses during and after the Holocaust* (Oxford: Oxford University Press, 2007).
65 Fackenheim, *The Jewish Return into History* (New York: Schocken Books, 1978), includes essays from 1967 through 1977.
66 Fackenheim, "Demythologizing and Remythologizing in Jewish Experience: Reflections Inspired by Hegel's Philosophy," in *The Jewish Return into History*, 112–26.
67 Fackenheim, "Midrashic Existence after the Holocaust: Reflections Occasioned by the Work of Elie Wiesel," in *The Jewish Return into History*, 252–72.
68 Fackenheim, "Demythologizing and Remythologizing," 114.
69 Fackenheim, "Demythologizing and Remythologizing," 116–20.
70 See Martin Buber, *I and Thou* (New York: Scribner's, 1970), 143–4.
71 Fackenheim, "Demythologizing and Remythologizing," 122.
72 Fackenheim, "Demythologizing and Remythologizing."
73 Fackenheim, "Demythologizing and Remythologizing," 123.
74 Fackenheim, *To Mend the World* (New York: Schocken Books, 1980), 331.
75 See Fackenheim, *What Is Judaism? An Interpretation for the Present Age* (New York: Summit Books, 1987), esp. 286–9. The book is filled with midrashic texts, as one might expect. For references, see the index.
76 See Fackenheim, *What Is Judaism?*, 286, where Fackenheim frames the dialectic as one between divine intimacy and divine infinity or what we might call divine presence and divine transcendence, proximity and distance.
77 Fackenheim, *What Is Judaism?*, 287.
78 Fackenheim, *What Is Judaism?*, 288–9.

79　Fackenheim, *What Is Judaism?*, 289.
80　Fackenheim translates the midrash, ascribed to Shimon bar Yochai, from *Sifre* differently here than he had earlier, but I take him to be referring to the same text.
81　Fackenheim, *What Is Judaism?*, 290.
82　Fackenheim, "Demythologizing and Remythologizing," 124.
83　Fackenheim, "Midrashic Existence after Auschwitz," 262.
84　Fackenheim, "Midrashic Existence after Auschwitz," 263: "Midrash does not shrink from paradox, but confronts it and yet in the very act of confrontation reaffirms the bond."
85　See especially 263–4, which are a paraphrase of these earlier accounts.
86　Fackenheim, "Midrashic Existence after Auschwitz," 265.
87　Fackenheim, "Midrashic Existence after Auschwitz," 265.
88　Fackenheim, "Midrashic Existence after Auschwitz," 266.
89　In *God's Presence in History*, Fackenheim had claimed that the fragments of the post-Holocaust commandment regularly come into conflict with one another. To try to respond to them all would leave anyone mad – religious or secular. But he claimed that "the Voice of Auschwitz commands Jews not to go mad" but to face up to the contradictions and endure them (*God's Presence in History*, 92). But that madness is insanity, irrationality, and such. Here the madness differs.
90　Fackenheim, "Midrashic Existence after Auschwitz," 268. The models for such a lapse he finds in Kierkegaard and in Hegel.
91　Fackenheim, "Midrashic Existence after Auschwitz," 268. For a fascinating discussion of Wiesel, see Naomi Seidman, *Faithful Renderings: Jewish–Christian Difference and the Politics of Translation* (Chicago: University of Chicago Press, 2006), ch. 5.
92　Fackenheim, "Midrashic Existence after Auschwitz," 269.

Chapter 9

1　This rhetorical turn, as one finds it in *To Mend the World*, is a central theme of Susan Shapiro's critique in "'For Thy Breach Is Great Like the Sea; Who Can Heal Thee?,'" *Religious Studies Review* 13, no. 3 (1987): 210–13. Sol Goldberg suggested to me that a useful comparison might be Michael Walzer, *Interpretation and Social Criticism* (Cambridge, MA: Harvard University Press, 1993).
2　Timothy Gould, *Hearing Things: Voice and Method in the Writings of Stanley Cavell* (Chicago: University of Chicago Press, 1998).

3　Stanley Cavell, *A Pitch of Philosophy: Autobiographical Exercises* (Cambridge, MA: Harvard University Press, 1994).

4　Cavell, *Themes Out of School: Effects and Causes* (Chicago: University of Chicago Press, 1988), 48–9.

5　Around 1980, when Cavell first explicitly begins to use the expression "voice," he takes the human voice that is obscured or hidden by philosophy to be "voice" and does not yet use that expression for the way traditional philosophy expresses itself. See Gould, *Hearing Things*, 95, where Gould points out that what is lost "outside of language-games" is "voice," that is, the human voice of the ordinary.

6　Gould puts this point in terms of philosophy's desire for transcendence: "For Cavell, the drive to emptiness in our words is inseparable from the wish for transcendence. And he interprets the wish to speak outside of language-games as a version of the wish for transcendence." *Hearing Things*, 17.

7　Gould, *Hearing Things*, 207–8.

8　Gould, *Hearing Things*, 209: "In Cavell's reading, Shakespearean tragedy measures the cost of our extraordinary efforts at once to know and to not know." This is the cost of avoiding love, as in *King Lear*, and demanding too much of knowledge, as in *Othello*.

9　Stanley Cavell, *Little Did I Know: Excerpts from Memory* (Stanford: Stanford University Press, 2010). There is an important passage in *A Pitch of Philosophy* where Cavell calls attention to the continuing compelling character of the project for him of discovering his voice in philosophy and its connection with recollection: "The moment I felt that something about ordinary language philosophy was giving me a voice in philosophy, I knew that the something was the idea of a return of voice to philosophy, that asking myself what I say when, letting that matter, presented itself as a defiance of philosophy's interest in language, as if what philosophy meant by logic demanded, in the name of rationality, the repression of voice (hence of confession, hence of autobiography). Thus when in my second paper in philosophy, the first in response to reading Wittgenstein ('The Availability of Wittgenstein's Later Philosophy,' placed as the introduction to my dissertation), I identified the *Investigations* as a form and work of confession, I set words out that I am following to this moment" (69). For discussion, see Gould, *Hearing Things*, 52–5.

10　Gould, *Hearing Things*, 24.

11　Gould, *Hearing Things*, 21–2.

12　Gould, *Hearing Things*, 47.

13 Cavell's use of the concept of voice is then extended to the female voice and its various valences, which he goes on to explore in two film genres: romantic comedies and melodramas of the unknown woman. See his *Pursuits of Happiness: The Hollywood Comedy of Remarriage* (Cambridge, MA: Harvard University Press, 1984), and *Contesting Tears: The Hollywood Melodrama of the Unknown Woman* (Chicago: University of Chicago Press, 1997). As Cavell puts it, in *Pursuits of Happiness*, "skepticism [is] the wish to transgress the naturalness of human speech" (74; see also *Hearing Things*, 141). In ch. 3 of *A Pitch of Philosophy*, Cavell takes up opera in the same spirit, as a vehicle for examining how women find their voice, as in *Contesting Tears*.

14 Gould, *Hearing Things*, 141. It means abolishing the genuine otherness of the other as it is experienced in our everyday lives.

15 See Fackenheim, *The Jewish Bible after the Holocaust: A Re-reading* (Bloomington: Indiana University Press, 1990).

16 Gould, *Hearing Things*, 86; see also 58, 61.

17 Gould, *Hearing Things*, 131.

18 Gould, *Hearing Things*, 185. Cavell's *A Pitch of Philosophy* is cast as using autobiography as a vehicle for discovering his voice and expressing it in his past and present readings and writings.

19 There is a rare occurrence of the first person in "Judaism and the Idea of Progress," published in *Judaism* in 1955. See Fackenheim, *Quest for Past and Future* (Bloomington: Indiana University Press, 1968), 83: "It is well for the theologian to use, from time to time, the autobiographical form of discourse. To be sure, what matters in theology is truth, and this truth must be universal in some sense (though it is not easy to define this sense). But it is doubtful whether any theologian can wholly achieve the ideal of universality. For unlike matters of science, theological matters are of intimate personal concern to us. Our personal experience here inevitably enters into our conclusions, and this experience is necessarily partial and limited. In writing autobiographically the theologian puts, so to speak, his cards on the table. The reader can judge for himself whether the writer's experience has affected the universality of his conclusions; and if he finds this to be the case he can discount them."

20 This point, which he makes in his memoirs many years later, is already clear in "Judaism and the Idea of Progress" as well as in many of the essays in *Quest for Past and Future*. There he notes that for the individual Jew, to live a Jewish life takes more than a coherent theory; it takes a commitment. But with regard to that commitment, he makes a personal acknowledgment: "Nevertheless I cannot recall any point at which I made

this commitment. I always seemed already to have made it, though perhaps unaware of what the commitment was. And I venture to suggest that many of my fellow Jews may be in a similar position. The example of the liberal may be a case in point. For he somehow knows that he should continue to be a Jew, whether he likes it or not; yet he cannot give good reasons why he should. Jewish theology teaches that God often hides His face. Perhaps ours is one of those times. Perhaps it is a time in which many of us know some of His will, without knowing that it is His will" (94).

21 The paper referred to in note 19 above includes a very rare early comment on Nazism; see "Judaism and the Idea of Progress" in *Quest for Past and Future*, 87: "My third and most fundamental criticism of the progress view arose from the brutal fact of Nazism. This evil phenomenon, whose very possibility still defies comprehensibility, gave the final lie to the view that history is necessary progress ... A view still popular in America holds that history progresses necessarily but intermittently; relapses may occur, but these become ever less serious. But to me Nazism was, and still is, not a relapse less serious than previous relapses, but a total blackout."

22 Fackenheim, "On the Self-Exposure of Faith to the Modern Secular World: Philosophical Reflections in the Light of Jewish Experience," in *Quest for Past and Future*, 278–305.

23 The essay from the conference in California appeared in Walter Capps, ed., *The Future of Hope* (Minneapolis: Fortress, 1970), but the conference was held in 1968. Some of the same material that appeared in the *Commentary* essay was also used in the first chapter, "These Twenty Years: A Reappraisal," of *Quest for Past and Future*, which also appeared in 1968. I believe that Fackenheim, Schwarzschild, and the others first met Elie Wiesel at the Segal Conference in 1966, at which the theme of the next *Judaism* symposium was discussed.

24 Fackenheim, "On the Self-Exposure of Faith to the Modern-Secular World," in *Quest for Past and Future*, 281.

25 This section of the essay summarizes the conclusions of Fackenheim's "On the Eclipse of God" in *Quest for Past and Future* and anticipates the fuller account in ch. 2 of *God's Presence in History*.

26 Fackenheim, "On the Self-Exposure of Faith to the Modern-Secular World," 302.

27 Fackenheim, "On the Self-Exposure of Faith to the Modern-Secular World," 303. Here we have an early formulation of what would become, in Fackenheim's contribution to the *Judaism* symposium, the 614th commandment.

28 Fackenheim, "On the Self-Exposure of Faith to the Modern-Secular World," ibid.

29 Fackenheim, *Quest for Past and Future*, 335n48. Schwarzschild's comments were from the *Judaism* symposium "Toward Jewish Unity," held in 1966; they were published in *Judaism* 15, no. 2 (1966): 157. This was one year before the first symposium on the Holocaust. In his comments, Schwarzschild refers to an "experience that many of us shared last summer … [at] a gathering in the Canadian Province of Quebec … where a number of us, from all over the spectrum of Jewish life, gathered for a week's intensive study and conversation." This was, I believe, the first of the Segal Conferences, held in 1965. I am not sure if Wiesel was present at that meeting or whether he was invited but only came the following year. But it is clear that for Fackenheim and others, Wiesel represented the capacity of Jewish faith to suffer Auschwitz yet survive.

30 Both papers are reprinted in Fackenheim, *The Jewish Return into History* (New York: Schocken Books, 1978). They are chs. 2 and 3, 19–24 and 25–42.

31 There was an early anticipation of these three contradictions in Fackenheim's description of the contemporary situation in "On the Self-Exposure of Faith to the Modern Secular World," 303.

32 See Benjamin Pollock, "Thought Going to School with Life?" in Sharon Portnoff, James A. Diamond, and Martin D. Yaffe, *Emil L. Fackenheim* (Leiden: Brill, 2008), 58–87.

33 See Fackenheim, "The 614th Commandment," in *The Jewish Return into History*, 21.

34 Fackenheim, "The 614th Commandment," 21–2. Fackenheim repeats this confession, using many of the same words, yet with significant modifications, in Fackenheim, "Jewish Faith and the Holocaust: A Fragment," in *The Jewish Return into History*, 30–1. We will discuss the passage shortly.

35 Fackenheim, "The 614th Commandment," 22.

36 Fackenheim, "The 614th Commandment."

37 Fackenheim, "The 614th Commandment."

38 For this enumeration of the four fragments of the 614th commandment, see Fackenheim, "The 614th Commandment," 23–4.

39 He often repeated this point, reminding me that he was so distressed about giving the presentation that when he and Rose left for the airport to fly to New York, they left Rose's suitcase at home.

40 The paper begins by itemizing three modern events of momentous importance for Judaism – the Emancipation, the Holocaust, and the State of Israel. Fackenheim states this in the first sentence of the paper, which focuses on the latter pair. See Fackenheim, "Jewish Faith and the Holocaust: A Fragment," in *The Jewish Return into History*, 25–6.

41 Fackenheim, "Jewish Faith and the Holocaust," 26.

42 Fackenheim, "Jewish Faith and the Holocaust," 26.
43 Fackenheim, "Jewish Faith and the Holocaust," 27.
44 Fackenheim, "Jewish Faith and the Holocaust," 29.
45 Fackenheim, "Jewish Faith and the Holocaust," 30.
46 Fackenheim, "Jewish Faith and the Holocaust," 30.
47 See I Corinthians 1:23–25, where the crucified Christ is called a "*scandalon*" (stumbling block) to the Jews.
48 Fackenheim, "Jewish Faith and the Holocaust," 30–1.
49 Fackenheim, "Jewish Faith and the Holocaust," 37. The discussion of Jewish–Christian relations occurs at 32–40.
50 Fackenheim, "Jewish Faith and the Holocaust," 38.
51 Of special interest is "The People Israel Lives," first published on 6 May 1970 in the *Christian Century* for a series called "How My Mind Has Changed" and reprinted in *The Jewish Return into History*. In that essay, for example, reflecting on the way in which an honest encounter with the horrors of the Holocaust should place everything in question, he admits: "I am filled with shame of mind as well as of soul when I consider that my earlier theology had ruled it out on neat a priori grounds, when it implied that nothing new could happen in Jewish religious history between Sinai and the messianic days" (47–8). In the essays in *The Jewish Return into History*, the use of testimony, narrative paraphrases, and such, collected and juxtaposed in careful ways and then interpreted, often dialectically, is widespread. There are especially powerful cases in two essays on the State of Israel: "Israel and the Diaspora: Political Contingencies and Moral Necessities; or, The Shofar of Rabbi Yitzhak Finkler of Piotrkov," originally delivered at McGill University on 27 November 1974, and "The Holocaust and the State of Israel: Their Relation," delivered as a lecture several times in the early 1970s and then published in the *Encyclopedia Judaica Yearbook* in 1974.
52 W.H. Walsh, review of *The Religious Dimension in Hegel's Thought*, in *The Philosophical Quarterly* 23, no. 90 (1973): 77–9.
53 Stanley Cavell, *In Quest of the Ordinary: Lines of Skepticism and Romanticism* (Chicago: University of Chicago Press, 1988), 14.
54 Cavell, *In Quest of the Ordinary*, 14. For discussion, see Gould, *Hearing Things*, 175.
55 Fackenheim, *To Mend the World* (New York: Schocken Books, 1982), 249.
56 I have discussed the analysis and argument of the digression elsewhere, both in this book and in *Beyond Auschwitz*; also, it is the theme of my paper "The Central Problem of Fackenheim's *To Mend the World*."
57 See Fackenheim, *To Mend the World*, 162–3.

58 There is an allusion here to Adorno's famous remark: that Auschwitz has paralysed our metaphysical capacity.

59 Fackenheim, *To Mend the World*, 249.

60 I am omitting from consideration a large volume of newspaper articles, letters to the editor, and other more journalistic writings. These pieces, mostly published in Israel and Canada, typically focused on recent events and were highly politicized and highly charged. Fackenheim's political views tended to be very realistic, almost as if his earlier insights about the religious significance of survival itself were being translated straightforwardly in his mind into questions about the security and survival of the State of Israel. Most often, his writing and his thinking came to be associated with the political right in Israel and with right-wing Zionism in general. The tone of these writings is highly polemical and strident.

61 I set aside, that is, the essays in *Jewish Philosophers and Jewish Philosophy*, ed. Michael L. Morgan (Bloomington: Indiana University Press, 1996); as well as *What Is Judaism?* and *The Jewish Bible after the Holocaust*, and other so far unpublished lectures and papers.

62 See Michael L. Morgan and Benjamin Pollock, eds., *The Philosopher as Witness* (Albany: SUNY Press, 2008), chs. 1 and 2. The essays are: Fackenheim, "In Memory of Leo Baeck and Other Jewish Thinkers in 'Dark Times': Once More, 'After Auschwitz, Jerusalem'"; "Hegel and 'The Jewish Problem.'" Both were given at the conference in Fackenheim's honour of his eighty-fifth birthday in 2001. See also Fackenheim, *An Epitaph for German Judaism: From Halle to Jerusalem* (Madison: University of Wisconsin Press, 2007). The lectures and essay appear at 221–64. In these works we find an increased use of autobiographical recollection – beyond what we find in earlier essays and books, and akin to what one finds, say, in Cavell's *A Pitch of Philosophy* and *Little Did I Know*.

63 Fackenheim, "In Memory of Leo Baeck," 3.

64 Fackenheim, "In Memory of Leo Baeck," 4.

65 Fackenheim, "In Memory of Leo Baeck," 5. Once again, Fackenheim challenges philosophy not to suppress or repress the Holocaust.

66 See *An Epitaph for German Judaism*, 210–11, for another account of this return to Halle and Fackenheim's thoughts about Handel.

67 On Heydrich and Curt Lewin, see *An Epitaph for German Judaism*, 208–10.

68 Fackenheim, "In Memory of Leo Baeck," 11.

69 See also *An Epitaph for German Judaism*, 210–11.

70 How might we understand this literary strategy? If we take it to be a conscious decision on Fackenheim's part, why has he abandoned the lyrical and narrative style of his earlier writings for this fragmented,

cryptic, condensed one? One possibility is that he learned the style from Celan, who saw the Holocaust as having fractured language and left it in bits and pieces. Fackenheim attended and gave a paper on Celan at a conference, at the University of Oregon. The conference, "Ethics after the Holocaust," was held on 5–8 May 1996. For me, however, one way to understand his method is to treat it as realizing the possibilities suggested by Walter Benjamin's concept of the dialectical image and of taking history to be a pile of debris. Analogously, Fackenheim presents a bundle of reports, observations, memories, and so forth with a bare sense of order; the reader is left to construct the more elaborate picture or image or narrative that is hinted at by the order, using the pieces Fackenheim provides. One should not forget the idea that his writing seems intentionally compressed, minimalist, and written in haste, as if time is running out and everything needs to be said at once.

71 Fackenheim, "In Memory of Leo Baeck," 12.
72 Fackenheim, "On the SS Murder of My Uncle Adolf Goldberg," Appendix D, in *An Epitaph for German Judaism*, 254.
73 Gould, *Hearing Things*, 24.
74 Stanley Cavell, *The Senses of Walden* (New York: Viking, 1972), 92–3. For discussion, see Gould, *Hearing Things*, 125–7.
75 Fackenheim, *To Mend the World*, 28.
76 Fackenheim, *To Mend the World*.
77 Fackenheim, *To Mend the World*, 221.
78 Fackenheim, *To Mend the World*.
79 See Michael L. Morgan, "Foreword," in *An Epitaph for German Judaism*, ix–xxv.
80 Quoted by Morgan in "Foreword," xxi.

Chapter 10

1 He was aware that Marxists and others elaborated the analysis of such a crisis and delivered a critique of these features of modernity, even if he only rarely focuses on their work. I am thinking of the Critical School of Adorno and Horkheimer and their colleagues, and also, for example, of someone like Arendt.
2 In some cases, it is not deemed possible to provide such an account; in others, it is not necessary. But arguably it is a lapse in any account that is framed by a notion of the divine–human relationship.
3 It is especially valuable to consider Fackenheim's concept of revelation with that of those predecessors and to compare his reflections with the

engagement of several of his contemporaries with revealed texts – for example, Heschel, Soloveitchik, Scholem, and others such as Borowitz, Hartman, and Novak.

4 Both are indebted to Heidegger, although to different depths and in different ways, and both might usefully be compared to Buber. Both are philosophers, although Levinas's commitment to Husserl and phenomenology is much more direct than anything one finds in Fackenheim. Levinas's debt to Kant is stronger than Fackenheim's, I would argue, while Fackenheim's debt to Hegel is much more determinative for him. In fact, Hegel is to Fackenheim the way that Heidegger is to Levinas – or possibly Husserl. Yet both felt a deep sense of loss and debt with regard to those who died during the Holocaust, and both were very serious Zionists. See Michael L. Morgan, *Discovering Levinas* (Cambridge: Cambridge University Press, 2007); and *The Cambridge Introduction to Emmanuel Levinas* (Cambridge: Cambridge University Press, 2011).

5 See Emmanuel Levinas, "Meaning and Sense" and "God and Philosophy," both in *Emmanuel Levinas: Basic Philosophical Writings*, ed. Adriann Peperzcak, Robert Bernasconi, and Simon Critchley (Bloomington: Indiana University Press, 1996). For discussion, see Morgan, *Discovering Levinas*, ch. 7, and *The Cambridge Introduction to Emmanuel Levinas*, ch. 6.

6 Thomas Nagel, *The View from Nowhere* (Oxford: Oxford University Press, 1989).

7 See ch. 7 in this book.

8 The role of confronting the threats to human dignity and the assault on the "divine image" in humankind is pre-eminent for someone like Jean Améry, *At the Mind's Limits* (Bloomington: Indiana University Press, 1980); and also to Irving Greenberg, "Cloud of Smoke, Pillar of Fire," in *Auschwitz: Beginning of a New Era?*, ed. Eva Fleischner (New York: Ktav, 1974).

9 See Luc Ferry and Alain Renaut, *Heidegger and Modernity* (Chicago: University of Chicago Press, 1990); *Why We Are Not Nietzscheans* (Chicago: University of Chicago Press, 1997); and *French Philosophy of the Sixties: An Essay on Antihumanism* (Amherst: University of Massachusetts Press, 1990).

10 See Michael André Bernstein, *Foregone Conclusions* (Berkeley: University of California Press, 1994).

11 I have said something about such a view in the first chapter of *Interim Judaism* (Bloomington: Indiana University Press, 2001).

12 See Donald Davidson, "On the Very Idea of a Conceptual Scheme," *Proceedings and Addresses of the American Philosophical Association* 47 (1973–4): 5–20.

13 See John McCumber, "The Holocaust as Master Rupture: Foucault, Facken-
    heim, and 'Postmodernity,'" in *Postmodernism and the Holocaust*, ed. Alan
    Milchman and Alan Rosenberg (Amsterdam: Rodopi, 1984), 239–64.
14 See Richard Bernstein, *Radical Evil* (Cambridge: Polity, 2002), ch. 6; also
    in *The Cambridge Companion to Levinas*, ed. Robert Bernasconi and Simon
    Critchley (Cambridge: Cambridge University Press, 2002), ch. 12.
15 See Emmanuel Levinas, "Useless Suffering," in *Entre Nous* (New York:
    Columbia University Press, 2000), ch. 8, 91–102.
16 See ch. 5 in this book; see also Fackenheim, *An Epitaph for German Judaism*
    (Madison: University of Wisconsin Press, 2007), 56–7, and "Hegel and
    'The Jewish Problem,'" in *The Philosopher as Witness*, ed. Michael L. Morgan
    and Benjamin Pollock, 16.
17 See Fackenheim, *The Religious Dimension in Hegel's Thought* (Bloomington:
    Indiana University Press, 1967), 31; quoting Hegel, *Lectures on the Philoso-
    phy of Religion*, trans. E.B. Speirs and J.B. Sanderson (London: Kegan Paul,
    1895), I:65; see also G.W.F. Hegel, *Lectures on the Philosophy of Religion*,
    vol. I, *Introduction to the Concept of Religion*, ed. Peter C. Hodgson (Berkeley:
    University of California Press, 1984), 212.

Index

252, 254, 264, 275–6, 282, 285–6,
304, 311, 315n3, 341n23, 342n44,
344n77, 345n95, 347n139, 360n27;
on Bible, 227, 361n34; on creation,
41; on law, 29, 37–8, 107; on new
thinking, 60, 68, 208, 254, 315n3;
on revelation and love, 15, 17–19,
23–8, 26, 32–9, 158, 160, 164, 202,
224–5, 232, 253, 264, 273, 295, 298,
300–1, 317n28, 317n43; works by,
"Atheistic Theology," 225; *Star of
Redemption*, 17, 19, 34, 225–6, 236,
315n3; "The Builders," 37, 107
Rossi, Philip, 85
Rousseau, Jean-Jacques, 260
Ruge, Arnold, 151
rupture, 7, 45–6, 49, 77–9, 200, 206–7,
210, 212, 214–17, 245, 268–9, 286,
306, 309, 314n7. *See also* epoch-
making event; Holocaust

Sabra and Chatila, 349n8
Sachsenhausen, 358n6
sacrifice, 107–13, 132, 244, 268; child,
110–12, 335n89; self-, 73, 108,
112–13, 152, 206. *See also* martyrdom
salvation, 150, 232, 272, 328n8. *See
also* redemption
Sandel, Michael, 216
Santa Barbara, 257
Sartre, Jean-Paul, 41, 55, 78, 125,
156, 187, 191, 198, 308, 314n10,
320nn25–6, 325n30; works by,
Anti-Semite and Jew, 41
Satan, 118
scepticism, 40, 144, 197, 207, 248–52,
272, 296, 303, 317n38, 366n13
Schelling, Friedrich Wilhelm Joseph,
9, 30, 41, 82–3, 121, 123, 130–1, 134,

192–6, 208, 255, 274, 276, 327n2,
337n123, 338n129
Schleiermacher, Friedrich von, 20
Scholem, Gershom, 314n9, 359n11,
372n3
Schwarzschild, Henry, 349n8
Schwarzschild, Steven, 259, 349n8,
367n23, 368n29
science, 16, 59, 62, 132, 144–5, 188,
197–8, 204, 208, 217–18, 296–8,
303–5, 352n2; absolute, 166;
Hegelian, 133, 136–7, 205, 210,
297, 343n64; social, 59
secularism, 13, 164, 181, 257–8, 297;
Jewish, 297
secularity, 75, 153–5, 172, 180, 183,
258
self, 58, 60–1, 67, 87, 134–6; 199,
208–9, 215, 217–18, 301–2, 310,
320n24, 341n18, 354n27, 357n66;
atomistic, 250; authentic, 41, 199;
autonomous, 37; hermeneutical conception, 6, 44, 47, 198,
215, 319n13; historically situated
and embedded, 6, 37–8, 40, 43,
45, 47, 49–50, 56, 198, 209, 308;
as a process, 40–1, 49, 51, 134;
recipient of revelation, 17, 37; self-
choosing, 41, 43, 50–1, 56, 67, 199,
320n24, 320n26; self-constitution,
35, 38–41, 51, 55–6, 134, 198–9,
341n18; self-deception, 116; self-
definition, 67; self-determination,
34, 37, 55–6, 62, 87, 94, 98, 104,
180; self-making, 35, 40–1, 67,
186, 196–9, 320n26, 324n19; self-
understanding, 23, 50, 67, 138;
as a struggle between finite and
infinite, 67, 87, 91, 310–1. *See also*
agent and agency; freedom